May Yahweh the Father
bless you and keep you!

May Yahweh the Son
make his face shine upon you
and be gracious to you!

May Yahweh the Holy Spirit
lift up his countenance upon you
and give you peace!

God Bless,
Judy Jacobson
judyjake@comcast.net

The Holy Spirit

It started with jealousy.
I wanted a gift.
The Holy Spirit whispered, "Then ask me."
I obeyed.
God gave me information.
I was told to write a book.
I thought it was so I would have a purpose.
So I obeyed.
Writing became a passion.
There was a sweetness to his words.
My mind was being renewed.
Little did I know, the book I was writing was for me.
It was titled,
How to Communicate with My LORD and Savior.
I said, "Hineni. Here I am, LORD."
He replied, "I've been longing to hear those words your whole life.
Come on in, my dear child.
Stay a while.
Let's talk."
I asked the Holy Spirit for a gift.
What I received was an intimate relationship with HIM.
First came obedience … then understanding.
A life reborn.

Contents

Acknowledgments ix
Introduction xi

Chapter 1: What's in a Name? 1
Chapter 2: God's Divine Name 4
Chapter 3: Proper Names 14
Chapter 4: The Ark of the Covenant 17
Chapter 5: Sacred Fire 31
Chapter 6: Shekinah Glory 45
Chapter 7: The Spirit of Prophecy 61
Chapter 8: Urim and Thummim 77
Chapter 9: Satan 104
Chapter 10: The Silent Years 119
Chapter 11: Noah's Ark 141
Chapter 12: The Ark of Jesus 148
Chapter 13: The Word Became Flesh 165
Chapter 14: My Beloved Son 183
Chapter 15: The Great I AM 200
Chapter 16: The Passover Lamb 219
Chapter 17: Our High Priest 235
Chapter 18: The Holy Spirit 252
Chapter 19: The Name above All Names 270
Chapter 20: Love Languages 285
Chapter 21: The Antichrist 303
Chapter 22: The Great Physician 323
Chapter 23: To Those Who Conquer 338

Chapter 24: The White Stone...358
Chapter 25: YHWH Shammah 367
Chapter 26: Conclusion..383

Notes 387

Acknowledgments

Thank you God for providing me with all of the inspiration needed to write this book. I am humbled by this experience and by the way everything took place. I felt you by my side on a daily basis throughout this entire process. Thank you for providing me with a clear mind, wisdom, and understanding while fitting all of your puzzle pieces together. I can honestly say that I now know what it means to have a personal relationship with my heavenly Father, my LORD, and my Savior.

Thank you to my husband, Jake, for pushing me to write a book before I even had a topic, for convincing me that I had some important information that I needed to share with others, and for always being the optimist in my life. Thank you for loving me.

Thank you to my dear sister in Christ, Rachel Buggs, for listening to me talk almost daily about what God was revealing to me. Your wisdom and insight on the pieces of this puzzle influenced the words found throughout these pages. Your words of encouragement that were placed directly on your lips by God inspired me to complete what seemed like an impossible task. Also, thank you for your loving friendship.

Thank you to Sherryl Myrick, my dear friend, for all of your hard work in editing this book. Your expertise in the English language is a special gift from God and is priceless. Thank you for all of your valuable comments. I couldn't have completed this work without you.

And finally, thank you to my boys, Nick, Zach, and Sam. You are my daily joy sightings, my gifts from God. I feel truly blessed to have you in my life. Always remember to keep your eyes on your heavenly Father and his Son, Jesus, and your life is guaranteed to be filled with peace, love, and joy.

Introduction

I want to tell you a little bit about myself—about who I am and who I am not. I am a wife to my incredible husband, Jake, who is the love of my life and my soul mate. I cannot imagine my life without him. I am also a mother to three terrific teenage boys—Nick, Zach, and Sam—who continue to teach me about God every single day. They love God with all their hearts, and I know that God has great plans for them.

I am a follower of Jesus Christ, and I proclaim him publicly as my LORD and Savior. What I am not is a Bible scholar. I do not claim to know all there is to know about the Bible, as I have only been studying God's Word now for about thirteen years. Before that, I had not opened my Bible since I was a child, memorizing verses for first communion and confirmation classes.

I love to ponder the truth about all things, and I am a puzzle maker. My family knows that when I am putting a puzzle together, they won't see much of me until it is finished. I have this uncanny ability to pick out a random piece of a puzzle, even if it looks like every other sky-blue piece available, and find where it fits. Maybe that is the engineer in me.

When I started this book five years ago, I was not a writer. In fact, I have had no formal training. I had not written anything formal since college research papers other than some short openings for various Bible studies on various topics. I am, however, a very logical thinker, and if something makes sense to me, then I become a very passionate speaker on that topic.

I have just recently, over the last five years, become very bold in my faith and will share truths about Jesus and God with anyone who will listen. My favorite books of the Bible are Genesis, the Gospels, and Revelation, and for several years now, I have been interested in biblical prophecy. Storytelling has always been a favorite pastime of mine, which I'm sure you will gather from the numerous stories I will share throughout the pages of this book.

Since I am not a trained writer, you may be asking, "Then why are you writing a book?" My answer is that God told me to. Trust me, writing a book has never been on the list of things I wanted to accomplish before I died. It's actually kind of funny how it all came about. Back in January of 2011, my husband gave me a newspaper article and said, "You need to do this." So I began to read the article—and kept reading and reading, waiting to get to the part I thought he wanted me to do. You see, the whole article was on writing books and blogs and, like I have said, I was not a writer. So I asked my husband, "What exactly do you think I should do?" And he said, "I think you should write a book." I replied, "Why in the world would I write a book?" He said, "Because you have information that other people need to know about, and I think they need to be informed."

What my husband wanted me to write a book about was the knowledge I had acquired over the years about nutrition and healthy eating, which had become a passion of mine. So I told him that I would think about it. After pondering on his request for about a week, I agreed to write a book. However, I knew the topic was not supposed to be about nutrition but instead on how I came to know Jesus Christ. At that point, I thought it was going to be a short, personal testimony of my journey with my LORD and Savior. What I didn't know is that God had different plans. Oh, he did want me to write a book, but it wasn't going to be short. And the topic he wanted me to write about was *new* information about his divine name that he wants all of his children to thoroughly understand. What I have come to find out is that it is definitely information people need to know. Not only will this new information change your understanding of scripture, but it will also enrich your relationship with your LORD and Savior.

In writing this book, I have come to realize that I love writing, and it really has become my passion. I guess God knew that would be the case since he is the one who created me. Throughout this book, I share a lot of my own personal stories because I am well aware that my stories are really God's stories, and isn't it really God's everyday life stories that make our faith grow stronger?

I hope that after reading God's story, along with my own personal testimony of how I came to know Jesus Christ, you will gain a little more insight into God's plan and will have one more piece of God's incredible puzzle. After the names and specifics of my stories are all but forgotten, my prayer for you is that you are left with one thought: *Wow! Isn't God amazing?*

Chapter 1

What's in a Name?

What's in a name? Names have been in existence since the beginning of humanity. We see in Genesis that, in the very beginning, God started naming parts of his creation. We see that he called the light "day" and the darkness "night." The firmament was called "heaven," the dry land "Earth," and the waters that were gathered together "seas." The garden was named "Eden." And in Genesis 2:19, we see that "God formed every beast of the field and every bird of the air, and brought them to the man to see what he would call them; and whatever the man called every living creature, that was its name."

So why aren't humans just called "man" and "woman," as we were originally named? Why instead do we each have individual names? Why not labels, or titles, according to our kind? Part of the answer is found in Genesis 1:27: "So God created man in his own image, in the image of God he created him; male and female he created them." God created a rich and timeless tradition, starting in Genesis, when he gave Adam the first name, which means, "formed from earth." In turn, Adam named his wife Eve, meaning "mother of life." Their children were named Cain and Abel. Since then, humans have kept this tradition of parents' naming their children.

If we were merely another species of God's creation, we would all have one name, such as "lion," "bird," or "ant," as named by Adam. But because we are special creations to God, made in his own image, we have each been given individual names. You see, from the very beginning, God wanted a relationship with human beings. He even said that it wasn't until he made males and females that he felt that everything he created was "very" good. Because he made us in his image, we were unlike anything else he had created. We were special! We were unique! It is only because God made us spiritual beings that we are able to commune with him. What our unique names do is enrich our unique relationships with our Creator.

In ancient Israel, it was believed that a name was filled with power and vitality. At the human level, a name represents the innermost self or identity of a person. Names are an integral part of who we are. We are all unique, and God reveals this individuality in Isaiah 43:1, saying, "Fear not, for I have redeemed you; *I have called you by name*, you are mine." When people want to know someone intimately, the first thing they ask the other person is his or her name. Consequently, the naming of a child has always been a significant event.

The evolution of names has been shaped by both religious and cultural influences. In ancient times, people were generally given one name, called a given name. This given name often related to a circumstance surrounding a child's birth. Moses's name means "drawn from the water." Pharaoh's daughter gave Moses this name because she physically drew him out of the river. Other times, a name was given that had the meaning of a trait the parents hoped a child would possess. For example, *Hannah* means "gracious" and *Ira* means "watchful." Also a name could be connected with plants, animals, or simple objects. *Tamar* means "palm tree," *Tabitha* means "gazelle," and *Esther* means "star."

In later ancient history, some utilization of second names became more common. These names were usually given to demonstrate a person's identification with a particular family, clan, or father. The use of *bar* in the name Simon bar-Jonah indicates that Simon is the son of Jonah. This practice of having two and even three names has been brought into modern times.

Throughout the Old and New Testaments, we see God having a continued interest in names. Many times God changed a person's given name, such as when he changed *Abram* to *Abraham*, *Saria* to *Sarah*, *Jacob* to *Israel*, *Simon* to *Peter*, and *Saul* to *Paul*, so that their new names adequately reflected their new identities in God's kingdom. Also, throughout history, we see God informing fathers and mothers what to name their children. Isaac, Ishmael, John the Baptist, and Jesus were all given their names because God sent angels to tell Abraham, Hagar, Zechariah, Mary, and Joseph what they were to name their children. Out of obedience, the parents followed God's orders.

So what's in a name? Names are not only a celebration of our humanity but also a reminder of our individuality, a reminder that we are uniquely made in the image of God. Jeremiah 1:5 says, "Before I formed you in the womb I knew you." And after each and every one of us was born, it was the will of the LORD our God for our parents to name us so that we could begin an intimate relationship with him.

Names are wonderful gifts. They are given to us as a gift immediately after God gives us his incredible gift of life itself.[1]

Chapter 2

God's Divine Name

So now that we know how important names are to God, you might ask yourself, *Why doesn't God have a name?* I had never thought of it before, but imagine my surprise when, in February 2011, I stumbled on the fact that the God I worship does indeed have a divine name. Who knew? For my entire life, my prayers had always started with "Dear God" or "Dear Lord."

It's interesting how I even came upon God's name. One day in February I was on a biblical prophecy website, and the preacher kept referring to God as *Yahweh*. In fact, he never referred to him as *God* or *Lord*. I became very intrigued by this, so of course I had to find out why. After a little research throughout my Bible, here is what I found out. In Genesis 32:29, after Jacob wrestled with God throughout the night, Jacob asked God, "Tell me, I pray, your name." God replied, "Why is it that you ask my name?" In other words, Jacob was asking the God he worshipped, "Who are you?"

It's not an uncommon question. In fact, the question, "What is your name?" is one that humans ask one another quite often. When we become interested in the person we have just been talking to, we have a desire to know who he or she is. In Jacob's case, after wrestling with God for an entire night, his question was normal, especially since God had just given Jacob his new name—Israel. Placing a name with a person's face helps us to start identifying the character of that individual.

Once we have a name, then we can start asking other questions about that person, and a relationship begins to develop. It's almost as if our individual names are how we categorize in our brains the specifics about all the people we know in our lives. I can't imagine relationships ever developing if we just addressed people as, "Hey, you," every time we saw them. If we didn't have names to file away important details about individuals, I would think our relationships would become very confusing.

Because names are so important, Moses asked God the very same question that Jacob asked him. After God appeared to Moses in the form of a burning bush, God instructed Moses to lead the Jewish people out of Egypt. It was at that time that Moses and God had the following conversation: Moses said to God, "If I come to the people of Israel and say to them, 'The God of your fathers has sent me to you,' and they ask me, *'What is his name?'* what shall I say to them?" (Exo. 3:13). Keep in mind that Moses had been living in the desert, raising sheep and a family, for the entire forty years since he had left Egypt. So the day that God spoke out of a burning bush to him was far from an ordinary day. Nothing like this had ever happened to Moses. If I were Moses, I would also have wanted to know who was speaking to me, considering he was probably having a hard time believing what he was seeing in the first place. So God, who also knows the importance of names, replied to Moses.

> God said to Moses, "**I AM WHO I AM**." And he said, "Say this to the people of Israel, '**I AM** has sent me to you.'" God also said to Moses, "Say this to the people of Israel, '**YHWH**, the God of your fathers, the God of Abraham, the God of Isaac, and the God of Jacob, has sent me to you': **this is my name for ever, and thus I am to be remembered throughout all generations**." (Exo. 3:14–15)

You see, God does have a name! It is a divine name, given to Moses by the God of Abraham, Isaac, and Jacob. His divine name is YHWH (Yahweh), and per his instructions to Moses, he wanted to be known by this name for all generations. The fact that God has a divine name was news to me, even though I grew up in a Christian home, went to a Christian school until sixth grade, and completed both First Communion and Confirmation. Over the most recent ten years of my life, I had also been going to church regularly and had participated in in-depth Bible studies. And yet, no one had ever told me that God has a divine name. I began wondering if any of my friends knew this important piece of information. Apparently, God's name was not being passed down from generation to generation as commanded or surely I would have learned of it before now. Upon asking other Christians over the next year whether they knew that God had a divine name, the overwhelming response was, "No, what is it?" So my next question was, "What went wrong?" and then, "Why don't we call God by his given name?" I thought that God wouldn't have given his name to Moses if he didn't want us to know it and furthermore address him by his given name.

When I first looked at these Scriptures, I discovered that my version of the Bible didn't say, "*YHWH*, the God of your fathers, the God of Abraham, the God of Isaac, and the God of Jacob, has sent me to you." My version says, "*The LORD*, the God of your fathers, the God of Abraham, the God of Isaac, and the God of Jacob, has sent me to you." The word *LORD* was in all capital letters, and next to it was the number of a footnote that referred me to the bottom of the page. The footnote read, "The word LORD, when spelled with capital letters, stands for the divine name YHWH." To say the least, I was very confused at this point. It was definitely something I had never noticed before, and it made no sense to me. I wondered, *Why in the world would a title be used in place of God's divine name?* And a more important question, *Why was God's divine name of YHWH placed in a footnote and used nowhere else in the sixty-six books of the Bible?* I had just discovered that my God's name is YHWH, which means "I AM WHO I AM," and I was horrified that it had been moved to a footnote in my translation, as if it no longer mattered. At this point, God's divine name was a footnote, but who knows in future translations if his name would be left out of the Bible altogether.

I had to find out what had happened. Why did the translators of my Bible and the majority of all other translations replace God's divine name with a title? It sounded to me like the work of Satan. In my research, I found that in the original Hebrew Scripture, God's divine name of YHWH was used 6,828 times.[1] What that means is that in my version of the Bible, *YHWH* was replaced with *LORD* 6,828 times—not one time, not ten times, not one hundred times, but 6,828 times! Obviously, from the way the original Scripture was written, YHWH wanted us to know and remember his name—from generation to generation.

So why do we refer to YHWH as *God, Lord, Father, Almighty, Savior*, and *Creator*? These are all titles. These titles are indeed characteristics of the God I serve, and they are descriptive, but they are also very impersonal. It's like calling humans *man* or *woman*. Any mother will tell you that being called *Mom* by her own child in a crowded department store can be very confusing. In fact, as my children got older, they started calling me *Judy* when we were in crowded places. Since almost every mother in America is called by the same title, my children knew that if they called me by my given name instead of my title, they would have a better chance of getting my attention.

I wonder if YHWH enjoys being called by his title of "God" since this same title is also used for every other god that is worshipped throughout the world. The definition of *god* is "the being perfect in power, wisdom and goodness whom men worship as creator and ruler of the universe." The definition of *father* is "a man who has begotten a child." *Almighty* means "having absolute power over all." A *savior* is "one that saves from danger or destruction." *Creator* means "one that creates by bringing something new or original into being."[2] The problem with all of these titles is that none of them, in and of themselves, completely describe the God of Abraham, Isaac, and Jacob. Titles also do not leave room for all the personal knowledge and experiences that we have with our God. Only the name YHWH completely describes who God is and what he has done for all of man and creation. It's like me being called a wife, mother, sister, and friend. All of those titles describe the different roles I play in life, but I am so much more than my titles. I am Judy. That is my name. And for those who know me, calling me by my titles just doesn't work in a relationship. Likewise, YHWH is so much more than his titles.

In his initial conversation with Moses, God not only gave Moses his name but also its meaning. YHWH said, "I AM WHO I AM." He said, "I AM," which is like saying, "I exist." What that means to me is that YHWH is the one and only true living God, who is and always has been the same yesterday, today, and tomorrow. He is a loving God who wants to have a personal relationship with each and every one of his children. He gave Moses his divine name so that we could *call on him by name*.

YHWH's Name in Scripture

When you know that God has a divine name and you put his name in the place of the capital-letter LORD, it gives Scripture a whole new meaning. Let me give you an example. In my Bible and your Bible, Psalm 8:1 reads, "*O LORD, our Lord*, how majestic is thy name in all the earth." But that is not how King David originally wrote and sung this verse. He wrote this verse to say, "*O YHWH, our Lord*, how majestic is thy name in all the earth." Now that makes more sense because King David was not writing these words about just any lord. He was writing this song about the Lord of all lords. He was writing about YHWH's majestic holy name. Can you see how the true meaning of this Scripture changed when God's divine name was changed to a title?

Here are some more verses where I have replaced *LORD* with *YHWH* so that you can see their true meaning.

> **YHWH** is my shepherd; I shall not want. He makes me lie down in green pastures. He leads me beside still waters. He restores my soul. He leads me in paths of righteousness for his **name's** sake. (Ps. 23:1–3 ESV)

> Sing praises to **YHWH**, O you his saints, and give thanks to his **holy name**. (Ps. 30:4 ESV)

> Blessed be **YHWH**, the God of Israel, who alone does wondrous things. Blessed be his **glorious name** forever; may the whole earth be filled with his glory! (Ps. 72:18–19 ESV)

> But thou, O **YHWH**, art enthroned for ever; thy **name** endures to all generations. (Ps. 102:12)

> Nations will fear the **name of YHWH**, and all the kings of the earth will fear your glory. (Ps. 102:15 ESV)

And finally, these verses were spoken by YHWH himself: "I am YHWH, that is my name; my glory I give to no other, nor my praise to carved idols" (Isa. 42:8 ESV); "For I am YHWH your God, the Holy One of Israel, your Savior" (Isa. 43:3a). Remember, YHWH's name was removed 6,828 times; therefore, this is just a sampling of verses where his name is used. There are over one hundred verses concerning God's divine name in Psalms alone. By knowing this fact, I hope that you will never read the Old Testament the same way again. Any time you see the word *LORD* or a reference to God's name used in a verse, I pray that it will pop off of the page for you and that the verse will take on a whole new meaning—a very intimate and personal meaning.

So let's go back to the history of YHWH's name. What I learned is that because of God's holy character, the Jewish people removed the name of YHWH from ordinary speech during the period of the second temple, around 300 BC. In its place, they substituted the Hebrew word *Adonai*, which in English means "Lord."[3] Because the Jewish people became so fearful that they were taking YHWH's name in vain, they decided it would be better not to use it regularly. So they literally stopped saying it and writing it.

I can envision the devil sitting on the people's shoulders, saying, "Don't say it. It's too holy, so don't say it." Even though they had been saying YHWH's name daily since the time God gave it to Moses, the Jewish people became convinced through the religious leaders that YHWH didn't want them to use his name anymore. Satan must have felt victorious on the day that decision was made. Who could have imagined that Satan could actually influence YHWH's chosen people to stop saying YHWH's name after all of those years? But it actually worked.

It was at this point in history that YHWH's divine name went missing from daily speech and the written word. During this same time frame, it was recorded in oral Jewish history in what is called the Talmud that five other things went missing from the second temple. The missing items were the ark of the covenant, the sacred fire, the Shekinah glory, the spirit of prophecy, and objects that were used by the high priest called the Urim and Thummim.[4] With all of these things missing, God's presence in the second temple and in Jewish society was completely absent. In fact, this time period is referred to as the 430 years of silence. There were no prophets, no voice of YHWH, and no visible presence of God. The temple was basically dead. Therefore, since the scholars who translated the Hebrew Bible into Greek in the third century BC didn't know any better, they adopted the use of *Adonai* in place of YHWH. In addition, it became common to use the word *HaShem*, which means "the name," in the place of YHWH's divine name.[5] This is still the tradition today in Jewish synagogues. Christianity has followed suit by translating the Greek use of *Adonai* as "LORD" in most English Bibles.

YHWH's Name

We do not know how to pronounce God's divine name of YHWH, because the Hebrew language of the day used only consonants. However, when YHWH's name was said daily, everyone knew how to pronounce it. It is only after the Jewish people stopped saying it out loud for hundreds of years during the silent years that the pronunciation was lost. What we do know is that the Hebrew Scriptures reveal that his name is four letters long and spelled *Yod-Hey-Waw-Hey*, best transliterated into English "Y-H-W-H." In Hebrew it looks like this:

Encountering the Great I Am

YHWH's four-letter name is read right to left and is also referred to by the Jewish people as the *tetragrammaton*, which simply means "four-letter word." The word *Jehovah*, which is often used to refer to God's name, is an artificial form of God's divine name that arose from the erroneous combination of the consonants of *YHWH* and the vowels of *Adonai*. This hybrid form of God's divine name can be traced back to a work by Raymond Martin in AD 1270 and is invalid, as there are no "J" sounds in the Hebrew language. Other scholars will tell you that *Yahweh* is the correct pronunciation, but that is just a guess as well. For all we know, there may be two vowels inside each pair of consonants or none at all. Or maybe one of the consonants is silent. Since there are over forty renditions of how to pronounce YHWH, no one really knows how to say it. All of the scholars have their own beliefs, and they all believe they know the truth. But there is only one truth. So unfortunately, until we hear God or Jesus speak it again, we will not know the correct pronunciation. Until that day, the most widely used pronunciation of YHWH is "Yahweh" or "YAH-way."[6]

The fact that we don't use God's divine name of YHWH in our everyday speech is why I think, in today's society, so many people say and believe that there are many ways to God. "Well, which god are you talking about?" "I am talking about the God of Abraham, Isaac, and Jacob, and the one who sent Jesus to be our Savior." So unless you refer to God every time in this way, how do you really know the person you are talking to is thinking of the same God you are thinking of? Referring to God as YHWH would clear up all that confusion. Even Muslims say they believe in the God of Abraham, whom they call Allah. Because of this, people will say that the God of the Muslims, the God of the Christians, and the God of the Jews are the same God. But what they don't understand is that YHWH sent his only Son, Jesus, to save us from our sins. In addition, Jesus says over and over in Scripture that it is only through him (Jesus) that we get to the Father (YHWH). So in reality, the Muslims may think they are praying to the God of Abraham, but they are taking the wrong path to get to him and will never reach him unless they come to believe that Jesus is their LORD and Savior. The same can be said about the Jewish people. When Jesus spoke the words "No one comes to the Father, but by me" (John 14:6), he was speaking to his twelve *Jewish* disciples. Therefore, the Jewish people also need to believe that Jesus was the Son of God before they will ever reach YHWH, the God they worship.

What is so ironic about the Jewish people being fearful to use God's name in vain is that many Jewish people who have come to know Jesus Christ as their LORD and Savior will readily testify that, before they recognized Jesus as their Messiah, the only time the name *Jesus* was used in their household was as a curse word. By taking Jesus's name in vain, their biggest fear of breaking the third commandment came to fruition without their even realizing it.

Before Jesus was born, I wonder if YHWH was in heaven thinking, *Okay, they wanted to know my name. I gave it to them, and now they don't even use it. Jacob and Moses practically begged me for my name. What a shame they stopped saying it. Let's try this again. This time I'm going to tell a woman my desires. "Mary, you are going to have a baby and his name will be Jesus." And until the end of time, Jesus's name will be spread throughout the world. This time his name will be passed down from generation to generation, from mothers and fathers to sons and daughters. Not even Satan will be able to remove my Son's name from my Word.*

One Title Missing

While pondering all of the titles we use for YHWH instead of his divine name, I came to realize that there is one title missing and, in my eyes, this title is the most important. We never refer to God as *lover*, and that is what I think he would want to be referred to more than anything else, for there is no other relationship that is deeper and more intimate than a love relationship. In fact, the Bible is the greatest love story ever told. It's about a courtship that begins in the garden of Eden and culminates at the wedding feast of the Lamb.

You see, YHWH is and always will be our pursuer, the ageless romancer who calls us to be his lovers. With all of his being, YHWH wants us to be intimate with him and, in return, he will love us with an unconditional love that is out of this world. It is a love like no other—a love so great that he sent us his Son to be our Savior in order for us to have eternal life. When we feel and accept YHWH's love, we will then be able to love our neighbors as ourselves. In the end all God really desires is a loving relationship with his children. Maybe that is why YHWH describes himself as being a jealous God. He feels cheated when we don't give him the time and love that he desires from us. "For I YHWH your God am a jealous God, visiting the iniquity of the fathers upon the children to the third and the fourth generation of those who hate me, but showing steadfast love to thousands of those who love me and keep my commandments" (Exo. 20:5b–6).

So now we know that the God we worship—the God of Abraham, the God of Isaac, the God of Jacob, and the God who sent his Son, Jesus, to be our Savior—is so much more than just titles. He is definitely our God, our Father, our Creator, our Lord, and Savior, but he is also our lover.[7] For he is "I AM WHO I AM." He is the living YHWH.

> For all the peoples walk each in the **name of its god**, but we will walk in the **name of YHWH our God** forever and ever. (Micah 4:5 ESV)

Chapter 3

Proper Names

After searching my entire Bible for YHWH's divine name, I happened to read the preface. I figured I might as well look everywhere for the puzzle pieces and, lo and behold, I found a paragraph speaking about YHWH's divine name. The publisher discusses why YHWH's name was removed from Scripture and replaced with the title *LORD*.

> For two reasons the Committee has returned to the more familiar usage of the King James Version [of replacing YHWH's name with LORD]: (1) the word "Jehovah" does not accurately represent any form of the Name ever used in Hebrew; and (2) **the use of any proper name** for the one and only God, as though there were other gods from whom He had to be distinguished, was discontinued in Judaism before the Christian era and **is entirely inappropriate for the universal faith of the Christian Church**.[1]

What? Did you catch that? The preface of my Christian Bible states that God's divine name of YHWH is "entirely inappropriate" for the universal faith of the Christian church. What could they possibly have been thinking when they made this decision? They obviously had blinders over their eyes. This is hard to even grasp. The Christian faith was made possible only because YHWH, the Jewish people's one and only true God, decided to send his Son, Jesus, into the world to save all of mankind. YHWH could have decided to save his chosen people alone, but because of his love for mankind he sent us Jesus. And why would YHWH have given Moses his proper name if it were entirely inappropriate? These few sentences confirmed for me exactly why God was asking me to write this book.

Make no mistake—names are extremely important to YHWH. If they weren't, then the Bible wouldn't talk much about them. The exact opposite is true. From Genesis to Revelation, it is clear that names and the meanings of names are incredibly important to him. Throughout the Old and New Testaments, YHWH makes sure that we become well aware of all the characters that will eventually determine our eternal future, whether it is YHWH himself, his Son Jesus, Satan, or the Antichrist. He makes us aware of their proper names, as well as their titles and descriptions, for, in the end, he wants all of our names written in his Book of Life so that we can spend the rest of eternity with him. He loves us that much. In the book of Revelation alone, names are written on hands and foreheads, thighs, robes, white stones, gates, pillars, and foundations. Satan's name is revealed to us in both Hebrew and Greek so that we will clearly know our enemy. Those of us who have YHWH's name sealed on our foreheads will be spending eternity with our Father in the new heaven and new earth. Unfortunately, those who have been sealed with the Antichrist's name either on their hands or foreheads will be spending eternity in hell with Satan. Once a person is sealed, there is no turning back.

So have I convinced you that proper names are important? YHWH surely does think so. And since YHWH is "I AM WHO I AM," I'm choosing to go with what he thinks.

In the previous chapter, we learned that there were five elements missing from the temple during the same time that the Jewish people decided YHWH's divine name was too holy to speak. What I hope to convey is how each of these elements, along with YHWH's name, was used by God for communication with his people. At the time of the second temple, all these elements were missing; hence, communication with YHWH ceased for 430 years. It was only after this time period, with Jesus's birth, life, death, and resurrection, that YHWH brought all the missing elements back, including his name.

God's ultimate goal is to have a personal relationship with all of us who believe in his name. In order for that to occur, there has to be communication. Both parties have to be engaged. Both have to be listening and speaking to each other. All that follows is what YHWH has shown me through his Word. I will be discussing all of YHWH's elements of communication in detail so that you have a clear understanding of how God communicated with his believers in the past, how he currently communicates with us, and his plans for the end of times. It is simply masterful how he works everything out and how his divine name is interwoven throughout. I hope you enjoy YHWH's incredible story.

> Because he cleaves to me in love, I will deliver him; I will protect him, because **he knows my name.** (Ps 91:14)

Chapter 4

The Ark of the Covenant

Whether you are a Bible reader or not, you have probably heard about the infamous ark of the covenant sometime in your life, either from Indiana Jones movies or from your priest or preacher. Throughout history, the ark of the covenant has always been considered a valuable and sacred artifact. The fact that this holy object simply vanished over twenty five hundred years ago makes it even more intriguing.

But do the majority of people or, for that matter, believers of the Christian or Jewish faith really understand what its purpose was or what it looked like? I know that I didn't until I started writing this book, when YHWH instructed me to find out everything I could about the ark of the covenant through his Word. At that point, I vaguely knew that the ark was a sacred box of some kind that the Jewish people carried around with them. Thankfully, I know more about it now. Our preacher always tells our congregation, "You really should read your Bible. You will be amazed by what you discover." Of course, he is right.

The ark of the covenant was indeed a box, and it was considered extremely holy by the Jewish people. Several chapters of Exodus, beginning with Chapter 25, are devoted specifically to YHWH giving Moses very clear and precise instructions on how to build the ark, as well as the tabernacle that was to hold it. YHWH instructed Moses to make the ark of acacia wood to house the Ten Commandments. It measured two and a half cubits in length, one and a half cubits in width, and one and a half cubits in height (five feet by three feet by three feet). The inside and the outside of the ark were overlaid in pure gold. On its feet, four gold cast rings were attached, with two rings on one side of it and two on the other side. Two acacia wood poles overlaid with gold were placed through the rings at the feet of the ark so that the ark could be carried from place to place. A mercy seat of pure gold, measuring two and a half cubits in length and one and a half cubits in width (five feet by three feet), was placed on top of the ark. Over the mercy seat, two cherubim of gold were placed, one on each side. The wings of the cherubim were spread open, overshadowing the mercy seat, while their faces were turned toward it. The ark of the covenant was built to be an exact replica of YHWH's throne in heaven.

Eventually, three items were placed inside the ark of the covenant. They were the Testimony (which we know as the Ten Commandments), Aaron's budded rod, and a golden urn holding an omer of manna (Heb. 9:4). We will discover the significance of these three items throughout this chapter.

After the instructions for building the ark of the covenant were given, YHWH told Moses the reason it needed to be built, for the ark of the covenant was to have a very special purpose, indeed. YHWH told Moses, "*There I will meet with you*, and from above the mercy seat, from between the two cherubim that are upon the ark of the testimony, *I will speak with you* of all that I will give you in commandment for the people of Israel" (Exo. 25:22). In other words, YHWH was telling Moses that it would be over the mercy seat of the ark of the covenant that he would communicate with Moses and tell him all that the Israelites needed to know about his commandments, which would be placed within the ark itself. It was here, over the mercy seat, that Moses would hear YHWH's voice.

The Ten Commandments

And **God spoke** all these words, saying,

"**I am the YHWH your God**, who brought you out of the land of Egypt, out of the house of slavery.

"You shall have no other gods before me.

"You shall not make for yourself a carved image, or any likeness of anything that is in heaven above, or that is in the earth beneath, or that is in the water under the earth. You shall not bow down to them or serve them, for I **YHWH** your God am a jealous God, visiting the iniquity of the fathers on the children to the third and the fourth generation of those who hate me, but showing steadfast love to thousands of those who love me and keep my commandments.

"You shall not take the name of **YHWH** your God in vain, for **YHWH** will not hold him guiltless who takes his name in vain.

"Remember the Sabbath day, to keep it holy. Six days you shall labor, and do all your work, but the seventh day is a Sabbath to **YHWH** your God. On it you shall not do any work, you, or your son, or your daughter, your male servant, or your female servant, or your livestock, or the sojourner who is within your gates. For in six days **YHWH** made heaven and earth, the sea, and all that is in them, and rested on the seventh day. Therefore **YHWH** blessed the Sabbath day and made it holy.

"Honor your father and your mother, that your days may be long in the land that **YHWH** your God is giving you.

"You shall not murder.

"You shall not commit adultery.

"You shall not steal.

"You shall not bear false witness against your neighbor.

"You shall not covet your neighbor's house; you shall not covet your neighbor's wife, or his male servant, or his female servant, or his ox, or his donkey, or anything that is your neighbor's." (Exo. 20:1–17 ESV)

The first thing I noticed in reading the Ten Commandments is that YHWH *spoke* his commandments out loud for all to hear, *before* he engraved them in stone and gave them to Moses. The next thing I noticed is that in order to initiate their relationship, like any relationship, YHWH first introduced himself to the people. He said, "I am YHWH your God." The first thing he wanted them to know was his name, for YHWH knew that he had just delivered his people out of a foreign land, where the Egyptians worshipped over eighty different gods. By first introducing himself, YHWH ensured that there would be no confusion among his people concerning who had just delivered them out of slavery. By speaking his name out loud, YHWH also ensured that his people knew how to pronounce it because they heard it spoken by YHWH himself.

What I find so extraordinary is that YHWH didn't show up one day, give the Ten Commandments, and then demand for the Israelites to become his people. Instead, YHWH knew that for an intimate relationship to develop, he would have to prove to the Israelites through his actions that he was trustworthy to follow and to listen to. Therefore, he *demonstrated that he could be trusted* by miraculously delivering them out of the bondage of slavery while protecting them along the way. Then, only after they were safe in the wilderness, YHWH introduced himself as their God. Finally, he gave his people rules to live by that would not only bless them and make them fruitful but also make them unique among all of the other nations. Built into these rules was even a command for an entire day of rest every week. Everything YHWH did for the Israelites was because of a promise that he had given Abraham a long time ago: to make his descendants a great nation and to deliver them into a special land. By not breaking his promise to Abraham, YHWH further proved to the people that he was a God who could be trusted.

In the Ten Commandments, *YHWH's name* can be found eight times. It appears three times in the fourth commandment alone, concerning the Sabbath day. Therefore, not only were God's commands placed into the ark of the covenant, *YHWH's name was as well*. Not only was God's divine name given to the Israelites through Moses and by YHWH speaking it himself, but it was also engraved in stone eight times by YHWH's own finger and finally placed into the ark of the covenant for safekeeping.

The whole reason YHWH did all of this was so that he could dwell among his people, something he has always desired from the day he created man. That is why he instructed Moses to build the ark of the covenant and the tabernacle that would house the ark. Although a tent cannot contain the glory of God, YHWH wanted the tabernacle built so that there was somewhere he could place his glory, through his name and his commandments, as a daily reminder to the people that he was their God and they were his people.

> **I will dwell among the people of Israel and will be their God.** And they shall know that I am YHWH their God, who brought them out of the land of Egypt that I might dwell among them. **I am YHWH their God.**" (Exo. 29:45–46 ESV)

> God spoke to Moses and said to him, "**I am YHWH**. I appeared to Abraham, to Isaac, and to Jacob, as **God Almighty**, but by my name YHWH I did **not** make myself known to them." (Exo. 6:3 ESV)

YHWH told Moses that he did not introduce himself to Abraham, Isaac, and Jacob as YHWH but as El-Shaddai, which is translated as "God Almighty."[1] And before YHWH introduced himself to Abraham as God Almighty, YHWH was simply known as Creator God, or "Elohim."[2] What this tells me is that YHWH reserved his divine name strictly for the people of Israel, whom he redeemed out of Egypt. These people were the ancestors of Jacob's (Israel's) twelve sons, who went to Egypt when there was a great famine in the land. It was only to these chosen people that God gave his divine name. What an awesome gift from God—a special name for a special people! Obviously, YHWH was interested in a very personal relationship with the Israelites. Just by receiving YHWH's divine name, they knew the God they worshiped even more intimately than their ancestors did. In addition, they were the only people in history who had ever received YHWH's Word, first spoken and then engraved in stone by his own finger.

What was even more incredible is that YHWH told Moses it would be over his name and his Word, over the mercy seat of the ark of the covenant, that he would meet and speak with them—something that had never been done before. It was as if the giving of his name and the Ten Commandments written in stone was proof that YHWH existed. Once there was proof of God's existence, then communication could be established between him and his people. The cornerstone of this communication all began with the giving of his divine name. It made their relationship real and personal.

The Ten Commandments that were placed in the ark formed the foundation of YHWH's covenant with Israel. While God was on Mount Sinai giving Moses the Ten Commandments, he also gave Moses the rest of what is referred to as "the law." Included in the law were the instructions for the seven feasts that YHWH required the Israelites to hold once a year. These biblically ordained feasts, along with the weekly Sabbath day, formed the backbone of worship and communication with YHWH in the tabernacle and later in the temple. More will be revealed about these important feasts in future chapters.

Aaron's Rod

The second item that was placed into the ark of the covenant was Aaron's budded rod. A rod or staff was used to symbolize power and authority. The distinction between them in biblical times is not clear. In the Old Testament, the two words are often translated from the same Hebrew word and seem to be used interchangeably. In the New Testament, the English words *rod* and *staff* are used several times and are always translated from the same Greek word. Staffs were simply dead pieces of wood used by shepherds to guide and correct sheep. Rods were also often used as walking sticks to assist people as they traveled over rough terrain.

Aaron's rod that was placed in the ark of the covenant was a very special rod that is mentioned in the Scriptures in connection with the exodus of Israel from Egypt. This particular rod went by many names. It was called the rod of Moses, the rod of Aaron, the rod of Levi, and most significantly the rod of God. Even though this rod played such an important role in the delivery of Israel from Egyptian bondage, it had a very humble beginning. Aaron's rod began simply as a shepherd's rod, which Moses used in tending his father-in-law's flocks in the land of Midian.[3]

On the same day that YHWH appeared to Moses from the burning bush and introduced himself, he said to Moses:

> "I have **seen** the affliction of my people who are in Egypt, and have **heard** their cry because of their taskmasters; I **know** their sufferings, and **I have come down to deliver them** out of the hand of the Egyptians, and to bring them up out of that land to a good and broad land, a land flowing with milk and honey. … **Come, I will send you to Pharaoh that you may bring forth my people, the sons of Israel, out of Egypt.**" (Exo. 3:7–8, 10)

Feeling inadequate for this task, Moses questioned God's wisdom in choosing him to deliver Israel out of Egypt. Moses supposed that no one would believe that YHWH actually appeared to him and would therefore not listen to his commands. YHWH responded to Moses:

> YHWH said to him, "What is that in your hand?" He said, "**A rod**." And he said, "Cast it on the ground." So he cast it on the ground, and **it became a serpent**; and Moses fled from it. But YHWH said to Moses, "Put out your hand, and **take it by the tail**"—so he put out his hand and caught it, and **it became a rod in his hand**—"that they may believe that YHWH, the God of their fathers, the God of Abraham, the God of Isaac, and the God of Jacob, has appeared to you." (Exo. 4:2–5)

YHWH performed this miraculous sign to show Moses that he would not be alone in this endeavor. Even after this, Moses still insisted that he did not possess sufficient ability in public speaking to convince Pharaoh to release the Israelites from slavery. Moses pleaded with YHWH to send another person. It is at this stage in the story that we are introduced to Aaron, Moses's brother. YHWH replied to Moses:

> "Is there not **Aaron, your brother, the Levite**? I know that he can speak well; and behold, he is coming out to meet you, and when he sees you he will be glad in his heart. And **you shall speak to him and put the words in his mouth**; and I will be with your mouth and with his mouth and will teach you what you shall do. **He shall speak for you to the people; and he shall be a mouth for you, and you shall be to him as God**. And you shall **take in your hand this rod**, with which you shall **do the signs**." (Exo. 4:14b–17)

And that is exactly what happened. Together, Moses and Aaron went to Pharaoh's court in Egypt where, under Moses's instructions, Aaron spoke all of the words that YHWH gave Moses to speak. Together, Aaron and Moses performed sign after sign, urging Pharaoh to release their people from slavery. Even after nine plagues of blood, frogs, gnats, flies, cattle disease, boils, fire and hail, locusts, and darkness were sent by YHWH, Pharaoh would not let the Israelites go. Scripture tells us that God purposely hardened Pharaoh's heart so that both the Egyptians and the Israelites would see and understand all of YHWH's power and authority. It wasn't until the tenth plague, YHWH's final demonstration, with the death of all the firstborn children in the land, that Pharaoh finally let the people go. Through it all, Aaron used the rod of God to perform these signs. Upon commandment of YHWH, Aaron and Moses performed many more miracles using this rod after they were brought out of Egypt, including parting the Red Sea and making water flow from a rock.

So how and why did Aaron's rod, the rod of God, come to be placed in the ark of the covenant alongside the Ten Commandments and YHWH's divine name? Well, as it always seems to happen when someone new comes into authority, like Moses and Aaron had, there will be individuals who question the authority and start to grumble.

When it became apparent to the people that Moses and Aaron were YHWH's chosen leaders, a rebellion began, led by a man named Korah. Korah, along with 250 other men, was not happy with the current situation. They started questioning Moses and Aaron on why they were exalting themselves above everyone else. What they didn't understand is that by questioning Moses and Aaron, what they were actually doing was questioning YHWH's will for his people.

As you might imagine, things did not end well for Korah and his friends, because going against YHWH's will never seems to work out. In Numbers, we learn that the earth swallowed up the men's families on that exact day, and the 250 men were consumed by fire from heaven. The next day, the entire congregation assembled in protest against Moses and Aaron, saying, "You have killed the people of YHWH" (Num. 16:41). When YHWH saw what was happening, he instructed Moses and Aaron to move away from the congregation because he was going to consume them all immediately. As soon as Moses and Aaron realized that YHWH was going to kill all of the people for their disobedience, they both fell onto their faces, pleading with YHWH to forgive them. Moses quickly instructed Aaron to make atonement for the people in order to stop the plague of death that YHWH was setting in motion. So Aaron did exactly as Moses instructed. He got fire from the altar, went into the midst of the congregation, and put incense on the fire to make atonement for the people. Because Aaron obeyed Moses's commands, Aaron caused the plague that was unleashed by YHWH to stop. "And he *stood between the dead and the living*; and the plague was stopped" (Num. 16:48).

Because of Aaron's selfless sacrifice of running into the midst of the congregation where the death was occurring, even after YHWH had told Aaron and Moses to move away from the people, only 14,700 people died on that day. That may sound like a lot of deaths, but considering that God was ready to take out all two million-plus people for their disobedience, Aaron's actions truly showed his love for his people by willingly risking his life for them. Because of Aaron's incredible act of bravery, the murmurings from the people on whether Moses and Aaron were worthy of leading them probably ended, but in order to ensure that their questioning stopped for good, YHWH gave Moses very specific instructions.

> YHWH said to Moses, "Speak to the people of Israel, and **get from them rods, one for each father's house**, from all their leaders according to their fathers' houses, twelve rods. Write each man's name upon his rod, and write Aaron's name upon the rod of Levi. For there shall be one rod for the head of each father's house. **Then you shall deposit them in the tent of meeting before the testimony, where I meet with you. And the rod of the man *whom I choose* shall sprout**; thus I will make to cease from me the murmurings of the people of Israel, which they murmur against you." Moses spoke to the people of Israel; and all their leaders gave him rods, one for each leader, according to their fathers' houses, twelve rods; and the **rod of Aaron was among their rods**. And Moses deposited the rods before YHWH in the tent of the testimony. And on the morrow Moses went into the tent of the testimony; and behold, the **rod of Aaron** for the house of Levi **had sprouted and put forth buds, and produced blossoms, and it bore ripe almonds**. Then Moses brought out all the rods from before YHWH to all the people of Israel; and they looked, and each man took his rod. And YHWH said to Moses, "**Put back the rod of Aaron before the testimony, to be kept as a sign** for the rebels, that you may make an end of their murmurings against me, lest they die." (Num. 17:1–10)

Not only had Aaron's rod, a dead branch, sprouted, but it had also put forth buds, blossoms, and ripe almonds all at the same time. From a dead branch came ripe fruit. Aaron's sprouted rod was a miraculous sign to the people that YHWH had definitively *chosen* Aaron for leadership. The position in which Aaron was placed was as their high priest. The priesthood was meant to bring life and fruit to the congregation and was an incredibly important position. This post was meant for a special man of God's choosing. Only YHWH would make this decision, and no one would change his will. After Aaron's dead branch sprouted, blossomed, and bore fruit, it became obvious to the congregation of Israel that Aaron, the man who had saved them all from death, was to be their high priest.

What is so ironic about the rebellion led by Korah, is that Korah was from the tribe of Levi. As a Levite, he was in the tribe that was being exalted by God to do service in the tabernacle of YHWH and to stand before the congregation to minister to them. His tribe was chosen out of all twelve tribes to be brought near to YHWH. But I guess that wasn't going to be enough for Korah.

Isn't that always how it seems to be? We can be blessed so many times by our God, and yet it never seems to be enough. There always seems to be something to complain about in life. Rarely are people satisfied with what God has given them and are truly content. Instead of being content with all the miraculous events that YHWH had already done for them, Korah and his men wanted more. It was their pride that convinced them that they needed the same power as Moses and Aaron.

Moses and Aaron, on the other hand, were very humble men. Remember, from the very beginning, Moses did not want to be in the position he was in. He pleaded with YHWH to ask someone else to take his place. And we just learned what Aaron was willing to do in order to save his people from death. In addition, both of these men knew the source of the power that came from the rod. There was no question in either of their minds by whose authority they were able to accomplish all that they did. All of the miracles and signs that occurred in order to deliver their people out of the hands of their enemy were only possible because of the God they served. YHWH was the source of their power; and by being firsthand witnesses to YHWH's divine power, both Moses and Aaron felt extremely honored and humbled to be chosen by YHWH to be his leaders. YHWH instructed Moses to place Aaron's rod in the ark of the covenant as a reminder to the people that God had chosen Aaron to be his high priest.

Manna

The third item that was placed in the ark of the covenant, alongside the Ten Commandments, YHWH's divine name, and Aaron's budded rod, was an omer of manna placed in a golden urn. One month into the Israelites' journey from Egypt, the food they had carried with them was gone and the people were getting very hungry. They started complaining that they would have been better off back in Egypt as slaves with an abundance of food than out in the wilderness—freed from slavery but dying of hunger. YHWH heard the people's complaints.

> Then YHWH said to Moses, "Behold, **I am about to rain bread from heaven** for you, and **the people shall go out and gather a day's portion every day.**" (Exo. 16:4 ESV)

> And when the dew had gone up, there was on the face of the wilderness a fine, flake-like thing, fine as frost on the ground. When the people of Israel saw it, they said to one another, "**What is it?**" For they did not know what it was. And Moses said them, "**It is the bread that YHWH has given you to eat.**" (Exo. 16:14–15 ESV)

Since the Israelites didn't know what it was, they just called it manna. The literal meaning of the word *manna* is, "What is it?"[4] The Israelites were perplexed because it was a mystery food. YHWH called it bread from heaven. For forty years, the Israelites rose in the morning and, like clockwork, found this strange substance on the ground. For forty years, the people did not have a name for it other than manna, "What is it?" Well, whatever it was, they were thankful for it. All the people had to do was gather the manna daily in the morning, and it provided them with all the physical nourishment they needed. If they didn't gather it in the morning, it would be gone by the heat of the day. On the days they missed gathering their daily food, they would go hungry until the next morning, when there would be more available.

Now the house of Israel called its name manna. It was like coriander seed, white, and the taste of it was like wafers made with honey. Moses said, "This is what YHWH has commanded: **'Let an omer of it be kept throughout your generations, so that they may see the bread with which I fed you in the wilderness, when I brought you out of the land of Egypt.'**" And Moses said to Aaron, "Take a jar, and put an omer of manna in it, and place it before the YHWH to be kept throughout your generations." **As YHWH commanded Moses, so Aaron placed it before the testimony** to be kept. (Exo. 16:31–34 ESV)

For forty years, YHWH provided the Israelites with daily nourishment. For forty years, they learned to rely on YHWH's provisions for their physical needs. And not once in those forty years did they wake up and not find manna, other than on the Sabbath days. It was available every morning for them to gather. Daily YHWH sent bread from heaven until the day the Israelites entered into the promised land with Joshua. Only after the first day when the people ate the fruit of the land of Canaan did the manna cease (Joshua 5:12). At that point the manna was no longer needed because the fruit of the promised land was finally available to the people.

I find it significant that Aaron's rod and an omer of manna were placed in the ark of the covenant next to the Word of God—the Ten Commandments written by his very finger. Any one of these items alone spoke of the power, authority, and love of YHWH for his people. Any one of them alone spoke volumes of who YHWH, "I AM WHO I AM," truly was. Through these three items YHWH was communicating to his people, "I am your Provider. I am your Protector. I am your Deliverer. I am your Savior. I am YHWH, your God."

God could have stopped right there communicating with the Israelites, but that was not enough for YHWH. Instead, YHWH decided to place all these items together in the ark of the covenant in order to represent a new covenant with the people. These items, which represented his provisions, his protection, his wonders, and his very words, were placed alongside his new covenant name; and over the ark of the covenant, over these very items, YHWH began speaking to his people.

The Israelites were not even a few months into their journey with YHWH, and yet they already knew so much more about the God of their fathers Abraham, Isaac, and Jacob. In Egypt, all they knew were the stories that had been passed down from generation to generation about how their God had communicated with their forefathers. They had all probably been told, more than once, what Joseph said to his eleven brothers so long ago, when he had given them all a promise and a prophecy. Joseph said, "I am about to die; *but God will visit you*, and bring you up out of this land to the land which he swore to Abraham, to Isaac, and to Jacob" (Gen. 50:24).

It had been hundreds of years since Joseph had made this promise to his brothers, and since then all that could be heard from YHWH was silence. That is, until about 1447 BC, when God did indeed "visit" them and in a big way. Bringing the Israelites out of the land of slavery would be his first step in completing his promise to their forefathers of bringing them into the promised land. With YHWH's visit came a whole new way of communicating so that an intimate relationship could develop. The promise given to Abraham by *El Shaddai*, God Almighty, was starting to come true. God was about to make Abraham's offspring a great nation. It all started with a special covenant name— YHWH— spoken to Moses out of a burning bush, meant for a special people—Israel.

> "I will dwell among the people of Israel, and will be their God." (Exo. 29:45)

> "**I am YHWH**." (Exo. 20:2a)

Chapter 5
Sacred Fire

> "**When you walk through fire you shall not be burned, and the flame shall not consume you.** For **I am YHWH your God**, the Holy One of Israel, **your Savior**." (Isa. 43:2b–3 ESV)

When I first heard about the five elements missing from the second temple, along with YHWH's name, I had no idea what any of them were, including the sacred fire. I quickly learned that the sacred fire was considered the heavenly fire that came down from above to light the very first sacrifice in the tabernacle in the wilderness and then again in the temple that was built by King Solomon.

From the beginning of time, YHWH has used fire as a communication device between himself and the world. With the Israelites, he used the element of fire in the same way that he used his name, the ark of the covenant, and everything that was placed inside of the ark to explain who he is. Remember, the first time YHWH ever spoke to Moses was through fire in the form of a burning bush. The Bible tells us about that moment:

> Now Moses was keeping the flock of his father-in-law, Jethro, the priest of Midian, and he led his flock to the west side of the wilderness and came to Horeb, the mountain of God. And the angel of YHWH appeared to him in a **flame of fire** out of the

> midst of a bush. He looked, and behold, **the bush was burning, yet it was not consumed**. (Exo. 3:1–2 ESV)

What an unbelievable sight this burning bush must have been! When Moses became fearful and turned away from the bush, YHWH called to him from out of the bush. "Moses, Moses!" And he said, "Here am I." ... And he said, *"I am the God of your father, the God of Abraham, the God of Isaac, and the God of Jacob"* (Exo. 3:4, 6). YHWH wanted Moses to know who was speaking through the fire and to not be afraid. God had something to say to Moses. It was out of this burning bush that God gave Moses his name of YHWH, or "I AM WHO I AM," along with instructions to deliver his people out of Egypt. Obviously, the element of fire was important to YHWH as a communication tool and is also an element of who God is or he wouldn't have used this way to reveal himself.

Fire has been an important part of all cultures and religions, from the beginning of time to the modern day, and was vital to the development of civilization. It has been regarded in many different contexts throughout history but especially as a constant of the world. Fire does everything from warm us on a cold winter night to cause the mass destruction of a forest. Fires cook our meals, which warm our bellies; and yet, fire can also destroy an entire house of belongings with just one match or lightning strike. A lit candle warms our hearts and bears light. A fire can be critical in keeping us alive in survival situations, but it will burn our skin if we get too close. Fire is used to refine metals and to make gold and silver pure. Fire is a must for human survival in this world, and yet it will also be used on the Day of YHWH for judgment of the world.

Whether YHWH uses a fire to mesmerize us, by allowing us to watch its colorful flames dance around a burning log, or whether we stand in awe of the destruction it can cause, fire grabs our attention. And even if the result of fire is destruction, in its place something new always seems to come forth, for YHWH always brings a message—and new life—when he speaks through fire.

I just love the story of the prophet Elijah, who gathered all of the people of Israel at Mount Carmel to prove to them, once and for all, who they were worshipping as their God. Elijah came near to all the people, and said, *"How long will you go limping* with two different opinions? *If YHWH is God, follow him*; but if Ba'al, then follow him" (1 Kings 18:21). In other words, "How long are you going to have it both ways? There is only one true God. You cannot follow both YHWH and Baal. So do yourself a favor. Make up your mind and decide who is God, and then follow him." So to help the people with this important decision, Elijah instructed King Ahab to gather all of Israel, along with the 450 prophets of Baal and the 400 prophets of Asherah. He said:

> "Let two bulls be given to us, and let them choose one bull for themselves and cut it in pieces and lay it on the wood, but put no fire to it. And I will prepare the other bull and lay it on the wood and put no fire to it. And **you call upon the name of your god, and I will call upon the name of YHWH, and the God who answers by fire, he is God**."
> (1 Kings 18:23–24a ESV)

So the prophets of Baal chose a bull, prepared it, and called on the name of Baal from morning until noon, saying, "O Baal, answer us!" But there was no voice, and no one answered.

> And at noon Elijah mocked them, saying, "Cry aloud, for he is a god. Either he is musing, or he is relieving himself, or he is on a journey, or perhaps he is asleep and must be awakened." And they cried aloud and cut themselves after their custom with swords and lances, until the blood gushed out upon them. And as midday passed, they raved on until the time of the offering of the oblation, but **there was no voice. No one answered; no one paid attention**. (1 Kings 18:27–29 ESV)

I imagine that the 850 prophets of Baal and Asherah were humiliated and frustrated at this point. Elijah was ridiculing them and making it obvious to the people watching that it was a lost cause—not to mention that they all had blood gushing out of their bodies from cutting themselves. They must have looked a mess and just wanted the day to be over.

It was at this time that Elijah took twelve stones to represent the twelve tribes of Israel and built an altar in the name of YHWH. Around the altar Elijah built a trench and then laid wood upon it. The bull was prepared and laid upon the wood. He then told the people of Israel to fill four jars with water and pour it on the burnt offering and on the wood. Elijah said to the people, "Do it a second time." And they did. Then he said, "Do it a third time," and they did it a third time. The altar, the wood, and the offering became so wet that the water ran off the altar and filled the trench. Only after everything was prepared did Elijah say:

> "O YHWH, God of Abraham, Isaac, and Israel, let it be known this day that you are God in Israel, and that I am your servant, and that I have done all these things at your word. **Answer me, O YHWH, answer me, that this people may know that you, O YHWH, are God**, and that you have turned their hearts back." Then the **fire of YHWH fell** and consumed the burnt offering and the wood and the stones and the dust, and licked up the water that was in the trench. And when all the people saw it, they fell on their faces and said, "**YHWH, he is God; YHWH, he is God.**" (1 Kings 18:36b–39 ESV)

Elijah's purpose for this day in history was to forever clarify in the hearts of the Israelites who YHWH was. Elijah wanted his people to know without a doubt *whom* they needed to worship. Just as important, he wanted them to know that when they sought God with all their hearts, souls, and minds, YHWH would reveal himself to them. And not only would he answer them quickly, he would answer with great power and clarity. When YHWH answered Elijah on this day through fire, there was no wondering in the Israelites' hearts from whom the answer had come. There was no doubt that YHWH was their God.

Did you notice that the prophets of Baal spent all day asking their god to answer them and to show them a sign that he was the one true god? Scripture even describes them as limping about their altar, asking Baal to answer them. In the end there was no voice heard from Baal. Perhaps some of these prophets of Baal started questioning their beliefs as they continued to walk around and around the altar with no answer. Their faith in Baal started wavering to the point that even the way they walked around the altar started to show their weakness. Because they were not sure if what they believed was the truth anymore, their physical walk no longer conveyed the confidence they once held.

In contrast, when Elijah asked YHWH to show a sign from the heavens through fire, the results were amazing. Not only did the wood and bull burn up, but the stones and the water were burned up as well; all that was left was dust. Only the one true God is capable of that. And did you notice that Elijah had to ask only once?

I have found in my own walk with YHWH that when I am searching for the truth about him, and if what I am asking is his will, he is very quick to answer. And why wouldn't he be? YHWH wants us all to know everything there is to know about him, so when we ask for the truth, we can be confident that is exactly what he will provide. Remember, YHWH is a God who desires intimate relationships with his children.

This event was by no means YHWH's first time speaking to the nation of Israel in such a powerful way. As I previously stated, the very first sacrifices that were placed upon the altar in the tabernacle and upon the altar of Solomon's temple were also consumed by fire sent from heaven. This fire that came from above to light these first sacrifices was considered YHWH's sacred fire.

The Tabernacle

After Moses delivered the people of Israel out of Egypt, YHWH instructed the people to build not only the ark of the covenant but also the sanctuary in which the ark of the covenant would reside. In the book of Exodus, we see that YHWH made his wishes very clear on how he wanted the tabernacle to be built—the tabernacle where his presence would dwell.

> YHWH said to Moses, "Speak to the people of Israel, that they take for me an offering; **from every man whose heart makes him willing you shall receive the offering for me**. And this is the offering which you shall receive from them: gold, silver, and bronze, blue and purple and scarlet stuff and fine twined linen, goats' hair, tanned rams' skins, goatskins, acacia wood, oil for the lamps, spices for the anointing oil and for the fragrant incense, onyx stones, and stones for setting, for the ephod and for the breastpiece. **And let them make me a sanctuary, that I may dwell in their midst**." (Exo. 25:1–8)

YHWH told his people that if they built a sanctuary for him, then he would dwell in their midst. But we must not forget that the Israelites had just come out of Egypt, in the middle of the night, after being slaves for 430 years. Where in the world were they to obtain such fine and expensive materials in order to build a sanctuary for their God? Well, of course, YHWH had thought of that. When YHWH told Moses how he would bring his people out of Egypt, he said that at the same time he was performing all of his signs and wonders in front of the Pharaoh, he would also give the Israelites favor in front of the Egyptians. God told Moses that the people would receive the Egyptians' gold, silver, and fine clothing when they asked. Because that is exactly what happened, all of the materials needed for the construction of YHWH's sanctuary were available. So the people heeded Moses's instructions for the building of the sanctuary exactly as YHWH commanded them. The Bible records, "And in the first month in the second year, on the first day of the month, *the tabernacle was erected*" (Exo. 40:17).

After the sanctuary was erected, the ark of the covenant was placed inside the tabernacle behind a veil so that it was separated from the rest of the structure. This area of the tabernacle is referred to in Scripture as the Holy of Holies because of the holiness of God's divine name, the Ten Commandments, Aaron's rod, and the omer of manna that was placed inside the ark of the covenant. In order to consecrate the newly built tabernacle and everything that went inside of it, Moses and Aaron were instructed to go through an elaborate series of anointings and sacrifices in order to consecrate Aaron, Aaron's sons, the tabernacle, and the altar. After all of this was accomplished, the Bible tells us,

> **Then Aaron lifted up his hands toward the people and blessed them**, and he came down from offering the sin offering and the burnt offering and the peace offerings. And Moses and Aaron went into the tent of meeting, and when they came out they blessed the people, and **the glory of YHWH appeared to all the people**. And **fire came out from before YHWH** and consumed the burnt offering and the pieces of fat on the altar, and when all the people saw it, they shouted and fell on their faces. (Lev. 9:22–24 ESV)

This display of fire by YHWH in front of all the people of Israel was confirmation that God had accepted their sacrifices for their time and effort in constructing a sanctuary that would house YHWH's name and Word. This display of fire confirmed to the people that YHWH had indeed come to dwell among them.

But wait a minute—before we go any further, notice in the previous verses that the sanctuary was built with materials offered by people whose *"hearts made them willing to sacrifice"* what was considered the riches of the world, and in return they would receive the presence of YHWH into their midst. These people proved they were willing to sacrifice their riches because of their desire to have their God dwell among them. I believe it was these material sacrifices for YHWH, along with their sacrifices of time in building the tabernacle—not the actual sacrifice of the animal—that was lit on fire by YHWH. What mattered to God on that day was the sacrifice that was coming from his children's hearts because YHWH's desire was to dwell among people who wholeheartedly believed in his holy name.

Solomon's Temple

After forty years of dwelling in the wilderness, the people of Israel were finally led into the promised land, and the tabernacle and the ark of the covenant came with them. The ark of the covenant stayed in this portable sanctuary until King Solomon, the son of King David, completed the first permanent temple in 950 BC.[1] YHWH allowed Solomon to build this temple because of a promise he had made to King David so that his name could reside among his people in his chosen city of Jerusalem.

> "But YHWH said to David my father, '**Whereas it was in your heart to build a house for my name, you did well that it was in your heart**. Nevertheless, it is not you who shall build the house, but your son who shall be born to you shall build the house for my name.' Now YHWH has fulfilled his promise that he made. For I have risen in the place of David my father and sit on the throne of Israel, as YHWH promised, and **I have built the house for the name of YHWH**, the God of Israel. **And there I have set the ark**, in which is the covenant of YHWH that he made with the people of Israel." (2 Chron. 6:8–11 ESV)

After Solomon's temple was constructed and all of the anointings and sacrifices were complete, Solomon prayed an elaborate prayer to YHWH, asking him to dwell among them.

> As soon as Solomon finished his prayer, **fire came down from heaven** and consumed the burnt offering and the sacrifices, and **the glory of YHWH filled the temple**. And the priests could not enter the house of YHWH, because **the glory of YHWH filled YHWH's house**. When all the people of Israel saw the fire come down and the glory of YHWH on the temple, they bowed down with their faces to the ground on the pavement and worshiped and gave thanks to YHWH, saying, "**For he is good, for his steadfast love endures forever**." (2 Chron. 7:1–3 ESV)

These sacred fires that came down from heaven to light the very first sacrifices during the dedication of the tabernacle and Solomon's temple were kept lit continually so that every sacrifice given to YHWH from then on would be burned by the same fire that he originally sent from heaven.

My Own Sacred Fire

Throughout history, YHWH has communicated with his people through fire. For the people who witnessed these sacred fire events firsthand, it may have been their first experience of seeing YHWH's power and glory up close and personal. It may have been their very first experience in feeling God for themselves. These events may have been the defining moments that clarified for them who YHWH was and what he was capable of, for we all know that a personal experience with God can be very powerful and convicting.

In writing this chapter about sacred fire, it became very clear to me why YHWH gave me this piece of his story. Believe it or not, my very first communication with God came through sacred fire. Through fire YHWH spoke to me in a very powerful way. I remember the experience as if it happened yesterday.

At the age of thirty, YHWH moved my family and me to Atlanta, Georgia, next to a family who had a very strong faith. We immediately became friendly and ate dinner with our neighbors often. The first thing that I noticed about this family was their prayer before the dinner meal. Every time we ate dinner with this family, a different person would pray. In addition, the Holy Spirit led them in the words they spoke.

In contrast, my family always said the same prayer before mealtimes, regardless of whether we were eating breakfast, lunch, or dinner. The prayer was always the same because it was our denomination's tradition. And because it was tradition, the prayer never changed. However, the problem with tradition is that the meaning of the tradition gets lost over time. The words we spoke before mealtimes were said simply from memory, not because we truly meant them. Those words no longer held any meaning, at least not for me. Therefore, discovering a new way of praying before mealtime was refreshing, and it was a practice that we almost immediately instituted in our own household. By doing this, we discovered how to pray from our hearts instead of our minds.

It was during one of our dinners with our new neighbors that the subject of evolution became the topic of conversation. Our neighbors' teenage girls, Kristen and Meridith, were talking about how Kristen's science teacher was teaching lies in school about the creation of the world. I remember hearing them say that the way the Bible describes creation is how they believed the world came into being. Being an engineer and a very logical thinker, or so I thought, I had always believed in evolution, even though I also thought I believed there was a God. So I began debating with them about the subject and tried to convince them that the teacher was actually correct.

Well, these young girls would have nothing to do with my thinking. They knew what they believed and would not be convinced of any other theory. I left their house thinking, *How is it that thirteen- and fifteen-year-old teenage girls can have such a strong faith in biblical creation when the rest of society is telling them that they are wrong?* I became a little jealous that I didn't have what they had. I began asking myself, *How do I get their faith?*

YHWH also, in his infinite wisdom, plopped me down in a job where I met a girl named Kristy. She had a love for God and Jesus that I had never seen before in anyone. Her whole outlook on life was positive, and I could see it on her face daily. Our boss used to say that she was a ray of sunshine because that is exactly what she was. Everyone liked to be around Kristy, and if anyone was ever in a bad mood, she was always able to cheer them up. She was the first person I met who talked daily about God. She gave him credit for everything, and she never tried to hide her faith. She always had a Bible on her desk for everyone to see. I loved working with Kristy.

Because of the influence of my neighbors next door, the daily reminder of Kristy's strong faith, and the knowledge of what was possible, I became jealous. I began to want more. I began to seek the truth. At this point in my life I believed there was a God but that was about it. My husband and I attended church when we felt guilty for not going in a while, and I prayed occasionally. However, I did not have a personal relationship with YHWH, nor did I even know that was possible. I was pretty much cruising through life on my own. Then, one night as I was driving home from the airport, I began praying to God that he would send me a sign that he existed—and not only that he existed but also that he cared about the well-being of my family and me. I cried and prayed for the entire hour-ride home, pleading for God to answer me.

It was a prayer like I had never prayed before. It was a prayer that came directly from my heart. I needed to know with certainty that there was a God. I truly desired the faith that my neighbors and friend exhibited, but I first needed to know that he existed. I didn't want to limp along in life not really knowing the truth. I needed a sign from YHWH just for me. Throughout my childhood I had heard of all the miraculous stories written in the Bible, but that was no longer enough for me. I needed proof of my own. Once and for all, I needed to resolve my question of God's existence so that I, too, would know with certainty *whom* I should worship.

Like I mentioned before, when we ask YHWH for the truth about himself, he is pretty quick to answer. That next morning, my young son Nicholas woke up early because he wasn't feeling well. Soon after I let him get in bed with me, he proceeded to throw up on my pillow. So much for going to work that day! God obviously had different plans. I immediately got out of bed; gathered my pillow, pillowcase, and other articles of clothing that needed to be washed; and threw everything into the washer. After the wash cycle was complete, I put everything into the dryer.

On this particular day, our builder was at our house because we were having our kitchen remodeled. Around lunchtime, our builder found me outside to tell me that something in the house just didn't smell right. We pinpointed the problem to be coming from the laundry closet. I opened the bi-fold doors, and even though everything appeared to be normal with my washer and dryer, there was a definite smell. It wasn't until I opened the dryer door that I discovered what had happened. It was obvious from what I saw that a raging fire had occurred in my dryer.

Not only were all of the contents of the dryer in ashes, but also the interior walls of the dryer were solid black, and the metal was severely deformed. Everything inside the dryer had been consumed by fire.

When I opened the dryer door on that day and saw all of the destruction, YHWH spoke to me very clearly. It was not an audible voice but an internal voice inside my spirit. And what he said is this: "Judy, this is life without me, perfectly white on the outside, black and charred ashes on the inside." I knew exactly what God meant by his words. He wanted me to know that in order to have true joy and peace in my life, I needed to let him into my heart. I needed to stop pretending that everything in my life was a rose. Instead, I needed to include him in every aspect of my life so that my life could actually smell like a rose. He wanted the condition of my heart to match what I was portraying to everyone around me. As it was, my outside persona portrayed a perfect life; however, my heart was anything but whole. It was broken into many pieces and full of ashes.

Immediately upon hearing YHWH's voice, I remembered that I had just asked him the night before to send me a sign: first, that he existed and, second, that he was watching over my family and me. As soon as I opened the dryer door and he spoke to me so clearly, I knew that God existed. I had never experienced anything like this before, and there was no doubt in my mind *who* had spoken. Finally, for the first time in my life, the question of God's existence could no longer be denied. Once I started thinking about the circumstances, I also knew that YHWH cared deeply about my family and me. Not only was there no smoke in the house due to this fire, but also the fire did not burn down our house. At the time this event occurred, the dryer vent was located only three feet below our seventeen-year-old wooden deck. At some point, I imagine that there were flames licking the bottom of our deck, and yet it did not catch on fire. The destruction was contained to our dryer. In addition, all of the contents of the dryer were mine. I had asked God to provide a sign, and that is exactly what he gave me. He knew that I would be able to see his truth and symbolism about him through a modern-day appliance.

YHWH spoke to me through fire on that day, and for that I am forever grateful. Hearing his voice through the remnants of the fire is what started my personal walk with YHWH, and my life has never been the same since. On that very day, God said to me, "I see your heart and the ashes that fill it. Bring your heart to me, my child, and let me show you what I can do with it. If you put your trust in me and let me be your God, I will take your heart, I will heal it, and I will make the ashes white as snow." Once YHWH personally answered my question about his existence, all of a sudden his words become truth. My belief in God from that day forward was no longer based on what I had been taught about him throughout my childhood; my belief in God was now based on YHWH personally speaking to me through his sacred fire. In the matter of a day, YHWH became real and his words became truth because I heard his voice for the very first time. After that day, without a doubt in my mind, I finally knew the truth about the creation of the world in which we live—*for the Bible clearly tells me so.* Kristen and Meridith would be so proud.

What amazes me is how fast YHWH spoke truth into my life. From the time of my prayer spoken the previous night, God revealed himself to me in fewer than twelve hours. Like I said before, when we ask to know the truth about him, he communicates very quickly. The key is in the asking. In order to hear YHWH's voice, we have to be pursuing him with all that we have. Just as Elijah asked YHWH to answer him, we must also do our own asking.

I relive this story of how YHWH personally introduced himself to me every time I tell it to a new person I meet, for it is my way of spreading the truth about YHWH. And it is YHWH's way of reminding me of what he has done for me. Stories that begin with "I remember when" always have a way of making our faith stronger.

Go Ahead, Ask

So when have you asked YHWH a question about himself? Have you ever asked him to verify for you, once and for all, his existence? Have you ever asked him to reveal himself to you in a personal way? Asking God about his existence was the first step in my personal walk with my heavenly Father, and I believe it needs to be the first step for all of us.

When you ask YHWH to reveal himself to you, you can be assured that he will because God's greatest desire has always been for us to find him. The apostle Paul wrote,

> For as I passed along and observed the objects of your worship, I found also an altar with this inscription: '**To the unknown god.' What therefore you worship as unknown, this I proclaim to you**. The God who made the world and everything in it, being Lord of heaven and earth, does not live in temples made by man, nor is he served by human hands, as though he needed anything, since he himself gives to all mankind life and breath and everything. **And he made from one man every nation of mankind** to live on all the face of the earth, having determined allotted periods and the boundaries of their dwelling place, **that they should seek God, and perhaps feel their way toward him and find him**. (Acts 17:23–27a ESV)

The whole purpose for your existence is to seek YHWH and to find him. That is why he created you. And finding him is what YHWH wants for your life. I promise you, if you start seeking him with all your heart, mind, and soul, he will reveal himself to you. After my sacred fire incident, I could finally say with confidence that I knew there was a God—a God who loved me enough to speak to me. I didn't know he had a name yet, but I knew he existed, and that was a step in the right direction. My personal relationship with my heavenly Father had been initiated.

When Moses asked God, "What is your name?" God told Moses to say to the Israelites, "Tell them, 'I AM' has sent me to you." From YHWH's own words of "I AM," he was revealing to Moses, "I exist." He spoke the words of his existence to Moses out of a burning bush. Some thirty-four hundred years after YHWH spoke to Moses, YHWH spoke in the same manner to me out of my burning dryer and said, "Judy, I exist." And we know from the prophet Elijah's own words that the God who speaks through fire is the only God who is truly worthy of our praise and worship. On that day, what was forever engraved on my heart was, "*YHWH, now he is God.*"

Chapter 6

Shekinah Glory

Remember when you were a child and you spent time lying in the grass, just gazing at the sky to see what you could see in the clouds? Remember all the animals that you saw in the clouds, how what first looked like a bunny changed into a bear and then finally into a dog jumping over a log? Well, one summer evening not too long ago, I found myself lying on a lounge chair just looking at the sky to see what I could see, doing the same thing as I had done as a child so long ago. It was around dusk, and there were beautiful, white, billowy clouds in the sky. The sun was just about to go below the horizon for the night, and the crescent moon was already visible. As I lay on my chair, I kept asking YHWH, "What do you want me to see, LORD? What do you want me to see?" At first there was one very large, white cloud directly in front of me that had the light from the sun glowing upon it. It was spectacular. What immediately came to my mind is that I was looking at YHWH's glory shining on that beautiful cloud. But then I noticed some darker clouds trying to pass over and block out this shiny white cloud from my sight. I remember thinking that I didn't want these dark clouds to succeed in covering YHWH's glory, this beautiful sight.

Again I asked, "What do you want me to see, LORD?"

At this point, it dawned on me exactly what I was looking at. I was looking at a pillar of a cloud. It stretched all the way from the horizon vertically up into the sky, and it was big. This must be how YHWH led the Israelites by day—the cloud that led them through the wilderness. That very day I had been writing about what I was seeing.

> And YHWH went before them **by day in a pillar of cloud** to lead them along the way, and **by night in a pillar of fire** to give them light, that they might travel by day and by night. The pillar of cloud by day and the pillar of fire by night did not depart from before the people. (Exo. 13:21–22 ESV)

As I was looking at this pillar of cloud, I said to myself in my mind, *It was by a pillar of cloud that God led the Israelites by day.* As I was finishing my sentence—*and it was by fire that God led them by night*—I saw lightning fill the cloud that I was gazing at, and I heard a roll of thunder. I couldn't believe what I had just seen and heard! I was mesmerized. I was seeing and hearing YHWH's Shekinah glory right before my very eyes. But God wanted to show me more.

Again I asked, "What do you want me to see, LORD?"

As the sky kept changing, I saw the face of a child in the clouds, with YHWH's glory illuminating just her face. I thought to myself, *YHWH's glory is in our children. Oh, how God's glory is in our children.* The clouds continued to change as the dark clouds crept in, and I was sad to see that YHWH's glory was fading and it would soon be dark. But right before what looked like his glory had faded, I saw two large eyes form in the clouds with an outstretched arm, and I thought to myself, *Those must be the eyes of God.* There was no face—just two big, beautiful eyes looking directly at me, with his outstretched arm being extended to the world. Immediately I felt warmth inside my soul.

Finally, the sky changed again from black, white, blue, and gray to every color in the rainbow, and I was looking at the most beautiful sunset I had ever seen. Every color imaginable was there in the sky for me to enjoy. It felt as if YHWH had created the sunset just for me to see. What a special gift!

So I asked him again, "What do you want me to see, LORD?"

Without hesitation, YHWH replied, *"I want you to see me!"* I lay in my chair trying to soak in his words, with tears streaming from my eyes. After about five minutes, I stood from my chair and did something I had not done in probably forty years. I twirled around like a small child would twirl in the grass, with my arms out wide and my eyes turned to the sky saying, "I see you, LORD! I see you!" What an incredible revelation! What I realized from this night of gazing at YHWH's glory is that not only do we have a burning desire in our hearts for God to see us, but God also has a burning desire in his heart *for us to see him*. With all his heart, YHWH wants us to seek him and find him. He wants us to see, hear, and feel his presence above and beyond anything else.

So the next time you are looking into the sky and see one of YHWH's clouds, think about his glory, and you just might see his very eyes looking back at you. But keep in mind that you will only see what you want to see. If you only expect to see bunnies, then that is exactly what you will see. However, if it is YHWH's glory that you expect, then watch out, because you will begin to see him everywhere.

Visible Signs and Wonders

YHWH's Shekinah glory—isn't that really what we all want to see? Isn't it the visible signs and wonders from God that really make our faith strong? Jews and Christians use the word *Shekinah* to describe the visible presence of YHWH.[1] Although the word *Shekinah* is not found in the Bible, it can be thought of as God's glory and physical manifestations that he uses to let his people know that his presence is with them. Because YHWH's greatest desire has always been to have a personal relationship with his people, his Shekinah, or physical manifestations, were simply his way of letting his people see, hear, and feel his divine presence in our three-dimensional world without actually seeing him. Scripture tells us that no one has yet ever seen YHWH face to face, not even Moses. Even when Jacob wrestled with God throughout the night, it wasn't really God himself but his Shekinah in human likeness that Jacob saw face to face.

King Solomon understood this about the eternal presence of YHWH: "But will God indeed dwell on the earth? Behold, *heaven and the highest heaven cannot contain thee*; how much less this house [temple] which I have built!" (1 Kings 8:27). So the Shekinah was not actually YHWH but a physical manifestation of YHWH's presence among his people so that people could experience God with their senses and therefore believe that he existed. God knew that his people would need to see the unseen in order to have faith.

YHWH's Shekinah was first evident to the Israelites when Moses led them out of Egypt on the way from Succoth to Etham. It was here on the edge of the wilderness that the pillar of cloud appeared to the Israelites to lead them along their way. It was here that a pillar of fire, a sacred fire, appeared to give them light by night. And from that day forward, the pillar of cloud and the pillar of fire did not depart from the people. But YHWH's Shekinah glory did more than just lead the Israelites by day and night. It also protected them from their enemies and fought for them.

> And Moses said to the people, "Fear not, stand firm, and see the salvation of YHWH, which he will work for you today. For the Egyptians whom you see today, you shall never see again. **YHWH will fight for you**, and you have only to be silent." (Exo. 14:13–14 ESV)

> Then the angel of God who was going before the host of Israel moved and went behind them, and the pillar of cloud moved from before them and stood behind them, **coming between the host of Egypt and the host of Israel**. And there was the cloud and the darkness. And it lit up the night without one coming near the other all night. (Exo. 14:19–20 ESV)

> And in the morning watch YHWH in the pillar of fire and of cloud looked down on the Egyptian forces and threw the Egyptian forces into a panic, clogging their chariot wheels so that they drove heavily. And the Egyptians said, "Let us

flee from before Israel, for **YHWH fights for them against the Egyptians**." (Exo. 14:24–25 ESV)

The Israelites were led and protected by the pillar of cloud by day and fire by night for their entire forty years in the wilderness. They never had to ask themselves if they were where God wanted them to be or if God's presence was with them, for YHWH's cloud and sacred fire let them know. When the pillar of cloud moved, they moved. When it stopped, they stopped. And they never doubted that YHWH was with them and was protecting them, because daily they saw his Shekinah glory dwelling among them.

Three months into their journey from the land of Egypt, the Israelites came into the wilderness of Sinai. Since their departure from Egypt, they had already seen the cloud and the fire that led, protected, and fought for them. They had witnessed the parting of the Red Sea and had crossed over, unharmed by their enemies. They had seen, tasted, and been nourished by the manna that YHWH rained down on them from heaven. And they drank bitter water that had been made sweet by the hand of God. But there was more to come in the wilderness of Sinai.

> And YHWH said to Moses, "Behold, I am coming to you in a thick cloud, that **the people may hear when I speak with you**, and may also believe you forever." (Exo. 19:9 ESV)

> On the morning of the third day there were **thunders and lightnings**, and a **thick cloud** on the mountain and a very **loud trumpet blast**, so that all the people in the camp trembled. (Exo. 19:16 ESV)

Then Moses brought the people out of the camp to **meet** God.

> Now Mount Sinai was wrapped in smoke because **YHWH had descended on it in fire**. The smoke of it went up like the smoke of a kiln, and the whole **mountain trembled greatly**. And as the sound of the trumpet grew louder and

louder, Moses spoke, and **God answered him in thunder**. (Exo. 19:18–19 ESV)

Not only did YHWH make his presence known through the silence of a pillar of cloud and fire, but his presence was also made known very noisily and dramatically at Mount Sinai. It was God's way of saying to his people, "Take notice and listen." YHWH made himself known through thunder, lightning, the earth shaking, and finally a trumpet blast. He then descended upon the mountain in a sacred fire. He wanted everyone to know, without a shadow of a doubt, *who* was speaking. It was at this time that God introduced himself as YHWH and spoke the Ten Commandments for all his people to hear.

What is interesting to me is that I previously believed that YHWH had just given the Ten Commandments to Moses on two stone tablets and Moses delivered them to the Israelites. That is what the movies I had seen had portrayed. But that is not what happened. (That's why it's good for us to read our Bibles.) Through Scripture it becomes clear why YHWH chose to speak audibly to the Israelites.

> "**To you it was shown, that you might know that YHWH is God**; there is no other besides him. **Out of heaven he let you hear his voice**, that he might discipline you. And on earth **he let you see his great fire, and you heard his words** out of the midst of the fire." (Deut. 4:35–36 ESV)

And the people responded,

> "Behold, YHWH our God has shown us his glory and greatness, and **we have heard his voice** out of the midst of the fire. **This day we have seen God speak with man**, and man still live." (Deut. 5:24 ESV)

YHWH wanted witnesses. He planned this event so that there would be approximately two million witnesses who could account for who they heard speaking. YHWH planned for everyone to hear his voice coming from his sacred fire. He wanted his people to experience

Encountering the Great I Am

his presence directly so that when they passed this story down from generation to generation, there would be passion in their voices. He spoke directly to his people so that there would be no doubts concerning from whom the Ten Commandments and the law came. On that day, YHWH was *seen* in the thick cloud, the thunders, the lightning, the shaking of the earth, the smoke and fire, and the trumpet blast. In addition, the people heard YHWH's voice. Loud and clear, with all of their senses, they felt his presence and heard his commands. His physical presence was not actually seen through the thick cloud, and yet they believed because of what all their other senses told them. From that day forward, YHWH became their God and they became his people. I cannot think of a better way of starting a relationship than so directly.

YHWH's Shekinah glory that day showed the power behind his name. On that day, the people of Israel knew a little more about their God, who described himself as "I AM WHO I AM." But even after this spectacular showing of YHWH's power and glory on Mount Sinai, Moses still needed further clarification from God on what all this meant for him and for the people. Moses needed to verify whom YHWH was going to send with them on this journey.

> Moses said to YHWH, "See, you say to me, 'Bring up this people'; but **you have not let me know whom you will send with me**" … And he [YHWH] said, "**My presence will go with you, and I will give you rest.**" And he [Moses] said to him, "If your presence will not go with me, do not bring us up from here. **For how shall it be known that I have found favor in your sight,** I and your people? **Is it not in your going with us, so that we are distinct**, I and your people, from every other people on the face of the earth?" (Exo. 33:12a, 14–16 ESV)

Moses knew the power of YHWH's presence. He had witnessed YHWH's Shekinah glory for himself through the burning bush, through all of the signs and wonders of delivering the people out of Egypt and destroying their enemies, and now on Mount Sinai. Moses knew without a doubt that if YHWH went with them, then it would make them distinct from all the other nations on the face of the earth. What an incredible promise for YHWH to give Moses! YHWH had already done so much for the people of Israel, so for YHWH to promise that he would be with Moses through it all was significant. It gave Moses great peace to know that no matter what took place from this point forward, YHWH would be with him. YHWH's daily presence meant more to Moses than any inheritance of land could ever mean.

But God didn't stop there; in order to seal his promise, YHWH actually allowed Moses to see his presence without the covering of a thick cloud. With the exception of his face, YHWH allowed Moses to see his entire being so that Moses would believe his promise of going with the people.

> And YHWH said to Moses, "This very thing that you have spoken I will do, for you have found favor in my sight, and I know you by name." Moses said, "**Please show me your glory**." And he said, "**I will make all my goodness pass before you and will proclaim before you my name 'YHWH.'** And I will be gracious to whom I will be gracious, and will show mercy on whom I will show mercy. But," he said, "you cannot see my face, for man shall not see me and live." And YHWH said, "Behold, there is a place by me where you shall stand on the rock, and while my glory passes by I will put you in a cleft of the rock, and I will cover you with my hand until I have passed by. Then I will take away my hand, and you shall see my back, **but my face shall not be seen**." (Exo. 33:17–23 ESV)

This all took place exactly as YHWH promised it would. As much as Moses wanted to see God's presence, it appears that *God wanted Moses to see him as well*. So after Moses presented himself to God on top of Mount Sinai the next morning to receive the Ten Commandments, Scripture tells us that YHWH descended in the cloud and stood with Moses, proclaimed his name of YHWH, and physically passed all of his glory before him (Exo. 34:1–7). This was all the proof Moses needed to confidently move on with what YHWH had commanded of him.

After God physically revealed himself to Moses, Moses remained in YHWH's presence for forty more days and nights. "When Moses came down from Mount Sinai with the two tablets of the testimony in his hand, as he came down from the mountain, Moses did not know that the *skin of his face shone because he had been talking with God*" (Exo. 34:29). YHWH's glory shone so brightly while Moses was in his presence that Moses's face radiated God's light to everyone else, even after Moses was no longer in his presence. What a testimony to the true power of YHWH's Shekinah glory! When we spend enough time in God's presence, his light will not only penetrate us, but it has the ability to radiate through us onto others so that they can also see and feel it for themselves.

Trip to Wyoming

After writing these chapters about YHWH's sacred fire and Shekinah glory, I thought I was finished writing all God wanted me to write on these subjects. What I didn't know is that he was not finished speaking. YHWH had more signs to give me, more of his glory for me to see, more revelations to behold. It was at this point that God took me on a family vacation to Jackson Hole, Wyoming. What is noteworthy about this vacation is that we had originally planned it for the previous summer. However, just before booking our flights, I got this odd feeling that we were not to take the trip. I had no solid reasons why we needed to delay; I just knew that it wasn't supposed to happen that year, so we made other plans.

Well, I know now, without a doubt, after spending eight glorious days in Wyoming, that God did want me to experience that part of his creation but not until I was knee-deep into writing this book. He needed me to wait a year for what he was about to communicate to me so that his message would be fully understood. He needed me to have his name and everything I had discovered about his sacred fire and Shekinah glory front and center in my mind. He needed me to be pondering his name and the meaning of his name in order to understand what he was about to show me. The odd feeling that I had felt a year prior was YHWH's Holy Spirit instructing me to delay my trip. At the time, I had not recognized it as the Holy Spirit's voice.

I had visited Jackson Hole with my parents and siblings as a teenager. We stayed at a dude ranch, and I remember it fondly as being the best vacation I had ever experienced. We spent our days riding horses, hiking through the mountains, whitewater rafting, going to rodeos, having our dinners by campfires, playing games with the other families, and just simply hanging out, all with the spectacular Grand Teton Mountain Range as our backdrop. Every day there was something new to see, hear, and feel.

It was an unforgettable vacation for me and something I wanted my boys to experience as well. So as we were flying into the Jackson airport and I caught my first glimpse of the Grand Tetons, I couldn't help but be excited. I was thinking of all that we were going to share together over the next eight days, and I couldn't wait. I had expectations of fun and excitement. What I was not prepared for was all that God had planned for me.

Upon arriving at the ranch, the first thing we all noticed, after the beauty of our surroundings, of course, was that there was no cell phone coverage anywhere on the ranch. Although we had already decided as a family that we were going to unplug from all electronics, we all knew that we probably wouldn't follow that rule 100 percent of the time. So YHWH made sure we honored our decision to unplug by making it impossible to connect with the outside world simply because of our location. I guess he wanted to make sure that he had our full attention. It ended up being the best blessing he could ever have given us because it gave us the quiet time we so desired—to think, to relax, to ponder, and to just be. For one week our job was to see, hear, smell, feel, taste, and experience YHWH's beautiful creation with absolutely no outside distractions. It was a job I was more than willing to complete.

It didn't take me long to figure out how much I was going to enjoy my week in Wyoming. On our very first horseback-riding adventure, we were led through the most beautiful forest I had ever seen. Not only were the trees luscious and green, but also there were wildflowers in every color under the sun absolutely everywhere we looked. Being a lover of flowers, I was simply amazed by this rainbow of blooms that blanketed the forest floor.

Our days at the dude ranch quickly became very comfortable, our lives slowed down, and we took in YHWH's Shekinah glory that was all around us. Daily we received gifts from him in the form of wildflowers, in the wildlife, in the mountains, in the peace of the silence, and in one another. Our week progressed as hoped. I was reliving my childhood vacation, this time as an adult, seeing everything through the eyes of my boys, and yet this vacation to Wyoming was different from the last time I was there. This time I was seeing YHWH's creation as a true believer, as one who had developed a personal relationship with him through his Son, Jesus Christ.

What I didn't realize when I made our vacation plans is that I had booked our accommodations at a Christian dude ranch. So it wasn't until we arrived that I realized that not only was everyone who worked at the dude ranch a Christian, but everyone who was staying there was Christian as well—another unexpected gift. I was surrounded by YHWH's beautiful landscape and God's beautiful children. Scripture tells us that when two or more are gathered in Jesus's name, Jesus promises that he will be in their midst (Matt. 18:20). Was Jesus ever present during this week! I cannot even begin to recount all the amazing stories that I heard from YHWH's children about how he was using them for his kingdom. So not only was God physically nourishing me during this week, but through hearing his stories my spirit was also being fed.

What I heard during this week from YHWH's children were their life stories. I heard about their pasts, from where they had come, how they had been redeemed, and where God had taken them. Even though their individual pasts varied from being pleasant to horrifying, what they all had in common was some sort of difficult family circumstance, tragedy, sexual abuse, or even death that defined their lives. They all had experienced some sort of "fire" in their lives prior to becoming Christians. At some point, they had all experienced some tragedy or crisis and desperately needed someone to extinguish the smoldering fire that resulted. Fortunately for all of them, when they put their trust in Jesus Christ, they found their Savior. The result of finding and following Jesus was obvious in their current lives. Not only had their fires been extinguished, but what had resulted were transformed lives. Every single one of these individuals was currently living abundantly with peace and joy.

Trip to Yellowstone

So it was during a day trip to Yellowstone National Park that YHWH tied up some loose ends for me about his sacred fire and his Shekinah glory. As we entered the park, it became very clear that the forests before us were different from the wildflower-infested forests near the ranch. Immediately upon entering the park, it was obvious that we were looking at the remains of a devastating fire. Our guide explained that in 1988, a series of thirty-one fires had scorched approximately 1.2 million acres of land, leaving behind a landscape of unsightly blackened tree trunks as far as the eye could see. We couldn't believe the destruction and thought of how incredibly powerful the fires must have been. There had been fires in Yellowstone prior to 1988, but nothing to this degree had ever happened. Since it was a policy to let all fires burn out naturally, that is what occurred with these.

What complete and utter destruction we saw that day! We began to question whether letting the fires burn out naturally was a good idea. The landscape was so depressing to look at, and to be completely honest it was ugly. However, when we took our eyes off all of the devastation for just a moment and looked below the scraggly black tree trunks, we saw hope—hope for new life. For approximately the first ten feet off the forest floor, all we could see was the new growth of what looked like millions of new saplings. It was really interesting to see such a conflicting sight of death and destruction alongside an overwhelming abundance of new growth all in one place. Our guide explained to us that the majority of trees in the park are called lodgepole pines. YHWH created these particular pines with a very special, intelligent design. The pinecones that these trees produce and drop each year are sealed by a resin, which keeps the pinecone sealed until the intense heat of a fire cracks the bonds and releases the seeds inside. Then, and only then, do the seeds inside these pinecones become available for sprouting and for new growth.

So in 1988 when these fires were devastating the landscape, YHWH's plan for new growth was already taking place. In fact, YHWH's plan for new growth could *only* take place if a very intense fire occurred. In other words, fire is the catalyst by which new life occurs for this particular pine tree. What a heavenly design! At the exact moment when the heat was the most intense, as the fire was consuming the trees, YHWH was opening the seeds for new life. Talk about a grand plan! Talk about God being there in the darkest moments, and not only being there, but also being active! During these forest fires, YHWH was not just sitting back watching the devastation take place. Oh, he was watching the devastation take place, but what he was really interested in watching was all the pinecones that he had been dropping over all these years, doing exactly what he planned for them to do—release all of their seeds.

As I was taking all of this information in, I couldn't help but think of the lives of the individuals who had shared their stories with me that week. All of a sudden, I looked at the individual tragedies that defined their lives in a whole new way. I was able to see their "fires" as the catalysts that brought them new life. I imagined all of the seeds that YHWH must have personally been dropping year after year after year into their lives so that when their individual tragedies were taking place, his seeds were in place. The seeds YHWH dropped were the gospel seeds of a loving God, a loving Father, who sent us his only Son, Jesus, to save us from ourselves.

During the destruction of these personal fires, YHWH was watching his seeds of new life being broken open so that they were available to sprout. New life was already being generated before their intense fires had even been extinguished. YHWH had not only planted the seeds through fellow believers but had opened the seeds of new life in the midst of their darkest moments. Somehow, *in the midst of their fires, God spoke to them* just as he had to Moses through the burning bush. His voice was probably loud and clear in the midst of their tragedies. In a way similar to how YHWH spoke to me through my sacred fire, he said to them, "This is life without me." These individuals all came to realize that they didn't want the black, charred lives that they had been living, which resulted in only ashes. They all decided that they wanted new life, and that is what the all-powerful YHWH was able to accomplish. God said to them, "Give me your mess, and let me show you what I can do with it." Through his Son, Jesus, YHWH forgave them of their sins and then began the process of mending their broken hearts.

Even though every one of these individuals walked through the fire and felt the intense heat that it put forth, the flames did not consume them. The evidence of new life in all of their lives was dramatic. The smiles on their faces gave them away. It was obvious that they had since spent a long time in YHWH's presence, just like Moses had, because their faces reflected God's glory for everyone to see. YHWH's light had penetrated the darkness of their hearts and had healed them. YHWH's light radiated from them and was evident in their peace, their joy, and the works they were doing for their LORD and Savior's kingdom. The way God was able to turn around the lives of all these individuals is mind-boggling. Once his gospel seeds were broken open, YHWH was able to accomplish the impossible with the charred landscape of their lives when hope was reestablished. Through it all, YHWH made their lives very distinct. Now, instead of ashes, all that could be seen was YHWH's Shekinah glory shining off of them into other people's lives.

The Aftermath

In the aftermath of the fires in Yellowstone, studies were done on the resulting damage, and what the researchers found out was shocking. Not only were a small portion of animals found dead, but less than 1 percent of the soils were heated enough to damage the other plant seeds and roots found throughout the forest. In other words, *the life that existed below the forest floor was barely touched.* And over the entire area they found anywhere from *50,000 to 1,000,000 seeds* of the lodgepole pines *per acre*. Not only did YHWH have a plan for new growth, but he also ensured there would be new life because of the large seed densities. As an added bonus, in the several years following 1988, spectacular displays of wildflowers were seen throughout the burned areas. Because complete sunlight was now hitting the entire forest floor, YHWH showed his Shekinah glory by giving a rainbow of blooms for all to enjoy until the new tree growth was established. Before the fires occurred, the sun's light did not hit the forest floor. If there were seeds ready for germination, nothing would have happened anyway because sunlight was not available to them. With no sunlight, the seeds would have simply died.

For YHWH to show his glory at Yellowstone National Park, it took a sacred fire and the life-giving power of the sun he created. Likewise, many times it takes a sacred fire in our own lives before we allow the life-giving power of YHWH's only Son, Jesus, to shine upon us to give us new life. What sacred fires accomplish is clearing out all of the dead branches and debris that clutter our own lives so that Jesus's glory can shine upon us and produce spectacular wildflower displays. Through Jesus, new life sprouts and communication with our heavenly Father begins. At that point, YHWH's Shekinah glory is revealed for all to see.

Once we start living for YHWH's kingdom, sacred fires can be seen through a different lens and their purposes become clearer. Sacred fires come from heaven so that we can hear, see, and feel YHWH's Shekinah glory all around us, know that he exists, and understand that only he is capable of sprouting new life within us. The purpose of sacred fires is so that YHWH can have a personal relationship with us. The more time we spend in relationship with YHWH, the more our faces and lives start reflecting his glory and begin spreading his gospel seeds into other people's lives. So don't be too quick to try to extinguish the fires in your life or in the lives of others. Remember, the seeds of new life are set free through intense heat. Some fires need to be free to burn to accomplish their true purpose.

YHWH wants each and every one of us to hear his voice, feel his presence, and see his Shekinah glory. He wants to lead us through our daily lives and protect us at night, when the enemy seems so real. He wants to fight for us. YHWH wants to speak to us in a still, small voice, as well as loudly, in order to grab our attention. He wants us to see him in the clouds and the stars, the trees and flowers. He wants us to see him in our parents, husbands, wives, and children. God wants us to see him everywhere. He wants his Shekinah glory to shine on us *so that we can reflect his glory to others*. Remember, YHWH's greatest desire is for us to "see him" so that his presence in our lives will make us distinct from all the other people who are upon the face of the earth.

Chapter 7

The Spirit of Prophecy

"Before I formed you in the womb **I knew you**, and before you were born **I consecrated you**; **I appointed you a prophet** to the nations." (Jer. 1:5 ESV)

The three Hebrew words used in the Old Testament to designate the prophets are *navi*, *roeh*, and *hozeh*. Each of these words designates one who is a spokesperson for God. The usage of *navi* is illustrated by Exodus 4:15–16, which we previously discussed in the chapter on the ark of the covenant. In this passage, YHWH clearly stated that Moses was to be "as God" in relation to Pharaoh, and Aaron would be the intermediary. Aaron's role was to speak to Pharaoh the exact words Moses gave him. YHWH further clarifies the role of Moses and Aaron: YHWH said to Moses, "See I make you as *God to Pharaoh; and Aaron your brother shall be your prophet*" (Exo. 7:1). So in the land of Egypt, in front of the Pharaoh, Moses was as God, and Aaron acted as his prophet, or his spokesman. Therefore, from this Scripture we can see that a man who is designated a prophet is one who speaks forth or announces the declarations of God.[1]

The two words *roeh* and *hozeh* are rendered "seer" and are practically synonymous in meaning. The word *seer* refers to a person designated as a prophet who on occasion "sees" the message that God gives him. After seeing the message, as in a vision or dream, the prophet declares the message to the people. In the Greek language, the word for "prophet" is *prophetes*. This Greek word had a wider significance than the Hebrew words. It signified one who spoke for the god *and* interpreted the god's will. The Greek *prophetes's* role was to act as an interpreter for the muses and the oracles. Therefore, we must be careful to distinguish the biblical prophet from the *prophetes* of the Greeks.

The biblical prophets were not interpreters. They uttered the actual words, which God had given to them, without any modification or interpretation upon their parts. The Bible itself gives an accurate description of a prophet's role: "I will raise up for them a prophet like you from among their brethren; and *I will put my words in his mouth*, and he shall speak to them all that I command him" (Deut. 18:18). The prophet YHWH was to raise up was said to be like Moses. Just as Moses, God's first prophet, was a mediator between God and the nation, so all the future prophets would also serve as mediators.

So why would God allow a prophet to speak for him? Consider what the Israelites said to Moses after God appeared to them at Mount Sinai.

> Now when all the people saw the thunder and the flashes of lightning and the sound of the trumpet and the mountain smoking, the people were afraid and trembled, and they stood far off and said to Moses, "**You speak to us, and we will listen; but do not let God speak to us**, lest we die." (Exo. 20:18–19 ESV)

Because the people were afraid when they heard YHWH's voice, God granted their request of speaking to them through Moses. From that time forward, YHWH decided to communicate with his people through a mediator, now that his people were fully aware of the source of the mediator's words.

> And YHWH said to Moses, "Thus you shall say to the people of Israel: 'You have seen for yourselves that **I have talked with you from heaven**.'" (Exo. 20:22 ESV)

So God spoke to the people of Israel through Moses, then through Joshua (Moses's successor), and finally through the prophets. They served as spokesmen for God to the nation of Israel. This arrangement was truly unique. People who heard the words of the prophet heard the very words of YHWH himself.

Some of the famous prophets of the Old Testament after Moses and Joshua include Samuel, Elijah, Elisha, Jonah, Amos, Hosea, Joel, Isaiah, Micah, Obadiah, Nahum, Jeremiah, Habakkuk, Zephaniah, Daniel, Ezekiel, Zechariah, Haggai, and Malachi. There are simply too many prophets throughout the entire Bible to name them all. There were also prophetesses, or women who possessed the same gifts as the prophets. The four women in the Old Testament who had the gift of prophecy were Moses's sister Miriam, Deborah, Huldah, and the unnamed wife of Isaiah.

So whom did YHWH choose to place in this incredibly important role of being his spokesperson? What were the qualifications of his prophets? Who would God be able to trust with his words? Just like YHWH chose Aaron out of all his people to be their high priest, YHWH also handpicked each and every one of his prophets. Scripture states that before they were formed in their mothers' wombs, God knew these men, and before they were even born, he consecrated and appointed them as his prophets. Also, just as Moses was humble in thinking he was not capable of speaking for God, these chosen men were humble as well. When Jeremiah was told he was to be a prophet to the nations, he surely did not think he was capable of performing this important job. Jeremiah told God that he was only a youth and therefore did not know how to speak. To calm Jeremiah's fears, the Bible says YHWH put forth his hand, touched Jeremiah's mouth, and said, "Behold, I have put my words in your mouth" (Jer. 1:9).

Upon Isaiah's appointment to prophet status, Isaiah declared to God that he was lost and a man of unclean lips. Isaiah felt like he did not deserve to see the vision God was giving him; he did not feel worthy to be YHWH's spokesman because of his own sins. So a seraphim took a burning coal from the altar of God and touched Isaiah's mouth with it, and God said, "Behold, this has touched your lips; your guilt is taken away, and your sin forgiven" (Isa. 6:6–7). In response to God's gift of forgiveness, when Isaiah was then asked by God, "Whom shall I send, and who will go for us?" Isaiah confidently replied, "Here I am! Send me."

YHWH calmed these men's fears of incompetence and youth and forgave them of their sins. By physically touching each man's lips, God gave each one of them the confidence and the ability to become his prophets. With their sins forgiven, God was now going to use them for his service. They were given the strength and power they needed to complete the task God was asking them to do. Now all they had to do was to trust YHWH and continue to be obedient to him.

Of course, the men YHWH chose to be his prophets were humble men. Being humble simply means having a fear of God. Instead of being full of pride in themselves, being humble ensured that God's words would not be interpreted by these men for their own gain. Because these men feared God, YHWH could be sure that his words would be delivered to the people exactly as they were placed in the prophets' mouths. Proverbs 9:10 says, "The fear of YHWH is the beginning of wisdom." God's prophets each met this requirement, or they would never have been chosen in the first place. But simply fearing God was not enough. In addition, each of these men knew the words of God. Scripture had been spoken and written about YHWH before their times. Jeremiah and Ezekiel, for example, were not only prophets but also priests. Both of these men had probably been memorizing Scripture since they were children. Again, YHWH would not have chosen them to be his prophets if they didn't have his words and commandments written in their minds and on their hearts.

So once the prophets were chosen, how did God choose to speak to them? How did God place his words in their mouths? Over the ark of the covenant, God spoke clearly and distinctly to Moses—as a man speaks to a friend. However, to the prophets who followed Moses, Scripture tells us that YHWH revealed all of his messages through dreams and visions through the Holy Spirit.

> **"Hear my words: If there is a prophet among you, I YHWH make myself known to him in a vision; I speak with him in a dream**. Not so with my servant Moses. He is faithful in all my house. With him I speak mouth to mouth, clearly, and not in riddles." (Num. 12:6–8a ESV)

By speaking to the prophets in dreams and visions, not only did the prophets hear God's voice, but they also were able to see with their eyes YHWH's Shekinah glory, his visible presence. Through these dreams and visions, God would reveal to the prophets what he wanted them to say and to whom he wanted them to speak.

For forty years God spoke directly to Moses from his own mouth. After Moses died, God appointed Joshua as Moses's successor to lead the Israelites into the promised land. Joshua, too, was a humble man who had personally served Moses and YHWH for the forty years in the wilderness. He had heard YHWH speak to the people from Mount Sinai and was the only person allowed to go with Moses for the first leg of his trip up the mountain to receive the Ten Commandments. Joshua was a man who feared God and obeyed his commandments. Before Moses died, God instructed Moses to lay hands on Joshua so that he could be commissioned for service and be filled with the spirit of wisdom. When YHWH commissioned Joshua to be Moses's successor, YHWH swore to Joshua, "I will be with you" (Deut. 31:23). Like Moses, Joshua was filled with the Holy Spirit of YHWH and had God's presence with him until the day he died.

After Moses died and Joshua became God's spokesman to the people, God continued to speak directly with Joshua. We know from Scripture that Israel served YHWH all the days of Joshua and also all the days of the elders who outlived Joshua (Joshua 24:31). It wasn't until after this time, when a new generation arose that had never felt YHWH's presence or known of the work he had done for Israel, that Israel started rebelling and worshipping idol gods. They began disobeying God's commandments and law. It was at this time that YHWH began communicating with his people through prophets.

So what were the words that YHWH placed into the mouths of the prophets to speak? For the most part, the messages sent from God were pleas for his people to come back to the law. They were invitations to the people to repent of their sins so they could receive forgiveness. YHWH longed for his people to come back to the covenant that had been made between him and the Israelites so long ago in the wilderness. More than anything, he wanted them to once again become his people so he could be their God. Peace and prosperity were promised to those who chose to change their evil ways and return to loving YHWH with all their hearts, minds, strength, and souls. However, for those who chose to continue worshipping idol gods, the prophets gave them warnings of the future doom and destruction they would experience if they did not change their ways. Sometimes the messages YHWH gave the prophets to speak were of a future Messiah who was to come and who would save them from all of their sins. These messages told of a time when the Messiah would bring with him a kingdom of peace.

To say the least, the prophet's job was by no means an easy one. Prophets were sent to the people with messages that were hard to hear. The people often refused to believe they were sinning and therefore did not heed God's invitations to repentance and forgiveness. As a result, instead of accepting the messages and turning from their wicked ways, the people often attacked the messenger. There are countless stories of prophets being attacked and imprisoned, and many times their lives were threatened. No wonder pages of Scripture are filled with prophets pouring out their souls in grief. They loved their people and longed for them to repent and receive forgiveness, but time and time again the people refused to listen. Because of their circumstances, many times the prophets became frustrated, disheartened, and weak. It was during these difficult times that the prophets themselves often turned from God and ran from the duty YHWH had given them to do. We see Jonah running to the sea and Elijah running to a cave—as if God wouldn't be able to see where they were going. But instead of punishing the prophets for disobedience, God let them run, and then he met each one of them exactly where they were.

YHWH showed his prophets compassion and understanding for the difficult job he had given them to do. He allowed them to rest in his presence for a while, and he calmed their fears. He reminded them of who he was, that he was with them always, and that he would protect them from their enemies. Once they were finally rested, nourished, and at peace, God would send them back to service. God knew very well the difficult job he was asking his prophets to complete. He also knew that his messages would most likely fall on deaf ears. Prophets were not to worry about whether the people listened to them. All they were to do is what God commanded them to do. The following words are what YHWH spoke to Ezekiel in a vision when he called him to be a prophet.

> And he said to me, "Son of man, stand on your feet, and I will speak with you." And as he spoke to me, the Spirit entered into me and set me on my feet, and I heard him speaking to me. And he said to me, **"Son of man, I send you to the people of Israel, to nations of rebels**, who have rebelled against me. They and their fathers have transgressed against me to this very day. The descendants also are impudent and stubborn: I send you to them, and you shall say to them, '**Thus says the Lord God.**' **And whether they hear or refuse to hear (for they are a rebellious house) they will know that a prophet has been among them**."
> (Ezek. 2:1–5 ESV)

Biblical Prophecy

I have been studying biblical prophecy pertaining to future events now for several years. I am fascinated with this subject. As I said before, I love puzzles, am an engineer by education, and am a very logical thinker. The book of Revelation is one of my favorite books of the Bible; I have read it so many times that I have lost count. I look at the prophetic books of the Bible, like Revelation, Ezekiel, and Daniel, as a large puzzle that needs to be put together, and I am always up for a challenge. In addition to Bible studies, I have read numerous books about biblical prophecy. All of them have been very intriguing and enlightening. As I am reading these books, the individual theories are convincing and believable—that is, until I read another book on prophecy whose theories wildly conflict with the ones I just read, and once again I am put into a state of confusion to determine the truth. About the only thing the theologians do agree on are prophecies that were made about future events that have already come true. For example, being on this side of the cross, the various interpreters of prophecy do all agree on the prophecies concerning Jesus's birth, death, and resurrection. That is simply because prophecy is always easier to discern after the event has taken place.

In Revelation alone there are numerous opinions on how Jesus's second coming and the tribulation that precedes his coming will unfold. Will the rapture of the church happen at the beginning of the tribulation, the middle, or the end? Some people adamantly believe that the rapture will occur at the beginning of the tribulation; therefore, the church will not have to go through any suffering. However, equal numbers of people believe that the rapture of the church occurs at the end or the middle of the tribulation. All sides sincerely believe they know the truth, and yet we all know that there can only be one truth. There will be only one way that Jesus will come back onto the scene.

So what are those of us who are searching for the truth to do? Considering that one third of the Bible is prophetic in nature, largely concerning future events that have yet to take place, I find it extremely important to know and understand what YHWH is trying to tell us through the prophets of old. If their words, which were given to them by YHWH and Jesus, were not important, then I believe we would not have these books of the Bible. God's Word is available for us to read over and over again. What I have found in my own experience is that reading other people's opinions of the meaning of Scripture is a good start, but that is all it is—a start. After we examine other people's interpretations of prophecy, it is then up to us to do some investigation on our own. It is not wise to take another person's opinion as truth, by blind faith. We need to open our own Bibles, read God's Word for ourselves, and ask God to reveal to us the deep, mysterious, and hidden things about him that he wants us to know.

Because the prophetic books of the Bible are known to be confusing, I think most believers don't even attempt to read these books—either that, or they believe that these books of the Bible do not apply to them. They believe it is just "Old Testament stuff" that they don't need to pay attention to. Some may also think that since Jesus came and died for us in order to save us from our sins, the New Testament is all we need to pay attention to. This is so far from the truth. To believe that Jesus fulfilled *all* Old Testament prophecy is false, for even Jesus gave us future prophecy concerning himself that has not yet been fulfilled. Our eternal future may lie in what is coming ahead of us, events still unknown. Revelation says that when the Antichrist comes, he will be able to deceive many. What he will be preaching is guaranteed to look a lot like the truth, but it will not *be* the truth. Those who do not know Scripture will be easily deceived, and unfortunately the consequences will be eternal death. Please do not let yourself be deceived by Satan simply because you do not know Scripture. Now is the time to investigate on your own what your Father in heaven wants you to know about him and his Son, Jesus. Today is the day to start reading his very words that he placed in the mouths of the prophets so long ago. YHWH's and Jesus's words are as critical for us today as they were to the people they were spoken to centuries ago.

Dreams and Visions

At the same time I was scouring the Bible for everything I could find about prophets and their roles as spokesmen for God, I was also starting a new study of the book of Daniel. Daniel was one of those humble men chosen by YHWH to be his prophet to a foreign, Gentile nation. It is clear from the very first chapter of Daniel, when he refused to defile himself with the king's food and wine, that Daniel had a fear of YHWH and knowledge of Scripture. As a result of his obedience, God gave Daniel learning, skill in all letters, and wisdom. He was also given an understanding of all visions and dreams and was appointed and consecrated a prophet of YHWH to the nation of Babylon. From that point on, Daniel was known to have wisdom and understanding that surpassed that of any of the other magicians and enchanters of the kingdom.

In Chapter 2 of Daniel, King Nebuchadnezzar has had a dream that is very troubling, and he wanted the wise men of Babylon to not only tell him what the dream meant but to also tell him what the dream was about. When no magician or enchanter was able to accomplish this seemingly impossible task, the king became angry and put out a decree that the wise men were to be slain. When Daniel heard of his fate, that he would perish along with all the other wise men of the nation if the king was not given an interpretation of his dream, Daniel asked the king for a chance. The king complied and gave Daniel an appointment for the next day.

At this point, Daniel did what only a man who feared God knows to do, and that was to seek mercy of the God of heaven concerning this mystery. I think it is likely that Daniel did not sleep that night but instead filled the night with prayer, begging God to reveal to him the king's dream. As a result of humbling himself before YHWH in prayer, "the mystery was revealed to Daniel in a vision of the night" (Dan. 2:19). Because of this vision, not only was Daniel able to tell King Nebuchadnezzar what his dream was about, but he also was able to give him the interpretation of the dream. What Daniel did on the night of seeking mercy and prayer was to ask God for wisdom. No doubt he was praying like never before for understanding and knowledge. Because Daniel knew Scripture, he probably knew the proverbs of Solomon, the wisest man to ever live, and he chose to do exactly as Solomon advised.

> My son, if you **receive** my words and **treasure** up my commandments with you, making your **ear attentive** to wisdom and **inclining your heart** to understanding; yes, if you **call out** for insight and **raise your voice** for understanding, if you **seek** it like silver and **search** for it as for hidden treasures, **then you will understand** the fear of YHWH and **find the knowledge of God**. (Prov. 2:1–5 ESV)

Daniel simply cried out to God, asking for knowledge and an understanding of the king's dream, and that is exactly what Daniel received. Because Daniel was able to explain the king's dream and give its interpretation, he was able to save his own life and the lives of his three friends and all the wise men in Babylon. When Daniel spoke to the king the next day, he gave YHWH all the glory.

> Daniel answered the king and said, "No wise men, enchanters, magicians, or astrologers can show to the king the mystery that the king has asked, **but there is a God in heaven who reveals mysteries**, and he has made known to King Nebuchadnezzar what will be in the latter days." (Dan. 2:27–28a ESV)

Now, I personally do not have a dramatic story of a vision or dream given to me by YHWH that saved my physical life. However, after studying these first few chapters of Daniel in depth, and knowing about a prophet's role, God gave me knowledge and understanding on yet another way he chooses to speak to believers.

I am a prolific dreamer and have always had the ability to remember my dreams. I used to wow my friends with the retelling of all the crazy nonsense that occurred night after night. But I have to say that my dream world has changed since I started writing this book. Since writing about YHWH's divine name, I have been having more vivid and colorful dreams. For approximately the first six months during this time, my dreams largely consisted of me in search of something. Whether it was a piece of clothing, a person, a school book, a classroom, or my class schedule that I was searching for, I was never able to find it. I would spend my entire night searching for that one item and never locate it. In these dreams I became very frustrated, and yet I never gave up the search. I often woke up feeling very anxious.

For six months, these dreams occurred almost every night. I even remember praying to God several nights in a row that he would take these dreams away from me and instead replace them with dreams about him. I thought, *Surely God would rather I dream about him than a missing item.* But these prayers were never answered. During this time, I would hate the thought of going to bed because I already knew what I would be doing in my dreams. It wasn't until I began studying Daniel and reading the verses in Proverbs on wisdom, about seeking and searching for God's hidden treasures, that YHWH gave me insight into what these particular dreams were all about.

One day I realized that over the previous months, day in and day out, I had been seeking and searching God's Word for wisdom and understanding in the writing of this book. I had been seeking and searching YHWH's mysteries and hidden meanings in the Bible. I had been crying out for insight and raising my voice to God for understanding when the meaning escaped me. I had been asking for clarity and wisdom from his Word and had been asking him to place his words in my mouth because I wanted this book to be his work and not mine. Once I realized this, YHWH explained to me that my dreams were simply an extension of what I was doing during the day. Just because I was sleeping did not mean that I wasn't still seeking and searching.

So why is it that in my dreams I never found what I was looking for? Doesn't YHWH always want us to find what we are looking for when we are searching for meaning in his Word? Of course he does. But sometimes God is the one who has to give us this wisdom in order for us to have complete knowledge and understanding. YHWH is the only one who can explain his hidden and mysterious things. Sometimes God has to physically place his words in our minds and on our lips as he did for his prophets.

I have found this to be true in my writing. On numerous occasions I came across several Scripture passages that I just did not understand, but somehow I knew that they were important. If I was still confused about their meaning after pondering them for several days, in prayer before bed I would ask God to enlighten me. I can't even count how many times after praying this prayer that, by the time I woke up, I knew what God was saying through his Scripture. Upon waking, the meaning that I was looking for was right there in my brain and on my lips. I asked God for the meaning of his Word, and he gave it to me generously. But just like Daniel, I had to take the first step and ask. And just like Daniel knew where the meaning of the king's dream had come from, I clearly knew where my understanding of the Scripture came from. I knew God had given me the wisdom I had asked for: he placed it in my brain while I was in an unconscious state. Suddenly, I knew why I never found what I was looking for in my dreams—because I had already looked while I was awake and couldn't find it. It was God who needed to give me the understanding and knowledge because it was only through him that I would discover it. YHWH does what only YHWH can do: he brings what is hidden in the darkness into the light.

I now see my dreams in a whole new light—God's light, that is. It is at night that God wants to reveal his glory to me because he knows that it is in the darkness that his glory shines the brightest. No longer do I consider my dreams crazy nonsense. I now know that my dreams are one more incredible way in which YHWH speaks to me. In addition, because I asked for even more knowledge and understanding, YHWH has also taught me over the years how to interpret my dreams, with the help of the Holy Spirit, in order to find their hidden meanings.

So never dismiss how YHWH wants to speak to you. If you think that your dreams are senseless, think again. I have come to understand that dreams are simply personal, modern-day parables given directly to us by our Creator in order to speak truth into our lives. Dreams are incredible "word pictures," and we all know that pictures are worth a thousand words.

The Voice of YHWH

The Old Testament is filled with stories of people hearing God's voice. Adam, Noah, Abraham, Isaac, Jacob, Joseph, Moses, Joshua, King David, Daniel, and the prophets all heard God speak on a regular basis, if not daily. All of these men led extraordinary lives, not because they were extraordinary men but because of the extraordinary voice that was guiding and instructing them. These men heard YHWH's voice daily, either directly from him or through dreams, visions, prophets, or angels of the LORD. And because they were obedient to what they heard, Christians today are still studying these men's lives thousands of years later.

Unfortunately many Christians today do not hear YHWH's sweet voice, even though they have the Holy Spirit living within them, because no one has taught them how. In all of my years of attending church, not once do I ever remember hearing a sermon preached on how God's children hear his precious voice. Not once were the various methods of hearing YHWH's voice taught to me through a preacher or Sunday school teacher. Oh, I learned how to pray, but I was never taught how to *hear* God's voice. There is a distinct difference. Prayer is a powerful way for believers to speak to YHWH, to allow their voices to be heard. But even if you pray every day, that doesn't mean you know how to then listen for God's reply to your prayers. Since the ways in which YHWH speaks are not being taught in the churches, I believe most Christians don't hear their heavenly Father's voice. When someone is unaware that something is even possible, then why would that individual ever expect to experience it? And since most Christians are not expectant to hear YHWH's voice daily, his personal words for them go unheard.

Various Ways of Communication

You see, it is YHWH's voice that gives you life and makes you extraordinary. If you are not hearing God's voice, then you need to start investigating his various ways of communication. From this day forward, make sure to never limit his voice or the ways he is capable of getting a message to you. And please don't ever make the mistake of placing YHWH's voice into the box of Sunday mornings at church. The ways that God communicated with the characters of the Bible are the same ways he communicates with believers today. Finally, always remember that there are no coincidences. If you remember these things and start searching out his voice daily, you can be sure that your relationship with your heavenly Father will come alive and your life will be completely transformed.

So what can you do today to start your own relationship and daily communication with your heavenly Father? It all comes down to how you position yourself. You need to regularly step out of the chaos of the physical world and into YHWH's spiritual world so that you can hear his spiritual voice. Here are some ideas:

- Read your Bible daily, knowing that God can speak directly to you through the words you are reading.
- Go to church in order to hear YHWH's voice spoken through your pastor.
- Join Bible studies and small groups in order to study his Word with others.
- Pray daily.
- Then intentionally listen for God's reply. (Prov. 20:12; Jer. 33:2-3; John 10:27; John 16:13-15)
- Pay attention to your dreams. (Joel 2:28; Job 33:15; Acts 2:17)
- Know that Jesus still appears to people in visions. (Joel 2:28; Job 33:15; Acts 2:17)
- Ask YHWH's Holy Spirit to help you interpret your dreams and visions for meaning.
- Spend quality time being silent in YHWH's presence.
- While doing so, take notice of the words, thoughts, or phrases that come into your mind that you know are not your own. (1 Corin. 12:8)
- Analyze the words that complete strangers, possibly angels, speak into your life as perhaps being direct words from God. (Heb. 13:2)
- Intentionally look for YHWH's personal messages through his creation and things that surround you. (Ps. 1-4; Rom. 1:20)
- Remember, there are no coincidences.
- Pay attention to the lyrics of a song God places on your lips.
- Know that YHWH may choose to speak to you through friends and family.
- Understand that God still uses his children to speak prophecy into other people's lives. (Joel 2:28; Acts 2:17; 1 Corin. 12:10, 14:1,5,39)
- Be bold and ask other people who hear God's voice to teach you how to recognize and find it.
- Surround yourself with other believers who are searching out his voice as well.
- Ask YHWH to awaken all of your senses to his voice.

- Read books on discerning the voice of God.
- Start each day with questions such as: "Father, what do you want me to know today?" "What is your will for me today?" "What does love demand of me today?"
- Expect a reply before the day is over.
- Finally, when you do hear YHWH's voice in a new way and it fills your heart to overflowing, rejoice with your heavenly Father.

Let the mystery of YHWH's voice be the hidden treasure that you seek, search, and cry out for. If you seek his voice, you will find it. That is guaranteed! But remember that the word *seek* is an action word. You must intentionally search for God's voice in order to show him your interest in hearing him before he will respond. But respond he will because there is nothing that makes YHWH happier than his children searching for an intimate and personal relationship with him. So expect to hear God's voice. Understand what is possible, and then strategically position yourself, both physically and spiritually, in order to make it happen. And finally, when you start hearing YHWH's voice, know that it will begin transforming you from the ordinary to the extraordinary. Make sure that you record in a journal all that YHWH tells you over the years so that you too will have proof that you serve a living God who still speaks to his children.

Once you hear YHWH's voice regularly, never forget that you too may be commanded to speak to other believers the words he places in your mouth or the visions he places in your sight. Like the prophets of old, the words YHWH gives you may not be for you alone. His words may, in fact, be meant to save the eternal life of another. They may be meant for the person sitting right next to you. Never fail to speak God's wisdom just because you are afraid of how other people will receive his words. Just like the prophets of old, you need to be ready to speak when YHWH commands you to, regardless of whether his words fall on deaf ears.

"It is written, 'Man shall not **live** by bread alone, **but by every word that proceeds from the mouth of God.**'"
(Matt. 4:4)

Chapter 8

Urim and Thummim

> When Saul saw the army of the Philistines, he was afraid, and his heart trembled greatly. **And when Saul inquired of YHWH, YHWH did not answer him, either by dreams, or by Urim, or by prophets.** (1 Sam. 28:5–6 ESV)

When I first heard about the Urim and the Thummim going missing along with YHWH's divine name during the silent years, I asked myself many questions. First of all, *What were they?* Second, *What was their purpose?* And finally, *Why had I never heard of them before now?* As I started looking into these mysterious objects, I got this feeling that I was going to discover something truly unique and amazing, just like the day I discovered that my God has a divine name.

Well, YHWH does not disappoint. Not only are the Urim and Thummim truly unique and amazing objects, but they also have everything to do with YHWH's divine name and communication with him. I have come to realize just how important it is to understand the purpose of the Urim and Thummim to truly understand God's plan for our salvation. As described in the previous chapter, YHWH spoke to the prophets through dreams and visions. In this chapter, we will discover that YHWH used the Urim and Thummim to speak to the high priest. As the prophets represented God to the people, Aaron, the high priest, represented the people before God. Through the use of the Urim and Thummim, the high priest was able to discern YHWH's will for the people of Israel. But before we get into what these objects were and how they worked, we need to first discuss the role of the high priest. As we look into the critical role that he played, we will discover the purpose of the Urim and Thummim.

Priesthood

We know that YHWH chose Aaron from the tribe of Levi to be his high priest. Therefore, Aaron became God's high priest, and the Levites became God's priestly tribe. The Levites served as assistants to Aaron and to Aaron's sons, who would eventually become Aaron's successors upon his death. Together, the roles of the high priest and the Levites were to take care of the duties of the tabernacle and the duties of the altar. This entire tribe was to serve YHWH daily in all that they did. "Behold, I have taken the Levites from among the people of Israel instead of every first-born that opens the womb among the people of Israel. The Levites shall be mine" (Num. 3:12).

Priesthood was a special assignment given by God to a special tribe. The Levites' job importance could not be overstated, because their job responsibility was huge. They were responsible not only for taking care of the physical structure of the tabernacle itself but also for everything that was located inside of the tabernacle, which included the ark of the covenant containing God's Word and his divine name. Because the ark of the covenant was in the tabernacle, the tabernacle was the very place where YHWH's Shekinah glory dwelled among the people. In addition, the altar that was found in the tabernacle held the sacred fire that was to be kept continuously burning so that all future sacrifices would be consumed by the same fire that was sent from heaven. YHWH described priesthood as a gift: "And you and your sons with you shall attend to your priesthood for all that concerns the altar and that is within the veil; and you shall serve. *I give priesthood as a gift*, and any one else who comes near shall be put to death" (Num. 18:7).

YHWH would not allow the important job of priesthood to be placed into just anyone's hands. Therefore, whoever was not from the tribe of Levi and attempted to enter the tabernacle would be put to death. Also, if anyone questioned YHWH's authority on any of these matters, he would be put to death as well, just like Korah was when he questioned the authority of Moses and Aaron before the LORD. So, because priesthood was such a special position, God gave Moses specific instructions on what the priests were to wear. Along with precise instructions on how the ark of the covenant and the tabernacle were to be built came specific instructions on the high priest's garments while he was in the tabernacle. Since he was going to be near the presence of YHWH daily, close to his written Word, his divine name, his sacred fire, and his Shekinah glory, Aaron's garments needed to be very special indeed.

> "And you shall make **holy garments** for Aaron your brother, **for glory and for beauty**. You shall speak to all the skillful, whom I have filled with a spirit of skill, that they make Aaron's garments **to consecrate him for my priesthood**. These are the garments that they shall make: a breastpiece, an ephod, a robe, a coat of checker work, a turban, and a sash. **They shall make holy garments** for Aaron your brother and his sons **to serve me as priests**." (Exo. 28:2–4 ESV)

The tabernacle was considered holy because of what was contained within—the ark of the covenant. The tabernacle was also holy because of God's visible presence that resided over it through the cloud by day, the fire by night, and the sacred fire that burned in the altar. Therefore, wherever the tabernacle resided, the ground under it was considered sacred as well. In order for Aaron and his sons to serve as priests, they also had to be consecrated, or made holy, before they could enter the tabernacle and commence their duties. So the high priest's garments were made as YHWH commanded. The high priest was clothed exactly as God wanted him to be.

> And Moses said to the congregation, "This is the thing that YHWH has commanded to be done." And **Moses brought**

Aaron and his sons and washed them with water. And he put the coat on him and tied the sash around his waist and clothed him with the robe and put the ephod on him and tied the skillfully woven band of the ephod around him, binding it to him with the band. And **he placed the breastpiece on him, and in the breastpiece he put the Urim and the Thummim**. And he set the turban on his head, and on the turban, in front, he set the golden plate, the holy crown, as YHWH commanded Moses. (Lev. 8:5–9 ESV)

Aha, our first clue! After Moses cleansed Aaron with water, Moses dressed Aaron with all of the priestly garments, which included the Urim and the Thummim. From this verse we know the Urim and Thummim were part of the garments that made the high priest holy in YHWH's presence.

You Shall Put

Our second clue about the Urim and Thummim comes from knowing that there are absolutely no instructions from God for making the Urim and Thummim. The very first time we hear of the Urim and Thummim is while Moses is with YHWH on Mount Sinai, when he is receiving precise instructions on the construction of the rest of the garments.

> "And in the breastpiece of judgment **you shall put** the Urim and the Thummim, and they shall be **on Aaron's heart, when he goes in before YHWH**." (Exo. 28:30 ESV)

YHWH said to Moses, "you shall put," not "you shall make." For the breastpiece, ephod, robe, coat, turban, and girdle, God said, "you shall make," but that was not the case for the Urim and Thummim. From the phrase "you shall put," we can safely conclude that the Urim and Thummim were items that YHWH *gave* Moses to place in the breastpiece of judgment. What this means is that the Urim and

Thummim were not made by the people but by the very hand of God, which makes them extraordinarily special. Also, from this verse we know that every time Aaron went into the presence of YHWH, the Urim and Thummim were to be physically located upon his heart, which we all know is a very special place of the human body.

Without the heart there is no physical life. We also know that the condition of our hearts directly determines the physical strength and health of our bodies because the heart's purpose is to deliver oxygen-rich blood to all of the body's parts. God describes the blood that our heart pumps as "life of the flesh" (Lev. 17:11). Spiritually speaking, the condition of our hearts directly determines our ability to love God, others, and ourselves. The health of our souls is directly related to the amount of love our hearts are capable of giving. When we receive love from someone else, it is like receiving life. Therefore, just by the placement of the Urim and Thummim in the breastpiece directly "upon" Aaron's heart, we can safely conclude that these objects were of extreme importance and *just perhaps* were needed for "life."

We have seen so far that YHWH entrusted Moses and the Israelites to build his tabernacle, the ark of the covenant, and all of the high priest's garments, but not the Urim and the Thummim. So what could they be? Don't you just love puzzles? So far we have a few of the pieces of this mystery, but we need to keep digging. The picture will soon become clear. There are only seven verses in the Bible about the Urim and the Thummim. Hopefully, seven verses are enough for us to determine what these items were. I'm starting to think they are one of those hidden and mysterious things that only YHWH can reveal when we search and seek for his truth and ask for the wisdom and understanding that only he can provide. So to find out more about what these objects could have been, we first need to know all there is to know about the breastpiece into which the Urim and Thummim were placed.

Breastpiece of Judgment

"You shall make a **breastpiece of judgment**, in skilled work. In the style of the ephod you shall make it—of gold, blue and purple and scarlet yarns, and fine twined linen shall you make it. It shall be square and doubled, a span its length and a span its breadth. **You shall set in it four rows of stones**. A row of sardius, topaz, and carbuncle shall be the first row; and the second row an emerald, a sapphire, and a diamond; and the third row a jacinth, an agate, and an amethyst; and the fourth row a beryl, an onyx, and a jasper. They shall be set in gold filigree. **There shall be twelve stones with their names according to the names of the sons of Israel**. They shall be like signets, **each engraved with its name**, for the twelve tribes." (Exo. 28:15–21 ESV)

Imagine twelve sparkling gems of all colors, set in gold, covering the breastpiece of judgment, which is made out of blue, purple, gold, and scarlet materials, all made for glory and for beauty. Inscribed on these precious stones are the names of the twelve tribes, one name per precious gem. It must have been a sight to see. Aaron must have looked like royalty when he wore his priestly garments. But this breastpiece was not made simply for glory and for beauty. It was a significant piece of the high priest's holy garments and played a very important role in allowing the high priest to enter into God's presence. In addition to the twelve stones placed on the front of the breastpiece, there were two onyx stones that were placed on the shoulders of the ephod that attached the breastpiece to the rest of the garments.

"You shall take **two onyx stones**, and engrave on them the names of the sons of Israel, **six of their names on the one stone, and the names of the remaining six on the other stone**, in the order of their birth. As a jeweler engraves signets, so shall you engrave the two stones with the names of the sons of Israel. You shall enclose them in settings of gold filigree. And you shall set the two stones on the shoulder pieces of the ephod, **as stones of remembrance for the sons**

of Israel. And Aaron shall bear their names before YHWH on his two shoulders for remembrance." (Exo. 28:9–12 ESV)

Now we are getting somewhere. There were a total of fourteen stones located on the high priest's garments: twelve on the breastpiece and two on the shoulders of the ephod, all with the names of the tribes of Israel inscribed on them. The purpose of these stones was that when the high priest went into YHWH's presence, God's people were brought to his remembrance. From this verse, one extremely important role of the high priest comes to light. Every time he went in before YHWH, he represented the people before God; therefore, the way in which his garments were constructed were meant to continuously remind YHWH of the covenant with Israel—that he was their God and they were his people.

So before we go any further, let's take a moment to ponder what it was about the high priest's garments that would have made them holy. What allowed Aaron to stand in YHWH's presence on holy ground to remind God of his covenant with the people of Israel? Was it the red, purple, blue, and gold material used in the construction of the garments that made them holy? No, the rich colors of the materials did make the garments beautiful and radiant, but not holy. Was it the brilliant, precious gems of all different colors of the rainbow that covered the breastpiece and the ephod that made them holy? The stones did indeed make the garments sparkle with beauty and glory, but no, the stones themselves did not make the garments holy.

Was it the names of the twelve tribes that were inscribed on these precious gems that made the garments holy? No, by no means would the names of the tribes make anything holy. YHWH knew very well that his people were not righteous people, and their names were far from holy. When I considered all of these facts, there was only one conclusion that I could draw. What made the high priest's garments holy was not the garments themselves. What made the garments holy and allowed Aaron to be in YHWH's presence were the items that were placed *inside* the garments, the items that were made by God himself: the Urim and Thummim.

The ark of the covenant was similar in this way. Was this extraordinarily beautiful box covered in gold holy because of the materials it was made out of? No, the ark of the covenant was holy because of what was placed *inside* of it: the Ten Commandments that were inscribed by YHWH's own finger, on which he had written his divine name; the manna he rained down from heaven to nourish his people; and the budded, blossomed, and fruited rod of Aaron. These items inside the ark of the covenant are what made it holy. Likewise, was the tabernacle holy because of the materials that were used in its construction? No, the tabernacle was holy only because the ark of the covenant resided *within* it and YHWH's presence dwelled over it. So what was it about the Urim and Thummim that made the high priest's garments holy?

YHWH's Holy Name

At this point in my thought process, I asked myself, *What do the ark of the covenant and the tabernacle have in common?* It didn't take long for me to realize that both the ark of the covenant and the tabernacle were constructed to house God's divine name of YHWH.

> "**I have built the house for the name of YHWH**, the God of Israel. **And there I have set the ark, in which is the covenant of YHWH** that he made with the people of Israel."
> (2 Chron. 6:10–11 ESV)

Could it be possible from what we know so far of YHWH's divine name that the Urim and the Thummim were also objects that he inscribed his holy name upon, like the stone tablets given to Moses and placed in the ark of the covenant? Could it be that YHWH's holy name is what made the high priest's garments holy, once the Urim and Thummim were placed inside the breastpiece over Aaron's heart?

Think about it. Aaron had all of the tribes' names written on the breastpiece and the ephod. Aaron's role as high priest was to stand as the nation of Israel's representative of the covenant between God and his people. So as we think of God's covenant, what name is missing? The covenant was between YHWH and the Israelites. The fourteen stones located on the breastpiece and the ephod represented the Israelites. Aaron's job was simply to be the people's representative, the mediator who stood between them and God. So how else would YHWH's holy name be represented on the high priest's garments?

When I first began researching what the Urim and Thummim were, along with their purpose, I soon came to realize that it would not be an easy task. As I said, there are only seven passages in the Bible that address these objects. Therefore, I did what most people in America do when they have a question and need an answer: I went to the Internet. The first six articles I found that were written about the Urim and Thummim indicated that they were believed to be stones with the words *yes* and *no* inscribed on them. These articles described the high priest pulling these stones out of the breastpiece and rolling them to determine YHWH's will concerning whatever situation was brought to the high priest for discernment. As I was reading these opinions (which all seemed to agree with one other), I immediately knew that they were wrong. Even before I did my own research in the Bible for clues, I knew without a doubt that the Urim and Thummim were not stones with the words *yes* and *no* inscribed on them. I don't know how I knew that these opinions were wrong; I just did.

First of all, the way these objects were described in these articles made them sound too much like how an Ouija board operates. A question is asked to a spirit, and the spirit leads a person's hand to move to either "yes" or "no." Second, the first thing I noticed in reading the verses in the Bible about the Urim and Thummim is that these words were capitalized. I thought, *Would these two words be capitalized if they were simply stones with* yes *and* no *written on them that the high priest physically rolled?* I surely did not think so, because only proper nouns are usually capitalized. In addition, if the Urim and Thummim were stones with *yes* and *no* written on them, why would YHWH have needed to inscribe them himself? If that were the case, then I would think anyone could have made them, just like the rest of the priestly garments.

Additionally, what we will soon discover from the remaining verses concerning the Urim and Thummim is that the high priest did indeed use these objects in communication with YHWH. Therefore, if they were stones with the words *yes* and *no* written upon them, every question asked by the high priest would have to be carefully phrased so that a yes-or-no answer from God would be sufficient. I don't know about you, but the God I know has never answered my questions or prayers with a simple yes or no. YHWH's answers to my prayers have always been a little more complicated than that. And finally, I already knew the meanings of the words Urim and Thummim. And by now, you know how important the meaning of names is to God.

Light and Perfection

The word *Urim* comes from a common Hebrew verb meaning "to be or to become light," "to shine," "to give light." In addition, the second meaning of *Urim* is "flame." The word *Thummim* means "perfection." So together, the words *Urim and Thummim* mean "light and perfection."[1] Hmm ... interesting. I have never known of the words *yes* and *no* as having the meaning of "light and perfection." But if we consider that the Urim and Thummim possibly had YHWH's name written upon them, it is easy to see how they would mean "light and perfection."

On the very first day of creation, YHWH spoke into the darkness and created light. On the fourth day, God created the lights—the sun and the moon and the stars—and he placed them in the heavens to light our way. God's Word is described as being "a lamp to my feet and a light to my path" (Ps. 119:105). And YHWH himself will eventually be our everlasting light. "The sun shall be no more your light by day, nor for brightness shall the moon give light by night; but *YHWH will be your everlasting light*" (Isa. 60:19). We also know that YHWH is the epitome of perfection in all that he is and all that he does. There is no one more perfect than God. A simple look at creation or how the human body operates gives us an idea of YHWH's ability for perfection. Therefore, the meaning of "light and perfection" for the words *Urim* and *Thummim* give these items an even greater significance.

What did ring true with me from the first six opinions I read is that the Urim and Thummim were most likely stones. That seemed to make sense to me, considering the high priest's garments already had fourteen stones on them. These fourteen stones were "as stones of remembrance for the sons of Israel." So to say the Urim and Thummim were stones is plausible. And since Scripture does describe YHWH, Jesus, and believers as stones, it is also plausible that these stones had God's divine name inscribed on them in order to represent him in the covenant with his people. "Trust in YHWH forever, for *YHWH God is an everlasting rock*" (Isa. 26:4). "Come to him, to *that living stone* [Jesus], rejected by men but in God's sight chosen and precious; and *like living stones be yourselves built into a spiritual house*, to be a holy priesthood, to offer spiritual sacrifices acceptable to God through Jesus Christ" (1 Peter 2:4–5).

Role of the High Priest

Before I tell you about the other theory I came upon, which described what the Urim and the Thummim were and how they operated, let's continue to look at some more verses describing the role of the high priest to discover how critical a position he held in representing the people of Israel.

> "So **Aaron shall bear the names** of the sons of Israel in the **breastpiece of judgment upon his heart**, when he goes into the holy place, to bring them to continual remembrance before YHWH. And in the breastpiece of judgment **you shall put the Urim and the Thummim, and they shall be upon Aaron's heart, when he goes in before YHWH**; thus **Aaron shall bear judgment of the people of Israel upon his heart before YHWH continually**." (Exo. 28:29–30)

We must not miss that the breastpiece was called the *breastpiece of judgment*. It was made very specifically for the judgment of the people of Israel, and Aaron was the one chosen to bear judgment of the people upon his heart before YHWH continually. Wow! Talk about job responsibility.

> "… and Aaron shall **take upon himself any guilt** incurred in the holy offering which the people of Israel hallow as their holy gifts." (Exo. 28:38)

> So YHWH said to Aaron, "You and your sons and your fathers' house with you **shall bear iniquity in connection with the sanctuary**; and you and your sons with you **shall bear iniquity in connection with your priesthood**." (Num. 18:1)

> "And you shall attend to the duties of the sanctuary and the duties of the altar, **that there be wrath no more upon the people of Israel**." (Num. 18:5)

Can you imagine it? As high priest, not only was Aaron now responsible for his own sins but also for all of the sins that occurred in relation to the sanctuary, the priesthood, and offerings to YHWH from the people of Israel. Before God, Aaron continually bore all of these sins of the people on his own shoulders. Talk about job stress! Aaron was asked to do all this for one reason: so that the people would not have to feel God's wrath for their sins.

So with all this guilt laid upon Aaron for all the sins committed by the people day in and day out, in order for Aaron to stand holy in front of YHWH, wouldn't he have to be forgiven of all of these sins? Otherwise, he would not be considered holy to stand in front of God on sacred ground. With all that guilt on his shoulders, there is no way YHWH would even allow him into his sanctuary, let alone the Holy of Holies, where the ark of the covenant was placed. There is only one way that Aaron would be considered holy enough to enter into YHWH's presence, and that is if God forgave Aaron of all of these sins on a regular basis. Therefore, before Aaron could even serve as high priest, there was an elaborate set of sacrifices and ceremonies that took place in order to consecrate both him and his garments and to forgive him and his sons of their personal sins.

> Then Moses took some of the anointing oil and of the blood which was on the altar, and sprinkled it upon Aaron and his garments, and also upon his sons and his sons' garment; **so he consecrated Aaron and his garments**, and his sons and his sons' garments with him. … "And you shall not go out from the door of the tent of meeting for seven days, until the days of your ordination are completed, for it will take **seven days to ordain you**. As has been done today, YHWH has commanded to be done **to make atonement for you**. At the door of the tent of meeting you shall remain day and night for seven days, performing what YHWH has charged, lest you die; for I have so commanded." (Lev. 8:30, 33–35)

So Aaron and his sons' sins were forgiven through the blood of the sacrifices that were upon the altar. Through this seven-day ritual they were consecrated and made holy. But what about the people's sins that were placed on Aaron's shoulders? How were their sins forgiven? YHWH made provisions for that as well. Along with all the daily duties of the sanctuary and the duties of the altar, YHWH commanded the people of Israel to hold seven feasts. One of these seven feasts occurs in the seventh month of the Jewish calendar and is called the Day of Atonement.

> "And it shall be a statute to you for ever that in the seventh month, on the tenth day of the month, you shall afflict yourselves, and shall do no work, either the native or the stranger who sojourns among you; for **on this day shall atonement be made for you, to cleanse you; from all your sins you shall be clean before YHWH**. It is a sabbath of solemn rest to you, and you shall afflict yourselves; it is a statute for ever. **And the priest who is anointed and consecrated** as priest in his father's place shall make atonement, **wearing the holy linen garments**; he **shall make atonement for the sanctuary,** and he shall make

> atonement for **the tent of meeting** and for **the altar,** and he shall make atonement **for the priests** and **for all the people of the assembly**. And this shall be an everlasting statute for you, that **atonement may be made for the people of Israel once in the year because of all their sins**." (Lev. 16:29–34)

The Day of Atonement was a Sabbath day of solemn rest and fasting. It was, and still is, the holiest day of the year for the Jewish people. It was the only day that the high priest was allowed to enter the Holy of Holies in the tabernacle or temple to approach YHWH where his Spirit resided above the mercy seat of the ark of the covenant. It was there in the Holy of Holies that the high priest would sprinkle sacrificial blood over the mercy seat and ask God for forgiveness of sins for the nation of Israel. Because of how sacred the ground was in the Holy of Holies, every year when the high priest approached the ark of the covenant, he was putting his life on the line for the people. He was literally standing between life and death. As he approached, God would judge his people of their sins. If God forgave the people of their sins, then the people would once again be in righteous standing before God for one more year. However, if their sins were not forgiven, then the wrath of God would come upon the high priest and all of the people, and all would be lost. So every year, on the Day of Atonement, the high priest would ask YHWH to forgive the nation of their sins, and every year their sins would be wiped clean.

When we consider the importance of the high priest's garments in bringing into remembrance the covenant between YHWH and his people, along with the role he played yearly during the Day of Atonement, it becomes clear that the Urim and Thummim were not merely objects engraved with the words *yes* and *no*. However, if we consider that maybe these items had God's divine name written on them, we can see how God would daily be reminded of the covenant he made with his people. Because of his holy name alone, YHWH would be willing to forgive the Israelites of their sins on the Day of Atonement so that he could be their God and they could be his people. YHWH would be reminded throughout the year, through his holy name in the high priest's garments, that it was a loving relationship that he truly desired with his people.

Once the people's sins were forgiven, the high priest could then use the Urim and Thummim for the other significant purpose that YHWH had planned for them. Once the people's sins were atoned for, direct communication between Aaron and YHWH became possible so that the people would know YHWH's will for them. It's as if, once the people's sins were wiped clean for one more year, the static from the telephone line was removed, thus making communication with God crystal clear. This makes perfect sense to me because it seems like everything God has ever done and will ever do for mankind has been for the purpose of communication.

Communication Devices

By pondering the first two verses concerning the Urim and Thummim, we have already discovered that these extraordinary objects were physically located in the breastpiece over Aaron's heart. We were also able to deduce that YHWH himself made these objects. Finally, we realized it must be the Urim and Thummim themselves that made the high priest's garments holy. In contrast, four of the remaining five verses enlighten for us the other incredible purpose these objects served. What will become clear after examining the remaining verses is that the Urim and Thummim were used by the high priest as a communication device for determining YHWH's perfect will for his people.

> Moses spoke to YHWH, saying, "**Let YHWH, the God of the spirits of all flesh, appoint a man over the congregation** who shall go out before them and come in before them, who shall lead them out and bring them in, that the congregation of YHWH may not be as sheep that have no shepherd." So YHWH said to Moses, "**Take Joshua the son of Nun, a man in whom is the Spirit, and lay your hand on him. Make him stand before Eleazar the priest and all the congregation, and you shall commission him in their**

> **sight**. You shall invest him with some of your authority, that all the congregation of the people of Israel may obey. **And he shall stand before Eleazar the priest, who shall inquire for him by the judgment of the Urim before YHWH."** (Num. 27:15–21a ESV)

After Aaron died, his son Eleazar inherited the role of high priest, along with the priestly garments. When YHWH told Moses that he would not be going into the promised land, he told Moses to appoint Joshua, the son of Nun, to take his place. As part of this commission, Joshua was to stand before Eleazar so that he could inquire from YHWH his perfect will. It was only after confirmation from the Urim and Thummim, through the high priest, that Joshua was appointed as Moses's successor to lead YHWH's people. Just as YHWH communicated with the people through his budded rod that Aaron was to be his high priest, likewise, YHWH used the Urim and Thummim to communicate who would bring his people into the promised land after Moses's death. Joshua's appointment to become Moses's successor was an extremely significant event, so much so that YHWH instructed Eleazar to inquire of the Urim and Thummim so the people would receive YHWH's undeniable confirmation that Joshua was his chosen man.

In the next verse pertaining to the Urim and Thummim, it becomes obvious that King Saul, the first king of Israel, communicated with YHWH through the use of the Urim, as well as by dreams and by prophets. "When Saul saw the army of the Philistines, he was afraid, and his heart trembled greatly. And when Saul inquired of YHWH, *YHWH did not answer him, either by dreams, or by Urim, or by prophets*" (1 Sam. 28:5–6). When Saul failed to obey the voice of God, YHWH removed his Spirit from Saul and no longer answered him, even during a time of war. Because of Saul's disobedience, all communication lines with YHWH previously available to Saul were completely severed.

The last two verses that give us a clue to the use of the Urim and Thummim are almost identical. They both address the same situation but are found in two different books of the Bible.

These sought their registration among those enrolled in the genealogies, but it was not found there, so they were excluded from the priesthood as unclean. The governor told them that they were not to partake of the most holy food **until a priest with Urim and Thummim should arise**. (Neh. 7:64–65, Ezra 2:62–63 ESV)

Both of these verses state that until a high priest arose who could consult the Urim and Thummim on his genealogy, whoever sought priesthood would not be allowed to serve YHWH as a priest or be allowed near his presence. Because of the significant role the priests played, until YHWH confirmed that these individuals had the right genealogy, they would not be allowed to eat the most holy food found within the temple. By repeating this same message two times in the Bible, YHWH is making it very clear to us that this determination could *only* be made through the Urim and Thummim.

From these four verses concerning the Urim and Thummim, some of the critical decisions that were determined by their use become very clear. Moses, King Saul, and the governor Nehemiah all had some very important questions for YHWH. These questions had to do with determining Moses's successor, a war with the Philistines, and verifying genealogy for the priesthood. These situations required that God's perfect will be made known to them so that they knew without a doubt the path he wanted them to take. The situations and questions posed by these men required a complete answer from YHWH, not a simple yes or no.

Divine Communication

It wasn't until I read another theory of what the Urim and Thummim were, and how these two objects possibly worked, that I knew what I was reading was true. Again, I don't know how to explain how I knew other than to say that it just fit with everything God was revealing to me through the Bible about the Urim and Thummim and his divine name.

Now remember, we know that the breastpiece had four rows of three stones (twelve stones in total) with the names of the twelve tribes written on them. There was one name written on each stone. Each tribe's name consisted of two to six letters. In total there were fifty letters on the breastpiece. The high priest would use the Urim and Thummim when an answer to a critical question was needed from YHWH.

According to this theory, the Urim and Thummim were stones with YHWH's two separate divine names inscribed upon them. When a question was brought to the high priest, he would begin by meditating on the holy name written upon the Urim. This would cause the letters on the stones of the breastpiece that were necessary for the answer to raise or light up. The Urim was therefore called the "Illuminator." However, the high priest would still not be able to answer the question since he would not know the order of the letters that were raised or illuminated. It wasn't until the high priest contemplated on the holy name written upon the Thummim that the letters would be put in order, giving him the answer to the question. The second name was therefore called Thummim, the "Completer," because it was through this name that the answer was completed. Through the Urim and Thummim, the high priest would gain a level of divine inspiration approaching prophecy.[2]

This theory rang true with me for several reasons. Of course the Urim and Thummim were capitalized in Scripture because, according to this theory, they represented God's divine names. By being God's divine names, that also explained to me why these words would have the meaning "light and perfection," not only because *light* and *perfection* describe YHWH but also because of the way the Urim and Thummim were designed by God to operate. According to this theory, the way in which an answer was determined was by God first "illuminating" his answer with lights after the high priest contemplated the name written on the Urim. The answer to the question was then "perfected" when the high priest contemplated the name written on the Thummim. The Urim "illuminated" the answer, and the Thummim "completed" the answer—thus light and perfection.

This opinion also revealed why the high priest's garments were considered holy. In the same way that the ark of the covenant, the tabernacle, and the temple were holy because they had YHWH's name within them, the high priest's garments were also holy because YHWH's divine names were located inside of them. By wearing the holy garments with God's divine names written within them, the priests were *clothed with the power* to ask YHWH for forgiveness of the people's sins and then for communication. YHWH physically placed his names upon Aaron's heart because it was from the heart that YHWH chose to communicate with his people all that he wanted them to know. The reason YHWH made the Urim and Thummim instead of instructing Moses to make them is because only he could personally inscribe his own divine names upon these stones. So far, Moses only knew of one divine name for God, and that was the name YHWH.

Two Divine Names

You may already be asking yourself, *I thought God only had one divine name. So what is the second divine name that was inscribed on the Thummim?* Well, I can only think of one other name in history that was used to *bear judgment* on the nation of Israel, and that is the name Jesus! When you consider the trinity, you know that Jesus is YHWH's second divine name. At the time YHWH inscribed the Urim and Thummim, only YHWH knew the Thummim's name, Israel's future Messiah, and that is why only he could engrave them.

YHWH and Jesus! Light and Perfection! The Father and the Son! One God, two divine names! So the pieces of the puzzles are starting to fall into place. And of course, the Urim was called "the Illuminator" because it had YHWH's divine name written on it. The Thummim was called "the Completer" because it had Jesus's name written on it. It just makes sense. The word *Urim* means "light" because YHWH illuminated for us through the law in the Old Testament what man needed do in order to be righteous in his presence. The word *Thummim* means "perfection" because it was Jesus who came to fulfill the Old Testament law so that we could be forgiven of our sins and truly made righteous before God. Jesus's name was the name inscribed on the Thummim because Jesus, the Son of God, was sinless and was therefore considered by YHWH to be perfect.

The fact that there are only seven verses about the Urim and Thummim does not surprise me. The number 7 in the Bible represents spiritual completion and perfection.[3] God's divine names are definitely complete and perfect. Because God's divine names were physically placed over the heart of Aaron, the high priest was allowed to wear a holy crown on his forehead that read, "Holy to YHWH."

> "And you shall make a plate of pure gold, and engrave on it, like the engraving of a signet, '**Holy to YHWH**.' And you shall fasten it on the turban by lace of blue; it shall be the front of the turban. It shall be **upon Aaron's forehead**, and Aaron shall take upon himself any guilt incurred in the holy offering which the people of Israel hallow as their holy gifts; **it shall always be upon his forehead, that they may be accepted before YHWH.**" (Exo. 28:36–38)

The holy crown placed on Aaron's head became a visual representation of what God's divine names over Aaron's heart accomplished: making Aaron holy to stand in God's presence on holy ground. When you consider all that the priests had to be in charge of, it sounds like an incredibly stressful job. So why does YHWH describe priesthood as a gift? YHWH said to Aaron, "You shall have no inheritance in their land, neither shall you have any portion among them; *I am your portion and your inheritance* among the people of Israel" (Num. 18:20).

It wasn't because of *what* the high priest received in return for his position but because of *whom* he received. The priest's job may have been stressful, but can you imagine the satisfaction he must have felt by daily being allowed to be in YHWH's presence? Daily the priests worked for YHWH, and daily they were rewarded with the visible presence and clear communication with their God.

God's Perfect Will

Wouldn't it be nice to receive YHWH's perfect will so clearly, as the high priests did? Where are our Urim and Thummim to use whenever we need them? When I looked at my own experiences to see if I had any stories about God's perfect will being given to me is such a clear way, YHWH reminded me of two. I have already mentioned that God moved me to Atlanta, Georgia, when I was thirty years old, but I haven't yet explained the specifics of how this move came to be. After my husband, Jake, and I got married, we moved to St. Louis, Missouri, where we lived for three years. During that entire time my husband begged me to move farther south to a city where we could live on a lake. My husband was from Wisconsin and had always lived on a lake; he wanted the same experience for our future children. So after three years of hearing him beg me to move, I finally caved in.

At the time, I was employed with a company that had southern offices in Atlanta, Dallas, and Houston. I had spent some time in the Dallas area but had never been to any of the other cities. We knew we wanted to live on a lake, so we took out a map and a ruler and actually measured the distance to the closest lake to each of these three cities. Atlanta won since the nearest lake was only thirty miles away from the downtown area. So the next day I went into my office and asked my boss if there was any way I could be transferred to Atlanta. He didn't seem too positive about it, but I asked him if he would call his boss and see what he thought. It wasn't even thirty minutes later that my boss came into my office and told me that, if I wanted to be transferred to Atlanta, there was an opening available. The job position would be as an underwriter instead of an engineer, which was perfect for me because my first child was on his way. This new position would mean no more travel. Hallelujah!

So the next step was to visit Atlanta for the first time. We had a three-day weekend coming up, so we used it to accomplish three things. We needed to find daycare for our new son, we had to find my husband a job, and we needed to find a house. We had three days to accomplish three very daunting tasks. We arrived early on a Friday because my husband had two job interviews on that day. On Saturday we went to every daycare facility that had an opening for an infant. And finally, on Sunday we looked at every house on the lake that was in our price range, which totaled fifteen houses. We then flew home to Missouri. By the end of the day on Sunday, to say the least, we were completely exhausted. While we were in Atlanta, we were able to find a daycare that we liked for our son and, by the end of Sunday, we put a bid on the only house on the lake that we liked. After we got word on Monday morning that the owners of the house accepted our bid, we immediately put our house in Missouri on the market. Within a week, we had a buyer. On that same Monday, my husband received a job offer from one of the companies he had interviewed with on Friday. He accepted the offer; it was a perfect fit for his talents. Three days, three daunting tasks, and three miracles. I remember saying, "I guess God really wants us to move to Atlanta." Things couldn't have gone smoother than they did. But you see, when it's YHWH's perfect will, that's how it goes. Miracles take place that otherwise would seem impossible.

When I was thinking of all the miracles that took place to get us to Atlanta, I asked the question, "But why Atlanta? Why not Dallas or Houston?" I realized that it was Atlanta because YHWH knew exactly where he was going to place me, right next to a family that loved God with all their heart, mind, and soul. He also knew that by taking the new job position, I would be working with a girl named Kristy, who loved him as well. YHWH knew that in Atlanta people who knew him and had personal relationships with him would surround me. And because of the jealousy that YHWH knew I would soon feel, he was sure I would begin my own search for him and ask for a sign to show me that he existed. All that took place in our move to Atlanta had nothing to do with our dream of living on a lake. All that took place had everything to do with YHWH wanting to reach us, to begin relationships with him. That is why our move was made so easy. God wanted us to know him, and he knew it wasn't going to occur where we were currently living. So he physically picked us up and placed us where he wanted us to be. Living on his beautiful lake just came as a bonus. I believe it was YHWH's bait to accomplish his goal.

Encountering the Great I Am

But the story doesn't end there. Because of our move, I finally came to hear my God's voice for the first time ever through his sacred fire. Finally, I knew that he existed. But that knowledge can only take a person so far into a relationship with YHWH. The Israelites knew that YHWH existed because they heard his voice, and yet they still did not live the life he desired for them. Sixteen months after my first son Nicholas was born, my second son Zachary was born. After the birth of my first two boys, I continued working the job God had placed me in. However, seventeen months after Zachary's birth, I became pregnant with my third son, Sam. It was at this point that YHWH laid on my heart the desire to stay home with my children. I knew this desire was from him because for twelve years I had been a career woman. But over the previous two years it was becoming a challenge to do both of my jobs well—as a mother and an engineer. I also started realizing all that I was missing because I had chosen to have my boys taken care of by others. All of those "firsts" in my small children's lives were being seen by their caregivers and not by me. I was becoming jealous once again.

My husband and I started dreaming about what life would be like if I were able to stay home with our children. Although we knew our lives would be simpler and more fulfilling if I stayed home, we had one problem that we could not seem to resolve. Unfortunately, the mortgage on the house that we had bought three years prior was based on both of our salaries. Financially, it was just not going to work for me to quit my job. So we started to pray. One thing we had going for us was that my husband did, on occasion, receive small bonuses and commissions. We looked at our budget and came up with a plan. We were going to have to sock away all of our extra cash and start sacrificing everything out of our lifestyle that was not entirely necessary.

We had a vision, we began to put our plan into action, and through it all we prayed for YHWH's will. That is when God stepped in. YHWH did exactly what only YHWH can do. He performed another miracle. Over the next nine months, my husband received not one raise but two. Did you catch that? My husband got two raises in a matter of nine months! I had never heard of that happening to anyone, let alone us. What a blessing! And do you want to know the real kicker? My husband's raises over this nine-month period made up my entire salary. We couldn't believe it. I had to pinch myself to make sure I wasn't dreaming. If my husband and I had been unbelievers at this time in our lives, we would either have considered it extremely good luck or maybe thought that my husband's talent is what warranted such a raise. But we both knew that was not the case. Because we were believers, we knew a miracle when we saw one. We knew who was making our dream come true. Not only had YHWH chosen to bless us with the reality of me staying home with my children, but he also gave us the added bonus of enough money to be able to stay in our current home.

But was it our dream, once again, that YHWH was making come true, or was it his perfect will that was being accomplished? Again, is that why everything went so smoothly? Remember who we were living next to: a family that was a perfect role model for us on how to bathe our children in the faith of YHWH. God didn't want us to have to move away from this family. He wanted us planted exactly where we currently lived. But YHWH had even more plans. Not only would staying home with my children allow me to raise them and therefore not miss out on their childhoods; staying home would free up my time to learn more about him and his Son, Jesus. God knew that with more time, I would start opening my Bible and begin to read his Word. With more time, YHWH knew I would meet another stay-at-home mom who loved him with all her heart and who would eventually invite me to join a woman's Bible study. By reading and studying his Word more often, he knew my life would start looking a lot more like what he desired it to look like. In addition, the truths I learned from his Word would allow me to pass these truths down to the next generation so that my boys would know him from an early age. YHWH knew that staying home with my children would allow me time to start doing his will for his kingdom. Why *wouldn't* my heavenly Father allow me to stay home with my children? My dream and his will for my life matched perfectly, and therefore he performed another miracle.

Aligning with God's Will

So when you kneel before YHWH with your list of prayers, start thinking of God's bigger picture and ask yourself, "What is God's perfect will for my life?" Start asking yourself, "Will God's answering this prayer for me bring me any closer into a relationship with him?" If you can honestly answer yes to that question, then there is a pretty good chance that your prayer will be answered. But only YHWH knows what his perfect will is for your life. In what might seem to you like a prayer that needs to be answered, he might have a better solution—one that brings you even closer to him than you could ever have imagined. For me, what simply looked like decisions to move to another city and to stay home with my children became springboards for the development of a loving relationship with my heavenly Father. Each step was perfectly planned out by YHWH before I even knew what was happening.

So without even knowing you, I can tell you right now what YHWH's perfect will is for your life. It is to spend quality time reading his Word daily and to tuck this into your heart for later use. It is to teach your children God's words and his values. It is to join a small group in your church and form a community of believers so that when hard times come, you can feel his love for you. YHWH's will for you is to serve him in his kingdom in whatever role he asks of you. It is to tell your "God stories" to whomever will listen. It is to be bold and speak the words he places in your mouth for others to hear. It is to obey his commandments. It is to know that YHWH truly exists and that he loves you dearly.

YHWH wants more than anything for you to know him, to feel his presence, to see his Shekinah glory everywhere you go, and to hear his voice daily. He wants you to love him with all your heart and to love others the way he loves you. It is God's perfect will for you to want more than anything his perfect will for your life and to come to him in your time of need. He wants to be not only your LORD but also your Savior. YHWH's perfect will for your life is to have his two divine names written upon your heart, personally inscribed by him. His divine will for you is for you to stand righteous in his presence because he has a lot he wants to share with you. Ultimately, it is God's will for you to ponder both of his divine names so that "light and perfection" are brought into your own life.

Are we, as human beings, righteous simply because God physically created us in his image? No, of course not. Being made in YHWH's image certainly makes us extraordinarily beautiful, radiant, and intelligent, like no other animal on earth. However, we are only made holy when God places his Spirit within us, which is given to us in the name of God's precious Son, Jesus. It is the placement of Jesus's name in our hearts and in our souls that makes us righteous and able to stand in YHWH's presence, to hear YHWH's voice, and to ask for his will for our lives. It is what God places in us that makes us holy, just like the ark of the covenant, the tabernacle, the temple, and the high priest's garments. It is YHWH's Spirit, in Jesus's name, that resides in us that lets us communicate with our heavenly Father. So you see, believers in Jesus Christ do have the Urim and Thummim available to them just like the high priests did. However, what we need to remember and understand is that in order to receive the clear communication we all desire, we must ponder on *both* the holy names of YHWH and Jesus will *all* of our hearts, souls, minds, and strength.

Aaronic Blessing

For the Israelites, if YHWH forgave the people of their sins during the Day of Atonement, the high priest would then go outside, lift his hands, and pronounce the Aaronic blessing on the people.

> "**YHWH** bless you and keep you;
> **YHWH** make his face to shine upon you, and be gracious to you;
> **YHWH** lift up his countenance upon you, and give you peace."
> (Num. 6:24–26 ESV)

God had one purpose for this blessing. He told Moses that Aaron should speak it so that YHWH's name would be placed upon the people of Israel (Num. 6:27). By placing his name on the people, they would therefore receive his blessings of peace and of communication with him. Through this blessing, not only was God's divine name upon the heart of the high priest, but it was also placed upon the people's hearts.

I proposed at the beginning of this chapter that since the Urim and Thummim were placed upon Aaron's heart, perhaps they were needed for life. What we have discovered is that the names inscribed on the Urim and Thummim—YHWH and Jesus—are the very names *that created life*. What we will discover in future chapters is that *only* when these names are inscribed upon our hearts and we ponder on them daily will we receive peace, an abundant life in this world, and everlasting life one day in the future.

> "O YHWH, we wait for thee; **thy memorial name is the desire of our soul.**" (Isa. 26:8)

Chapter 9

Satan

Be sober, be watchful. Your adversary the devil prowls around like a roaring lion, **seeking some one to devour**. (1 Peter 5:8)

Satan, devil, adversary, beast, Abaddon, Beelzebub, Apollyon, Antichrist, deceiver, dragon, enemy, murderer, tempter, accuser, thief, Serpent of Old, ruler of this world—the list goes on! The Bible calls Satan by many different names. In fact, except for Jesus Christ, there are more names for Satan in the Bible than for anyone else. Each of Satan's names adds a little more to the description of how evil he actually is. But life for Satan as the king of the bottomless pit was not always like this. Satan, at one point in creation, had a different name and a different position in God's kingdom. The book of Isaiah tells us that YHWH once described Satan as "Day Star, son of dawn!"

> "You were the **signet of perfection, full of wisdom and perfect in beauty**. You were in Eden, the garden of God; every precious stone was your covering, carnelian, topaz, and jasper, chrysolite, beryl, and onyx, sapphire, carbuncle, and emerald; and wrought in gold were your settings and your engravings. On the day that you were created they were prepared. **With an anointed guardian cherub I placed you**; you were on the holy mountain of God; in the midst of the stones of fire you walked.

> **You were blameless** in your ways from the day you were created, **till iniquity was found in you**." (Ezek. 28:12b–15)

At one time, Satan was a beautiful angel. His name was Day Star, which referred to the morning star and literally means "bringer of dawn."[1] He ushered in the morning light from the darkness. YHWH created him as the seal of perfection, a perfect creation, full of beauty and wisdom. He was adorned in precious stones and gold. He walked where YHWH walked. Day Star's position was one of the highest possible for angels. Scripture tells us that he was one of the two guardian cherubs that covered the throne of God.

> "**Thou art the anointed cherub that covereth**; and I have set thee so." (Ezek. 28:14a KJV)

> "**O YHWH of hosts**, God of Israel, **that dwellest between the cherubims**, thou art the God, even thou alone, of all the kingdoms of the earth: thou hast made heaven and earth." (Isa. 37:16 KJV)

Day after day, Day Star overshadowed the throne of YHWH with his wings, while his face never turned away from God. Life couldn't have been any better for this angel—of course, until the day God removed Day Star's light and he was cast down to the earth.

> "How you are **fallen from heaven, O Day Star, son of Dawn**! How you are cut down to the ground, you who laid the nations low! You said in your heart, '**I will ascend to heaven; above the stars of God I will set my throne on high;** I will sit on the mount of assembly in the far north; I will ascend above the heights of the clouds, **I will make myself like the Most High**.'" (Isa. 14:12–14)

> "Your **heart was proud** because of your **beauty**; you corrupted your wisdom for the **sake of your splendor**. I cast you to the ground." (Ezek. 28:17a)

This mighty angel grew proud because of his beauty. Satan became envious of YHWH's position and his power in the universe and wanted it for himself. Satan's heart became hard. Even though he already was the most perfect reflection of God's glory, it wasn't enough. He wanted more. In the beginning, Day Star had an intimate relationship with YHWH and Jesus, but he was still dissatisfied. He wanted to be God and have all his glory. Day Star wanted his own glory so that he himself could sit on the very throne that he was created to protect. So Day Star rebelled against his Creator. Therefore, it is not surprising that Jesus tells us that he "saw Satan fall like lightning from heaven" (Luke 10:18). Once he was cast to the ground along with all the other rebellious angels, Day Star was renamed: "They have as king over them the angel of the bottomless pit; his name in Hebrew is *Abad'don*, and in Greek he is called *Apol'lyon*" (Rev. 9:11).

From this time forward, Satan, Devil, Abaddon, and Apollyon would forever be his names. The original Hebrew word *Satan* means "adversary." *Devil* is translated from the Greek word "diabolos," the root from which we get such words as *diabolic* and *diabolical*, used to describe something wicked or sinister. *Diabolos* means "an accuser, a slanderer."[2] The words *Abaddon* and *Apollyon* mean "ruin and destruction."[3] The angel that used to usher in light from the darkness was now only capable of producing darkness. There was no more God-given light left in Day Star. Because of his own choices, Satan now only had the power of being the *destroyer* of people's lives. His new names reflected his new position in the universe as being YHWH's adversary, enemy, and opponent.

Many people have asked the following question: "So if God made everything, why did he create Satan, who is so evil?" Well, now you can answer them, "God didn't create Satan; he created Day Star." In the beginning, Day Star was good and pure and beautiful. It was his own rebellion, his own pride, that caused him to become so evil and to be renamed. When God allowed free will, it created the possibility of evil's being introduced into the world. And as we all know, with every free will decision, there are consequences, both good and bad.

Garden of Eden

Satan has been around since the beginning of time. He was in the garden of Eden, tempting Adam and Eve to disobey God. After YHWH created the heavens and the earth, on the sixth day the Creator decided to create man. God said, "Let *us* make man in *our own image, after our likeness*; and let them have dominion over the fish of the sea, and over the birds of the air, and over the cattle, and over all the earth and over every creeping thing that creeps upon the earth" (Gen. 1:26).

I have read this verse so many times over the years, but it wasn't until the day I typed this verse that I understood for the first time why Satan is so angry. For the first time, YHWH opened my eyes to see the creation of man from Satan's point of view. Remember what Satan used to look like. God described him as being "perfect in beauty," and he was given great duties from YHWH himself. He had a purpose, and he radiated light. And yet, for some reason, Day Star wanted to ascend higher than YHWH. He wanted to be like the Most High. Therefore, because of his pride and self-righteousness, he was thrown down to the earth. So I can only imagine that on the day God created man in his and his Son's image, Satan must have become infuriated. Now, not only was he cast out of heaven, but also he would forevermore be surrounded by humans who were all made in YHWH's image. What a slap in the face! All of a sudden he realized that daily he would have walking and talking reminders of his enemy: men and women all made in God's image and reflecting his glory—the glory Satan himself used to reflect. And, as if that weren't enough, YHWH planned on giving these men and women individual names so that he could begin relationships with them. To make matters worse, man was given dominion over the entire earth. They were made in God's image, lived in the garden of Eden, were designed to have a relationship with God, and were given a purpose for their lives. Talk about being unfair! At this point in time, Satan was no longer beautiful, his home was no longer heaven, and he no longer had a purpose in life. He was miserable and in pain!

Hitting Rock Bottom

Just thinking about Satan's life, I have gained a new perspective on what it means to hit rock bottom, or in his case, the bottomless pit. I wonder at this point if he ever questioned his actions or felt the urge to repent. I wonder if he missed his former glorious life. Because YHWH is only good, if Satan truly repented of his deeds, God would have forgiven him of his iniquity, and life on earth over the last approximately six thousand years would have been completely different. But Satan had too much pride to ask for forgiveness. So, like a lover scorned, Satan went into attack mode. His new purpose in life would forever be revenge. Since he no longer had a relationship with YHWH, his new goal in life would be to do everything in his power to prevent relationships from forming between God and this new being called "man." He would do everything he could do to make mankind's life miserable. All he would have to do is convince these humans to disobey YHWH, and they would be punished just like he was. Problem solved. Satan found his new mission in life. And he knew he would have help from all of the other miserable angels that had been cast out of heaven along with him. People often say that misery loves company.

There was no time to waste. Why not try out his new life of deception with YHWH's first humans, Adam and Eve? Since in Satan's previous life he had walked with YHWH in the garden of Eden as Day Star, he had intimate knowledge of the two trees that were in the middle of the garden and their purpose. He knew all he had to do was convince Eve to eat of the Tree of Knowledge of Good and Evil and he would have a game-changer. When Eve told the serpent that she was not allowed to eat or touch the fruit of that tree or she would die, Satan responded: "*You will not die.* For God knows that when you eat of it your eyes will be opened, and *you will be like God*, knowing good and evil" (Gen. 3:4–5). What a lie! Since we know one of Satan's names is the Father of Lies, we can be sure that he knew from the very beginning what the consequences of eating that fruit would be for Adam and Eve. It is likely it was because of him that there was even a tree in the garden of Eden called the Tree of Knowledge of Good and Evil. Before Satan's rebellion, there would have been only a Tree of Good. He knew that death would be man's consequence for disobeying God, and that would make him very happy. Adam and Eve would receive a worse consequence than what he got. Oh sure, he was unhappy, but he was still alive. God didn't kill Satan after his disobedience because at that point in history there was no such thing as death; there was only good. However, once Satan rebelled, there was good *and* evil. So when Satan was in the garden of Eden, he used his evil ways to convince Eve that she would not die if she ate the fruit. Once she gave in, he knew death would be the consequence.

And that is exactly what happened. From that moment on, because he caused it, Satan held the keys to death and Hades. He caused death to become a fact of life for man; for it was Satan who introduced evil into this world through his rebellion. Once evil was introduced, then death easily became the consequence for sin.

So you might ask the question, "Now that death was possible, why could YHWH not just go ahead and kill Satan and be done with all this nonsense?" The answer may be confusing, but because Satan held the keys to death and Hades, he was safe for the moment from experiencing his own death. And if you think about it, he really no longer had life or light in him anyway, so he could at that point only be considered the walking dead.

But remember who YHWH is. He is all knowing; he is omniscient. God knew from the beginning of time that Satan would become proud of his beauty, rebel, and introduce evil into this world, and he wasn't surprised at how easily Adam and Eve were deceived. He was well aware of the risk of giving his creations free will and that death would become the consequence of sin. I'm sure this knowledge saddened God deeply, and yet he already had a plan in place to resolve all of these issues. It would take a while, but YHWH would not lose this battle. One day, God's only Son, Jesus, would obtain the keys to death and Hades back from Satan, and eventually Satan and all his demon friends would be destroyed for eternity. As Adam and Eve were being sent out of the garden of Eden, YHWH said,

> "Behold, the man has become like **one of us, knowing good and evil**; and now, lest he put forth his hand and take also of the tree of life, and eat, and live for ever"—therefore YHWH God sent him forth from the garden of Eden, to till the ground from which he was taken. He drove out the man; and at the east of the garden of Eden he placed the cherubim, and a flaming sword which turned every way, **to guard the way to the tree of life**. (Gen. 3:22–24)

If you recall, there were two trees in the middle of the garden of Eden. One was the Tree of Knowledge of Good and Evil, but the other one was called the Tree of Life. YHWH knew that Adam and Eve would eat the fruit from the Tree of Knowledge of Good and Evil. That is exactly why he planted the Tree of Life at the same time. He knew the fruit of its tree would be needed to reestablish a relationship with his creation. The Tree of Life was Jesus Christ, who would eventually bring eternal life to YHWH's creation and give YHWH the keys to death and Hades. In fact, I believe it was Jesus whom God was talking to in these verses. However, until the time was right for Jesus to walk on this earth, sacrifices would have to be made for the sins of man that would now be a part of everyday life. YHWH was willing to make the first sacrifice for Adam and Eve. "And YHWH God made for Adam and for his wife garments of skins, and clothed them" (Gen. 3:21). God knew that Adam and Eve could now see their sins and feel their nakedness and the need to be clothed. They now had a taste of good and evil and discovered the consequences that came with their choices. Their hearts were laid bare for YHWH to see. I'm sure that God felt sorry for them both. He definitely did not want this for his creation.

Because of YHWH's unconditional love for Adam and Eve, he himself sacrificed the first animals to make atonement for their sin of disobedience. And then he personally clothed them with garments made out of the skins of animals before sending them out of the garden. The garments made out of this sacrifice represented a physical covering of their sin. Upon leaving, God placed guardian cherubim at the east of the garden to protect the Tree of Life. No one was going to mess up

YHWH's desire of communing with man, not even Satan, even if it took him to eternity. God would ensure that man's future would be protected.

The Art of Deception

Satan now had the keys to death and Hades, Adam and Eve were kicked out of Eden, and YHWH was deeply saddened. What a productive day! Satan was rather proud of his accomplishments. But he didn't want to get ahead of himself. He knew very well what the Tree of Life was for and would have known Jesus while he lived in heaven. There was still work to be done. Once Adam and Eve started populating the earth, he was going to be very busy keeping all of their offspring distracted from wanting a relationship with God. It was time to come up with a game plan. Satan knew that if he were going to be successful he would need to be very deceitful and sneaky. He would have to go into the world in a disguise, and he would have to teach his fellow demons how to do this as well.

> For such men are false apostles, deceitful workmen, disguising themselves as apostles of Christ. And no wonder, **for even Satan disguises himself as an angel of light**. So it is no surprise if his servants, also, disguise themselves as servants of righteousness. Their end will correspond to their deeds. (2 Corin. 11:13–15 ESV)

Satan could think of no better way to disguise himself than as an angel of light. Even he knew that no one would be fooled into following an angel of darkness, the one and only angel of death. He had to make the world believe that he was someone else. Satan used to be Day Star, son of Dawn. In his previous life, he ushered in the morning light. Even though there was no more God-given light left in him, he would have to fake it. What an awesome plan! He would become the master of disguises. It was such a great plan because Satan knew that deceived people do not know that they are being deceived. Once people are deceived, they start making really bad decisions on their own. The resulting consequences of their choices then bring these individuals even further down into misery. At this point they become so depressed that a relationship with God is far from their minds.

Deception is like receiving a counterfeit one hundred dollar bill. It is specifically designed to look very much like an authentic bill. The creator of the counterfeit bill knows that untrained eyes will just key in on the many similarities of what they know a one hundred dollar bill looks like and accept it as being real. So unless the receivers have knowledge of the slight differences between the two and are trained to see them, they will miss the clues. They will be deceived and left with the fake.

When you ponder the light from the sun and the moon, you gain an even better understanding of how deceptive Satan can be.

> And God made two great lights, the **greater light to rule the day, and the lesser light to rule the night**; he made the stars also. And God set them in the firmament of the heavens to give light upon the earth, to rule over the day and over the night, and to **separate the light from the darkness**. And God saw that it was good. (Gen. 1:16–18)

We know that the sun is the source of all light and life on this earth, so why does it seem like the moon has its own source of light as well? The untrained eye—someone who knows nothing about the revolution of the earth and the moon around the sun—would believe that the moon must produce its own light because that is how it appears. The person with the untrained eye would be deceived. It would take an explanation from a trained scientist of what was really going on to convince the person otherwise. That expert would explain that the moon is not a light source. It only looks like the moon produces light because the rotation of the moon around the earth allows for the sun's light to reflect onto the moon. At night you are not seeing the light of the moon; you are seeing a reflection of the sun's light on the moon. If the person had only investigated the truth prior to coming to the conclusion that the moon made its own light, he would not have been deceived.

What the deceiver of the world knows about humans is that we rely on our senses much more often then we rely on confirmed truth before making our decisions. Relying on our senses in all arenas of life is a lot easier than searching out the truth. Finding the truth takes time, and who really has enough time in the day to do that? So all Satan has to do is look similar to the truth and play on the humans' senses, and the deceived will think they are receiving the true light that produces life.

The Encounter

As I was writing this chapter on Satan, YHWH led me to a movie titled *The Encounter*, directed by David A. R. White.[4] Before watching it, I had no idea what it was about because my husband and I picked it simply by its name.

In the first scene, five individuals are traveling separately through town. Because the bridge is closed on the road they were traveling due to flooding, they have no other option but to wait out the wicked storm indoors. So very quickly into the movie, five strangers find themselves together, in the middle of the night, in the middle of nowhere, at a strange diner. The beginning of this movie looked so familiar, like many scary movies I had seen in my past. So imagine my surprise when the owner of this diner introduced himself to these five individuals as Jesus Christ. I couldn't believe what I was seeing and hearing. How refreshing! This movie was so not going to be about death and destruction. It was going to be about Jesus bringing people out of their destructive lives into the light. What a blessing!

The Encounter is an incredible movie about Jesus and all that he has to offer mankind. While I watched this movie, YHWH instructed me to focus on Satan and the tactics he uses to deceive people, including the different ways he prevents God's people from hearing his voice.

The five characters in this movie are from diverse backgrounds. One is a male CEO of a restaurant chain and a former football player. The husband and wife are a typical, middle-class married couple. The young teenage girl is from an abusive family. And then one is a strong believer. What is interesting about these five characters is that four of them already know about Jesus and what the Bible says about him. However, at this point in their lives, their faiths varied greatly, from being an atheist to a strong believer. The teenage girl is the only character in this movie who had not yet been introduced to Jesus.

Throughout the CEO's entire adult life, he had been surrounded by Satan's false light of power, fame, success, and fortune. Even though his mother and father had had intimate relationships with God, as a young teenager he just saw his family as being poor. Because of his family's position in society, he felt they received no respect. So he decided at a young age that his life's mission would be to make a *name for himself*. His goal in life was to obtain the respect and fame from society that he felt his parents never had, and therefore he would never have to answer to anyone but himself.

So that is exactly what he did. He became famous, rich, and self-sufficient. He made sure that he needed no one. This man's pride was so strong that he had no need for YHWH in his life. He truly believed that everything that came his way did so as a result of his own power and glory. He had achieved everything he ever pursued in life and more, and he answered to no one. There was absolutely no convincing him that a relationship with Jesus was necessary. Just like Satan, this man's pride blinded him to the truth that the only light that filled his life was the light of the material world.

> "For you say, **I am rich, I have prospered, and I need nothing**, not realizing that you are **wretched, pitiable, poor, blind, and naked**." (Rev. 3:17 ESV)

This man thought he was on top of the world. Satan had definitely succeeded in stepping into this man's life and convincing him that all he needed was to be accepted by man and society and life would be bliss. And yet, it wasn't. Deep down, this man's inner life was a mess.

Encountering the Great I Am

He was bitter and angry. His heart had been so hardened over the years that he had no love left to give. What he was in dire need of was a Savior.

Because of his spiritual blindness, this man could not see how abundant his parents' lives had been. They were not rich by society's standards, but they were rich by YHWH's standards. They had intimate relationships with YHWH through Jesus. His parents probably heard God's voice on a daily basis, and because of it their lives had been abundant. In contrast, the only voice this man had ever heard was his own and, as a result, his life was a mess.

And then there was the husband and wife. The wife truly believed that she was a believer in YHWH and Jesus. She went to church every Sunday and even taught Sunday school. She had been a member of a church for as long as she could remember and thought of herself as a good person. But for as much head knowledge as she had about YHWH and Jesus from the Bible, she had absolutely no heart knowledge of them. Even after hearing the gospel so many times throughout her life, she had truly never understood what it meant to believe in Jesus Christ and to follow in his footsteps. She had no idea what it meant to surrender her life to her Savior because she had never done so.

She was still in complete control of every aspect of her life. She did not have a personal relationship with YHWH because Jesus's name had never made it into her heart. In fact, she had never truly heard Jesus's voice—that is, until this night. Satan had deceived this woman into believing that her church attendance and service were all that were needed for salvation. As long as a personal relationship with YHWH never developed, then Satan would win this woman's soul. He just had to keep convincing her that all was well.

This woman's husband was a timid man. He was a believer in YHWH and Jesus and did, on occasion, hear God's still, small voice. However, because of his wife's strong personality and his desire to please her, his decisions would often go against what he knew God wanted him to do. He chose making his wife happy over obeying YHWH. His relationship with his wife had become more important than his relationship with God. Because of this, he would never live the abundant life that YHWH had in store for him. Satan had won the deception game of making this man believe that this earthly life is more important than the eternal life promised to those who completely surrender their lives to Jesus.

The abused teenage girl's entire young life had been anything but pleasant. At some point she had heard about God and Jesus, but because her life had been so difficult, she felt that God must not really exist. And if God did exist, then she wasn't so sure that she was worthy of his love. She therefore never pursued a relationship with YHWH or asked him to save her from her wretched life. Instead, she was on the road, literally running from her life. She had bought into Satan's deceptive lies that YHWH only loves the loveable, that he doesn't exist, or that he just didn't care about her or her situation. She often questioned where God was when horrible things were happening to her. What she didn't understand was that YHWH was right by her side the whole time, patiently waiting for her to ask for his Son to be her Savior, to save her from her existing life. But she never asked, "Do you exist?" If she had, YHWH would have answered her loud and clear.

And finally, out of the five characters, there was one true believer. She had long ago recognized her need for a Savior and therefore had surrendered her entire life to Jesus Christ. Because of it, she had an intimate relationship with her heavenly Father. She not only heard YHWH's voice on a regular basis, but she often heard him clearly. And because of it, her earthly life was abundant and filled with joy.

This woman was the only individual who had heard God's voice at the beginning of the movie asking her to stop for the hitchhiker—the abused girl on the run. Because there was open communication between her and YHWH, this woman is the only one who responded to his voice. The husband had also thought he heard God's voice when they were passing the teenager, but because his wife's voice was louder that YHWH's, they did not stop. Because the CEO's life was far from YHWH, he would never have heard God's voice even if he were speaking to him because he did not know what God's voice sounded like.

This movie is about a "close encounter" with Jesus. For one evening, these five individuals are in the very presence of YHWH's only Son, Jesus. While their faces are turned toward his, each individual is given

Encountering the Great I Am

the chance to learn the truth about who Jesus is—to see him, hear his voice, and feel his presence. After Jesus shares the truths about himself, he then asks them each individually to accept him as absolute truth and to follow him.

Of the five close encounters with Jesus, four of the people either come to know Jesus Christ as their LORD and Savior for the first time or rededicate their lives to him. Once Satan's lies were exposed, they came to personally know Jesus's love for them and surrender their lives to him. The CEO, however, is unable to see his need for Jesus as his Savior, even after encountering him face to face. This man decides to continue his life on his own, relying on his own abilities to conquer life. As a result, he is the only one who dies from his choice at the end of the movie. Satan eventually wins this man's soul. The deception worked. Because a relationship between this man and Jesus failed to develop, eternal death would be the eternal consequence of this man's decision to deny Jesus and instead accept Satan's false lights as truth.

If the devil could destroy us whenever he wanted to, he would have wiped mankind out a long time ago. But the fact remains that he can't. He does not have that power. Satan knows that the only way he can cause eternal death is to get us as far away from YHWH as possible. He intimately knows, from personal experience, that no personal relationship with YHWH means no eternal life with YHWH. No eternal life means that person will be exactly where Satan will be for eternity. Like I said, misery loves company.

In Satan's former life as Day Star, his face was always turned toward God. Every time YHWH spoke, Day Star heard him loud and clear due to their proximity. However, since Satan decided to forever turn his face away from God, he was cast out of heaven and out of YHWH's daily presence. Because he was no longer in proximity to YHWH, he no longer heard God's voice clearly. Satan, therefore, loves to use whatever method he can think of to keep people's faces also turned away from God so that they never *see* YHWH, *hear* YHWH, or *feel* his presence. Satan doesn't want people to get too close to YHWH because then they will stop believing the lies he personally speaks into their ears.

Now, I know the premise of this movie is simple, and Satan is far from simple in his tactics. Satan's tactics look different for every individual; he attacks our individual weaknesses and insecurities. Remember, he prowls around our lives like a lion waiting for the exact moment to attack. Therefore, it is useless to study all of Satan's counterfeit lies because there are so many of them. The only way to detect Satan's lies is to study the truth, the one and only truth about YHWH and his Son, Jesus, which can be found in the Bible. "Sanctify them in truth; thy word is truth" (John 17:17).

The experts who recognize counterfeit bills are individuals who spend an incredible amount of time studying with great detail an actual one hundred dollar bill. They don't study counterfeits; they know that the best way to detect a counterfeit is to study the real thing. They know that *only* by studying the real thing will they recognize a fake when they see it. Likewise, the best way for you to detect Satan's lies is to spend a great amount of time studying the truth, YHWH's truth. The first step in studying the truth is to keep your face always turned toward YHWH so that you are so close to your heavenly Father that when he speaks to you, you will hear him clearly.

> I love you, O YHWH, my strength. YHWH is my rock and my fortress and my deliverer, my God, my rock, in whom I take refuge, my shield, and the horn of my salvation, my stronghold. **I call upon YHWH, who is worthy to be praised, and I am saved from my enemies.** (Ps. 18:1–3 ESV)

Chapter 10

The Silent Years

Moses spent the last forty years of his life in complete service to YHWH. Their intimate relationship began when God introduced himself to Moses through a burning bush. Moses then saw and experienced firsthand the signs and wonders and plagues brought on by YHWH, through the use of "God's rod," that eventually released his people from the bondage of slavery in Egypt. He felt the very presence and might of the Almighty God as he led his people through the Red Sea, thereby destroying their Egyptian enemies. He was comforted daily by YHWH's Shekinah glory when he looked upon the cloud by day and fire by night that resided over the tabernacle and when it led them along their way. Moses spent many days in YHWH's very presence on Mount Sinai receiving the Ten Commandments, and he thanked YHWH daily for the provision of manna and water.

In the tabernacle, YHWH spoke to Moses over the mercy seat of the ark of the covenant. Moses also held the Urim and the Thummim, which YHWH personally placed in his hands, so that the high priest also could receive God's will for the people. Moses called on the name of YHWH daily concerning the people of Israel. Throughout those forty years, Moses and YHWH built a genuine, loving relationship based on daily communication and complete trust that God would provide the Israelites with all their needs. In return, Moses did all that was commanded of him.

Throughout all those years, Moses spoke to the nation of Israel as YHWH's prophet. Before his death, Moses made one last declaration to the people of Israel. He knew his life was coming to an end because YHWH had already made it known to him that he would not be entering the promised land with his people. Joshua, the son of Nun, would be bringing the people across the Jordan River into the land of milk and honey. Therefore, speaking to the entire nation of Israel, Moses declared to them one last time the words YHWH placed in his mouth to speak.

> "See, I have set before you today **life and good, death and evil. If you obey the commandments of YHWH your God** that I command you today, by loving YHWH your God, by walking in his ways, and by keeping his commandments and his statutes and his rules, then you shall live and multiply, and **YHWH your God will bless you** in the land that you are entering to take possession of it. **But if your heart turns away**, and you will not hear, but are drawn away to worship other gods and serve them, I declare to you today, that **you shall surely perish**. You shall not live long in the land that you are going over the Jordan to enter and possess. I call heaven and earth to witness against you today, that **I have set before you life and death, blessing and curse. Therefore choose life**, that you and your offspring may live, **loving YHWH your God, obeying his voice and holding fast to him**, for he is your life and length of days, that you may dwell in the land that YHWH swore to your fathers, to Abraham, to Isaac, and to Jacob, to give them." (Deut. 30:15–20 ESV)

Before his death, Moses wanted to remind God's people of the covenant that they had agreed to live by, with YHWH as their God. He wanted to remind the people he loved to love YHWH will all their hearts, minds, souls, and strength. Moses desired for his people to live long and blessed lives. From experience, he knew that the only way this would be accomplished was if they obeyed YHWH's voice and clung to him—the God who had been speaking and dwelling among them for forty years.

Worshipping Idol Gods

After Moses's death, Israel continued serving YHWH all the days of Joshua and all the days of the elders who outlived Joshua. It wasn't until a new generation arose, who had never felt YHWH's presence or knew of the work that he had done for Israel, that Israel started rebelling and worshipping idol gods. The prophet Jeremiah spoke these words to the people concerning their evil ways.

> "**For twenty-three years**, … the word of YHWH has come to me, and I have spoken persistently to you, but **you have not listened**. You have neither listened nor inclined your ears to hear, although **YHWH persistently sent to you all his servants the prophets, saying, 'Turn now, every one of you, from his evil way** and evil deeds, and dwell upon the land that YHWH has given to you and your fathers from of old and forever. Do not go after other gods to serve and worship them, or provoke me to anger with the work of your hands. Then I will do you no harm.' **Yet you have not listened to me, declares YHWH, that you might provoke me to anger.**" (Jer. 25:3–7 ESV)

God gave his people so many chances to change their ways. For approximately nine hundred years following the exodus of Israel from Egypt, God pleaded with his people to change their ways, to turn from evil. He was patient, and yet they continued to sin time and time again. Finally, he had had enough, and he would no longer keep from punishing them as a nation.

> "Therefore thus says YHWH of hosts: **Because you have not obeyed my words**, behold, I will send for all the tribes of the north, declares YHWH, and for Nebuchadnezzar the king of Babylon, my servant, and I will bring them against this land and its inhabitants, and against all these surrounding nations. I will devote them to destruction, and make them a horror, a hissing, and an everlasting desolation. **Moreover, I will banish from them the voice of mirth and the voice**

> **of gladness, the voice of the bridegroom and the voice of the bride, the grinding of the millstones and the light of the lamp.** This whole land shall become a ruin and a waste, and these nations shall serve the king of Babylon seventy years." (Jer. 25:8–11 ESV)

After nine hundred years of trying to be Israel's God, YHWH once again allowed an enemy to reign over them for seventy years as punishment for their behavior. Because the people had not heeded Moses's warning about blessings and curses, the worst possible event in history was allowed to take place in the promised land.

> And YHWH said to him, "Pass through the city, through Jerusalem, and **put a mark on the foreheads of the men who sigh and groan over all the abominations that are committed in it**." And to the others he said in my hearing, "Pass through the city after him, and strike. Your eye shall not spare, and you shall show no pity. Kill old men outright, young men and maidens, little children and women, **but touch no one on whom is the mark**. And begin at my sanctuary." (Ezek. 9:4–6 ESV)

So in 587 BC, YHWH gave the city of Jerusalem into the hands of Nebuchadnezzar, the king of Babylon.[1] Everyone and everything was given into the hands of the enemy, including men, women, children—the young, and the old. Everyone who did not have the mark of YHWH upon his or her forehead was killed by the sword. And all of the holy vessels and treasures of the temple of YHWH, as well as the treasures of the king and his princes, were taken to Babylon. Solomon's temple was completely burned with fire, and the walls of Jerusalem were broken down. The entire city was laid to waste and ruin, exactly as prophesied by Jeremiah. Only a remnant of believers, those who escaped from the sword and death, those who had YHWH's mark on their foreheads, were taken into exile to become servants once again in a foreign land.

Encountering the Great I Am

> How YHWH in his anger has set the daughter of Zion under a cloud! ... He has cut down in fierce anger all the might of Israel; he has **withdrawn from them his right hand** in the face of the enemy; ... He has broken down his booth like that of a garden, laid in ruins the place of his appointed feasts; **YHWH has brought to an end Zion appointed feast and sabbath**, and in his fierce indignation has **spurned king and priest**. YHWH has scorned his altar, **disowned his sanctuary**; he has delivered into the hand of the enemy the walls of her palaces; a clamor was raised in the house of YHWH as on the day of an appointed feast. ... Her gates have sunk into the ground; he has ruined and broken her bars; her king and princes are among the nations; **the law is no more, and her prophets obtain no vision from YHWH.** (Lam. 2:1, 3, 6, 7, 9)

Everything that made the people of Israel distinct from all the rest of the nations was taken away or destroyed when YHWH allowed the king of Babylon to conquer the city of Jerusalem and his temple. Moses had known from the very beginning that it was only YHWH's presence and communication with his people that made the Israelites distinct. So at the same time that YHWH was allowing Jerusalem and the temple to be destroyed, he was removing his presence from the city of Jerusalem. During the destruction of the temple, either the ark of the covenant was physically destroyed by the Babylonians or God physically removed it. I personally believe he removed it himself, before the destruction, because I don't think YHWH would have allowed his Word (The Ten Commandments) and divine name to be desecrated by a pagan nation. Also, if the Babylonians had taken the ark of the covenant, it would have been mentioned in Scripture, like all of the other treasures that were taken from the temple. The ark was covered in gold, and it would have been highly treasured by the Babylonians if it was in their possession. It would have been catalogued.

With the temple destroyed and the ark missing, the law was no more. There would be no more communication from YHWH over the mercy seat of the ark. Also, with the temple utterly destroyed, there would be no place to make sacrifices to YHWH and to celebrate the appointed feasts and Sabbath days that were the backbone of worship for their faith. The sacred fire that had been sent from heaven, that had burned on the altar and consumed the sacrifices and offerings of the people for so many years, was now extinguished. Scripture tells us that the priests were spurned or rejected by God, so we can be sure that he no longer spoke to the priests through the Urim and Thummim. And to make things even worse, Israel's prophets no longer obtained visions from YHWH.

All that occurred when YHWH removed his presence from the temple had been prophesied by the prophet Ezekiel. Chapters 10 and 11 of Ezekiel give a clear picture of a time when YHWH's Shekinah glory physically would leave the temple. All forms of communication with YHWH and his people ceased within a matter of days. YHWH removed his Spirit from among his people and ceased to dwell among them. The prophet Amos had also prophesied about this time period:

> "Behold, the days are coming," declares YHWH God, "when **I will send a famine on the land**—not a famine of bread, nor a thirst for water, **but of hearing the words of YHWH. They shall wander from sea to sea, and from north to east**; they shall run to and fro, **to seek the word of YHWH, but they shall not find it.**" (Amos 8:11–12 ESV)

Because of the famine of silence he was sending upon the land, YHWH knew the remnant of his people would yearn for communication from him—words from a prophet, a trumpet call, a lightning bolt sent from above, anything. He knew that they would long to hear his voice, would repent, and would cry out for him. But he would not give in to their pleas. He would remain silent.

Profaning YHWH's Holy Name

So why would YHWH remove all communication from among his chosen people? There are so many reasons, but really all that happened can be summed up in one sentence. God's chosen people were profaning his holy name, and he had had enough. They had been profaning his holy name by worshipping idol gods, from the time when they made a golden image of a calf in the wilderness until this time in history. Every time the people worshipped Baal or other idol gods made of gold, silver, bronze, iron, wood, and stone, they profaned the name of YHWH. Every time the people would bring their lame and diseased animals for sacrifice, when they were supposed to bring their blemish-free animals, they profaned the name of YHWH. Every time a prophet would speak his own words, for his own gain, in YHWH's name instead of speaking the words God placed in his mouth to speak, he profaned the name of YHWH. Every year when one of his seven feasts was not celebrated as ordained, the people profaned his name. Every time they didn't rest on the Sabbath day and focus on the one true God, they profaned his name.

The priest's behavior was no better. Scripture is filled with verses of priests throughout the years having no regard for the ways of YHWH when it came to their duties. There are stories of these chosen servants lying with women at the entrance of the tabernacle and the temple and treating the offerings with contempt. It is disgusting to think that the high priest had the very names of God located behind his breastpiece over his heart while he allowed these things to occur in the temple. Every time these atrocities happened, the name of YHWH was profaned. So YHWH removed the Urim and Thummim from the priests. Remember, the last two Scripture verses are about how a priest with the Urim could not be found to determine the genealogies of the returning people from Babylon. That is because God had already taken these items from the priests.

The Israelites claimed that YHWH was their God and they were his people, yet nothing could be further from the truth. So YHWH would not allow it to go on any longer. He removed all forms of his holy name from them. "As for you, O house of Israel, thus says YHWH God: Go serve every one of you his idols, now and hereafter, if you will not listen to me; but *my holy name you shall no more profane* with your gifts and your idols" (Ezek. 20:39).

I can only imagine what it must have felt like for the genuine believers of YHWH who were exiled into Babylon. They knew that their people had failed God. They must have mourned the loss of the temple, Jerusalem, the ark of the covenant, God's very presence, and his name. They must have longed to hear words from their God and to go back to their old ways of worshipping and hearing from YHWH. But that did not happen. For a period of seventy years, YHWH remained silent.

The Second Temple

At the end of their seventy-year punishment, exactly as YHWH had spoken through his prophets, the remnant of Israel was allowed to go back to their land, made possible by a decree from Cyrus, the king of Persia. God stirred up the spirit of Cyrus to proclaim that God had charged him to rebuild the temple of YHWH in Jerusalem. Therefore, Cyrus allowed "all who desired" to go back to Jerusalem. Cyrus provided the gold and silver, building materials, and the animals needed for this new house of God. In addition, Cyrus brought out all of the vessels that had been taken from Solomon's temple and returned them to the nation of Israel so they could be placed in the new house of YHWH that was being built. After years and years of delays, the second temple was finally completed in 515 BC under the direction of Zerubbabel, the governor of Judah, and Joshua, the high priest.[2]

As the temple was being rebuilt, there was a group Israelites who were disappointed with its construction. When the foundation was laid, the old men who had seen the first temple wept for sorrow, but the young men who had been born in exile shouted for joy (Ezra 3:11-13). Older Jews who could recall the grandeur of the first temple regarded Zerubbabel's temple as a poor substitute for the original. In their minds, it did not even begin to compare with the splendor of Solomon's temple.

No description of the second temple exists. Its dimensions were probably the same as Solomon's, but it was most likely much less ornate and expensive. The new temple had one lampstand, a golden altar of incense, a table of showbread, and a curtain that separated the Holy of Holies. According to Josephus, the Holy of Holies was empty since the ark of the covenant had disappeared. A single slab of stone marked its place.[3] The temple was rebuilt in the exact place that Solomon's temple used to reside, but besides its lack of physical splendor, there was another, more disturbing difference between Solomon's temple and this one. Even though the presence of YHWH was known to dwell in Solomon's temple, the Babylonian Talmud asserts that five things continued to be lacking in the second temple: the ark of the covenant, the sacred fire, the Shekinah glory, the spirit of prophecy, and the Urim and Thummim. It was also during this same time period that the use of YHWH's name was removed from ordinary speech and replaced in Scripture with *Adonai*, or *LORD*.

What this tells me is that even though YHWH himself commanded the second temple to be built, he had no intention at this point in history to return his glory, communication, or name to this sanctuary. So if God had no intention of bringing back communication with his people, then why did he want the temple to be rebuilt? Why did he send the prophets Haggai and Zechariah to encourage the people to rebuild the temple? What was its purpose? Without the presence of God, this temple would be just another elaborately built building. Because YHWH's Shekinah glory no longer resided there, the temple itself was considered dead and would never be holy. In order for this new temple to be holy, as Solomon's temple was, God would have to place his name inside of it. But because the ark of the covenant was missing, YHWH's divine name and his Word would never enter into this temple. Or would they? Remember, if God wanted his name, his Word, and his ark of the covenant to be in this new temple, then he would have simply given them back to the Israelites and life would proceed as it had before the exile to Babylon. If God wanted his name spoken by his people, he would have just sent a prophet to command them to use it again. But he had already told them to stop profaning his name, and so they literally stopped saying it and instead used the title of *LORD* when referring to him, thinking that would make him happy. They thought that by not saying his name, they would no longer profane it.

When I first thought about YHWH's name going missing from the Greek translation and his name not being spoken or used by God's people, I became angry. I remember thinking, *How could the powerful God I serve allow his divine name to no longer be used? How could he allow his name to be removed from Scripture? Wasn't YHWH's goal always to have communication with his people? Was all of this the work of Satan?* It was at this stage in my pondering that God said to me, "Judy, it's okay; I planned it this way. Let me show you what I did." In my own words, this is what YHWH said to me through Scripture:

> As a nation, the Israelites were profaning my name. Their hearts were hard. They didn't love me and were continuously disobeying my commandments and worshipping idol gods. Satan had prevailed in their lives, and therefore they were no longer hearing my voice. Their sacrifices were done out of tradition and nothing else. I asked them to stop saying my name because I knew they didn't love me. I couldn't have them acting like I was their God when I wasn't. Since we did not have a relationship, I corporately took all communication away. Oh, I still had believers, but only a remnant. The covenant that we had agreed to on Mount Sinai was broken by my people over and over again. However, I still loved my people. So I instructed them to build me a new temple. But this time, communication was going to be different. For a while I would remain completely silent. But after the silence I would perform a miracle. **Suddenly, my Name, my Word, and my Glory would come back into the temple when my beloved Son, Jesus, was physically brought into it. My Shekinah glory would return to the temple and to Jerusalem. Through my Son, Jesus, a new covenant would be written, with a new covenant name**, and all forms of communication with believers would once again be restored.

You see, God had a new plan with a new form of communication. YHWH was getting ready to send Jesus into the world. With his Son, a new covenant would be written with his people—with a new covenant name. With his Son, there would be a new name to ponder and to speak. YHWH explained to me that he *willingly* lowered his name to the title of *Adonai*, or *LORD*, so that the name of Jesus could be the *"Name above all Names."* Oh, what a sacrifice he made by lowering his name to a title. YHWH allowed his majestic name to no longer be spoken by his people *all* because of his Son, Jesus. This was not the work of Satan, as I first assumed. It was all God's plan from the beginning of time, and he did it all for his Name's sake!

> I give thanks, O YHWH, with my whole heart; before the gods I sing thy praise; I bow down toward thy holy temple and give thanks to thy name for thy steadfast love and thy faithfulness; **for thou hast exalted thy word [Jesus] above all thy name**. (Ps. 138:1–2)

Satan Loved the Silent Years

Satan must have loved the silent years. YHWH was not speaking through the prophets or the priests. The ark of the covenant had disappeared, along with the sacred fire and the Urim and Thummim. God's Shekinah glory could no longer be seen, and the people were afraid to say YHWH's name. What an awesome turn of events. Because God's voice was silent, Satan's voice could now be heard loud and clear. Without God speaking, Satan's work of leading people astray would be so much easier. Because Satan was allowed to speak freely during the silent years, these times were very tumultuous for the people of Israel.

However, even though God was silent, he was still working behind the scenes. YHWH accomplished a lot during these years in preparation for his Son. After Solomon's temple was destroyed, not only did YHWH have his temple rebuilt, but also for the first time he had synagogues built in individual communities so that the people had local houses of worship. In these synagogues, the law and the prophets were read every Sabbath day. By having his law and prophecies read every week in local places of worship, the people were hearing, sometimes for the first time, the prophecies about the coming Messiah. The newly built temple and the synagogues were the very places where Jesus would eventually speak YHWH's truth to his people and introduce himself as God's only Son. Maybe by hearing YHWH's Word read to them during the silent years, they would recognize Jesus for who he was when he finally came onto the scene. God also allowed the Roman Empire to conquer the known world so that roads would be built, connecting all of the cities. These roads eventually allowed Jesus's disciples to easily spread the good news to the ends of the earth about Jesus's death, resurrection, and ascension into heaven.

During this same time, YHWH arranged for his Word, his Scripture, to be translated from Hebrew to Greek before Jesus was even born. This was done so that the Gentiles would be able to read God's Word when they were brought into his new covenant. It was during these translations that he planned for his divine name, YHWH, to be rewritten as Adonai or LORD, so that when his Son came onto the scene there would only be one name to ponder—Jesus.

So while it seemed that Satan was in control over all these years when God seemed to be absent, the opposite was true. During all of the tragedy that occurred, YHWH was still present, watching over his people, watching over his Word to be performed. The book of Isaiah is filled with Scripture about the coming Messiah. With the Messiah, the old covenant would become obsolete.

> "Behold my servant, whom I uphold, my chosen, in whom my soul delights; **I have put my Spirit upon him**; he will bring forth justice to the nations. ... 'I am YHWH; I have called you in righteousness; I will take you by the hand and keep you; **I will give you as a covenant for the people**, a light for the nations, to open the eyes that are blind, to bring out the prisoners from the dungeon, from the prison those who sit in darkness. **I am YHWH; that is my name; my glory I give to no other, nor my praise to carved idols. Behold, the former things have come to pass, and new things I now declare; before they spring forth I tell you of them.**" (Isa. 42:1, 6–9 ESV)

God's presence would come back into the temple: "And the word of YHWH came to me, saying, 'Jeremiah, what do you see?' And I said, *'I see a rod of almond.'* Then YHWH said to me, 'You have seen well, *for I am watching over my word to perform it'"* (Jer. 1:11–12). YHWH's plan would soon come to fruition. His Word would soon become flesh. God was telling his people to watch, look, and listen to see what he was about to do. "Behold, I send my messenger to prepare the way before me, and *the Lord whom you seek will suddenly come to his temple*; the messenger of the covenant in whom you delight, *behold, he is coming*, says YHWH of hosts" (Mal. 3:1).

Do you remember what happened to the Israelites after their period of silence from God while they lived in Egypt? YHWH performed a miracle, a big one. After he sent Moses and Aaron to redeem his people from the hands of their enemy, YHWH introduced himself to his people, and the first covenant between God and his people was agreed upon. Well, this was going to be no different. Another 430-plus years of silence from God would occur before there would be another miracle—for miracles always seem to follow the silence. This time it would be YHWH's Son, Jesus, who would redeem his people from their enemy, Satan, who held his people in the bondage of slavery to sin. After Jesus reintroduced his Father to the people and then died for their sins, a new covenant would be written.

My Own Silent Years

As you might have already guessed, I have my own story that I would like to share with you about a time period in my life that can only be termed as my "silent years." These years began the day I went off to college. It is not a fun story to tell, but it is my story, nonetheless, of how God redeemed a very bad situation for his glory. It is a story of how YHWH turned what Satan meant for evil into something that has glorified him. I now know that YHWH wants me to tell my story, or should I say *our story*, for his Name's sake.

I grew up in a very loving home, and I remember attending church nearly every Sunday. I also attended a Lutheran school during all of my elementary years. Throughout my adolescent years I was introduced to the basics about the Christian faith, and I did learn the facts about Jesus. However, outside of church and school I do not remember my family openly talking about God and our faith, and I also didn't have any friends in my life who were strong followers of Jesus.

By the time I left for college, I think I can honestly say that I believed there was a God, and I also think I believed that Jesus lived and died for my sins, but that was really all there was to my faith. I did not have an intimate relationship with YHWH or know that was possible, even with everything that I had learned at church. In fact, I can say with certainty that the idea of real communication with God was foreign to me. Occasionally I would pray, especially for my mother whenever she was sick, but that was about it. While I was in college, the only times I ever went to church were when I was home for Christmas or summer break.

When I went to college I didn't know what it meant to be a Christian. All I knew was I was on my own, with all the freedoms that came with it. As a kid growing up I had always obeyed the rules, had made straight A's, and had never gone through a rebellious stage. I obeyed my parents because somehow I knew that was the right thing to do. In college, however, there was no one to tell me what I could and could not do, so I was free to do whatever I wanted. I remember my mom telling me before I left for college that she hoped that I would stay away from cigarettes. She was naive because she had never gone to college herself and had no idea about all the evils in the world that were waiting for me. Therefore, she never talked to me about alcohol, drugs, or sex; she had no frame of reference. So with no one guiding me while I was in college, I drank, I briefly tried drugs, and I had sex. Somehow I knew what I was doing was wrong, but everyone I knew was doing the same things that I was, so I made "everyone is doing it" my excuse. My grades were not suffering, so I thought I was making my parents proud.

During this time, Satan's world soon became my world. I was no longer hearing God's Word through church, so YHWH's voice became very silent. Also, I wasn't communicating with YHWH on my own, because I honestly didn't know how. Therefore, Satan's voice became very loud and clear. I found Satan's world to be fun—that is, until the consequences of living in his world started piling up. When I was twenty, after living for three years in Satan's world, I got pregnant in the spring of my junior year. All of a sudden my world came crashing down around me. *How could this be happening to me?* I couldn't believe it. I couldn't tell my parents because I *thought* that I was perfect in their eyes, and I knew they would be devastated. I couldn't tell my friends because I was so embarrassed. So I told no one except my boyfriend. We decided that an abortion was our only option. Because abortions were legal, we weren't really doing anything wrong, at least in society's eyes. I didn't have a relationship with YHWH, so I never even considered asking him what he thought I should do.

I took it upon myself to get my life back in order. I cleaned out my bank account so I could take care of my "problem." After it was over, I shoved my feelings way down deep and didn't shed one tear, which if you knew me would be hard to believe. I continued on with my life. The problem was taken care of, and I didn't have to burden my parents with any of it. Satan had me exactly where he wanted me—thinking that everything was once again right with the world. Boy, was I wrong.

It wasn't until fifteen years later that this experience came to the surface of my heart. At the age of thirty-five, I was happily married to my husband, Jake, and we had three wonderful boys, all under the age of five. At that point in my life, I knew that God existed because he had spoken to me through his sacred fire in my dryer just a year prior. Shortly after that incident, I had accepted Jesus Christ as my LORD and Savior. I had recently quit my job and was thoroughly enjoying staying home with my children. Because of more free time, I had also started opening my Bible to read God's Word on a regular basis.

Life couldn't have been more wonderful and was going along as planned—until out of the blue I started experiencing very strange, obsessive thoughts. For six months, every time I got into a car with my children, all I could think of was that we were going to get into a horrible crash and that one or all of my children were going to die. I had these thoughts every single day that I got into a car. I carried these thoughts with me all day long, and they got even more bizarre as the days passed. And like I said, this continued for six long months. I felt like I was on the verge of going crazy. And, once again, I remained silent and told no one about what was going on.

During those entire six months, I prayed with all my heart that YHWH would take these thoughts away from me. I didn't know where they were coming from. They were consuming me. Since God is always faithful, he answered my prayers but definitely not in the way I could ever have imagined. I remember the day very clearly. I went to a Mother's of Preschoolers group one morning, and the speaker of the day was talking about how we have to let our kids mourn all of the losses in their lives. The speaker explained to us that our children have to be allowed to mourn a bad grade, moving, loss of a friend, and so on. If they don't, they will stuff their feelings down deep, and it will eventually affect them.

I was very tearful during that meeting, and I wasn't sure why. It wasn't until I got into my car that morning that I asked God, "All right, God, what in my life have I not mourned?" Immediately, he replied, "You have never mourned the loss of your first child." His words struck me in my heart like a bolt of lightning. The truth of what he said was a revelation from heaven since no one else knew what had happened so long ago. So on that day, after fifteen years of denial, I finally began to mourn the loss of my first child. I finally allowed myself to cry and scream out in pain for what I had done.

During this process of grief, which took many weeks, YHWH instructed me to tell everyone close to me about my abortion so that what used to reside in the darkness was brought into the light for all to see. For the first time ever, I told my husband about it. I told my current friends, my college friends, and my parents. I had to confess my "deep, dark secret" so that it was no longer a secret. For once in my life, I could finally admit to everyone I knew that I was not perfect and acknowledge that I was a sinner in need of a Savior. I had broken one, if not all, of God's Ten Commandments.

I now believe that the word *abortion* is simply a clinical word for "premeditated murder." Therefore, through these several weeks, I had to come to terms with my LORD and Savior by my side that murder is the sin that I had committed. Romans 6:3 states that the consequences of sin is death. In the case of the sin I had committed, the actual death of my unborn child was the consequence of my sin. I don't know how I could look at it in any other way. If I had done nothing, I would currently be the mother of a thirty-year-old child. But instead, I intervened with the life that had been placed into my body.

In addition, the guilt I felt for all those years had been literally eating me alive for the last six months. The outward sign of my guilt was an obsession about death for my children and myself. What a perfect example of what the resulting guilt from sin will eventually do to a person if it is never addressed.

Having already birthed three children and having held them in my arms, I realized for the first time the tragedy of what I had done. I came to Jesus broken, on my knees, asking for forgiveness. And what do you think Jesus did? He forgave me, of course. You see, we had a relationship by this time, and it was becoming more intimate as our walk together progressed. Jesus knew that in order for me to have full communication with his Father, I would have to repent of all of my sins, especially those hidden in darkness.

Jesus was right. After repenting of my sin and receiving forgiveness, YHWH started communicating with me in a way I had only felt once before—when he told me he existed. Immediately all of my obsessive thoughts about something terrible happening to my children disappeared. God explained to me that because of the guilt I was feeling about my abortion, I was mistakenly thinking that since I took away one of God's children, he would surely take away one of mine. He assured me that taking one of my children's lives as revenge for my sin was something he would never do. He also helped me understand why, since the birth of my first child, I had this unexplainable desire to adopt another child. It wasn't because I truly wanted to adopt a child but because I was trying to replace the child that I had taken, as if that would make things better. I was supposed to have four children, not three. He further explained to me why I didn't always trust myself being alone with my firstborn child. It was because I thought that maybe I would hurt him, like I did my unborn child. YHWH explained all these things to me, he forgave me, and then he wrapped up all of my guilty feelings and took them away from me, never to be felt again. It was such a wonderful feeling. Suddenly, I felt so light on my feet. I really can't adequately put into words what a great experience it was.

But only YHWH knew that more healing would be required. Seven years after that experience, I was at a Bible study when my girlfriend sat down next to me. Her very first question to me that day was if I was okay in dealing with my abortion. She had heard of a Bible study that I might be interested in for women who had experienced abortion. Even though I felt like I was completely healed, I jumped on the idea because I always thought that there was going to be some way that I could use my experience to help others who have been through the same thing. So I signed up for a ten-week Bible study class titled *Forgiven and Set Free: A Post-Abortion Bible Study for Women* by Linda Cochrane.[4] It was amazing. I learned so many things about God's unconditional love and forgiveness. Surprisingly, I mourned some more. Seven years earlier, I knew without a shadow of a doubt that YHWH had forgiven me of my sin. However, it wasn't until I went through this process that I was finally able to forgive myself.

The two ministers leading the class had also had abortions and therefore knew what I was experiencing. At the end of this study we had a ceremony, at which time I named my child and dedicated it to YHWH's care. It was so powerful because naming my child was the one thing that had always been missing. If I had birthed my first child, I would have named it. Therefore, naming my child seemed like a very natural thing to do. God even took care of providing me with my unborn child's name. My husband and I always loved the name Jordan while we were having babies, and we were convinced one of our children would be named Jordan. By this point in time, we had three boys and did not plan on having any more children. Their names were Nick, Zach, and Sam. For some unknown reason, we never used the name Jordan, and I finally knew why. YHWH had other plans for that name. It was supposed to be my first child's name. So I named my child Jordan and dedicated him to God; and someday I know I will meet him or her in heaven.

It was as if naming my child was the last act I needed to do for complete healing to take place. By naming my child, I was accepting full responsibility for what had happened. Even though I did not choose to give my child the opportunity of life, what I did choose is to give a name to the child that once was growing inside of me, which is a gift second only to life itself. Once I named him and released him to God, I was in essence giving the entire situation over to YHWH, once and for all. Finally, after all those years, I knew in my heart what it meant to be a Christian and how it feels to be *forgiven* and *set free* by my LORD and Savior.

Hindsight Is Twenty-Twenty

In looking back at any situation, things always appear so much clearer. What I have termed my silent years were silent only because of my own disobedience. I had, through my adolescent years, been introduced to the gospel, Jesus Christ, and his heavenly Father through my parents, our church, and my school. It was no one's fault but my own that I did not have a relationship with Jesus. I had not pursued a relationship with Jesus and therefore did not know YHWH. I had not asked Jesus with my heart to be my LORD and Savior. We had no communication because of my decisions—and no one else's. Therefore, it was I who allowed Satan to steer me very far away from a godly life into a world of sin and disobedience. During those years, all of the pleasures of this world became my idol gods. Because of my pride and the need to be in control of my life, I allowed Satan to convince me that an abortion would be the best for everyone involved and that I should keep my experience a secret. Remember, Satan is the father of lies, and I fell for every deception he sent my way. During these years, I profaned the name of YHWH and Jesus with my actions over and over again.

And yet through all of those years I now see that YHWH never left my side. He continued to pursue me and love me, and he was waiting patiently for me to come to him. I now see my pregnancy in college as God trying to bring light and life into what had become a dark life in a sinful world. The life growing inside of me was meant to bring me out of Satan's world and back into God's world—out of the dark and into the light. At the time, I saw the life inside of me as only capable of producing the death of my dreams and visions and how I had determined my life should go. So I chose death instead of life, and since I chose death, all of the curses of death came along with it.

This experience was my defining moment in my relationship with YHWH. It was my "sacred fire." If I had never gone through what I did, I would never have felt the death and destruction that was taking place around me, and I would never have cried out for my Savior. It was during this sacred fire, which spanned many, many years, that God was watching his seeds of new life opening and beginning to sprout. It was one of those seeds that caused me to ask God for a sign that he existed. By showing me the true condition of my heart through the fire in my dryer, he knew I would have all the proof I needed of his existence because I knew that *only* YHWH would have known what I had hidden in the dark corners of my soul. I now believe the ashes in my dryer, that God allowed me to see, represented the ashes of my abortion.

> "**Fear not, for I have redeemed you**; I have called you by name, you are mine. When you pass through the waters, I will be with you; and through the rivers, they shall not overwhelm you; **when you walk through fire you shall not be burned, and the flame shall not consume you. For I am YHWH your God**, the Holy One of Israel, **your Savior**." (Isa. 43:1b–3a ESV)

Even though the consequence of my disobedience was the death of my unborn child, God assured me that even though I had felt the scorching heat of the fire, the flames would not consume me, just like the flames from my dryer did not consume my house. He would redeem me if I let him. YHWH let me know that if I followed his instructions and gave my heart to Jesus, he would start mending my heart back together and give me the new life that I so desired.

I often wonder what would have happened if I had not remained silent about my pregnancy, if I had told my friends and family. Maybe the outcome would have been different. Maybe I would have decided to have my baby and raise him and would currently have a thirty-year-old child. Maybe I would have met my LORD (YHWH) and Savior (Jesus) fifteen years earlier than I did. But I also know I can't go back in time, and truthfully, I don't think God would want me to if I could. I know that our relationship is what it is today because of my silent years so long ago. When the silence was finally broken, a miracle occurred—a big one. YHWH replaced the silence that filled my spirit and soul with an unconditional, loving relationship built on truth, trust, and a true desire to know my heavenly Father and to hear his voice. The relationship we built together was not based on my parents' faith but on my own personal experiences with God.

Now that I have heard God's voice, I never want to again experience a time when I don't. I now know what it feels like to yearn to hear his voice and therefore will always seek to hear him. The lesson I learned from feeling the intense guilt over sinning against YHWH is that I never want to feel that again. I have come to know why it is important to fear the LORD and to obey his commandments. What Satan meant for evil, YHWH has redeemed through his Son, Jesus Christ. What Satan meant to result in only death and curses, Jesus has transformed into blessings and peace. What Satan meant to take me far away from my heavenly Father has instead brought me extremely close into YHWH's presence. What used to tear me apart inside—knowing that I caused the death of my unborn child—now brings tears of joy to my eyes.

Today, because of my relationship with YHWH and Jesus, I am confident in my heart that Jordan has literally been in heaven singing and praising God from the day I took his or her life. I know that if given the choice, he would not trade his past thirty years in heaven in God's presence for thirty years on planet earth. God truly does work in mysterious ways. Who would have thought that through Jordan's death,

I would be given new life—spiritual life? What an awesome gift my heavenly Father has bestowed upon me. And to think, all I had to do to receive this gift of new life is give YHWH's Son, Jesus, my heart. Why did I wait so long?

> The angel of YHWH **encamps around those who fear him and delivers them**. (Ps. 34:7 ESV)

Chapter 11

Noah's Ark

An *ark* is simply defined as "something that affords protection and safety."[1] From a biblical sense, an ark provides salvation. In thinking about the ark of the covenant and its purpose of salvation, I came to realize that throughout the Old and New Testaments, there were three arks. Noah's ark was the first. Many people know the story; it was probably one of the first Bible stories they learned as a child, second to the story of creation.

God instructed Noah to build an ark out of gopher wood, and it was to have enough rooms in it to house two animals of every kind. After Noah completed this task, God ushered Noah and his family into the ark along with all the animals. God then flooded the earth for forty days and forty nights. When the waters had subsided, Noah sent out a dove to see if there was dry land, and when the dove finally brought back an olive leaf, Noah and his family knew that it was safe to leave the ark. Then God said to Noah, "Go forth from the ark, you and your sons and your sons' wives with you. Be fruitful and multiply, and fill the earth" (Gen. 9:1).

While rereading this Bible story from childhood verse by verse, several important facts came to light for me that I had never pondered before. First of all, Noah wasn't just any ordinary man living on the earth. Moses, who wrote the book of Genesis, tells us that Noah was a righteous man, blameless in his generation, and that he "walked with God" (Gen. 6:9).

> **YHWH saw that the wickedness of man was great in the earth**, and that every intention of the thoughts of his heart was only evil continually. And YHWH regretted that he had made man on the earth, and **it grieved him to his heart**. So YHWH said, "I will blot out man whom I have created from the face of the land, man and animals and creeping things and birds of the heavens, for I am sorry that I have made them." **But Noah found favor in the eyes of YHWH**. (Gen. 6:5–8 ESV)

In God's eyes, Noah was the only man worth saving. Of all the men on the earth at that time, there was only one man who loved God and walked with him. How quickly the earth had gone from paradise in the garden of Eden to an evil world, full of corruption and violence. How sad YHWH, the Creator of all the earth, must have felt! At that point in history he had a personal relationship with only one man. No wonder his heart grieved. So God made a covenant with Noah and said, "If you build an ark and fill it with all the animals of the earth, then when the waters come I will save you and your family from death."

The second thing I noticed were the dimensions of the ark that God asked Noah to build. It was approximately 450 feet long, 75 feet wide, and 45 feet high! Because of the ark's immense size, it became obvious to me that Noah, and I assume his sons, spent a very long time building it. We don't know when God gave his command to Noah to build the ark or how long it took. What we do know is that after Noah was five hundred years old, his sons Shem, Ham, and Japheth were born to him. We also know that when Noah was six hundred years old, the floodwaters came upon the earth. So some time during the hundred years in between, the ark was planned and built. Whether it took ten years, fifty years, or the entire one hundred years, we do not know.

I can only imagine what Noah's neighbors thought about his new construction project. They probably thought that he had lost his mind and ridiculed him daily. We also don't know how his sons felt about this new undertaking. Remember, the Bible tells us that God found favor with only Noah, so it is safe to assume that his sons were not walking with God either. Noah's sons probably thought their dad had gone insane. Also, no one truly knows if it had ever rained on earth before the flood. So when Noah told his family and neighbors that God was going to destroy the earth with a flood, they most likely had no concept of what Noah was talking about.

Finally, in reading these verses, it came to my mind that Noah did not have any power tools to make the task of building this boat any easier. Just cutting down one tree would have taken him a long time. Building this ark had to have been physically and emotionally draining, and yet Noah continued to build year, after year, after year, for possibly one hundred years.

With simple math, we know this means that for 36,500 days, Noah woke up knowing what his job for the day was going to be. I wonder if he, at some point, if not daily, doubted God's instructions. He probably asked more than once for reassurance that he was doing God's will. You see, Noah had an extremely daunting task in front of him, and he probably felt like the project would take him the rest of his lifetime to complete. But I imagine every time Noah doubted what he was doing, God, in his loving and patient way, would speak to Noah, either audibly or through his quiet voice, to reassure Noah that he was in charge. All Noah needed to do was follow YHWH's commandment to build the ark, and he would take care of all the details.

Just because Noah found "favor" in the eyes of YHWH did not mean that YHWH would not command Noah to do some very difficult things for him. We must not confuse being favored with receiving blessings. The ultimate blessing Noah was going to receive for all his hard work was salvation, but until then his daily life would be difficult. Daily, Noah sacrificed his life in obedience to God's commands and, finally, in the six hundredth year of Noah's life, the ark was completed. Bible history tells us that during this year, in the second month, on the seventeenth day of the month, the floodwaters came.

> **On that day all the fountains of the great deep burst forth**, and the windows of the heavens were opened. And rain fell upon the earth forty days and forty nights. On the very same day Noah and his sons, Shem and Ham and Japheth, and Noah's wife and the three wives of his sons with them entered the ark, they and every beast, according to its kind, and all the livestock according to their kinds, and every creeping thing that creeps on the earth, according to its kind, and every bird, according to its kind, every winged creature. **They went into the ark with Noah, two and two of all flesh in which there was the breath of life**. And those that entered, male and female of all flesh, went in as God had commanded him. **And YHWH shut him in**. (Gen. 7:11b–16 ESV)

This day must have been such a blessing to Noah to know that all his hard work, years of ridicule, and sometimes doubt and reassurance from God had paid off. He had obeyed God's commands, and for his obedience God saved him and his family exactly as he said he would. When God "shut him in," it was as if God was saying to Noah, "Job well done, my son. Now let me take care of the rest." YHWH had kept his covenant with Noah. As a result, one family, or eight souls, were saved from death on that day in history.

And when the waters subsided one year and ten days later and the earth was dry, Noah and his wife, his sons and their wives, and all the animals of the earth went forth by families out of the ark. What a glorious day that must have been. Having felt God's grace and mercy upon him and his family, Noah built an altar to YHWH in order to praise him. This pleased YHWH, and I can imagine he felt great joy. By making sacrifices to YHWH, Noah was communicating with God that he believed that YHWH was the one and only true God. After this event, YHWH blessed Noah and said:

> **"Behold, I establish my covenant with you and your offspring after you**, and with every living creature that is with you, the birds, the livestock, and every beast of the

earth with you, as many as came out of the ark; it is for every beast of the earth. I establish my covenant with you, that never again shall all flesh be cut off by the waters of the flood, and never again shall there be a flood to destroy the earth." And God said, "This is the sign of the covenant that I make between me and you and every living creature that is with you, for all future generations: **I have set my bow in the cloud, and it shall be a sign of the covenant between me and the earth.**" (Gen. 9:9–13 ESV)

The Covenant

The first time the word *covenant* is seen in Scripture is when God is speaking to Noah. Before the ark was even built, God promised Noah that if he completed the ark as commanded, he would establish a covenant with him. So after the floodwaters came and went, and the earth was dry again, God fulfilled his promise. The definition of the word *covenant* is "a written agreement or promise under seal between two or more parties, a formal, solemn, and binding agreement."[2] The covenant YHWH established with Noah was a promise that never again would he destroy the earth by water. What I find very interesting about this promise between Noah and God is that when God established this covenant with Noah, he used the word *covenant* seven times. There's that number seven again! Remember, in the Bible, the number seven means spiritual completion and perfection. What is also interesting is that God uses a physical "bow," or rainbow, in the clouds as a sign and a seal of their covenant. And wouldn't you know, there are seven colors in a rainbow! I find that to be simply amazing. So we can be assured that the rainbow covenant was a "perfect and complete" promise.

Maybe that is why seeing a rainbow in the sky is such a special event. Maybe, just maybe, after viewing a rainbow's beauty, we remember God's special promise to us all and see his spiritual completion and perfection. Because if you think about it, a rainbow typically occurs after a rainstorm, when light penetrates the darkness and brings forth brilliant colors for all to see. And who doesn't enjoy the peace and tranquility that comes when a storm has passed? A rainbow is just another glimpse into God's glorious creation and a reminder of his covenant to us all.

In thinking about this story and all that happened, it becomes clear that God essentially started creation over again with Noah. This time YHWH started it with one man whom he felt was righteous enough to save. Noah's instructions from God were to "be fruitful and multiply and fill the earth." Noah lived to the great old age of 950 years. I would imagine he never got tired of telling all his grandchildren, great-grandchildren, and great-great-grandchildren about the time when Grandpa built a huge ark for God that saved him, his family, and all the animals in the world from a great flood that covered the entire earth. Maybe that is why the story of this great flood can be found in most, if not all, of the histories of the world. In telling his story, undoubtedly Noah emphasized what an awesome God he worshipped.

The Driving Force: Faith

So what drove Noah to wake up every day for 36,500 days and continue to be obedient to God, to continue to honor him every day, even when everyone else was telling him he was crazy? It can only be explained this way: "*Now faith is the assurance of things hoped for, the conviction of things not seen. For by it the men of old received divine approval*" (Heb. 11:1–2). "*By faith Noah, being warned by God concerning events as yet unseen, took heed and constructed an ark* for saving of his household; by this he condemned the world and *became an heir of the righteousness which comes by faith*" (Heb. 11:7). You see, Noah had faith that what God said was true *was* actually true. Even though Noah had probably never seen a boat before and did not know how the whole earth could possibly be flooded by rain, Noah knew with all his heart that what God had spoken to him would come true. He therefore did not walk by sight but by faith alone. Because Noah walked with God, he was obedient to God's wishes. Regardless of what anyone else said to him, Noah knew who he was working and living for. He was walking in obedience because he knew that if he wasn't, he was walking in disobedience. And Noah knew that with obedience came rewards and life, and with disobedience came consequences and death. By being obedient, Noah saved his family from destruction and set a legacy for his family.

However, keep in mind that it wasn't until the flood finally came that Noah gained understanding. Remember, first comes obedience and then comes understanding. In fact, Noah's legacy of obedience became so timeless that we still talk about it to this day. Noah experienced God in a way that he would never have known if he had chosen not to obey. With his obedience came peace, joy, and life. Scripture tells us that Noah found favor in the eyes of YHWH. God considered Noah a righteous man who was found blameless in his generation. This does not mean that Noah was found sinless. God found Noah righteous for one reason only—and that is because Noah always kept his face turned toward him. This way, when God spoke, Noah heard him loud and clear. As a result, they had an intimate and loving relationship. YHWH's name was written on Noah's heart.

So what do you need to do to become obedient to God? What is he asking you to do? Can you honestly say that you have found favor in the eyes of YHWH? Are you walking with him? When the floods come, will you be inside the ark or will you be outside? Will you experience the rewards or the consequences? Now is the time to start asking yourself these questions. Now is the time to start walking "by faith" with your LORD and Savior, and I guarantee he will bring your life out of the darkness and into the light with all of his glorious colors radiating from your face.

Chapter 12
The Ark of Jesus

"And **I will give you shepherds after my own heart**, who will feed you with knowledge and understanding. And when you have multiplied and increased in the land, in those days, says YHWH, **they shall no more say, 'The ark of the covenant of YHWH.' It shall not come to mind, or be remembered, or missed; it shall not be made again.**" (Jer. 3:15–16)

Noah's ark was designed to save a family. All Noah had to do is be obedient to God's instructions to build the ark and then believe that the ark would provide him with salvation. The ark of the covenant that God instructed Moses to build was designed to save the nation of Israel. Placed inside this ark of the covenant were two stone tablets with YHWH's law and his divine name written upon them, Aaron's budded rod, and the manna given from heaven. The Israelites were told by YHWH that they would be his people and he would be their God. God asked his people to build the ark and to obey the covenant that was placed inside of it, and they would receive eternal salvation.

While thinking about Noah's ark and the ark of the covenant, it suddenly became very clear to me that there was a *third* ark. The ark that YHWH designed to save the world is what I have termed the "Ark of Jesus." What you will discover in the remaining chapters is that Jesus was the embodiment of everything the original ark of the covenant represented. He was God's Word in the flesh, and he came in YHWH's name. Jesus was God's rod, YHWH's righteous branch that sprouted new life and bore the fruit of the Holy Spirit. And finally Jesus was YHWH's manna, living bread sent from heaven to feed mankind. However, this time, the "ark" would not be built by man but by YHWH himself. The physical ark that would carry the new covenant into the world was simply Mary's womb, which YHWH filled with his Holy Spirit. The new covenant carried within Mary's womb was God's only Son, Jesus, who would in time bring salvation to the entire world. Those who believed in the Ark of Jesus, the new covenant, would be saved.

Why Mary?

So how did YHWH come to choose Mary for this astonishing task of bringing his new covenant into the world?

> In the sixth month, **the angel Gabriel was sent from God** to a city of Galilee named Nazareth, **to a virgin betrothed to a man** whose name was Joseph, of the house of David; and the **virgin's name was Mary**. And he came to her and said, "**Hail, O favored one, the Lord is with you!**" ... And Mary said to the angel, "How shall this be, since I have no husband?" And the angel said to her, "**The Holy Spirit will come upon you, and the power of the Most High will overshadow you**; therefore the **child to be born will be called holy, the Son of God**." (Luke 1:26–28, 34–35)

As it was with Noah, YHWH found favor with a virgin named Mary. Scripture doesn't tell us, but we can infer that Mary was found righteous and blameless in her generation because she, too, walked with God. Also, Mary's virgin body was pure, and that is exactly what YHWH needed to carry his Son, Jesus, into the world. When Mary heard what God was asking her to do, she responded to the angel Gabriel, "Behold, I am the handmaid of the Lord; *let it be to me according to your word*" (Luke 1:38).

Even though Mary had no idea how all of this was going to work out, she accepted God's will for her life. Even at her young age, she knew that God's will for her would be better than anything she could plan on her own. Although she knew this unexpected pregnancy would cause issues with her betrothed husband, Joseph, and the rumors would be plenty, she was willing to accept the Son of God's life into her womb.

So the Holy Spirit came upon Mary, and YHWH's Son, Jesus, was placed into her womb. Nine months later she delivered her firstborn son in the city of Bethlehem, exactly as prophesied. On the night of Jesus's birth, an angel of YHWH appeared to shepherds in a field and proclaimed, "Be not afraid; for behold, *I bring good news of a great joy* which will come to *all* the people; *for to you is born this day in the city of David a Savior, who is Christ the Lord*" (Luke 2:10–11). After finding Jesus wrapped in swaddling clothes and lying in a manger, the shepherds told everyone what they had seen and heard. How could they not have shared with others the wonderful news of the arrival of their Messiah when the news was so spectacular? With the announcement from the angels of the birth of the Messiah, and the proof of the shepherds seeing Jesus with their own eyes, it was obvious that the silent years were finally coming to an end. The long famine of not hearing YHWH's voice was broken. YHWH had once again initiated communication with his people. In time, God's second divine name would be brought back into the world and would become the *Name above all Names*, given among men, needed for salvation. People pondering the name of Jesus would bring great joy to YHWH.

God had made a huge sacrifice by asking his people to stop profaning his holy name. He knew his people would not understand this command and would simply stop saying his name, but that was a sacrifice YHWH was willing to make. His desire was for his people to long to hear from him, so that when Jesus was born and then finally started his ministry, they would be hungry for the truth. With Jesus's birth, *the ark of the new covenant* would once again return to the temple, this time designed and built by YHWH himself. The old covenant was starting to become obsolete, and very soon the *original* ark of the covenant would no longer be remembered or missed. "In speaking of a new covenant he treats the first as obsolete. And what is becoming obsolete and growing old is ready to vanish away" (Heb. 8:13).

The Name Jesus

So have you ever wondered why God chose the name Jesus for his only Son? The thought never crossed my mind until I was knee-deep into writing this book. Why wasn't Jesus named *Immanuel*, which means "God with us," exactly like the prophet Isaiah prophesied (Isa. 7:14, Matt. 1:23)? Why instead did God name his Son "Jesus," which was a very common name in the days he was born?

In its full form, Jesus's name in Hebrew is *Yehoshua*. The abbreviated form of *Yehoshua* is *Yeshua*. Yeshua's name in Hebrew letters is as follows and is read from right to left.

ישוע

Calling Jesus Yeshua instead of his given name of Yehoshua is like calling someone Mike instead of his given name of Michael. For ease of pronunciation, I will be using Jesus's abbreviated name of Yeshua (Yeh shoo wah) for the rest of this book. Yeshua translated into Greek is Iesous, and Iesous transliterated into Latin is Iesus. Derived from the Latin name Iesus, we arrive at Jesus. If you translate Yeshua directly into English, you get Joshua.[1] That is why you will sometimes hear people say that the name Jesus is the same name as Joshua.

Hebrew	**Greek**	**Latin**	**English**
Yeshua	Iesous	Iesus	Jesus
Yeshua			Joshua

When we know these facts about Jesus's name, it becomes even more interesting to know that the book of Joshua in the Bible foreshadows what Jesus came to do. After Moses died, we learned that Joshua was the man chosen by God to bring the Israelites across the Jordan River, defeat their enemies, and finally bring them into the promised land in order to give them their inheritance. What Joshua accomplished for the Israelites is what Jesus came to do for the world—to save us from our enemy Satan and to give us our inheritance.

God told both Mary and Joseph on separate occasions, through the angel Gabriel, to name their child Yeshua. "Joseph, son of David, do not fear to take Mary your wife, for that which is conceived in her is of the Holy Spirit; she will bear a son, and *you shall call his name Jesus [Yeshua], for he will save his people from their sins*" (Matt. 1:20–21). So why did YHWH give his beloved Son the common name of Yeshua when he had such a great purpose for him? There had been many sons, priests, and prophets all named Yeshua prior to our Messiah's birth. I believe Jesus received the name Yeshua partly as protection from the enemy. God did not want Satan to know the name of his only Son before it was time for Jesus's ministry and until Jesus was fully prepared to defeat the enemy. YHWH therefore gave his Son a common name so he could be raised like any other child without fear from his adversary. Although Satan knew Jesus while he dwelled in heaven, Jesus's name was not Yeshua at that time, or Satan would have known exactly who to look for on earth to destroy after the shepherds spread the word of the Messiah's birth.

I also believe that God did not want his Son to be named Immanuel, as the prophet Isaiah prophesied, because of all the impersonators claiming that their sons were the Messiah simply by naming him Immanuel. In addition, God surely didn't want people to believe his Son was sent from heaven simply because he bore the name that was prophesied in Scripture.

Jesus's name of Yeshua was not a holy name at the time it was given to him. It was simply a man's name. The name Yeshua does have an incredible meaning, however. Yeshua's name means, "YHWH is salvation,"[2] which accurately describes what God's Son came to accomplish while living on earth.

Scripture tells us that Yeshua "was for a little while made *lower than the angels*" (Heb. 2:9). You might ask, "If Yeshua was the Son of God, then how could he ever be considered lower than the angels?" First of all, I believe it is because Jesus willingly gave up his heavenly glory to become flesh and blood in order to live among us. And second, I believe he was considered lower than the angels because of the common name his heavenly Father gave him while he was flesh and blood. Jesus had to be made like his brethren in every respect (Heb. 2:17). Therefore, for a little while, Jesus would not have his Father's holy name of YHWH, which he had had since the beginning of time. "In the beginning was the Word, and the Word was with God, and the Word was God ... And the Word became flesh and dwelt among us" (John 1:1, 14). Since Jesus was the Word, and the *Word was God*, Jesus's name before he became man must have been YHWH.

The Naming Ceremony

According to God's law, the naming of a Jewish baby occurred on the eighth day of his birth instead of on the first day he was born. During this naming ceremony, it was also customary for every Jewish boy to be circumcised. Therefore, on the eighth day of Jesus's birth, Mary and Joseph named their child Yeshua, as God had instructed them to do. On this day Yeshua was also circumcised like any other Jewish boy. Circumcision of all Jewish males became customary for the nation of Israel because of a command Abraham had received from YHWH long before.

> And God said to Abraham, "As for you, you shall keep my covenant, you and your descendants after you throughout their generations. **This is my covenant**, which you shall keep, **between me and you** and your descendants after you: Every male among you shall be circumcised. **You shall be circumcised in the flesh of your foreskins**, and **it shall be a sign of the covenant between me and you**." (Gen. 17:9–12)

Just like the bow in the cloud was Noah's sign of YHWH's promise given to him, circumcision became the sign of the covenant that was made between Abraham, his descendants, and their heavenly Father. Circumcision was and still is considered an everlasting bond between God and his people for all time.[3] It is a bond that can never be broken. When Abraham was ninety-nine years old, God promised him that his descendants would have a special relationship with their Creator that would forever be symbolized by the covenant of circumcision. So Abraham circumcised himself, his son Ishmael, as well as all the men of his household on the same day God commanded him to do so. When Abraham's son Isaac was born, he also underwent circumcision on the eighth day as commanded, as did every other male born into Abraham's family from that day forward.

Circumcision has always been seen as more than a simple medical procedure; it is a connection with YHWH. At the ceremony, through circumcision, blessings, and prayers, the child takes his rightful place as a member of the nation of Israel. The act of circumcision suggests a change of state: the knife inscribes a circle, which is a symbol of unity, an everlasting covenant, one that has no beginning and no end. Circumcision is also seen as a form of ritual bloodletting, which has always been an integral part of offerings and sacrifices. Therefore, the act of circumcision is both an offering and a sacrifice to the covenant with God. The foreskin is the offering with which the people of Israel seal the covenant with YHWH.

So the day Yeshua was circumcised was the day he was brought into the covenant with YHWH. From that day forward, YHWH was his heavenly Father, and he was his Son. Yeshua's circumcision was his very first sacrifice of flesh given to YHWH for his plan of salvation, and it sealed the purpose for which he had come. From the time he was eight days old, Yeshua had a sign of God's everlasting covenant in his very flesh. Biblically, the number eight symbolizes new beginnings.[4] The day Jesus was brought into God's covenant was definitely a new beginning for the nation of Israel. "So shall my covenant be in your flesh an everlasting covenant" (Gen. 17:13b).

Jesus's Birthdate

The Bible does not tell us on what day Jesus was born. It is only because of tradition that Christians celebrate his birth on the twenty-fifth of December. There are theories on why this date was chosen as his birthdate, but the truth remains a mystery. However, when you consider the details given in Luke's account of his birth and dedication in the temple, we can figure out when Jesus was most likely born. What we do know is that right before Jesus's birth, Caesar Augustus declared that a census be taken for the entire Roman Empire. This meant that every citizen was required to travel back to the city in which he or she had been born in order to be enrolled. Common sense tells us that this event could not have taken place in December because it would have been the middle of the winter for this area of the world. Many travelers would have frozen to death considering it would have taken most of them several days of travel to get back to their birthplaces.

The Bible also tells us that in the region that Jesus was born, there were shepherds out in the fields, keeping watch over their flock by night. For the same reason of cold weather, we know that in December the shepherds would not have been out at night with their sheep. Instead, in order to provide their sheep with relief from the weather, the shepherds would most likely have been in caves. Finally, I would imagine that YHWH would not have sent his one and only Son into the world knowing that he would be born outside in a manger in the middle of winter. The elements would have been too harsh for a baby to survive. Therefore, many theologians believe that Jesus was most likely born in the fall instead of winter.

What we know to be true is that nowhere in Scripture does YHWH tell us to celebrate Jesus's birth, even though he gave Moses very specific dates and instructions on how and when the Israelites were to celebrate his seven ordained feasts. Instructions on how to celebrate these seven feasts, along with the Sabbath day, can be found in books of Exodus, Leviticus, Numbers, and Deuteronomy. These were very important celebrations that God wanted his people to remember yearly, from generation to generation. Unfortunately, most Christians know very little, if anything, about these feasts. What I have discovered over the past few years of studying God's feasts is how important they are in his plan for salvation and how they were put in place for the purpose of commemorating "communication events" between YHWH and his people, both for the old covenant and for the new covenant of Jesus.

Since God was so specific with the dates of his feasts, don't you think that he would be very specific with how and when he wanted us to celebrate Jesus's birth if he truly wanted us to? Considering all of these facts, the only conclusion that I can draw is that God doesn't require us to celebrate his Son's birth, because if he did he would have given us the specifics. The tradition of celebrating Jesus's birth did not even begin until approximately AD 300, which was 270 years after his death. Therefore, it is obvious to me that Jesus's birthdate of December 25 was simply a date chosen by man.[5]

We know that God did not command his believers to celebrate Jesus's birth; however, there is one date that Jesus did tell his disciples to celebrate. When Jesus said, "Do this in remembrance of me," it was the evening before he was sacrificed on the cross. When he said these words to his disciples, he was celebrating Passover with them. Passover just happens to be the first feast out of the seven feasts that God ordained his people to celebrate every year. We call this last meal Jesus spent with his disciples the Last Supper. What we know for sure is that this last Passover meal occurred on Nisan 14 of the Jewish calendar, as it had every year since God ordained this feast to take place. So it is not Jesus's birth that is critical, but instead it is the date of Jesus's death that God wants us to remember yearly. Even King Solomon said that the date of a man's death was more important than his birth because it was only at the time of a person's death that it would be known what that man accomplished while he lived (Ecc. 7:1). The date of Jesus's death is the date that the old covenant became obsolete and the new covenant began. More will be discussed about this important date in the chapter titled "The Passover Lamb."

If the Bible does not tell us when Jesus was born, and we are now convinced that he was definitely not born on December 25, what does the Bible say about his birth that might give us some clues? The purpose of finding out Jesus's birth is not so that we can celebrate this new date but so that we can get a better picture of how holy YHWH's name truly is and to get a better idea of how YHWH thinks. Let's consider Jesus's birth from God's perspective. Remember, he had remained silent with his people for approximately 430 years. It would seem likely that many of the people who believed YHWH was the one and only God had lost all hope that he would ever communicate with them again. So considering that the silence was now broken with the revelation to the shepherds of Jesus's birth, if you were God, how would you publicly introduce your Son to the world?

Witnesses

We know that when God introduced himself to his people on Mount Sinai, he had a lot of witnesses. His introduction and the giving of his name to his people was anything but quiet. The extraordinary way in which he chose to make himself known was intended to ensure that the people would have no doubt about what they saw or heard. He wanted his people to believe what they experienced to be true and therefore speak of this event for generations to come. He wanted the day he introduced himself to his people to be an encounter that would be remembered forever.

In contrast, Jesus's birth was a private occasion. The only witnesses to this incredible event were Mary, Joseph, and a few shepherds. In addition, Jesus's circumcision and naming ceremony, which occurred eight days later, was also private. It was most likely attended only by his parents and a priest or rabbi. So now that his Son was born into the world, how would YHWH accomplish introducing Jesus to his people in order to confirm what the shepherds were already telling people—that their Messiah had indeed been born?

From Luke's gospel, we know of one more event that occurred in the early days of Yeshua's birth. According to the Law of Moses (Lev. 12:2–8), when a woman bore a male child, she was considered unclean for seven days. Then on the eighth day the male child was circumcised and named. The mother would then experience purifying bleeding for and additional thirty-three days. Finally, at the end of these forty days, she was required to bring a sacrifice to the temple in Jerusalem as an offering to YHWH, which cleansed her from the flow of her blood: "And when the time came for their purification according to the law of Moses, *they brought him [Yeshua] up to Jerusalem to present him to the Lord* (as it is written in the law of the Lord, 'Every male that opens the womb *shall be called holy to the Lord*')" (Luke 2:22–23). At this same time of Mary's purification, Mary and Joseph were required to bring Jesus with them to fulfill the law of the firstborn. YHWH said to Moses, "*Consecrate to me all the first-born*; whatever is the first to open the womb among the people of Israel, *both of man and of beast, is mine*" (Exodus 13:1–2). This day in history served many purposes. Not only was Mary purified of her blood and Yeshua dedicated "holy to YHWH" according to the law for all firstborn sons, but it was also the day YHWH chose to publicly introduce his Son to his people.

The day of Yeshua's dedication was a very special day for YHWH. It was a day he had planned and designed centuries ago with the purpose of once again giving his people a living hope that he was their God and they were his people—to reassure them that he had not forgotten about them. He planned for this day to be very memorable so that it would be remembered and spoken of for generations to come. So what possible day would God choose to publicly reveal his Son to the world for the very first time?

The Day of Atonement: Jesus's Dedication

When you look at the seven feasts that God ordained and understand that they were originally designed as "communication events" from our heavenly Father, it becomes crystal clear that there is only one day of the entire year that YHWH would choose to introduce his one and only Son to his people, and that is the Day of Atonement.

Remember, the Day of Atonement was the day that the high priest asked YHWH to forgive him and the entire nation of their sins for an entire year. It was on this day that the high priest was allowed to enter into the Holy of Holies, where the ark of the covenant was placed, in order to approach YHWH, where his Spirit resided above the mercy seat. Only on this day was he permitted to sprinkle blood from the sacrifice over the mercy seat of the ark of the covenant while asking for forgiveness of the nation's sins.

However, we must not forget that during the time of Yeshua's birth, the ark of the covenant, YHWH's presence (Shekinah glory), and the Urim and Thummim were all missing from the temple. They had been missing for hundreds of years. So I would imagine that through these silent years, on the Day of Atonement, the high priest simply went through the motions. I guess he had no choice but to sprinkle blood into an *empty* Holy of Holies since there was no mercy seat to approach or to sprinkle blood over. All the high priest could do on this important day is humbly pray for redemption of their sins and hope for the best.

Because the new covenant of Jesus had yet to be established, the old covenant had not yet become obsolete. What I find truly amazing is that even with all these forms of communication missing throughout the silent years, God still chose to forgive his people of their sins year after year. This in itself was a miracle.

As previously discussed, the Day of Atonement is the holiest day of the entire year for the Jewish people. It occurs on the tenth day of Tishrei, which is the seventh month of the Jewish calendar. The seventh month is considered the holiest month of the year. There's that number seven again, which means spiritual perfection and completion. The Day of Atonement was, and is, considered the Sabbath Day of all Sabbath Days. It is a day of fasting and prayer. If the people received forgiveness of sins for one more year on this day, they received a day of great rest. If you consider God's purpose of introducing Yeshua to the people, there would not be a better day to introduce his Son as the "Savior of the world" than on the Day of Atonement—on the only day of the year the people of Israel were specifically looking to YHWH for salvation from their sins.

Because Yeshua was Mary and Joseph's firstborn son, then by law, the day Jesus was brought to the temple forty days after his birth was the day he was consecrated to YHWH. The dictionary defines *consecrated* as "dedicated to a sacred purpose, or hallowed."[6] Mary and Joseph knew that the day they brought Jesus to the temple to be dedicated holy to YHWH would be a very special day—one that would be cherished forever. So again, I ask: What day, of all days, would God choose to dedicate his son Yeshua to his sacred purpose? It must be the Day of Atonement. On this day, many people would be coming to the temple in Jerusalem to sacrifice, fast, and pray for forgiveness of the nation's sins. On this day there would be many witnesses, just as YHWH planned it. One of the witnesses was Simeon.

> Now there was a man in Jerusalem, whose name was **Simeon**, and **this man was righteous and devout, looking for the consolation of Israel, and the Holy Spirit was upon him**. And it had been revealed to him by the Holy Spirit that **he should not see death before he had seen the Lord's Christ**. And inspired by the Spirit he came in to the temple; and when the parents brought in the child Jesus, to do for him according to the custom of the law, **he took him up in his arms and blessed God** and said, "Lord, now lettest thou thy servant depart in peace, according to thy word; **for mine eyes have seen thy salvation which thou hast prepared in the presence of all peoples**, a light for revelation to the Gentiles, and for glory to thy people Israel." (Luke 2:25–32)

Simeon was in the temple that day because he was looking for the *consolation of Israel*. The word *consolation* means "the act or instance of consoling." The synonym of *consolation* is "comfort." To *comfort* means "to give consolation in time of trouble or worry" or "to give strength or hope."[7] Therefore, Simeon was at the temple looking for *hope* for the people of Israel in a time of trouble or worry. Why would Simeon have been doing that? There is only one conclusion. Simeon was at the temple on the Day of Atonement. It was on this day that all of Israel came to Jerusalem to fast and pray and to ask if YHWH would forgive them of their sins for one more year. All of Israel was praying for redemption on this day. If the high priest was able to come out of the temple and

Encountering the Great I Am

pronounce the Aaronic blessing in front of all who were gathered, then all was well for one more year.

When Simeon saw Jesus, he knew without a doubt that he had seen salvation in the form of this baby named Yeshua. Simeon said that he could now depart this life in peace. God brought his Son, Jesus, into the temple, to be dedicated holy to YHWH in front of all of Israel, *in the presence of all the peoples*, on the exact day that all of Israel was looking for salvation from their sins.

There was another person at the temple that day.

> And there was a prophetess, Anna, the daughter of Phan'u-el, of the tribe of Asher; she was of a great age, having lived with her husband seven years from her virginity, and as a widow till she was eighty-four. She did not depart from the temple, **worshiping with fasting and prayer night and day**. And coming up at that very hour she gave thanks to God, **and spoke of him to all who were looking for the redemption of Jerusalem.** (Luke 2:36–38)

The first thing you see about Anna is that she was worshipping with fasting and prayer at the temple night and day. She was doing this because it was the Day of Atonement, and she knew what her God commanded her to do on this day. This is the only feast and the only day of the year that God commanded his people to afflict themselves, which is another way of saying that he commanded them to fast.[8] Those who did not fast for the entire twenty-four hour day were cut off from the people (Lev. 23:26–32).

We see that with fasting and prayer Anna was keeping the commandment of YHWH on this day. *To afflict* oneself in biblical terms means to humble oneself before YHWH. God knew that with fasting comes clarity. On this day YHWH wanted people's minds to be extremely clear so that they were sure of what they were seeing and hearing. God had something very important to communicate to them. Because Anna was obedient to YHWH in her fasting and prayer, her mind was very clear so that she could receive the truth. Because she was seeking God through her fasting, she was sure of what she saw and heard when she came upon Simeon as he was pronouncing to the people that Jesus was their salvation. As a result of what she saw, she couldn't help but give thanks to God and to speak of Jesus to "all who were looking for the redemption of Jerusalem." To *redeem* means "to release from blame or debt, to free from the consequences of sin, or to atone for."[9] From this definition one can only conclude that Anna was also at the temple on the Day of Atonement, and she was speaking to all those looking for forgiveness or atonement of their sins.

Because the old covenant had not yet become obsolete, we know that, as was the custom, the high priest on this particular Day of Atonement was able to raise his hands toward heaven and pronounce the Aaronic blessing upon the people. YHWH once again forgave the people of their sins. Remember the words that the high priest would have said on this day:

> "**YHWH** bless you and keep you;
> **YHWH** make his face to shine upon you, and be gracious to you;
> **YHWH** lift up his countenance upon you, and give you peace." (Num. 6:24–26 ESV)

Before the silent years, this blessing was said by the high priest, using YHWH's divine name. Once YHWH's name became too holy to say (for fear of profaning it), the words "the LORD" were substituted for God's name in this blessing. However, there was one exception to this rule. On the Day of Atonement, the high priest would still invoke YHWH's divine name for all to hear.[10] Considering the purpose of this blessing was to place YHWH's divine name and blessings upon the people, what better day for Yeshua to be consecrated for his sacred purpose than on the day his Father's divine name was still spoken. The words of the Aaronic blessing carry so much meaning when we think of Simeon lifting up baby Jesus into his arms. Jesus was YHWH's ultimate blessing to the people, and on the day of his dedication, Simeon looked into Jesus's eyes and was able to see salvation. On that day he saw God's glory illuminated in Jesus's face. In time, Jesus's face would eventually shine upon all the people of the world, and he would be gracious to them. And in time, Jesus's countenance would be lifted up and sacrificed on the cross to die for man's sins so that peace could be upon us.

The Aaronic blessing was said so that YHWH's name would be placed upon the people of Israel and they would therefore *receive his blessings* (Num. 6:22–27). On the day of Jesus's dedication, the people received the blessing of looking into the face of the *new ark of the covenant and receiving the new covenant name: Yeshua.* Everyone who heard what Simeon and Anna said about Yeshua that day received great peace, knowing that the Messiah had finally been born.

One Final Note

On the day of Mary's purification and Yeshua's dedication, Mary and Joseph were required to bring a sacrifice. The law stated that a one-year-old lamb should be brought to the temple for a burnt offering and a young pigeon or turtledove for a sin offering. If she could not afford a lamb, then she could bring two turtledoves or two pigeons for her sacrifices (Lev. 12:6–8).

Being of humble means, Mary and Joseph could not afford a lamb, so they brought either two young pigeons or a pair of turtledoves for their offerings. What I find very intriguing about their inability to provide a lamb for their burnt offering is that by bringing Jesus into the temple with them on that day, they were actually carrying the Lamb of God in their arms. On this Day of Atonement, Mary and Joseph not only presented offerings for the purification of Mary, but they were also dedicating the one and only Lamb of God to YHWH. Thirty-three years later, this Lamb of God would save the people of the world from their sins and provide eternal salvation for all who believe in his name.

What foreshadowing God provided to Simeon, Anna, and all those who heard the good news and believed on that Day of Atonement in 3 BC! Their prayers of hearing from God had finally been answered.

Communication had begun again between YHWH and his people. The Messiah for whom they had been waiting all these years had finally been born, named, circumcised, brought into the covenant of God, and consecrated to YHWH's sacred purpose. YHWH had successfully achieved his goal. And because there were many witnesses on the day YHWH publicly introduced his Son to the people of Israel, it became a memorable day that would be written and talked about for centuries.

The day Jesus was brought into the temple was the day the new ark of the covenant suddenly entered into the temple after being lost for hundreds of years. The day Jesus was brought into the temple was the day God placed his Son's name onto his people, including all of the blessings that would be bestowed on those who chose to believe in the power of the Ark of Jesus. The day Yeshua was dedicated in the temple was a day when the names of the Urim and Thummim were both spoken out loud. For those who pondered the names of the Illuminator and Completer on this day came the ultimate promise of a future eternal salvation, which would one day be filled with light and perfection.

> **And he [Jesus] shall stand** and feed his flock in the strength of YHWH, **in the majesty of the name of YHWH his God**. And they shall dwell secure, **for now he shall be great to the ends of the earth**. (Micah 5:4)

Chapter 13
The Word Became Flesh

A few years ago, I studied the books of Genesis and Revelation at the same time. Both studies were very intensive and took eight months to complete. I thoroughly enjoyed reading and pondering both of these books of the Bible. Genesis is a book of beginnings. The universe is its stage; the glory of God is its theme; and humanity, sin, and redemption are its content. The book begins with creation and ends with Joseph's bones being placed in a coffin in Egypt. In between these two scenes, Genesis records the first marriage, the first family, the first rebellion against God, and sin's tragic consequences. We also see how God destroys the entire earth with a flood, with the exception of Noah and his family. The earth had become corrupt and was filled with violence due to Satan's presence. Finally, Genesis records how God, after the flood, chooses to begin personal relationships with Abraham, Isaac, Jacob, and finally Joseph in order to fight for mankind.

Genesis is a book about beginnings, and Revelation is a book of endings. At first glance, these two books appear dramatically different from one another. However, if you look at them more closely, you can see how they are really just mirror images of one another. In the book of Revelation, the universe is still the stage; the glory of God is still the theme; and humanity, sin, and redemption are still its content. The book of Revelation begins with God's Son, Jesus, speaking to his churches, which he has established and for whom he has fought for over thousands of years. It then reveals how God plans to destroy the earth because of how corrupt and violent it has become. The last rebellion of Satan takes place in the final chapters of this book. Finally, the book of Revelation closes with God creating a new heaven and a new earth so that YHWH, Jesus, and man can once again live together in paradise. Genesis begins with the first marriage, between Adam and Eve, and the first family; and Revelation culminates with the last marriage to ever take place, between Jesus Christ and his bride, the church. Those who are invited to the marriage supper of the Lamb are the people who are found in the Lamb's book of life. Together they form the very last family.

During the eight months I studied these books, I gained wisdom and understanding about both the beginning of time and the end of time. However, shortly after I completed these studies, I felt as if I didn't know what I was supposed to do next. I knew the beginning and the end of God's story, and, all of a sudden, in my mind, the story was over. What was left? How was I supposed to continue living, knowing that I was in the middle of God's story, where Satan's influences surrounded me wherever I turned? What was the purpose of my life when I knew how far mankind was from being back in paradise with YHWH and his Son, Jesus? I felt like King Solomon, who complained that everything in life was meaningless. All the things that used to bring me joy suddenly had no significance. Conversations with friends and family seemed trivial and empty. Daily chores and tasks were becoming increasingly more difficult for me to complete. I really was at a loss on how to continue in life. King Solomon was the wisest man of all times, and he had this to say about life on this earth:

> And I applied my mind to seek and to search out by wisdom all that is done under heaven. It is an unhappy business that God has given to the sons of men to be busy with. I have seen everything that is done under the sun, and behold, **all is vanity and a striving after wind**. What is crooked cannot be made straight, and what is lacking cannot be counted. (Ecc. 1:13–15 ESV)

I entered a very confusing and dark period of my life that lasted for several months. I didn't want to do anything or be with anyone. I cried all the time and just wanted to sleep. All of my symptoms clearly pointed to a diagnosis of depression. I hated life because *"what is done under the sun was grievous to me*; for all is vanity and a striving after wind"* (Ecc. 2:17). When I told my husband and friends about my situation, they recommended that I see a doctor and get my hormone levels checked out. They implied that I might need to start taking antidepressant drugs. Their suggestions all sounded reasonable, but I knew in my heart that there was something else going on. Like I said, I had just come off a very intensive study of two books of the Bible, so I started to think that maybe my depression was not a physical problem at all but perhaps a spiritual matter. I soon became convinced that I was physically well and that taking drugs would only mask the real issue. I knew my husband and friends were just trying to help me find an answer with their medical advice. Over these many months, life became very frustrating, as I did not know where or to whom to turn.

It wasn't until a woman whom I had just met at a gathering said something to me that I immediately realized was the key to my depression. She said, "Judy, in order to find meaning in this life, you have to model your life after the life of Jesus. Remember, he had to live in this world also. Why don't you start reading the Gospels and find out how Jesus handled life on this earth?" As soon as she said this, I knew that what she spoke was truth. Looking back in time, it was as if God put her in my life for that brief moment so he could speak directly to me through her. I had just met this woman and have never seen her since. YHWH knew that only Jesus could take away the darkness that currently enveloped me.

So I began over the next few weeks to look again at the Gospels. I began investigating everything there was to know about Jesus's life and how he spent his time on this earth. I thought about how the Son of God had to live in this world after residing in heaven from the beginning of time. I can only imagine the culture shock that he must have experienced. Jesus was with YHWH in the beginning of time in the garden of Eden, in paradise. We also know he will be with YHWH at the end of times in the new heaven and the new earth in paradise. What Jesus and I have in common is that Jesus also came to live on this earth in the middle of God's story. He also came to live in a time that was filled with the influences of Satan.

Miraculously, after studying the life of Jesus, in a matter of just weeks I was brought out of my darkness and into the light. After truly grasping that there was someone whom I could follow while here on this earth and that I was not here alone, I was able to find joy in my life once again. Suddenly, with the knowledge of the life of Jesus, everything in my life took on new meaning. As long as I did what Jesus commanded; lived my life loving YHWH with all my heart, my soul, and my mind; and loved others as much as I love myself, then I could live *in this world* without being *of this world*. This revelation gave me great peace.

I look back at that time period of darkness and thank God for the experience. Through it all, I came to know a critical truth about my purpose in life. Just like King Solomon came to understand the meaning of life, so did I: "Fear God, and keep his commandments; for this is the whole duty of man" (Ecclesiastes 12:13b). You see, nothing else matters in life except to love YHWH, your God, with all of your heart, soul, mind, and strength. Everything else is vanity and striving against the wind. Humans often come to realize this truth about life on this earth on their own when they reach middle age. It's called a midlife crisis. They start questioning the purpose of their lives. If this crisis hits and Jesus is not part of their lives, then their lives often end up a mess with divorces, adultery, drug or pornography addictions, alcohol abuse, and so on. They do not recognize that Satan is speaking into their lives. However, if they have Jesus to turn to when this crisis hits, as I did, then their crisis simply becomes a minor bump in the road because Jesus will explain to them their purpose in life.

It turns out that in my case of depression there were no physical issues causing my symptoms. My depression was a spiritual matter, after all. All I needed to do was turn to the one and only person who could help me, and that was my LORD and Savior, Jesus Christ, the Great Physician.

The Word of God

YHWH inspired Moses to write Genesis, the first book of the Bible, so that we would know who created us and for what purpose we were created. Jesus inspired the apostle John to write Revelation, the last book of the Bible, so that we would know who created us and for what purpose we were created. Both books agree that the only purpose for which we were created is to have a personal relationship with YHWH, our Creator, our Lord, our Father, our Savior, and our Lover. Jesus came to make these relationships possible for humanity and to model for us all exactly how to have a loving relationship with our heavenly Father. So what do we know about how Jesus lived his life on earth? By reading the four Gospels in the New Testament, I was able to learn a lot.

> **In the beginning was the Word, and the Word was with God, and the Word was God. He [Jesus] was in the beginning with God**. All things were made through him, and without him was not anything made that was made. In him was life, and the life was the light of men. **The light shines in the darkness, and the darkness has not overcome it**. (John 1:1–5 ESV)

As I was trying to figure out where to begin in describing the life of Jesus, God once again drew me back to his Son's birth and to the book of Exodus—to the story of Moses receiving the Ten Commandments. What most people don't realize about this story is that Moses received the Ten Commandments twice. The first time Moses ascended Mount Sinai, after God audibly spoke his commandments to his people, YHWH gave Moses the Ten Commandments written with his finger on two stone tablets that he himself provided. "And Moses turned, and went down the mountain with the two tablets of the testimony in his hands, tablets that were written on both sides; on the front and on the back they were written. *The tablets were the work of God, and the writing was the writing of God*, engraved upon the tablets" (Exo. 32:15–16 ESV). However, before

Moses descended the mountain, YHWH informed Moses that the people had made a golden calf that they were worshipping and sacrificing to. When Moses descended the mountain and saw how they were singing and dancing around it, out of burning anger Moses threw the two tablets that YHWH had given him and broke them at the foot of the mountain.

Moses then lay prostrate, fasting and in prayer before God, for forty days and forty nights, asking YHWH for forgiveness and atonement for the people's grave sin. YHWH was ready to destroy all of the people once again and start humanity over with Moses, just like he had with Noah. It took a lot of convincing, but YHWH finally changed his mind after Moses pleaded with God to let them live. After this event, Moses was allowed to receive the Ten Commandments a second time: "YHWH said to Moses, '*Cut for yourself two tablets of stone like the first, and I will write on the tablets the words* that were on the first tablets, which you broke" (Exo. 34:1 ESV). So Moses did as he was instructed. He cut the second set of stones with his own hands and took them up for God to engrave. God wrote his commandments once again; however, this time, God's words were engraved on stones *carved by human hands.*

Because I was thinking about the life of Jesus as I was reading this story in Scripture and I just happened to be fasting at this time, it became clear to me what the two sets of tablets represented. The first set of tablets represents YHWH's first covenant with the Israelites, along with the first covenant name of YHWH. The first set was carved by God and written by God. Written on these tablets were the words YHWH spoke on Mount Sinai to all the people, which represented truth and righteousness. Unfortunately, when the people profaned YHWH's name by making and bowing down to a graven image of a calf, they had already broken the first three commandments of this first covenant. When Moses broke this first set of tablets, it foreshadowed the breaking of the first covenant by the Israelites and YHWH's removing his holy name from the people. It had only been a matter of days since the people had seen YHWH's Shekinah glory on Mount Sinai, had heard his voice, and had agreed to God's covenant. So much had already taken place for the people to completely trust YHWH, yet they were already worshipping an idol made out of gold. God was furious and ready to eliminate the entire nation of Israel. At that time Moses interceded on behalf of the nation of Israel and asked that God spare their lives.

Once I realized that the first set of stone tablets represented the first covenant, the second set of stone tablets could only represent one thing, and that is the second covenant. Once sin entered this world in the garden of Eden, I would imagine that God was ready to eliminate all of humanity and start again. In fact, many times God threatened to do just that, and he actually did with the flood in Noah's time. And yet I also can imagine Jesus being right by God's side during these times, pleading with his Father to spare mankind. I can envision Jesus begging his Father to send him into the world to save the human race from their sins instead of destroying them. Even though Jesus knew that what he was asking of his Father would require him to become like man in every way, he was willing to make that sacrifice.

The Bible tells us, "In the beginning was the Word, and the Word was with God, and the Word was God" (John 1:1). God's Word had to become flesh in order for us to understand it, in order to understand his truth. Jesus is God's Word. YHWH illuminated his Word in the first covenant on the stone tablets that he provided his people. Jesus came to complete the illumination of what it meant to follow God's Word, and he became the second covenant. He came to show us how to live a sinless life by fearing God and keeping his commandments. For Jesus knows this is the whole duty of man.

YHWH did not carve the second set of tablets; Moses's human hands carved them. However, God engraved his Word on these tablets with his own finger, just like he had on the first set of stone tablets. Likewise, Jesus came into this world through the human process of birth, but not of conception: *"And the Word became flesh and dwelt among us*, full of grace and truth; we have beheld his glory, *glory as of the only Son from the Father"* (John 1:14). Jesus may have come into this world carved out of human flesh, but what was engraved into Jesus's heart, soul, and mind was the very Word of God. YHWH placed in Mary's womb, into the mortal flesh of Jesus, his Spirit and glory—his very essence.

Timeline of Events

While I was studying the giving of the Ten Commandments to Moses, I came across a timeline of events, beginning with the Israelites' exodus out of Egypt until the giving of the second set of stone tablets.[1] I learned that the Jewish people celebrate Moses's descent of Mount Sinai with the second set of tablets on the same day as the Day of Atonement. Once Moses descended the mountain for the second time, he placed the Ten Commandments, which had YHWH's name written upon them, into the ark of the covenant. "Then I turned and came down from the mountain, and *put the tablets in the ark* that I had made. And there they are, as YHWH commanded me" (Deut. 10:5 ESV). So Moses put God's Word in the ark of the covenant on the Day of Atonement. He presented the Word of God to all of Israel on this day. Is it just coincidence that Jesus was dedicated in the temple forty days after his birth on this same day on the calendar? Highly unlikely!

God's written Word (Ten Commandments), which represented the first covenant, was presented to the people on the Day of Atonement for all to see. Jesus, who represented the second covenant of God's Word, was also presented at the temple on the Day of Atonement for all to see. Jesus was the new Ark of the Covenant, and Yeshua was the new covenant name. The new covenant was replacing the first, so it makes sense that it was done on the same day. It also makes sense that YHWH removed the first ark of the covenant from the temple before Jesus's birth. It was removed so that when Jesus, the living, breathing Word of God, was being dedicated holy to YHWH, there would only be one Word of God in the temple. From that day forward, Jesus was God's living Word.

If I haven't yet convinced you that Jesus was dedicated on the Day of Atonement, maybe these facts about the months that Jesus was born, circumcised, and dedicated will change your mind. The Day of Atonement is always on Tishrei 10, as YHWH ordained it to occur every year. Since Jewish male children were dedicated forty days after they were born, we can conclude that Jesus was born 40 days earlier, which is Av 30, 3 BC. (Since a Jewish date cannot be converted to a date on the Gregorian calendar, if you want to remember Jesus's birthday, I would suggest you buy a Jewish calendar each year. But remember, Jesus didn't ask us to celebrate his birthday. Having said that, it is interesting to know the day of our Savior's birth for many reasons.)

The month of Av is the fifth month of the Jewish calendar, which falls in the autumn season in Israel, when theologians believe Jesus was most likely born. If we count eight days from Christ's birth, including the day he was born, we find out that he was named and circumcised in the sixth month of Elul, on Elul 7. He was then dedicated in the temple "Holy to YHWH" in the seventh month on Tishrei 10.

Jewish Month	**Jewish Date**	**Event**
Fifth	Av 30	Jesus is born
Sixth	Elul 7	Jesus is named and circumcised
Seventh	Tishrei 10	Jesus is dedicated "Holy to YHWH"

What I discovered about these months is the incredible meaning of their names. But before I reveal them, for it all to make sense I need to describe a few other events in the history of Israel that occurred during these months.

Jewish Month of Av

The month of Av has a turbulent history for the Jewish people. On the ninth day of this month in 587 BC, the Babylonians laid waste to Solomon's Temple, the first temple, by fire. On this same day, on Av 9 in AD 70, the Romans destroyed Herod's magnificent temple, the second temple, by fire. It seems quite amazing that both temples would be destroyed on the same date. But remember, YHWH prophesied through his prophets that these events would take place as punishment for profaning his holy name. The Jewish people remember the destruction of the temples with a feast called Tisha B'Av. This is not one of YHWH's seven ordained feasts; however, it has always been a day of great mourning for the Jewish people.

Remember also that Moses lay prostrate for forty days and forty nights before ascending the mountain to receive the second set of commandments. Therefore, Moses spent this entire month of Av asking forgiveness of the nation's sin of worshipping the golden calf. After God relented, Moses was instructed to carve a new set of tablets. According to the Jewish timeline, Moses carved them on Av 30. Interesting! Av 30 is the same day Jesus was born, according to my calculations. In addition, it is recorded in Numbers 33:38 that Aaron, the first high priest, died on the first day of this month, Av 1. So what possible meaning could there be for this month of Av that would describe all of those events?

There are actually several meanings for this fifth month. In the Babylonian language, the meaning of the fifth month is "torches" or "fiery." The Canaanite meaning for this month is "hostile." Well, those three words would definitely describe the beginning half of the month of Av in Jewish history, when Aaron died and both temples were destroyed by fire. And then there is the Hebrew meaning of the word *Av*, which means, "father." It also means "comforter or consoler of Av."[2] When I saw all of these meanings together in one place, after considering all of the things that occurred in this month, I couldn't believe it. Not only did such contrasting historical events occur in this month, but the various meanings of Av in the different languages described exactly what had happened, from death and destruction to the carving of the second set of tablets. And in the same month of Av in 3 BC, our heavenly Father sent his living and breathing Word of God into this world through the birth of his Son, Jesus. In addition, Israel's first high priest, Aaron, died at the beginning of this month, and Jesus, our final High Priest, was born at the end of this same month. Simply incredible.

In the history of this month, you could definitely say God became the comforter of Av. In addition, the biblical meaning of the number five is "grace" or "God's goodness."[3] Of course it is! This fifth month in Jewish history is full of God's grace in the bringing of his Son, Yeshua, the living Word of God, into this world.

Finally, it is interesting that the first and second temples were destroyed on Av 9 and that Jesus was born on Av 30. Historically, in this month of Av, three weeks to the day after the manmade temples were destroyed, Jesus's body became YHWH's new temple. "Jesus answered them, *'Destroy this temple, and in three days I will raise it up.'* The Jews then said, 'It has taken forty-six years to build this temple, and will you raise it up in three days?' *But he spoke of the temple of his body*" (John 2:19–21). "We heard him say, 'I will destroy this temple that is made with the hands, and in three days *I will build another, not made with hands*'" (Mark 14:58). After the temples built by human hands were destroyed, God built another through his Son, Yeshua. YHWH still desired a temple for his holy name to dwell in. YHWH never placed his name in the second temple, because he knew it would all too soon become Herod's temple. God's new temple became the body of his Son, Jesus, and YHWH's new name for the time being was Yeshua, *God's second divine name.* Jesus was born into this world in the month of Av in order to become YHWH's new temple. Jesus was born into this world to be the new covenant between man and God. And what better way to celebrate Jesus's birth than at his circumcision and naming ceremony, which occurred on the eighth day of his birth on Elul 7.

Jewish Month of Elul

According to Jewish history, it was on Elul 1 that Moses ascended the mountain of God for the second time, after carving the new tablets the day before. The name Elul is of Babylonian origin and is the sixth month of the Jewish year. In the Aramaic language, spoken by the Jewish people at the time that the names of the months were set, the word *Elul* means "search."[4]

"To search" is certainly an appropriate meaning for this period of time because the month of Elul has always been a time of repentance for the nation of Israel. Even though the people of Israel knew that Moses was allowed to go back up Mount Sinai a second time with new tablets of stone, they did not know if God was going to forgive them. Therefore, the month of Elul has always been a time for the Jewish people to search their hearts for evil and to repent in preparation for the seventh month when, as a nation, they ask God for forgiveness of sins on the Day of Atonement.

Jewish tradition teaches that YHWH is more accessible in the month of Elul and the first ten days of Tishrei, ending with the Day of Atonement. The mystical sages referred to this period as when "The King is in the Field."[5] This is based on the belief that when a king is enthroned in his palace, he is not easily accessible. But when the king is out in public, in the field, anyone may approach him. Not only is this a time when the farmer may approach the king, but it is a time when the farmer *should* approach him to show him respect and to take the opportunity to make his requests known. The month of Elul represents a time when the eternal King leaves the heavenly throne and descends to inspect this world.

Now remember, the Jewish people do not believe that Jesus is their prophesied Messiah, so what they believe about this month has nothing to do with when Jesus was born or any other event concerning him. So isn't it interesting that the month the Jewish people believe the *King is in the Field* is the first month that Jesus was alive on this earth? In this month of Elul, God's only begotten Son, Yeshua, was named and brought into the covenant with YHWH through circumcision. YHWH sent his Son into this world because he was concerned about the well-being of his people. YHWH wanted his people to have the rare opportunity to approach him, through his Son, Jesus, in order to express their needs face to face.

The Canaanite meaning of *Elul* is "to shout for joy."[4] In this month Jesus was given the name "Yeshua," which means "YHWH is salvation." YHWH sent his Son to save the world—including the Canaanites. No wonder the meaning of *Elul* is "shout for joy." We should all be shouting for joy because our Father in heaven saw our need for comfort and sent his Living Word to dwell among us.

Biblically, the number 6, for this sixth month of Elul, is the number for man.[6] God created the first Adam on the sixth day of creation. On that day, Adam was brought into a covenant with God. So much in the Old Testament is a foreshadowing of Jesus; likewise, Yeshua, the last Adam, was brought into the everlasting covenant with God through his circumcision in the sixth month of Elul. Unlike the covenant with the first Adam, which was broken through man's sin, the covenant with the last Adam is everlasting. The first Adam was made in the physical image of God; the last Adam was made in the spiritual image of God. The first Adam brought death; the last Adam brings life (1 Corin. 15:45–47). Can you see that the events of Jesus's birth, circumcision, naming, and dedication are starting to form a beautiful picture?

Jewish Month of Tishrei

Every year, after the nation of Israel spends an entire month confessing and repenting of their sins during the month of Elul, they are brought into the holiest month of Tishrei, with the celebration of the last three biblically ordained feasts. Remember, it was in the seventh month of Tishrei that God's firstborn Son, Yeshua, was dedicated in the temple "Holy to YHWH." What you will discover is that these three feasts were used by God to commemorate the introduction of Yeshua to his people.

Jewish Month	**Jewish Date**	**Feast**
Seventh	Tishrei 1	Feast of Trumpets
Seventh	Tishrei 10	Day of Atonement
Seventh	Tishrei 15-22	Feast of Tabernacles

Feast of Trumpets

There is little information in the Bible about the Feast of Trumpets, which is the first feast of this month. At first glance in the description of this feast, it appears to be simply a holy Sabbath day, celebrated with trumpet blasts on the first day of the seventh month. However, when we dig into what the blowing of the trumpet signaled, we get a clear picture of the great significance of this feast. Blowing of trumpets has always signified the calling of a Sabbath, new moons, or a solemn assembly, a warning of danger and action to be taken (such as gathering of the troops to war), or an announcement of the arrival of a king. Because the Feast of Trumpets was the first of the three feasts that occur in this holiest month of the year, it came to be called Rosh ha-Shana (Head of the Year). "In the seventh month, on the first day of the month, you shall observe a day of solemn rest, *a memorial proclaimed with blast of trumpets,* a holy convocation. You shall do no laborious work; and you shall present an offering by fire to YHWH" (Lev. 23:24b–25). This feast is celebrated with several different blasts of the shofar, a trumpet made from a ram or ibex horn, and it precedes the Day of Atonement by ten days. The ten days in between the Feast of Trumpets and the Day of Atonement are called the Days of Awe.

On the night Jesus was born, on Av 30, an angelic host proclaimed to shepherds in a field that their long-awaited Messiah had been born. Because the shepherds saw Yeshua for themselves in the place where they were told they would find him, wrapped in swaddling clothes and lying in a manger, it is likely that the word about the Savior being born in the city of David spread quickly throughout the land. So when the Feast of Trumpets began thirty days later on Tishrei 1, there was already a buzz in the air that Christ the LORD had been born. When the trumpets sounded on this day after Christ's birth, the people may have realized the meaning of this feast for the very first time. Blowing of the trumpets meant so much more than a Sabbath day, a new moon, a solemn assembly, or the arrival of a king. In the year Jesus was born, the Feast of Trumpets signaled the arrival of the King of all kings. YHWH had obviously ordained this feast long ago because he knew that at some point his Son would be announced to the world, and what better way to announce the coming of his Son than by blowing trumpets for an entire day? This day most likely energized the people even more for what was coming on the Day of Atonement, ten days later.

Day of Atonement

When Yeshua was brought to the temple by his parents to be dedicated on the Day of Atonement, there were more witnesses than normal because of their hope of the Messiah. Many people were at the temple on this day, hoping to see their King. YHWH surely did not disappoint his people when Yeshua was brought into the temple. Simeon and Anna were waiting there to proclaim to the people that Yeshua was their long-awaited salvation, so the anticipating crowds would receive confirmation of the rumors they had been hearing.

Feast of Tabernacles

The Feast of Tabernacles follows the Day of Atonement by five days. It is the only feast for which God commands his people to rejoice. It is an eight-day feast that commemorates YHWH's dwelling among the people. When Moses obeyed God by placing the tablets of stone into the original ark of the covenant, it confirmed for them that their sins were forgiven. From that day forward, for forty years in the wilderness, YHWH resided among his people through his Shekinah glory over the ark of the covenant. I can't think of a better month for Yeshua, the living Word of God, to also be presented to the people than during the same month that YHWH commanded his people to celebrate and rejoice. After Yeshua was consecrated for YHWH's sacred purpose during his dedication, he then dwelled among the people. God's Shekinah glory was among them once again, this time in human form. Because the long famine of silence, of not hearing from God, had finally ended with Jesus's birth, I can only imagine the great rejoicing that took place amongst the Israelites during this Feast of Tabernacles in 3 BC in order to celebrate the coming of their long-awaited Messiah.

Judy Jacobson

Meaning of Tishrei

So what is the meaning of the month Tishrei that could explain all that occurred in the seventh month? The Hebrew meaning of *Tishrei* is "to begin." The Babylonian meaning of this month is "beginning or beginnings."[7] That definitely describes what took place during this month in history. Not only did Moses present the Word of God to the Israelites in this month, but also many years later, Jesus, the living Word of God, was being presented in the temple. The first and second covenants were presented to the people on the same day of the calendar, on the Day of Atonement. On those days, the covenants began. Both were new beginnings: first for the Israeli nation, and then for the entire world.

What I find interesting is that the Canaanites have two meanings for this month. The first meaning of the word *Tishrei* is "to begin." Believe it or not, the second meaning is "to dedicate."[7] In this month, the new covenant of Jesus was *beginning* to be established because the Son of God was *dedicated* "holy to YHWH" on the Day of Atonement. Coincidence? Not a chance!

And again, the biblical meaning of the number 7 is spiritual completion and perfection. Are there any better words to describe the seventh month where the Word of God was presented, first in written form by Moses and then in human flesh in the form of YHWH's Son, Jesus? I just love the meanings of words and numbers. They bring such depth to whatever I am studying.

There is one more significant tradition that occurs between the days of Av 30, Jesus's birth, and Tishrei 10, the Day of Atonement. Because Moses was up on Mount Sinai receiving the word of God from Elul 1 to Tishrei 10, the Jewish people started a tradition of blowing trumpets throughout these entire forty days to commemorate the giving of God's Word. So by the time Jesus was born, this was a tradition that was kept every year. Therefore, because Jesus was born and dedicated over the same time period, trumpets were being blown the entire forty days between his birth and dedication, with more trumpets being blown on the Feast of Trumpets. Little did the Israelites know when they began this tradition that it would eventually signify their own Messiah's birth, circumcision, and dedication. Jesus's birth definitely warranted blowing of the trumpets for these forty days. The announcement of our "King in the Field" began the day he was born and continued until his dedication, with trumpets being sounded throughout the land. What is sad to me is that the Jewish people do not know that their Savior has already been born and has already died for their sins. They are still waiting for their Messiah to come.

Satan

Once YHWH broke the silence, Satan's life once again became difficult. Oh, how he must have thoroughly enjoyed the silent years, but even he knew they wouldn't last forever. Remember, Satan used to walk with God and Jesus in heaven. He knew that God's Son would eventually be sent to save the world. So when Satan heard the rumors that the Messiah had been born and brought to the temple, he wasted not time in redoubling his efforts. If Satan could convince someone to search out and kill this newborn baby, his problem would be solved. By physically destroying God's only Son, Satan would ensure that God's divine name would not be reintroduced into the world. Satan convinced Herod that his kingdom was in jeopardy with all the rumors of this boy born "the King of the Jews." As a result, after the wise men informed him that they had seen his star, King Herod ordered all of the male children two years and younger in Bethlehem and the surrounding region to be murdered. Satan's plot to kill the Messiah would have worked had it not been for YHWH stepping in to protect Jesus by sending an angel to warn Joseph of the impending danger. Because Joseph heeded YHWH's warnings and fled to Egypt with Mary and his son, Jesus was saved from death as a child.

What Satan did accomplish through the death of all the children in Bethlehem is that he made Mary's life very difficult. Not only would she have to live in a foreign land for many years, but she also had to live for the rest of her life with the weight of the reality that it was because of her son, a gift from God, that so many children died in her hometown. The pain of knowing what happened was likely hard to bear. It was probably at this moment that Mary realized exactly what God had asked of her in bringing his Son into the world. As the mother of the Son of God, she might have realized for the first time that her life had the potential of being filled with much heartbreak.

With the murder of all of these children, Satan was hopeful that he had accomplished his goal of destroying God's only Son, but of course he couldn't be sure. It wouldn't be until thirty years later when Jesus started his ministry that Satan would find out that he had failed.

> "For as the rain and the snow come down from heaven, and return not tither but water the earth, making it bring forth and sprout, giving seed to the sower and bread to the eater, so shall **MY WORD** [Jesus] be that goes forth from my mouth; **it shall not return to me empty**, but it shall accomplish that which I purpose, and prosper in the thing **for which I sent it**." (Isa. 55:10–11)

YHWH's Word (Jesus) would not return to YHWH empty. His Word would accomplish all that it had been asked to carry out, and it would succeed in all that it was sent to do. Until YHWH's Word watered the earth with living waters, bringing forth the gospel seed and daily bread to his people, Jesus would not return to YHWH. Satan's plans to destroy Jesus were therefore guaranteed to fail because nothing would keep Jesus from completing his Father's mission.

Chapter 14

My Beloved Son

"**Behold my servant, whom I uphold, my chosen, in whom my soul delights; I have put my Spirit upon him; he will bring forth justice to the nations.** He will not cry aloud or lift up his voice, or make it heard in the street; a bruised reed he will not break, and a faintly burning wick he will not quench; he will faithfully bring forth justice. **He will not grow faint or be discouraged till he has established justice in the earth**; and the coastlands wait for his law. Thus says God, YHWH, who created the heavens and stretched them out, who spread out the earth and what comes from it, who gives breath to the people on it and spirit to those who walk in it: '**I am YHWH; I have called you in righteousness; I will take you by the hand and keep you; I will give you as a covenant for the people, a light for the nations**, to open the eyes that are blind, to bring out the prisoners from the dungeon, from the prison those who sit in darkness. **I am YHWH; that is my name; my glory I give to no other**, nor my praise to carved idols. **Behold, the former things have come to pass, and new things I now declare; before they spring forth I tell you of them.**'"
(Isa. 42:1–9 ESV)

Before Jesus even walked on this earth, YHWH instructed his prophets, from Moses to Malachi, to prophesy about the coming Messiah, God's firstborn Son. The prophet Isaiah is known as the evangelical prophet because he gives the fullest and clearest explanation of the gospel of Jesus Christ in the Old Testament. I love these verses in Isaiah. In reading them, it becomes evident to me what God is trying to do. Through prophecy he is communicating his plans to the Israelites. He warns them that the *former things will come to pass, and new things YHWH will declare.* Before they spring forth, YHWH wants to tell his people about them so they can prepare themselves.

You see, it's all about communication. YHWH didn't want his people to be in the dark; he wanted his children to always be in the light. Therefore, every time he spoke to them through the prophets he made sure to give them more pieces of the prophetic puzzle. When YHWH's Son came into the world, he wanted his people to recognize him for who he was. God knows how much people dislike change, so God wanted to prepare them along the way. It's as if he were saying, "Be prepared. Change is coming. Before change comes, let me prepare you for it." And preparing his people for change is exactly what YHWH did. Not only did God reveal his plan to his people through the Old Testament prophets, but when Jesus finally came into this world, YHWH even sent a prophet immediately before Jesus's ministry to prepare the people for his coming. His name was John the Baptist. The day John's father Zechariah was visited by an angel of the LORD, the spirit of prophecy was back. The angel said to Zechariah,

> "Do not be afraid, Zechariah, for your prayer has been heard, and your wife **Elizabeth will bear you a son, and you shall call his name John.** And you will have joy and gladness, and many will rejoice at his birth, for he will be great before the Lord. And he must not drink wine or strong drink, and **he will be filled with the Holy Spirit**, even from his mother's womb. And he will turn many of the children of Israel to the Lord their God, and **he will go before him in the spirit and power of Elijah**, to turn the hearts of the fathers to the children, and the disobedient to the wisdom of the just, **to make ready for the Lord a people prepared**." (Luke 1:13–17 ESV)

Elizabeth did conceive, and approximately nine months later she bore a son whom they named John, exactly as they were told. John's name means "YHWH is gracious." On the day of John's circumcision and naming, the eighth day, John's father Zechariah prophesied for both the coming Messiah and his son John.

> And his father Zechariah was filled with the **Holy Spirit** and prophesied, saying, "**Blessed be the Lord God of Israel, for he has visited and redeemed his people and has raised up a horn of salvation for us in the house of his servant David**, as he spoke by the mouth of his holy prophets from of old, that we should be saved from our enemies and from the hand of all who hate us; to show the mercy promised to our fathers **and to remember his holy covenant**, the oath that he swore to our father Abraham, to grant us that we, being delivered from the hand of our enemies, might serve him without fear, in holiness and righteousness before him all our days. **And you, child, will be called the prophet of the Most High; for you will go before the Lord to prepare his ways, to give knowledge of salvation to his people in the forgiveness of their sins**, because of the tender mercy of our God, whereby the sunrise shall visit us from on high to give light to those who sit in darkness and in the shadow of death, to guide our feet into the way of peace." (Luke 1:67–79 ESV)

Six months before Jesus was even born, and thirty years before Jesus's ministry began, the priest Zechariah was prophesying about the Messiah to all who would listen. Zechariah's son John would be the one to prepare the way for the Messiah, who would bring salvation to the people. Six months before Jesus began his ministry, John began his—the very ministry that God had ordained from John's conception to be his life mission. John's early ministry began in the wilderness of Judea and in the Jordan valley. The main theme of his preaching was the approaching of the Messianic age and the need of adequate spiritual preparation to be ready for it. His mission was to prepare the people for the Messiah so that when the Messiah made his appearance, they would recognize and accept him. John called upon all to repent sincerely of their sins and to be baptized. John's baptism by water signified a turning away and cleansing from sin. John always knew that his ministry was subordinate to and temporary as compared to the one who was to come after him. One day, six months into John's ministry, while the multitudes of common people flocked to the Jordan River to be baptized, Jesus also came.

> Now when all the people were baptized, and when Jesus also had been baptized and was praying, **the heavens were opened**, and the **Holy Spirit descended on him** in bodily form, like a dove; and a voice came from heaven, "**You are my beloved Son; with you I am well pleased.**" (Luke 3:21–22 ESV)

All four Gospels—Matthew, Mark, Luke, and John—give a rendition of this story. Communication to the people that Jesus was the Son of God was of utmost importance to YHWH. So it doesn't surprise me that YHWH would choose to baptize his Son, Yeshua, on a day when multitudes of people were at the Jordan River hearing John the Baptist preaching a baptism of repentance for the forgiveness of sins. While John was preaching, he spoke the words found in Isaiah.

> "The voice of one crying in the wilderness: '**Prepare the way of the Lord**, make his paths straight. Every valley shall be filled, and every mountain and hill shall be made low, and the crooked shall become straight, and the rough places shall become level ways, **and all flesh shall see the salvation of God**.'" (Luke 3:4–6, Isa. 52:10 ESV)

There's that word *salvation* again. The prophet Isaiah used the word *salvation* when describing YHWH baring his "holy arm" before the eyes of all the nations (Isa. 52:10). Zechariah, John's father, prophesied about the coming Messiah as the "horn of salvation." Jesus was named Yeshua because it means "YHWH is salvation." Simeon the priest called Yeshua "salvation" as he held him in his arms at the temple on the day of his dedication. Finally, thirty years later, John the Baptist, while speaking the words of Isaiah, referred to the Messiah as the "salvation of God" on the exact day that Jesus came to John the Baptist to be baptized.

When the Holy Spirit descended upon Yeshua in bodily form as a dove, YHWH wanted there to be no doubt or speculation by the people of what was occurring. Therefore, YHWH chose this moment to audibly declare who Yeshua was in front of the multitudes. On this day, YHWH spoke out loud for all to hear. It was the first time YHWH had publicly spoken since Mount Sinai so long ago. At Mount Sinai, YHWH, the one and only God, introduced himself to his people. Approximately fifteen hundred years later, the same God publicly introduced Yeshua to his people as his beloved Son, his only begotten Son, who would bring salvation to the world. Scripture tells us that all who were present to hear God's voice had already received a baptism of repentance from John the Baptist. Therefore, on that day, their hearts were prepared to see and hear the truth. After hearing YHWH's voice for the first time ever, everyone present had the opportunity to see Jesus as the "salvation of God," God's "holy outstretched arm," just as Isaiah had prophesied. When John the Baptist saw Jesus following his baptism, John boldly declared what had occurred.

> **"Behold, the Lamb of God, who takes away the sin of the world!** This is he of whom I said, 'After me comes a man who ranks before me, because he was before me.' I myself did not know him, but for this purpose I came baptizing with water, that he might be revealed to Israel." **And John bore witness: "I saw the Spirit descend from heaven like a dove, and it remained on him.** I myself did not know him, but he who sent me to baptize with water said to me, **'He on whom you see the Spirit descend and remain, this is he who baptizes with the Holy Spirit.'** And I have seen and have borne witness that **this is the Son of God."** (John 1:29–34 ESV)

The people who witnessed this event must have been in complete awe. Not only had they been introduced to Yeshua, the person for whom John had been preparing the way for so many months, but they had also heard God's voice publicly acknowledge that Yeshua was his beloved Son. Once the Spirit of YHWH rested on Jesus, John knew with 100 percent confidence that his mission was complete. He knew without a doubt that Jesus was the Son of God, the Lamb of God who takes away the sins of the world. Because John had prepared himself his entire life for the mission God gave him, when the Messiah finally arrived, John knew who he was. His mind, body, and soul were all prepared for this one event. The day John declared that Jesus was the Son of God, John's God-given purpose of "preparing the way of the Lord" was finished. "There was a *man sent from God, whose name was John*. He came for testimony, *to bear witness to the light*, that all might believe through him" (John 1:6–8). The day Jesus was baptized is the day YHWH commissioned Jesus for his ministry, the very mission for which he was consecrated forty days after his birth.

Jesus Is Commissioned

Do you remember when Joshua, the son of Nun, was commissioned before Eleazar, the high priest (Num. 27:15–21)? If you recall, YHWH instructed Moses to lay his hands on Joshua and commission him in the sight of the entire congregation. During his commissioning, Joshua was instructed to stand before Eleazar, who inquired for him before YHWH by the judgment of the Urim. The commissioning of Joshua was an extremely important event since he was chosen to take Moses's place as the nation's leader to take them into the promised land. Since this commissioning required the approval of YHWH, the priest needed the judgment of the Urim to confirm this decision. So on this day, when Moses laid hands on Joshua and invested him with some of his authority, Moses became a witness for Joshua that it was God's will that he lead the people. In addition, Eleazar became a witness for Joshua through communication with YHWH by the use of the Urim. Two witnesses were needed because Jewish law requires at least two witnesses in order to provide conclusive proof of reality.

Just like Joshua was commissioned with Moses and Eleazar as his witnesses, Jesus was commissioned for his mission with YHWH and John the Baptist as witnesses. A priest with the Urim and Thummim would not be needed for the commissioning ceremony of Jesus, because *YHWH was the Urim and Jesus was the Thummim.* When YHWH spoke out loud, giving his beloved Son his approval, the people received all the proof that was needed. When John the Baptist also confirmed that Yeshua was the Lamb of God, it was a done deal. The day Jesus received his Father's Spirit, Scripture says that YHWH's Spirit physically "descended and remained" on Jesus. Even though Jesus always had the Spirit of YHWH within him, it wasn't until Jesus's baptism that Jesus was "anointed" by God. To be anointed by God is not only to be picked but *also to be empowered by him.* High priests, kings, and prophets were all anointed positions. Yeshua came to this earth to be all three. The Hebrew word *Messiah* and the Greek word *Christ* both mean "the anointed one."[1]

John the Baptist had been preparing his entire life for his ministry to be a witness for Jesus; Jesus had been preparing his entire life for his ministry to be a witness for his Father, YHWH. From the day Jesus was born, his parents, Mary and Joseph, were instruments in this preparation. It began with his circumcision and naming ceremony and was followed by his dedication in the temple. As a child, Jesus's parents took him to the synagogues and temple to hear and memorize Scripture. As a teenager, Jesus listened to and asked questions of the priests and teachers of God's Word. Jesus kept the Sabbath weekly and attended all the feasts yearly, just as God had ordained. Through the first thirty years of life, Jesus kept his eyes turned toward YHWH in everything he did. Jesus worshipped his Father the way God had hoped all of his people would, by learning his truth through his Word and keeping his commandments. If Jesus hadn't done all of these things, he would not have lived a sinless life.

Therefore, when God anointed him with his Holy Spirit, Jesus was prepared for his ministry and for the power that came upon him. The day Jesus was anointed, he received his Father's power because the Holy Spirit that descended and remained on Jesus *came in his Father's holy name of YHWH*. As a man with a common name, Yeshua was not given the power to accomplish his sacred purpose *until the day he was given his Father's powerful and holy name*. Before this day, Yeshua was simply a carpenter. Only after Yeshua received his Father's name, along with an anointing from his Father's Spirit, would he have the power to accomplish all that he had come to do. From that day forward, Yeshua would have the power to heal people both physically and emotionally, to cast out demons, to defeat death, and to baptize with the Holy Spirit and with fire.

The Jordan River

What I find so fascinating about Jesus's baptism and commissioning is that tradition tells us that it occurred in the Jordan River near the city of Jericho. The Jordan River is the same river whose waters YHWH stopped so that Joshua could lead the people into the promised land to defeat the enemy. Remember, Joshua, the son of Nun, and Yeshua, the Son of God, share the same name, just in different languages. The entire book of Joshua is a foreshadowing of what Yeshua came to complete. The day that Joshua was instructed to cross the Jordan River, God told him, *"This day I will begin to exalt you* in the sight of all Israel, that they may know that *as I was with Moses, so I will be with you."* God then said to the people, *"Behold the ark of the covenant of YHWH of all the earth is to pass over before you into the Jordan"* (Joshua 3:7, 11). On that day, Joshua did as God instructed and led the people across the Jordan River, with the ark of the covenant leading the way. With this miracle, YHWH exalted Joshua in the sight of all Israel, and Scripture tells us that they stood in awe of Joshua all the days of his life (Joshua 4:14).

So you see, Jesus had to be baptized in the Jordan River so that his Father, YHWH, could exalt him just as he did Joshua. The day Jesus was baptized was the day the *new* Ark of the Covenant of YHWH passed before the people into the Jordan. The day YHWH spoke at

Jesus's baptism is the day the people knew that God would be with Yeshua all the days of his life, just like he was with Moses and Joshua. No one knows for sure, but I would speculate that God made sure these two events in history, separated by thousands of years, took place in the very same location in the Jordan River. Tradition says that they both occurred east of Jericho. The first ark of the covenant was being replaced with the Ark of Jesus, so it only makes sense that it would occur in the same spot. When the original ark of the covenant came out of the Jordan River, the people followed Joshua to defeat the enemy and to enter the promised land. When Jesus came out of the Jordan River after being commissioned by YHWH for his ministry, he was prepared to do what he was sent to do: to defeat Satan and to bring his Father's people into their inheritance. All the people had to do is follow the Ark of Jesus, their newly commissioned leader, to the promised land—their heavenly Father's presence and loving arms.

Tempted by the Devil

Immediately following his anointing, Jesus was led by the Holy Spirit for forty days into the wilderness to be tempted by the devil. YHWH needed to know without a shadow of a doubt that his Son was ready for his ministry, so YHWH's Spirit led Yeshua into the wilderness for a one-on-one battle with their adversary and long-time enemy, Satan. The day YHWH commissioned Jesus was the day Satan knew that his plot to destroy the Messiah as a child had failed, so Satan was more than ready for this challenge of being alone with Jesus. All he had to do was get Jesus to disobey YHWH and his problem would be resolved. If he could convince Jesus to sin, just like he had Adam and Eve, then there would be no "salvation" for YHWH's people. So the question for Satan became, *What would tempt Jesus, the Son of God, to commit the ultimate sin of profaning the name of YHWH?*

Although Jesus and Satan were together for forty days, we only know of three questions that Satan used to tempt Jesus into sinning, even though I would imagine the temptations came daily. The questions posed by Satan that are recorded in Scripture would have been very enticing to any man with great power, let alone a man with the divine power and authority that Jesus was entrusted with through YHWH's name. The first thing Satan tempted Jesus with was to use his ability to turn a stone into bread. Satan knew that Jesus would be very hungry during this time, and he just might be tempted into using his anointing to satisfy his own fleshly desires for food. Jesus was indeed hungry because he ate nothing during these entire forty days. However, because Jesus was fasting during this time, along with his hunger came a great clarity for God's Word. He could see the truth for what it was and knew that his fleshly desire for food was only temporary. Therefore, when Satan tempted him to satisfy his hunger by turning a stone into bread, Jesus easily replied, "It is written, *'Man shall not live by bread alone, but by every word that proceeds from the mouth of God'*" (Matt. 4:4). Jesus knew with certainty that his heavenly Father's words were the only sustenance that he needed to survive. He knew that his much greater physical and spiritual needs were to be in complete communication with his Father through Scripture and prayer. Yeshua knew that it would be his Father's voice that would sustain him through this difficult trial.

Satan's second temptation was an attempt to get Jesus to desire all of YHWH's authority and glory as his own, which is what Satan had desired and which caused his own fall from God's grace. After showing Jesus all the kingdoms of the world in a moment of time, Satan said to Jesus, *"To you I will give this authority and their glory; for it has been delivered to me, and I give it to whom I will. If you then, will worship me, it shall be yours."* And Jesus answered him "It is written, *'You shall worship the Lord your God, and him only shall you serve'*" (Luke 4:6–8).

Just like John the Baptist, Jesus knew his part in God's story. He was not sent to earth to be God or to be worshipped by man. Jesus's whole mission on earth was to point YHWH's people to YHWH by being a witness for his Father. He was here to speak YHWH's truth and to do all that was commanded of him. He was here to serve. Jesus was not here to take God's glory for his own purposes but to provide "the way" for humanity to enter into a loving relationship with his Father. Jesus also knew that Satan was only capable of bestowing on him manmade authority and glory, and that is not what he desired. Jesus's only desire was to please the one and only God, YHWH, and to be blessed with the authority and glory that YHWH bestowed upon him. Therefore, he would never worship anyone but his Father; for if he did, he knew he would be profaning YHWH's holy name.

So Satan gave it one last try. This time he took Jesus to Jerusalem and set him on the pinnacle of the temple. Satan said to him, "*If you are the Son of God*, throw yourself down from here; for it is written, 'He will give his angels charge of you to guard you,' and 'On their hands they will bear you up, lest you strike your foot against a stone.'" And Jesus answered him, "It is said, '*You shall not tempt the Lord your God*'" (Luke 4:9b–12). Because Jesus knew all the stories written in Scripture, he knew that when people tempted YHWH, the results were never favorable. Again, Jesus knew his mission and place in God's story, and he wouldn't think of trying to rewrite what God had in store for him. He would only do what his Father commanded him to do. Jesus knew that God's will for his life would bring more blessings and glory than anything Satan could give him.

Having failed at tempting Jesus into sinning against YHWH, Satan took leave of Jesus until another opportune time. Satan was by no means finished and would surely be back. This battle may have been lost, but the war had just begun. Jesus had fought this fight with the enemy with the most powerful weapon he knew of: the Word of God. He had spent his entire life studying the truth and therefore would not be deceived by Satan's counterfeit lies. By using YHWH's powerful words against Satan's temptations, the temptations lost all their power. "For *the word of God is living and active, sharper than any two-edged sword*, piercing to the division of soul and spirit, of joints and marrow, and discerning the thoughts and intentions of the heart" (Heb. 6:12). Jesus knew that there was nothing more powerful in defeating the enemy than the words of his Father. Because Jesus was the Word of God, he also knew that the living and active Word of God was all that he would need to ward off Satan's temptations. Therefore, Jesus remained sinless, and Satan had no choice but to flee from his presence.

When we consider Satan's attack of Jesus in the wilderness, we can be certain that Satan knew that Jesus was the Son of God. If Jesus wasn't the Son of God, then Satan would not have spent so much time trying to get him to deny the name of YHWH, and he would not have planned on returning to attack Jesus at a later time. What Satan did not realize is that his encounter in the wilderness with Jesus would be written into God's Word by Matthew, Mark, and Luke. In the future, Satan's own words would be used as proof that even Satan knew that Jesus was YHWH's beloved Son.

Jesus's baptism, anointing, and testing were now complete. He therefore returned from the wilderness to begin his ministry in the power of YHWH's Spirit. One of his first stops was in his hometown of Nazareth. He went to the synagogue and stood up to read from the book of the prophet Isaiah. On that day, he opened God's Word and found the place where it was written, *"The Spirit of YHWH is upon me*, because he has *anointed me* to preach the good news to the poor. He has sent me to proclaim release to the captives and recovering of sight to the blind, to set at liberty those who are oppressed, to proclaim the acceptable year of YHWH" (Luke 4:18–19, Isa. 61:1–2). By Jesus reading God's words that YHWH had placed in his prophet Isaiah's mouth so long ago, not only was Jesus fulfilling Scripture, but he was also declaring the purpose of his ministry. He began his mission by declaring that he was coming in the "Spirit of YHWH" and that everything he would accomplish would be because of his Father's anointing. He declared that the power with which YHWH had entrusted him would be used to defeat the enemy so that he could release the prisoners Satan held in bondage.

Joshua, the son of Nun, was commissioned by YHWH to be his warrior in order to fight the enemy and bring his people into their inheritance of the promised land. Jesus, like Joshua, was also commissioned by YHWH to be his warrior to fight the enemy and bring his people into their inheritance. The difference between Jesus and Joshua is that Jesus would not need violence to complete his mission. Because Jesus was God's Word in the flesh, YHWH's divine Word and YHWH's divine name is all that he would need to defeat the enemy.

Two-Edged Sword

I want to end this chapter with an experience that happened to me during the process of writing this book. It is a story of the tactics Satan used while trying to distract me from doing God's work. It is likewise a story of how Satan ultimately lost this battle because I, too, had learned over the years how to use God's Word as my weapon against my adversary.

At the time, I was the small-group leader of seven couples from our church. Toward the end of our last session a few years ago, we were losing attendance and I was becoming very frustrated. Everyone seemed to be busy with end-of-school activities or had other valid reasons for not being able to attend. On the second-to-last meeting, I found out that only three out of fourteen people were going to be able to attend. Therefore, I decided to cancel that night's meeting. And the more I sulked, the more I just wanted to cancel our small group permanently. I convinced myself that people were just not interested in studying God's Word and that I was wasting my time. It wasn't until late that night that I realized what was really going on. I couldn't believe that I almost fell for Satan's oldest trick in the book. He was trying to deceive me into believing that we were too busy to discuss God's Word and that it would be better if we just canceled small group altogether. He wanted me to believe that my life would be easier without all of these frustrations.

In reality, what was really happening is that Satan didn't want us to learn how to "walk on water" with Jesus. You see, the book we were studying was *If You Want to Walk on Water, You've Got to Get Out of the Boat* by John Ortberg.[2] Satan didn't want us talking about this topic and was working behind the scenes to get us to stop. He wanted us to stay in our comfortable little lives, in our comfortable little boats, and to pay no mind to the will of our LORD and Savior.

So YHWH reminded me that night what Jesus had said to his disciples: "When two or three are gathered in my name, there am I in the midst of them" (Matt. 18:20). What Jesus's words meant to me on this night is that it didn't matter if only two people came to our meetings; I would still be doing his work of spreading his name. He encouraged me to not get hung up on the number of people in attendance because those were details that were not for me to worry about. I was encouraged to continue doing what he had called me to do. Once I realized what was happening, I texted my girlfriend my thoughts and told her how close I had come to buying into Satan's lie. She replied with such conviction with a text saying, *"The Devil Lost This One!"* I couldn't have agreed more. Knowing that Jesus would be present regardless of the attendance, I told our group that we *would* finish this book and we *would* learn to walk on water. I confessed to our group all the thoughts that had passed through my head and told them the devil would not win this fight. As a result, at our next session, we had twelve people in attendance. Because I had made the commitment to finish what God had asked me to do, YHWH took care of the details. The devil definitely lost that battle. I had heard YHWH's voice speaking truth to me through Jesus's words, and that is all that I needed to continue in his work.

However, I knew that Satan would be back because he had deceived me many times in the past. The difference between then and now, however, was that I was able to identify his lies more readily. In addition, because I had studied God's Word over the years and had tucked more and more of his truth into my heart, I had the same power that Jesus had to defeat the enemy's attacks. No longer was I powerless, because I too had the sword of the Spirit available to me.

Two Weeks Later

Two weeks later, my dear friend Rachel and I had the blessing of spending five hours one day talking to her dad about the book he was publishing on the subject of the second coming of Jesus. It was an incredibly awesome day. For five straight hours, we talked about God's Word and his glory and prayed for his truth to illuminate our lives. I went home feeling exhilarated and joyful. It did not take long, however, for my joy to be squelched.

As I was making dinner that night, my husband and I got into the silliest argument over what we were eating for dinner, of all things. The details of the argument are so ridiculous that I won't bother to disclose them. Our argument was very heated, and I ended up storming out of our house, huffing and puffing. Thankfully, as I was leaving my house, I thought (or maybe God suggested) to grab another book I was reading called *The 4:8 Principle: The Secret to a Joy-Filled Life* by Tommy Newberry.[3] The author of this book takes the biblical principle of Philippians 4:8 and teaches how this one simple truth can magnify the joy we experience in our lives. So after I calmed down from my anger, I sat down and read this powerful verse written by the apostle Paul: "Finally, brethren, whatever is true, whatever is honorable, whatever is just, whatever is pure, whatever is lovely, whatever is gracious, if there is any excellence, if there is anything worthy of praise, think about these things." As soon as I read these verses, it dawned on me what was happening. Immediately, I could clearly see that Satan was again in attack mode, and I knew why. Satan knew that YHWH had spoken to me through his Word for five hours that day, and he did not want me to ponder one minute longer on God's Word or the joy I was feeling from understanding his Word. So Satan used whatever he knew would distract me in order to rob me of this joy. He figured that an argument with my husband should do the trick. Little did he know that God would continue to fight for me through his Word.

From previous experiences, I knew that spiritual warfare from Satan always surrounded the birth of miracles, so I really should have expected this to happen after the miracle of spending an entire five hours studying the Word of God. By simply reading the apostle Paul's words, I knew that God's Word, which represented truth, purity, honor, love, grace, and excellence, was the only thing worth thinking about and praising. Because I had pondered his Word all day long, I knew that was the source of the joy I had been feeling. Through this revelation, I could clearly see that Satan was the source of the anger that had replaced it. Once again, God allowed me to see through the lies and see the truth. I saw the fight with my husband for what it was—just another attack by Satan. My mind was again able to ponder all that God had said to me that day. In addition, the anger that I had felt was replaced with joy once again.

Soon afterward, I made my way back to my house, and when I got back to our kitchen I checked my phone to see if anyone had called or sent a message. The message that was on my phone took my breath away. I am not kidding—when I turned my phone on, the words on my screen read, *"The Devil Lost This One!"* YHWH on this day, at that very moment, had sent me a message. The text my girlfriend had sent me two weeks prior was once again placed front and center on my phone for me to read. I was dumbfounded.

How in the world did that message get opened on my phone at that exact moment? I had taken my phone with me when I stormed out of the house, but I did not hear anyone texting me. I thought that maybe I had mistakenly pressed my message button to get that exact message back. However, when I checked my phone and realized that it would have taken me fourteen random presses to get to that place, I knew without a doubt whom the message was from.

Once again YHWH had *communicated* with me through modern technology, first through my dryer so long ago and now through my cell phone. To this day, I still don't know how it happened. What I do know, without a shadow of a doubt, is that God wanted me to know that since we had a personal relationship with each other, the devil had in fact *"Lost This One."* Just as Satan had lost the battle with Jesus in the wilderness, Satan lost this battle with me. I was no longer submitting to him or to his way of living, and I knew how to fight him with God's Word. But even more importantly than winning these battles against Satan, YHWH wanted me to know through his message to me that the devil had lost something even more valuable. Because of my relationship with his Son, Yeshua, *the devil had lost my soul.* My soul now belongs to my LORD and Savior, YHWH's beloved and chosen Son, whom he had anointed with his Holy Spirit and holy name to provide me with salvation. I could now count on the inheritance of peace and joy and a fulfilling life while on this earth, and in the future I could expect to live with Jesus and YHWH forever.

What a sense of awe I felt on that day for the God I serve! YHWH had done so much for me, and yet he continued to speak to me so often and in so many incredible ways. Once again he had fought the enemy on my behalf through his words, allowed me to feel his Shekinah glory, and allowed me to hear his sweet and loving voice.

So what about you? Are you aware of how to defeat Satan in your life with God's living and active Word? Remember, YHWH's Word, which is Jesus, is sharper than any two-edged sword. When you use God's Word against our adversary, Satan has no choice but to flee. Therefore, speak God's Word out loud against your enemy often, like Jesus did in the wilderness, and then enjoy the rest, peace, and joy that are sure to follow.

Chapter 15

The Great I AM

"You are my witnesses," declares YHWH, "and my servant whom I have chosen, **that you may know and believe me and understand that I AM HE**. Before me no god was formed, nor shall there be any after me. I, **I am YHWH, and besides me there is no savior. I declared and saved and proclaimed**, when there was no strange god among you; and you are my witnesses," declares YHWH, "and **I am God. Also henceforth I AM HE.**" (Isa. 43:10–13a ESV)

If you have ever bought a new car, you know that it can be a very exhausting experience. Most people will spend many, many weeks researching various makes and models, all the while comparing the pros and cons of the different vehicles. Due to the large expense of purchasing a new car, great care is usually made in first determining the family's needs in an automobile. The need is then weighed against the cost of the various makes and models, along with the pros and cons. Usually a great effort is made in taking cars for test drives, reading consumer reports, and asking friends for advice. As a result, when the purchase is finally made, there is a confidence that the right decision has been made for you and your family.

The last time I bought a new car for myself, it was a Honda minivan. I knew that I needed a family-friendly car. Since I had three small children, I decided to put aside my desire to drive a cool car and opted for the "mom mobile." The Honda was in our price range, it had a great reputation for reliability, it had automatic sliding doors (a must for a family of five), and it was the right size. I also had not seen many of these vehicles on the road, so I thought that maybe I would be driving something unique. Well, that thought lasted until the day I started driving my new car. From that day forward, I started to see Honda minivans absolutely everywhere. I was virtually surrounded by them on the roads. I was starting to think that every mom had surrendered her cool factor for the sake of her family. Why had I never noticed these cars on the road before? I think because I had spent a very long time focusing on this individual automobile and had researched everything there was to know about it, the Honda Odyssey became front and center in my brain. And because it was front and center, I started to see it everywhere.

The same thing happened to me when I was researching God's divine name. I became so focused on who YHWH said he was in the Old Testament that every time I saw his name referenced in the Bible, it popped out at me. Everywhere *LORD* was found in capital letters, I was able to replace it with God's divine name of YHWH, giving Scripture a whole new meaning. So when I started looking for God's divine name in the New Testament, the same thing happened. It's as if YHWH's name was illuminated for me to see clearly. Except this time, it wasn't YHWH who was talking when I saw God's divine name referenced. This time, as I was looking through the Gospels, Jesus is the one who was speaking.

YHWH said to Moses, "I AM WHO I AM. Tell them 'I AM has sent me to you.'" In the gospel of John, Jesus uses the words *I AM* over twenty times while describing himself. I had never noticed these verses before with such clarity because on all previous occasions, I had no reference that the God I serve has a divine name that means, "I AM WHO I AM." Now that I knew God has a divine name, Jesus's descriptions of himself took on a whole new meaning. It's as if, since I now knew the beginning of the story through the Old Testament, I could see Jesus's life with more clarity. It became very clear to me that the entire purpose of

YHWH's Word becoming flesh and blood was so that his Son, Yeshua, could personally tell humanity all about his Father, YHWH.

Jesus Christ is the most controversial man ever to walk this earth. There have probably been more conversations about Jesus than about all famous people who have ever walked on this earth. Jesus is the only human in all of history to ever claim that he was the Son of God and to be raised from the dead. And because of who Jesus claimed to be, there has been controversy about him ever since. No other major religions are based on someone claiming to be the Son of God. The majority of religions and cults are simply based on the claims of mortal men alone. Therefore, just as it is important to do research before buying a new car, it is extremely important for all of us to individually decide, through thorough research of our own, who we think Jesus is. Really, there is no more important question in life, especially when we weigh the cost of our decision in terms of eternal consequences.

In order to find out who Jesus is, it is necessary to read the entire New Testament, especially the Gospels of Matthew, Mark, Luke, and John. When we look at the Gospels, it is important to consider who Jesus claimed to be, who Jesus's witnesses came to believe he was, and why. In making up our minds on Jesus, we have to weigh all of the evidence. It also helps to compare prophecy about the coming Messiah in the Old Testament with facts written about Jesus to see if they coincide. Sounds like a lot of work, doesn't it? I never said it would be easy, but when we consider the time we spend doing other things in our lives and look at how fleeting the rewards are for the time we spend doing those things, it becomes clear that spending time investigating Jesus is well worth the effort.

So the first thing I want to do is provide a list of the things Jesus called himself. Then I will provide a list of what some of the witnesses, the people who experienced Jesus's presence firsthand, called him. My goal in this chapter is not to explain in detail everything Jesus and the witnesses claimed Jesus to be because that would fill an entire book on its own. My goal is to explain the main reason why Jesus said what he said and did what he did and what the witnesses called him based on their own encounters with him.

It is up to you to do your own research because a strong faith has to start with your own beliefs, not the beliefs of your parents, friends, or family. This research begins with reading everything you can get your hands on concerning Jesus, starting with the Bible. Belief based on someone else's research will not be strong, and it will eventually fail you in a time of crisis. Only a faith based on your own thorough research and findings will have the power to sustain you in a time of need. Through it all, I encourage you to start praying to God that he will reveal his Son, Jesus, to you in an extremely personal way so you will know without a shadow of a doubt that YHWH exists and Jesus is the Son of God.

Moses wrote about Jesus fourteen hundred years before he was born. *"If you believed Moses, you would believe me, for he wrote of me.* But if you do not believe his writings, how will you believe my words?" (John 5:46–47). Long before the Israelites were a nation living in the promised land, YHWH was already prophesying through Moses about his Son, Jesus. Remember that after God spoke to the Israelites on Mount Sinai, the people asked Moses to speak to them because they feared the voice of God? If you recall, YHWH granted their wish and revealed to Moses that he would send a prophet to the nation of Israel from among the brethren who would speak all the words that YHWH put in his mouth. As we have already discussed, from that day forward God spoke to the people through Moses, then Joshua, and then through the prophets. But if you look again at these passages in Scripture, you will discover that the future prophet Moses spoke about was actually Jesus.

> "YHWH your God **will raise up for you a prophet** like me from among you, **from your brothers**—it is to him you shall listen—just as you desired of YHWH your God at Horeb on the day of the assembly, when you said, '**Let me not hear again the voice of YHWH my God or see this great fire any more, lest I die**.' And YHWH said to me, 'They are right in what they have spoken. **I will raise up for them a prophet** like you from among their brothers. And **I will put my words in his mouth, and he shall speak to them all that I command him.** And whoever will not listen to *my words* that he shall speak in *my name*, I myself will require it of him.'" (Deut. 18:15–19 ESV)

The words that were given to the prophet Jeremiah also have more meaning when they are applied to Jesus: *"Before I formed you in the womb I knew you*, and before you were born *I consecrated you; I appointed you a prophet to the nations"* (Jer. 1:5). Before Yeshua was formed in Mary's womb, YHWH knew his Son because they were in heaven together before the world was even created. And before Yeshua was born in human flesh, he was consecrated, or set apart, for the sacred purpose of bringing YHWH's people back into a relationship with him. YHWH appointed Yeshua to be his prophet, but this time YHWH's prophet would not speak just to the nation of Israel but eventually to all the nations of the world.

Other prophets had come before Jesus, but they were not the ultimate fulfillment of YHWH's promise and were by no means sinless. No doubt the prophets who came before Jesus didn't say or do exactly what YHWH commanded of them at all times. We see through Scripture that, at times, the prophets even ran away from what God was commanding them to do when times became tough, as was the case with Elijah and with Jonah. Jesus, on the other hand, spoke every word that God ordained for him, and he did everything YHWH commanded of him. Since the Israelites feared God's voice and did not want to hear him speak, God in his infinite wisdom sent his Son, Jesus, to speak to his people instead. God knew that Jesus is the only person he could truly trust to speak his truth, and he couldn't think of a better way to speak his truth than in the extremely personal way of sending his Son in flesh and blood so that the people could hear, see, touch, and feel his presence. Jesus confirms many times through Scripture that he was sent to speak his Father's words: "For I have not spoken on my own authority; *the Father who sent me has himself given me commandment what to say and what to speak"* (John 12:49).

Knowing that Jesus came to speak only that which YHWH commanded of him gives me a new appreciation for Jesus's words because now when I ponder Jesus's words, I have to consider their ultimate source. Jesus's words and YHWH's words cannot be separated because, according to Jesus, they are one and the same. Remember also that Scripture tells us that Jesus was *YHWH's Word* that came and dwelt among us. Therefore, it was the Father who told the Son to describe himself as the "Great I AM," documented for us in the gospel of John. So let's look at exactly who Jesus claimed to be, through his Father's own words.

Who Jesus Claimed to Be

Description	Reference
Living Water	John 4:11–14
Messiah (Christ)	John 4:25–26
I have come in my Father's name	John 5:43
I am the bread of life	John 6:35, 6:48
I am bread from heaven	John 6:41
I am the living bread	John 6:51
I am the light of the world	John 8:12, 9:5
I am from above	John 8:23
I am not of this world	John 8:23
I am he	John 8:24
Son of Man	John 8:28
I am he	John 8:28
Before Abraham was, I am	John 8:58
I am the door of the sheep	John 10:7
I am the door	John 10:9
I am the good shepherd	John 10:11, 10:14
I and the Father are one	John 10:30
I am the Son of God	John 10:36
I am in the Father	John 10:38, 14:10–11
I am the resurrection	John 11:25
I am the life	John 11:25
I am Teacher and Lord	John 13:13
I am he	John 13:19
I am the way	John 14:6
I am the truth	John 14:6
I am the life	John 14:6

I am the true vine	John 15:1,5
I am he	John 18:5
I am he	John 18:8
I am a king	John 18:37

Jesus's words portray him as Life, Living Bread, Living Water, and the Light of the World. He claimed that he and the Father were "one" and that he was "in the Father." He stated that he was the Messiah, the Christ, and the Son of God, who was anointed with the Spirit of YHWH in his Father's holy name. Jesus claimed that he was the Door and the only way to the Father, as well as the Resurrection and the Life. The Jewish people knew exactly what Jesus was claiming when he spoke the words he did, such as "before Abraham was, I AM." Even though Jesus came to be the ultimate fulfillment of YHWH's prophet, the words YHWH gave Jesus to speak did not include the word *prophet*. With all of Jesus's "I AM" statements, the people knew that divinity is what Jesus was claiming. They knew through Scripture that God's holy name means, "I AM WHO I AM." That is why, when the Pharisees heard Jesus state time and time again, "I AM HE," they wanted to stone him and kill him, because claiming to be God was considered blasphemy, for which death was the consequence. But even with the threat of death from the religious leaders, Jesus continued speaking the words YHWH placed on his lips. Nothing would stop him from doing the will of his Father. Daily, Jesus prayed for God's words to be placed on his lips, and then he spoke them exactly as they were given to him. God confirmed that the words Jesus spoke were his own—through the daily miracles, signs, and wonders that followed him wherever he went. For if the words Jesus had spoken had not been from God, then Jesus would not have been able to heal the sick, cast out demons, turn water into wine, walk on water, feed the five thousand, and raise people from the dead. Jesus knew that everything he said or did was only possible because of his Father's name and Spirit that resided within him, and therefore he did not speak or act for his own glory but for the glory of the Father.

Jesus said to them, "Truly, truly, I say to you, **the Son can do nothing of his own accord, but only what he sees the Father doing; for whatever he does, that the Son does likewise**. For the Father loves the Son, and shows him all that he himself is doing; and greater works than these will he show him, that you may marvel." (John 5:19–20)

"For I have come down from heaven, **not to do my own will, but the will of him who sent me**; and this is the will of him who sent me, that I should lose nothing of all that he has given me, but raise it up at the last day. **For this is the will of my Father, that every one who sees the Son and believes in him should have eternal life**; and I will raise him up at the last day." (John 6:38–40)

The will of YHWH was for his Son, Yeshua, to bring his people back into a relationship with him. God's people had fallen very far away. Because of the people's disobedience and God's resulting silence, the generation of people during Jesus's time had never heard the voice of God through the prophets or through the Urim and Thummim. They also had never seen YHWH's Shekinah glory or his sacred fire. For many, the stories they knew about their forefathers' encounters with YHWH were just accounts from the Scriptures. Since they had never personally experienced God's presence during their lifetime, the stories they had heard over and over through their entire lives were probably very hard to believe. To make matters worse, since YHWH had stopped speaking to his people, the priests of the day started to use their own voices to fill the silence. As a result, the religious leaders made a "religion" out of God's law. What had started out as a relationship between God and his people had been transformed during the silent years into something that was difficult for people to follow, with all of the manmade rules. Therefore, Jesus came as a new covenant to reintroduce his Father to the people through his words, miracles, signs, and wonders. He came to be YHWH's Shekinah glory, YHWH's visible presence among his people. The people fortunate enough to witness Jesus's glory witnessed a glory that could only have come from the Father. "If I glorify myself, my glory is nothing; *it is my Father who glorifies me*" (John 8:54).

So now that we have a better understanding of why Jesus said what he said and did what he did, let's take a close look at what the witnesses, those who experienced Jesus's presence, called him after hearing the words YHWH gave him to speak.

What the Witnesses Called Jesus

Description of Jesus	**Witness**	**Reference**
Emmanuel (God with us)	Matthew	Matt. 1:23
King of the Jews	Wise men	Matt. 2:2
My Beloved Son	YHWH	Matt. 3:17
Teacher	Scribe	Matt. 8:19
Son of God	Two demons	Matt. 8:29
Son of David	Two blind men	Matt. 9:27
Son of God	Apostles	Matt. 14:33
O Lord, Son of David	Canaanite woman	Matt. 15:22
Christ, Son of the Living God	Peter	Matt. 16:16
My Beloved Son	YHWH	Matt. 17:5
Son of God	Roman centurion	Matt. 27:54
Holy One of God	Spirit of a demon	Mark 1:23–24
Son of God	Unclean spirits	Mark 3:11
Son of the Most High God	Unclean spirits	Mark 5:7
Elijah the Prophet of Old	Many witnesses	Mark 6:15
You are the Christ	Simon Peter	Mark 8:29
Good Teacher	A man	Mark 10:17
Son of David	A blind beggar	Mark 10:46–47
Son of the Most High	Angel Gabriel	Luke 1:32
Holy, the Son of God	Angel Gabriel	Luke 1:35
Savior, who is Christ the Lord	Angel of the Lord	Luke 2:11
Salvation	Simeon	Luke 2:30
Thou art my Beloved Son	YHWH	Luke 3:22
Son of God	Demons	Luke 4:41
Son of the Most High God	Demon-filled man	Luke 8:28

The Christ of God	Simon Peter	Luke 9:20
This is my Son, my Chosen	YHWH	Luke 9:35
The Word	Apostle John	John 1:14
Only Son from the Father	Apostle John	John 1:14
Lamb of God	John the Baptist	John 1:29, 35
Messiah (Christ)	Andrew	John 1:41
Son of God	Nathanael	John 1:49
King of Israel	Nathanael	John 1:49
Rabbi, Teacher come from God	Nicodemus	John 3:2
Savior of the World	Samaritans	John 4:42
The Prophet who is to come	Witnesses	John 6:14
Rabbi	Witnesses	John 6:25
Holy One of God	Simon Peter	John 6:69
The Prophet	Witnesses	John 7:40
The Christ	Witnesses	John 7:41
Prophet	Blind man	John 9:17
Christ, the Son of God	Martha	John 11:27
Teacher and Lord	Disciples	John 13:13
You came from God	Disciples	John 16:30
Innocent	Pontius Pilate	John 19:6
King of the Jews	Pontius Pilate	John 19:19
The Lord	Mary Magdalene	John 20:18
My Lord and My God	Apostle Thomas	John 20:28
Jesus is the Christ	Apostle John	John 20:31
The Son of God	Apostle John	John 20:31

The words used to describe Jesus varied depending upon the people who experienced him and the amount of time they spent in his presence. John the Baptist, who lived his entire life preparing the way for the Messiah, described Jesus as "the Lamb of God who takes away the sins of the world." Even though John the Baptist had never personally spent any time with Jesus, he knew who Jesus was the moment he saw him. In contrast, the apostle John, who spent three years in Jesus's presence, described Jesus as "God's Word sent to dwell among us." The Samaritans, who only spent two days with Jesus, came to the conclusion that Jesus was the Savior of the world, while still others described him as Teacher,

Lord, Rabbi, Prophet, Son of God, Son of David, the Messiah, Christ, and the King of the Jews.

Just like the Israelites did not know what to call the bread that rained down from heaven while they were in the wilderness, the Jewish people did not know what to call Jesus when he first appeared on the scene. Remember, when the Israelites first saw what we have come to know as manna, they had never seen it before and therefore did not know what to name it. Since they did not have a word to describe what they were seeing, they decided to call it manna, which means, "What is it?" Even though they did not know what the substance was or what to name it, the people quickly came to understand the importance of the mystery bread sent from heaven once they realized that it provided them with all the daily nourishment they needed to physically survive.

Similarly, when Jesus suddenly appeared in their land, the Jewish people did not know what to call him. Therefore, in attempts to describe him, Yeshua received many titles from the people who experienced a close encounter with him. The question in the land during this time was not, "What is it?" but instead, "Who is he?" They asked themselves, "Who is this mystery man who claims to be the Bread of Life sent down from heaven?" Over time, many of the witnesses came to understand that although they did not completely understand who Jesus was or what to call him, they knew in their hearts, because of the words he spoke and the miracles that followed his words, that he would provide them with all the daily spiritual nourishment they would ever need. Just like YHWH provided manna for the Israelites at a time of physical need for food, YHWH also provided Jesus, the real bread from heaven, at a time of great spiritual need of hearing YHWH's voice. YHWH sent his Son, Yeshua, at just the right time, when the people were hungry and thirsty to hear God's voice. They became eager to ask, to search, and to ponder the question, "Could this Jesus truly be our long-awaited Messiah?"

People from all walks of life were exposed to Yeshua's presence—from the very poor to the very rich, from the uneducated to the highly educated, from those who knew Scripture inside and out to those who knew no Scripture, from the sick to the healthy, from the Jews to the

Gentiles, and finally, from the demons of Satan to the angels of the LORD. Some people only needed one encounter with Jesus to know who he was, while others needed to experience him many times before they came to a conclusion. Some people, upon hearing his words spoken with authority, easily concluded that Jesus was the Son of God, while others needed the proof of his miracles, signs, and wonders before they could conclude that he had been sent from YHWH. Some just needed to hear Jesus's voice in order to make their conclusion, while others needed his physical touch to sense his compassion toward them in a time of need. Everyone's "close encounter" with Jesus looked different. As a result, the titles the witnesses used to describe Jesus varied; the words they chose were reflections of their own individual experiences with him.

The Heavenly Witnesses

What I find very compelling is what the demons and the angels called Jesus. Of course you would expect the angels, the ones who visited Mary and the shepherds, to describe Jesus as "Son of the Most High," "Holy," "the Son of God," and "Savior, who is Christ the Lord." Those titles for Jesus would have been expected because the angels were messengers of YHWH. However, when you look at the words the demons used to describe Jesus, you will see that they used the same words as the angels.

> And immediately there was in their synagogue a man with an unclean spirit; and he cried out, "What have you to do with us, Jesus of Nazareth? **Have you come to destroy us? I know who you are, the Holy One of God.**" (Mark 1:23–24)

> And whenever the unclean spirits beheld him, they **fell down before him** and cried out, "**You are the Son of God.**" (Mark 3:11)

> And crying out with a loud voice, he said, "What have you to do with me, **Jesus, Son of the Most High God**? I adjure you by God, **do not torment me**." (Mark 5:7)

While Jesus was casting the demons out of God's people, there was no confusion on their part as to who Jesus was. Like the angels, the demons had also experienced Jesus in heaven before they had been cast out of their heavenly home. Therefore, when the demons came in contact with Jesus on earth, they feared him because they also knew the power he received on the day he was baptized. Remember, even Satan himself witnessed that Jesus was the Son of God while they were in the wilderness together. When we consider that YHWH, Satan, the angels, and the demons are all part of the spiritual world, we have to value their witness of Jesus because the spiritual world is the world from which he was sent. Throughout our human lifetimes, we get only small glimpses of the spiritual world. The demons, however, live in the spiritual world in which YHWH, Jesus, and Satan also dwell, so they can be considered very credible witnesses. All the demons that described Jesus came to the same conclusion—that he was the Son of God, the Most High.

And then of course, there is Yeshua's heavenly Father, YHWH, who personally witnessed for Jesus on three occasions while he walked this earth. YHWH declared out loud at Jesus's baptism; during his transfiguration in front of Peter, John, and James; and once right before he died that Yeshua was indeed his beloved Son, his chosen. YHWH told those present to listen to his Son.

The people who were exposed to Jesus's presence during his lifetime came to their own conclusions regarding who Jesus was and whether they ultimately believed he was sent from heaven or not. The question of the day, "Who is he?" was such an important one during Jesus's time that even Jesus asked it of his own disciples.

> Now when Jesus came into the district of Ceasare'a Philippi, he asked his disciples, "**Who do men say that the Son of man is**?" And they said, "Some say John the Baptist, others say Eli'jah, and others Jeremiah or one of the prophets." He

said to them, "**But who do you say that I am**?" Simon Peter replied, "**You are the Christ, the Son of the living God**." And Jesus answered him, "**Blessed are you, Simon Bar-Jona! For flesh and blood has not revealed this to you, but my Father who is in heaven**." (Matt. 16:13–17)

But who do *you* say that I am? After spending many years together with these men, Jesus asked them point blank who they personally thought he was. By asking this question, Jesus was saying, "Disregarding other people's opinions, who do you think I am? What are your thoughts? What is your gut feeling about me?" When Peter replied, "You are the Christ, the Son of the living God," his response was based on his own personal experience of spending time with Jesus. Many other individuals had seen the same miracles and heard the same teachings that Peter had, but when asked the same question, they had a completely different answer. Some thought Jesus was John the Baptist, Elijah, Jeremiah, or one of the prophets, and perhaps some thought he was a crazy man. After Peter answered Jesus's question, Jesus explained that Peter had not come to this determination on his own. He stated that Peter had come to this conclusion only because his Father, YHWH, revealed this truth to him. Only those who received this truth from YHWH were able to acknowledge that Jesus was the Christ—their long-awaited Messiah.

Who Is Jesus?

In your own walk with God, this same question, "Who is Jesus?" becomes the most important question you will ever be asked. Just like the Israelites asked daily, "What is it?" of the manna, you have to ask yourself the question, "Who is he?" Putting aside all that you have heard or read about Jesus, there will come a time when Jesus will personally ask you, "But who do you say that I am?" To answer this question, you cannot rely on other people's experiences for the answer because, according to Jesus's own words, flesh and blood cannot reveal the truth about Jesus to you. Other people's experiences with Jesus are other people's experiences. They are not your own. Unless you have personally experienced Jesus, then you cannot answer this question with your heart and soul. Only if the Father has revealed to you the truth about Jesus will you honestly be able to answer this question. And only after YHWH reveals Jesus to you will you be able to undeniably acknowledge before men that Jesus is the Son of the living God. After this revelation there will be no shaking of your faith because your faith will no longer be based on faith alone; it will be based on an actual encounter with Jesus. The more experiences you have with Jesus, the more solid your relationship will become.

Immediately after I was introduced to these verses in my studies, I went out of town on a weekend trip to Nashville, Tennessee, with my husband. While on the airplane, I was pondering what it personally meant for the Father to reveal the truth about Jesus to me, and I started writing down my thoughts. All of my personal experiences with the Father and his Son over the years came flooding back to me. I was overwhelmed by YHWH's faithfulness in revealing himself and Jesus to me. Putting my thoughts on paper, I wrote at the top of a page, "Who do I say Jesus is?" Then I wrote the following:

> Jesus is my Lord
> Jesus is my Savior
> He is my friend, my comforter, and my companion
> He is my lover and my spiritual soul mate
> Jesus is the Son of God
> Jesus is YHWH

I can now say with 100 percent conviction and certainty that Jesus Christ, the Son of the living God, *is* the living YHWH. All of my previous thoughts about Jesus, which were based on other people's beliefs, have been replaced with my own convictions, based on my own personal experiences with him. I now know that the words Jesus spoke to his disciples and the stories found in Scripture are the absolute truth because I, too, have personally experienced hearing Jesus's voice and seen his miracles before my very eyes.

To me, Jesus is funny, loving, attentive, caring, and extremely strategic in everything he does. And it really hit me, as I was writing down all of these adjectives, that the gospel writers Matthew, Mark, Luke, and John did not convince me of these things—YHWH did! The Gospels only gave me a recorded history of Jesus. It was only after I personally searched with all my mind, heart, and soul about YHWH's existence that YHWH personally introduced me to his Son, Jesus. Only after YHWH sent Jesus into my life were my individual sins personally forgiven. And as a result of being made righteous through Jesus, an incredibly intimate relationship with my heavenly Father has formed.

After reminiscing about my personal relationship with Jesus and my heavenly Father, I decided that I needed to formally write down all that was swirling around in my brain. I wanted to start my journaling with the verses in Matthew that began all of these thoughts. I could not remember the exact location of these verses in Scripture, so I began to search the Gospels in order to find them. After about thirty minutes of searching with no luck, I finally gave up, knowing that I would locate them later.

When we got off the plane, my husband and I went in opposite directions. Since my husband had a business meeting, I caught a taxi to our hotel. On the ride to the hotel, I could not help but notice all of the churches that lined the street corners. As I was passing by a Baptist church, I got the feeling that I needed to go sit inside. I had no idea why; I just felt like it was something I needed to do. Even though I was raised Lutheran, my husband was raised Catholic, and we currently attended a non-denominational church, I really felt like YHWH wanted me to visit this Baptist church. It was an odd request since I had never made a practice of going to other churches while out of town and especially not on a weekday.

After checking into the hotel and finding my room, I took a moment to look out the large picture window. Would you believe, centered directly outside my window, was this same beautiful Baptist church! Again I heard, "Go sit in my church." As I was unpacking, my husband called to say he was going to have to take his clients to lunch, so I would have more alone time on my hands. So I went downstairs and got a bite to eat. After lunch, the thought was still there: *Go sit in my church.* So I obeyed. However, after walking a few blocks to get to this church, I was immediately disappointed to find the front doors and gate locked. When I walked to the two different sets of side doors, I found them to be locked as well. As I continued around the back of the church, I finally found the weekday entrance. Since I really didn't know why I was there in the first place, I asked the gentleman at the desk if I could sit in the sanctuary. He told me that the organist was rehearsing but that I was welcome.

It was a beautiful sanctuary, with stained glass windows that reminded me of a rainbow. As I was sitting in the pew, my ears were filled with beautiful sounds coming from the organ. As I started praying, I was suddenly overwhelmed by all of the thoughts of YHWH revealing his Son, Jesus, to me, so much so that the tears that came streaming out of my eyes were wetting my feet below. I thanked God for loving me so much that he was willing to send his Son to die on the cross personally for me and for revealing himself to me over and over again. I finished my prayer by asking YHWH to continue to reveal himself to me through Jesus. After I sat in silence for a while, not knowing what else to do, I thought, *Well, I guess that's it,* and I got up to leave.

Immediately upon exiting the sanctuary, I walked by a pillar that had a verse inscribed on it. It read, "Matthew 16:18." I said to myself, *Hmm … I wonder what that verse says*? Since I had my Bible in my purse from the plane ride, I was able to immediately look it up. I could not believe what I saw. This verse, and the three preceding it, was the *exact scripture* I had been searching for on the plane about YHWH revealing Jesus to us. I chuckled out loud in amazement.

I hadn't known why I needed to go to this church on this particular day, but YHWH did! Oh, how strategic he is. Once again, he wanted to reveal to me that he is an all-powerful and sovereign God who is capable of revealing himself to us whenever, wherever, and however he desires. He knew how much I wanted to find his verse, his words, and he wanted me to know them at that moment, as I was coming out of one of his churches. It could have waited until I got back home, but once again YHWH wanted to show me his power and glory. God obviously wanted me to pay attention to his Son's words to Peter, so he put an exclamation point on them by performing another miracle. He wanted me to know with certainty that Jesus's words are the absolute truth, and only he can reveal the truth about them with such clarity. The verse inscribed on the pillar of this Baptist church says, *"And I tell you, you are Peter, and on this rock I will build my church,* and the powers of death shall not prevail against it" (Matt. 16:18).

It was as if God were saying to me that day, "It is on the revealed Word of YHWH, the living Word, that I will build my church. It is not through head knowledge that I will build my church, but through everyday experiences, similar to what you have just experienced, that you will know that I am a living God. My Son, Jesus, is the revealed Word of God. He is the rock, the solid foundation upon which my church is being built. As a believer, because I have revealed Jesus to you, you too have become one of the living stones that is forming the pillars of my church."

Answering the question, "But who do you say that I am?" will be required of every single one of us. If you can honestly say from your heart and soul that Jesus is *"Christ, the Son of the living God,"* then Jesus calls you "blessed," for you have not come to this answer on your own. Your heavenly Father has revealed his Son to you. And because of this revelation from your Father, you too have become a living stone, a pillar in his church, and the powers of death will not prevail against you. Because you know Jesus, you can know for sure that your heavenly Father wants to know you personally. It is an overwhelming thought for me, and I hope it is for you too.

Once again, my heavenly Father revealed himself to me through his Word. I shudder to think that I almost didn't go to the Baptist church; I almost didn't listen to YHWH's voice that day. Only after he spoke three times did I finally obey. I could have turned around after I got to the first or second locked door, thinking I would find all the doors locked; but I didn't. My husband could have come back from his meeting as planned instead of going to lunch, which would not have allowed me enough time to do what God was asking of me. It makes me wonder how many instructions from YHWH I have missed in my walk with him due to circumstances or my own mind getting in the way. But on this particular day, I heard God's voice and I obeyed, and look at all that he revealed. First comes obedience and then understanding!

So who is Jesus to you? How do you describe him? Have you taken the time to research the greatest man to ever live? Through all of your research you may find out that it is not as exhausting as you first imagined. What you will most likely discover is that studying Jesus's life and the words he spoke is the most exhilarating experience you will ever have. Through it all, you just may have your very first close encounter with your LORD and Savior. What you might conclude, and I hope that you do, is that the prophet Isaiah had it right from the beginning—that Jesus is indeed Immanuel, *"God with us."*

Chapter 16

The Passover Lamb

> "Now is my soul troubled. And what shall I say? 'Father, save me from this hour'? No, for this purpose I have come to this hour. **Father, glorify thy name.**" **Then a voice came from heaven, "I have glorified it, and I will glorify it again.**" (John 12:27–28)

At this point in Jesus's ministry, he had not yet died on the cross, been raised from the grave, or ascended into heaven. And yet, according to YHWH's voice from heaven, his holy name had already been glorified through his beloved Son. YHWH's name was glorified every time temptation came Jesus's way and Jesus fought Satan's lies with the Word of God. YHWH's name was glorified when Jesus prayed daily for God's will on how to live and speak. YHWH's name was glorified when Jesus did not act on his own authority but obeyed God's voice in everything that was asked of him. God's name was glorified every time Jesus kept one of his Father's ordained feasts and the Sabbath days exactly as he was instructed. YHWH's name was glorified daily because Jesus loved God with all his heart, soul, mind, and strength.

Because Jesus had glorified his Father's holy name during his ministry, YHWH took time to speak out loud one more time to the Israelites to tell the people what he thought of Jesus. This was the third time YHWH spoke out loud while Jesus walked this earth. Three times the Father personally witnessed for his Son.

Jesus knew his time had come. Everything that he had been preparing for his entire life came to this moment when he was going to be sacrificed for the sins of the people. Jesus knew without a doubt the will of his Father was for him to lay down his life so that others could have a relationship with YHWH. He knew the will of the Father was to defeat the consequence of sin, which is death, so that Satan, the ruler of this world, would lose the power that he holds. The forgiveness of sins would allow the new covenant relationship to begin. With the new covenant, communication between the Father and his people would no longer be through priests and prophets but through YHWH's Holy Spirit.

Before the time came for Jesus to depart from the world and once again return to the Father, he had one more important task to complete. Jesus needed to spend one last night with his disciples celebrating Passover. This was the first of the seven biblical feasts that God ordained for his people to celebrate yearly. Jesus told his disciples that he "earnestly" desired to eat this last Passover with them before he suffered (Luke 22:15).

The Passover Feast

Why was it so important for Jesus to spend time celebrating this feast with his disciples, and why was he so eager to do so? This Passover celebration was critical for Jesus. His time on earth was about to come to an end, and yet he still had so many words he needed to say. He needed to make certain that the twelve men who had been entrusted to his care over the past three years were well aware of what was about to happen. All four Gospels talk about this particular Passover. In the Gospel of John, Chapters 13 through 17 are devoted solely to what Jesus told his disciples on this significant night. YHWH had given these twelve men, out of the world, to Jesus. Of all the people who came into contact with Jesus over the three years of his ministry, it came down to these few individuals. Jesus knew that it didn't matter who else came to the conclusion that he was the Son of God as long as these men did. He needed for them to believe without a doubt that he was indeed sent from the Father. Jesus knew what was going to be asked of his disciples after he died, rose again, and ascended into heaven. Therefore he needed them to be thoroughly prepared for their mission to take his name into the world.

The disciples were well aware of the meaning of this night because they had celebrated it yearly their entire lives. Passover was a celebration of YHWH leading his people out of Egypt, out of slavery and bondage. It was a celebration of a time when YHWH heard the cry of his people and freed them from their enemy's hand. The very first Passover was a night when the Israelites trusted YHWH to deliver them from death by being obedient to his commands. It was a celebration of what became the beginning of the first covenant between God and his people. The long-awaited promise of becoming a nation, given to Abraham, started on that first Passover night.

During Passover, the people were reminded that after the Israelites were led out of Egypt, YHWH had come to dwell in their presence. They were reminded of how he had led them by his cloud in the day and a pillar of fire by night out of the enemy's hand, and how he had spoken to them at Mount Sinai, and then through Moses, his Word, his sacred fire, his Shekinah glory, the high priests, the Urim and Thummim, and his prophets. The Israelites had not heard from God for the entire 430 years while they lived in Egypt, and yet, in the matter of one night, not only did they become their own nation, but also their God now dwelled among them.

The first Passover eve, Nissan 14, was a very important night for the people and God. Scripture tells us that it was a "night of watching by YHWH." YHWH was about to do something incredible for his people; he had to make sure it went exactly as planned. This night was going to be a night of great rejoicing because, on this night, YHWH would glorify his holy name through a miracle. "It was a night of watching by YHWH, to bring them out of the land of Egypt; *so this same night is a night of watching kept to YHWH by all the people of Israel throughout their generations*" (Exo. 12:42). And so he did; YHWH glorified his name on Nissan 14, the first Passover, exactly as planned.

I imagine Jesus talked at length to his disciples about the significant meaning of this night in history, as had been done in every Jewish household for thousands of years. But I imagine Jesus also told his men that *tonight*, Nissan 14, AD 30, YHWH would once again glorify his holy name. The night God started his first covenant with his people would be the same night God ended it and began a new covenant through his Son, Yeshua. The second covenant between God and his people would begin with his Son's death. Through Jesus's death, YHWH's people would once again be led out of the hands of their enemy—Satan. That is why YHWH commanded his people to keep this night of Passover as a "night of watching" throughout their generations, because he wanted his people to be ready for what he was going to do on this night in the future.

After celebrating Passover with his disciples, saying all that he needed to communicate, Jesus lifted up his eyes to heaven and prayed.

> "Father, the hour has come; **glorify your Son that the Son may glorify you**, since you have given him authority over all flesh, to give eternal life to all whom you have given him. **And this is eternal life, that they know you the only true God, and Jesus Christ whom you have sent. I glorified you on earth, having accomplished the work which you gave me to do**; and now, Father, **glorify me in your own presence with the glory that I had with you before the world existed**." (John 17:1–5 ESV)

Jesus stated that he had accomplished the work his Father had given him to do. So what did Jesus accomplish with his ministry? What was his purpose?

> "**I have manifested YOUR NAME to the people whom you gave me out of the world**. Yours they were, and you gave them to me, and they have kept your word. Now they know that everything that you have given me is from you; for **I have given them the words that you gave me, and they have received them and have come to know in truth**

that I came from you; and they have believed that you sent me." (John 17:6–8 ESV)

From Jesus's own words we can clearly see that the mission he was given by his Father was to "manifest" YHWH's holy name to the people. When used as an adjective, the word *manifest* means "readily perceived by the senses, especially by sight," or "easily understood or recognized by the mind, obvious." As a verb, *manifest* means "to make evident or certain by showing or displaying."[1] Jesus did all this and more while he walked on this earth. Yeshua, the beloved and chosen Son of YHWH, revealed the power and glory of his Father's holy name to all those who came into contact with him, especially to his disciples.

Regardless of what anyone else knew to be true about Jesus, these men that God had chosen for him had accepted Jesus's words as truth. They knew he was the Son of God and that he had been sent from the Father. Just like Moses had to prove to the people through his many signs and miracles that YHWH, the God of Abraham, Isaac, and Jacob, had sent him to lead the people out of Egypt to free them, Jesus had to prove to the people that YHWH, the God of Abraham, Isaac, and Jacob, had sent him. YHWH had told Moses to tell the people of Israel, "I AM has sent me to you." I can imagine YHWH telling Jesus to do the same during his ministry; and that is exactly what Jesus did.

The purpose of Jesus's manifesting his Father YHWH's name was not to receive worship from the people. Jesus manifested YHWH's name so that his disciples would know without a doubt *who* they would be following after Jesus performed his last miracle on earth—defeating his own death. Jesus wanted his disciples to know that by following him, they would, in fact, be following YHWH. He wanted his disciples to be certain that by following Jesus from this day forward and doing all that he would command them to do, they would be doing the will of their Father in heaven.

Judy Jacobson

The Passover Lamb

For centuries, the Passover lamb was chosen on the tenth day of the first month of Nissan and was kept until Nissan 14, when it was killed and eaten, as YHWH had commanded Moses so long ago. The lamb chosen was to be a male without blemish. This Passover celebration would be no different, but with one exception. On Nissan 10, on the day the lambs were being chosen by the people to celebrate Passover, Jesus, the Lamb of God, also entered into the city of Jerusalem. Most know this day as Palm Sunday. When the crowds saw Jesus coming into the city, they took branches of palm trees and went out to meet him, crying, "Hosanna! Blessed is he *who comes in the name of the Lord*, even the King of Israel!" (John 12:13).

On that day, a whole crowd of people worshipped Jesus for the name by which he came because they thought that Jesus would finally be taking his place as their king. What they didn't realize was that, on this day, Jesus was instead chosen by YHWH to be *"the Passover Lamb who takes away the sins of the world,"* just as John the Baptist had prophesied. Because Jesus was blemish-free, he met the requirement of the Passover lamb. Jesus remained in Jerusalem from this day until the day he died on Nissan 14. For all of this to make sense, you need to know that a Jewish day runs from sunset to sunset. So when Jesus was crucified during the morning hours on the day that followed the Passover celebration the night before, it was still considered the same day, Nissan 14.

On that first Passover night, YHWH gave the Israelites careful instructions on what to do with the Passover lamb after they killed it. They were instructed to first take the blood of the lamb, place it over the door frames of their homes, and then to eat the lamb. They were to eat in haste and be ready because on that very night YHWH was going to move the entire host of Israelites out of the hands of their enemy. It was going to be a night of intense watching and listening. The blood of the lamb was to be placed over their door frames for a very specific reason. YHWH said to the people through Moses,

> "**It is YHWH's Passover**. For I will pass through the land of Egypt that night, and I will smite all the first-born in the land of Egypt, both man and beast; and on all the gods of Egypt I will execute judgments: I am YHWH. **The blood shall be a sign for you, upon the houses where you are; and when I see the blood, I will pass over you, and no plague shall fall upon you to destroy you.**" (Exo. 12:11b–13a)

> "For YHWH will pass through to slay the Egyptians; and **when he sees the blood on the lintel and on the two doorposts, YHWH will pass over the door, and will not allow the destroyer to enter your houses to slay you.**" (Exo. 12:23)

Just as YHWH directed his people on what to do on the first Passover night, Jesus had instructions for his disciples on this night as well. He had specific instructions on what to do with his body (the ultimate Passover Lamb) once he was sacrificed so that *eternal death would pass them over*. These instructions were given to them during Passover (the Last Supper). "Now as they were eating, Jesus took bread, and blessed and broke it, and gave it to the disciples and said, *'Take, eat; this is my body'*" (Matt. 26:26). The unleavened bread that Jesus broke during this Last Supper represented his *sinless life*, which symbolically became *the flesh of the Passover lamb*. Jesus said that whoever eats of this bread, which represented his flesh, receives the *bread of life* sent from heaven. He also said, "I am the living bread which came down from heaven; *if any one eats of this bread, he will live for ever*; and the bread which I shall give for the life of the world *is my flesh*" (John 6:51).

Jesus then took a cup, and when he had given thanks, he gave it to the disciples, saying, "*Drink of it, all of you; for this is my blood of the covenant*, which is poured out for many for the forgiveness of sins" (Matt. 26:27–28). The wine that Jesus poured out for his disciples symbolically represented his *sinless blood*, which would be shed from his body. Jesus's shed blood would serve two purposes. Those who apply the blood of Jesus to the door frames of their hearts are led out of the hands of their enemy and are given the gift of communication with their heavenly Father just as the Israelites, who applied the blood to their literal door frames, were led out of Egypt and into the presence and voice of YHWH. In addition, we have been promised that those who believe that Jesus died for their sins and who drink his blood will one day be brought into his physical presence for eternity. Believers have been promised that on the Day of the LORD, when YHWH sees Jesus's blood over their hearts, his wrath will pass them over and they will be saved. "Truly, truly, I say to you, *unless you eat the flesh of the Son of man and drink his blood, you have no life in you; he who eats my flesh and drinks my blood has eternal life, and I will raise him up at the last day*" (John 6:53–54).

The apostle Paul gave us these same instructions.

> For I received from the Lord what I also delivered to you, that the Lord Jesus on the night when he was betrayed took bread, and when he had given thanks, he broke it, and said, **"This is my body which is for you. Do this in remembrance of me."** In the same way also the cup, after supper, saying, **"This cup is the new covenant in my blood. Do this, as often as you drink it, in remembrance of me." For as often as you eat this bread and drink the cup, you proclaim the Lord's death until he comes.** (1 Corin. 11:23–26)

Every time we participate in the Lord's Supper (communion), we are declaring that Jesus's body and blood, broken and poured out for us, have the power to give us everlasting life. When we eat the bread and drink the cup, *we proclaim that Jesus was and is the Great I AM*. We remember that it is because of Jesus's sacrifice on the cross that we have been forgiven of our sins, have been made completely righteous, are allowed to enter into YHWH's presence daily, and will one day live with him for eternity.

Betrayal

After the Passover meal was complete, Jesus went with his disciples across the Kidron Valley to a garden named Gethsemane. It was there that Judas, one of the twelve disciples, betrayed Jesus, which led to his crucifixion. But before we go any further into the details of this night, let's take a step back and look from Satan's point of view at what he was doing throughout Jesus's ministry.

We already know that immediately upon Jesus coming onto the scene, Satan tried to get him to sin in the wilderness. And, as was previously discussed, we know that Satan failed miserably. But do you remember what Scripture says happened next? "And when the devil had ended every temptation, he departed from him *until an opportune time*" (Luke 4:13). Satan knew with certainty that he would not be able to deceive Yeshua into sinning during his ministry, like he did Adam and Eve. He realized pretty quickly that dealing with Jesus was going to be a lot more difficult than he first imagined. Satan also knew that after the people witnessed all of Jesus's miracles, signs, and wonders, it was going to be very difficult to convince them that Jesus was not their long-awaited Messiah. Even his own demons witnessed to the people that Jesus was the Son of God. He would have to take a different approach. Satan thought that there had to be someone he could target to help him in his mission to rid the earth of Jesus's presence. Jesus may be the Son of God, but he was also flesh and blood and could be physically harmed, like any other human. So all he needed was someone on his side whom he could persuade to kill Jesus.

Now, keep in mind that Satan saw Jesus's entrance into the city of Jerusalem as the King of the Jews just like the crowds did. He likely had no idea that Jesus was sent as the Passover lamb, who would lead the people out of his grip by being raised from the dead. He believed that if he could just get someone to kill Jesus, then his problem would be solved—just as he had thought thirty-three years earlier that if he killed all the babies in Bethlehem, his mission would be complete. What Satan always seemed to forget, however, is who Yeshua's Father was and the lengths to which YHWH would go to protect his Son. So Satan decided that instead of focusing on the common man and worrying about who he thought Jesus was, he would target the religious leaders and the Roman governing bodies. He would concentrate his efforts on them because he could easily place doubt into their minds that if Jesus took his rightful place as King of the Jews, then they would lose their own power and prestige. He would speak to their pride and their desire to keep their riches and fame. If it all worked out as he planned, their desire to remain in power would overshadow any thoughts that Jesus just might be their Messiah. As a result, Jesus would be eliminated.

> But one of them, **Caiaphas, who was high priest that year, said to them**, "You know nothing at all; you do not understand that **it is expedient for you that one man should die for the people, and that the whole nation should not perish**." He did not say this of his own accord, but being high priest that year **he prophesied that Jesus should die for the nation, and not for the nation only, but to gather into one the children of God who are scattered abroad. So from that day on they took counsel how to put him to death**. (John 11:49–53)

When Satan heard Caiaphas speak these words, he must have thought, *Aha! My plan is working.* Even though the signs and miracles Jesus performed over and over again proved that he was the Son of God, through the deception of their own pride, the Jewish leaders could not see the truth. They enjoyed their positions and felt that if they accepted Jesus for who he said he was, they would lose their power and riches. Their hearts were hard, and therefore they could not see past themselves and see that the man who stood before them was indeed God's only Son.

Satan probably also thought that Caiaphas's plan would go much more smoothly if he had an "insider" to help him. So Satan targeted one of Jesus's trusted disciples by speaking doubt into his ears. What Satan didn't know is that his own plan played into exactly what YHWH willed for his Son. YHWH's intent was for Jesus to be killed so that his Passover Lamb would be sacrificed for the sins of the world. YHWH knew that Satan would use this opportune time to kill Jesus, so YHWH let the events play out. After Satan was allowed to enter into Judas's heart, Judas betrayed Jesus to the religious leaders with a kiss.

> Then Jesus, knowing all that was to befall him, came forward and said to them, "Whom do you seek?" They answered him, "Jesus of Nazareth." Jesus said to them, **"I AM HE."** Judas, who betrayed him, was standing with them. When he said to them, **"I AM HE" they drew back and fell to the ground**. (John 18:4–6)

Even though YHWH would allow the events of his Son's death to play out, he would still show his power and glory through it all. When Jesus said, "I AM HE" to the men who came to seize him, they fell to the ground. Only the Son of God has the power to make men fall to the ground simply by proclaiming his holy name.

The Trials

Over the next few hours, Caiaphas, Herod, and Pontius Pilate all tried Jesus. The final decision came down to Pilate, even though he himself believed that Jesus was innocent; he perceived that it was out of envy that the chief priests had delivered Jesus to him. Three times Pilate stated to the people that he found no crime in Jesus that deserved death and that he should be released.

> "You brought to me this man as one who was perverting the people; and after examining him before you, behold, **I did not find this man guilty of any of your charges against him; neither did Herod**, for he sent him back to us. Behold, nothing deserving death has been done by him; I will therefore chastise him and release him." (Luke 23:14–16)

But due to the urgent and demanding cries from the crowd that Jesus should be crucified, Pilate decided to give the crowd one more choice, and he hoped they would make the right decision. "After he had said this, he went out to the Jews again, and told them, 'I find no crime in him. But you have a custom that I should release one man for you at the Passover; will you have me release for you the King of the Jews?' They cried out again, 'Not this man, but Barabbas!'" (John 18:38b–40). Because the crowd's voice prevailed, the notorious killer Barabbas was released, and Jesus, a sinless man, took his place.

While reading the book *Jesus: The Greatest Life of All* by Charles R. Swindoll,[2] I came across an incredibly revealing fact about the meaning of Barabbas's name. His name is actually quite nonsensical, simply meaning "son of a father." This is odd, when most parents in biblical times gave their children much more meaningful names. Perhaps it was an alias, a clever "John Doe," that Barabbas himself adopted to protect his family when he joined a band of thugs and eventually became their leader. Nevertheless, by the time he was caught, he had become a notorious killer; and because of his deeds, Barabbas was to be executed by crucifixion. But instead, even though he was innocent of all sin, Jesus took Barabbas's place on the cross that day. When I was thinking of Jesus, the Son of God, taking the place on the cross of Barabbas, the "son of a father," I couldn't help but think of the great symbolism it portrayed. Jesus, though innocent, took the place of someone who deserved to pay the penalty of death for his wrongdoing. On that day Barabbas went free, and yet, the grace Barabbas received is merely an illustration of a greater, more personal truth.

It was *your place* on the cross; it was *my place* on the cross that Jesus took that day. Jesus died *for you;* Jesus died *for me*. The meaning of Barabbas's name was nonsensical because it was meant to represent us all. Jesus willingly became our substitute sacrifice for our wrongdoings so that we are no longer considered just another son or daughter of a father. Because of what Jesus did for us, we are now called *"sons and daughters of our heavenly Father."* No longer do we have nonsensical names, for we have been given a name that will last through eternity. We have become children of YHWH.

I can't help but wonder if Barabbas ever found out who gave him the gift of life that day. He had to have known the consequences for his behavior and yet, miraculously, he was saved from death. I wonder if, because of the gift he received that day, Barabbas ever repented of his sins and asked for forgiveness for all that he had done in his life. Did he ever get to know of Jesus's sacrificial love for him? Or instead, did Barabbas just think that he had a really lucky day and go back to his murderous ways?

The Crucifixion

With the people's decision made, Pilate handed Yeshua over to the Roman guards to be crucified. A crown of thorns was placed on his head, and he was spit on and mocked. He was humiliated, scourged, and beaten to within an inch of his life before he was made to carry his cross to a location called "the place of a skull," which, in Hebrew, is called Golgotha. He was nailed to a cross through his wrists and feet and placed between two other common criminals, and was continually mocked until he died. Above Jesus hung a sign made by Pilate.

> Pilate also wrote a title and put it on the cross; it read, "**Jesus of Nazareth, the King of the Jews**." Many of the Jews read this title, for the place where Jesus was crucified was near the city; and it was written in **Hebrew**, in **Latin**, and in **Greek**. The chief priests of the Jews then said to Pilate, "Do not write, 'The King of the Jews,' but, 'This man said, **I am King of the Jews**.'" Pilate answered, "What I have written I have written." (John 19:19–22)

YHWH used Pilate to let all the people know exactly whom they were putting to death. Because some of the people witnessing Christ's death had come from far places, due to the celebration of Passover, YHWH had Pilate write in three different languages that Jesus was the "King of the Jews." YHWH wanted everyone to know without a doubt that Jesus was truly his Son. As Jesus hung on the cross dying, bearing the incredible pain that had been inflicted on him, I am sure that he held onto his Father YHWH's promise that YHWH's holy name would be glorified again through him. Jesus had to believe with all of his body, soul, and spirit that YHWH was in control and that YHWH's will was perfect, regardless of the consequences. You wonder if, through all the pain and suffering, Jesus ever doubted God's words to him. Any mortal man surely would have, but Jesus was not just a mortal man. He was the Son of God, who knew that the will of his Father was for him to lay down his life for the sins of the world. That is why, right before he died, Jesus was able to say, *"Father forgive them, they know not what they do"* (Luke 23:34).

For *three hours* before Christ's death, Scripture says that darkness covered the land. Looking back into history, there was another time that darkness covered the land. Before the tenth plague, when YHWH killed all the firstborn in Egypt in order to free his children from the bondage of slavery, YHWH sent a ninth plague, which was a darkness that covered the land.

> Then YHWH said to Moses, "Stretch out your hand toward heaven that there may be darkness over the land of Egypt, **a darkness to be felt**." So Moses stretched out his hand toward heaven, and there was thick darkness in all the land of Egypt **three days**; they did not see one another, nor did any rise from his place for three days. (Exo. 10:21–23)

I imagine that the darkness YHWH sent before the death of his only Son, Jesus, was also a darkness *that could be felt*. People probably did not move during these entire three hours. Maybe the darkness was a visible manifestation of the agony YHWH felt for the pain that was being inflicted onto his Son. When Jesus could not hold on any longer, he cried out loud and said, "It is finished" (John 19:30), followed by, "Father, into thy hands I commit my Spirit!" (Luke 23:46). Having said these words, Jesus breathed his last breath. At the time Jesus gave up his Spirit, he became 100 percent completely separated from his Father. The consequences of taking on the sins of the world became real for him for the very first time.

What a huge sacrifice Jesus made for us! He had been in daily communication with his Father, and in a moment of time everything was taken away from him. Communication with the Father was no longer possible when Jesus released his Spirit, which his Father had given him, back into his Father's hands. All Jesus could do at the point of his death was to completely trust that his Father would do what he promised he would do so that his death would not be in vain. Jesus had to trust that YHWH would once again glorify his holy name by resurrecting Jesus from the dead.

Temple Curtain

Jesus's mission was now complete. He had successfully manifested his Father's holy name to his disciples and had become the sacrificial Passover lamb, exactly as his Father had commanded him. Now it was up to YHWH to complete the rest of the plan in order to bring YHWH's people safely out of Satan's hands and back into a relationship with him. At the very moment that Jesus cried out and gave up his Spirit to his Father, the temple curtain was torn in two from top to bottom, the earth shook, and rocks were split. At the moment that Jesus died, YHWH spoke again for his Son. YHWH did not speak audibly this time but through signs and wonders.

Have you ever wondered why YHWH chose to tear the temple curtain in two? It becomes clear when you remember that the curtain was used to separate the Holy of Holies from the rest of the temple. Only once a year was the high priest allowed to go behind the curtain and sprinkle blood over the ark of the covenant to ask forgiveness for the people's sins. But remember, the ark of the covenant had been missing since the destruction of Solomon's temple, so the high priest had been going into an *empty* Holy of Holies on the Day of Atonement for hundreds of years, sprinkling the blood of an animal sacrifice over absolutely nothing.

Whether or not the people knew the Holy of Holies was empty during the silent years we will never know. But what we do know is that by tearing the temple curtain in two, YHWH allowed his people to see the truth. He wanted his people to know that the ark of the covenant, which contained his holy name and his Word, could no longer be found in the physical temple. God wanted his people to know that his holy name and his holy Word could now be found in the new ark, the Ark of Jesus, his one and only beloved Son, who had just become the cornerstone of the new living temple. By tearing the temple curtain in two and exposing the truth, YHWH wanted his people to no longer look for forgiveness of their sins through the old covenant but to turn to the new covenant of Jesus and the new covenant name. He wanted them to realize that Jesus, about whom they had been pondering for three years, was indeed the Passover lamb of God. He was sent from heaven to take away the sins of the world, exactly as John the Baptist had prophesied. In essence, by tearing the temple curtain in two, YHWH himself was destroying the old covenant and the old covenant ways and replacing them with the new.

The first covenant that YHWH made with the Israelites started on Nissan 14, 1447 BC. And now, approximately 1477 years later, on Nissan 14, AD 30, the day Jesus died, the first covenant ended and a new covenant began. The missing ark of the covenant was replaced on the day Yeshua, the Son of God, was crucified. The new ark of the covenant was the Ark of Jesus. Those who believed in the power of this Ark would be saved from eternal death.

In speaking of a new covenant he treats the first as obsolete. And what is becoming obsolete and growing old is ready to vanish away. (Heb. 8:13)

Chapter 17

Our High Priest

> "**And I will raise up for myself a faithful priest**, who shall do according to what is in my heart and in my mind; and **I will build him a sure house**." (1 Sam. 2:35a)

After Jesus was removed from the cross, his dead body was given to Joseph of Arimathea and Nicodemus, religious leaders who were secretly disciples of Jesus. They wrapped his body in linen cloths with a mixture of spices and laid him in Joseph's tomb. After a stone was rolled in front of the tomb and Roman soldiers sealed it and placed a guard, Jesus's body was in the heart of the earth for three days and three nights, exactly as he himself had prophesied (Matt. 12:40). On the first day of the week, when the women came to the tomb while it was still dark, they saw that the stone had been rolled away. When they went into the tomb, they did not see Jesus's body.

> But Mary stood weeping outside the tomb, and as she wept she stooped to look into the tomb; and she saw **two angels in white, sitting where the body of Jesus had been lain, one at the head and one at the feet**. They said to her, "Woman, why are you weeping?" She said to them, "Because they have taken away my Lord, and I do not know where they have laid him." (John 20:11–13)

The angels replied,

> **"Why do you seek the living among the dead**? Remember how he told you, while he was still in Galilee, that the Son of man must be delivered into the hands of sinful men, and be crucified, and on the third day, rise." (Luke 24:5b–7)

At the end of the three days and three nights, YHWH raised his Son, Yeshua, from the dead. Since the consequence of sin is death, Jesus had to physically die for taking the sins of the world upon his shoulders, but because Jesus himself was sinless, death could not hold him. Therefore, on the third day, YHWH raised his Son from the dead, and Jesus took on his new role as his Father's High Priest. In the same way Aaron became the first high priest, YHWH chose Jesus to be his final High Priest.

Do you remember how YHWH proved to the Israelites that he had chosen Aaron for this important position? If you recall, YHWH instructed Moses to gather rods from the leaders of each of the twelve tribes, and Aaron's rod was among these. Moses then put the rods before the ark of the covenant, and the man whose rod sprouted was the man chosen to be YHWH's high priest. When Aaron's rod put forth buds, produced blossoms, and bore ripe almonds, there was no denying that Aaron was God's chosen man to fill this critical position. When Aaron's rod came to life, it was God's way of speaking to the people over the mercy seat of the ark of the covenant, through a physical sign and wonder, so that there would be no doubt. Even though Aaron's rod appeared to be simply a dead branch, when Aaron used his rod upon God's command, he was able to perform miracles, signs, and wonders before Pharaoh and the people of Israel. Aaron's rod became known as "God's rod."

We now know that what occurred in the Old Testament was just foreshadowing of what Jesus, the Son of God, came to fulfill. Throughout Old Testament Scripture, Jesus is described as "the righteous branch," and during Jesus's ministry it was obvious to many that Jesus was the true "Rod of God." Because Jesus spoke the words and did the work his

Father gave him to do, miracles, signs, and wonders followed him wherever he went. On the day of Jesus's crucifixion, when his dead body was placed into the grave, God's "righteous branch" was in essence placed before the ark of the covenant, upon the "mercy seat" of the broken first covenant. Placed at Jesus's feet and his head were two cherubim—the two angels Mary saw in white. Their wings were spread over Jesus, overshadowing him, with their faces turned toward his. This time the cherubim were not made of gold, like the ones over the ark of the covenant. The angels Mary saw were YHWH's cherubim, sent from heaven to protect Jesus's body. For three days and three nights the eyes of the cherubim never turned from Jesus's face until the day he was raised gloriously from the dead by his Father. When Mary came to the tomb and found it empty, the two cherubim said to Mary, "Why do you seek the living among the dead?" It was God's way of speaking to Mary over the mercy seat of the ark of the covenant. It was as if God were telling Mary, the mother of Jesus, "My Righteous Branch has been laid before my divine name and my divine Word and I have found him worthy. Because my Son never denied my name or my Word while he walked this earth, my beloved Son who was once dead is now alive forevermore."

Because Jesus humbled himself and physically stood between life and death in order to stop the plague of death from being the consequence for sin, his Father found his sacrifice worthy and therefore brought his Son back to life. On the day of Jesus's resurrection, God proved to his people through a miracle that he had chosen his beloved Son, Jesus, not only to be his Prophet and Passover Lamb but also his High Priest. "For every high priest chosen among men is appointed to act on behalf of men in relation to God, *to offer gifts and sacrifices for sins*" (Heb. 5:1). All of the previous high priests served YHWH until their deaths. Since death could not hold Jesus, we know that he lives forever and will therefore serve YHWH as his High Priest throughout eternity. Because of his exalted position, Jesus is allowed to act on behalf of men in relation to God forevermore.

Remember that before Jesus, the high priests could only enter into the Holy of Holies and approach the ark of the covenant once a year to ask for forgiveness of sins for the people. They could enter only after they had made atonement for their own sins. Because Jesus was sinless, he had no personal sins to atone for and therefore had the right to enter into the Holy of Holies and into the presence of YHWH. However, as High Priest, he still needed to make atonement for the sins of the world. By physically taking on the punishment of death, even though he was innocent, Jesus was in effect placing the guilt, shame, and rebellion of the world on his own shoulders. Because he was sinless, he did not deserve the death of a notorious murderer; however, Jesus still offered himself as a substitute sacrifice for the sins of mankind in order to fulfill his Father's will. He laid down his own life as the perfect sacrifice, as a substitute for our own lives, as our Passover Lamb—so that eternal death with pass us over at his second coming.

> **But when Christ appeared as a high priest of the good things that have come**, then through the greater and more perfect tent (not made with hands, that is, not of this creation) **he entered once for all into the Holy Place, taking not the blood of goats and calves but his own blood, thus securing an eternal redemption.** (Heb. 9:11–12)
>
> **Therefore he is the mediator of a new covenant, so that those who are called may receive the promised eternal inheritance**, since a death has occurred which redeems them from the transgressions under the first covenant. (Heb. 9:15)
>
> **For Christ has entered**, not into a sanctuary made with hands, a copy of the true one, but **into heaven itself, now to appear in the presence of God on our behalf**. Nor was it to offer himself repeatedly, as the high priest enters the Holy Place yearly with blood not his own; for then he would have to suffer repeatedly since the foundation of the world. But as it is, **he has appeared once for all at the end of age to put away sin by the sacrifice of himself**. And just as it is appointed for men to die once, and after that comes judgment, **so Christ, having been offered once to bear the**

sins of many, will appear a second time, not to deal with sin but to save those who are eagerly waiting for him. (Heb. 9:24–28)

When I think about the blood that flowed from Jesus's body from all the torture that he experienced—shed for our sins—I can picture it flowing over the mercy seat of God's broken law, completely covering it. Jesus knew that his innocent life was the only sacrifice that would be sufficient to cover all of the times throughout history that his Father's law was disobeyed and his holy name taken in vain. Therefore, as our High Priest, Jesus spoke to his Father over the mercy seat, asking for the forgiveness of the world's sins. Having found his Son's sacrifice of his own life more than sufficient for the sins of the world, YHWH appointed his Son as the mediator of the new covenant.

Feast of Firstfruits

As the mediator of the new covenant, our new High Priest had one more duty that he had to attend to after he was raised from the dead. During the Feast of Passover and Unleavened Bread, there is a third feast called the Feast of Firstfruits. The original Feast of Firstfruits was a celebration of the spring barley harvest, which occurred just days after Passover. YHWH required the Israelites to bring to his temple the first sheaf of the barley harvest or, in other words, the first fruits, as a wave offering. A sheaf is a bundle of grains in the amount that would provide a daily portion of bread. It wasn't until the sheaf was waved before God and accepted that the fresh barley grains could be eaten (Lev. 23:9–14). Along with the sheaf, the high priest had to offer a male lamb without blemish as a burnt offering to YHWH. Therefore, until Jesus presented himself to the Father and was accepted as the first fruit of the dead and as the Lamb of God who takes away the sins of the world, the gift of the new covenant would not be made available to God's people. The day Jesus was raised from the dead, he said to Mary, "Do not hold me, for *I have not yet ascended to the Father*; but go to my brethren and say to them, I am ascending to my Father and your Father, to my God and your God" (John 20:17).

> But in fact Christ has been raised from the dead, **the first fruits of those who have fallen asleep**. For as by a man came death, by a man has come also the resurrection of the dead. For as in Adam all die, **so also in Christ shall all be made alive**. But each in his own order: **Christ the first fruits, then at his coming those who belong to Christ**. (1 Corin. 15:20–23)

Mary found Jesus alive on the Feast of Firstfruits. On this day, Jesus ascended into heaven as our High Priest and presented himself as the "first fruit" raised from the dead. He presented his body as the sheaf, or daily portion of "bread from heaven." When God accepted Jesus's offering, God gave Jesus the power and authority to give his disciples the fruit of the new covenant. That is why, when Jesus appeared to the disciples that night, he said to them, "Peace be with you. As the Father has sent me, even so I send you." And when he said this, he breathed on them and said to them, *"Receive the Holy Spirit"* (John 20:21–22). Jesus's disciples, with the exception of Judas, were the first to receive the gift of the Holy Spirit. They were the first to receive the fresh new grain, the new fruit of the new covenant, the fruit from the Tree of Life. With the Holy Spirit, the disciples now had the ability to communicate with YHWH in the name of Jesus. From now on they would not have to rely on human priests or prophets to communicate with their heavenly Father, because they could now speak to him directly.

After breathing the Holy Spirit upon the disciples, Jesus continued to appear to them and to many others for forty days. At the end of the forty days, Jesus led his disciples out as far as Bethany and, lifting up his hands, blessed them. While he was blessing them, he was carried up into heaven, and they returned to Jerusalem with great joy and were continually in the temple blessing God. Being our eternal High Priest, it is very likely that Jesus would have spoken the Aaronic blessing to his disciples. Just as the high priests of the Old Testament would pronounce this blessing on the people after their sins were forgiven, it would make sense for Jesus to do the same thing for his disciples since their sins had also been forgiven.

> "**YHWH** bless you and keep you;
> **YHWH** make his face to shine upon you, and be gracious to you;
> **YHWH** lift up his countenance upon you, and give you peace." (Num. 6:24–26 ESV)

As Jesus was carried up into heaven, his countenance was once again being lifted up before his disciples, and it brought them great peace. Remember, the purpose of the Aaronic blessing was to place YHWH's name upon the people, and that is exactly what Jesus was doing. As his disciples' new High Priest, Jesus placed his name upon the men who would bring the new covenant name to the world.

While looking through the Old Testament for prophecy on Jesus, I came across this passage in Zechariah, which gives a beautiful picture of YHWH clothing his Son, Yeshua, with the garments of the high priest after dying for the sins of the world. (Remember, Joshua and Yeshua are the same names in different languages.)

> Then he showed me **Joshua the high priest standing before the angel of YHWH, and Satan standing at his right hand to accuse him**. And YHWH said to Satan, "**YHWH rebuke you, O Satan**! YHWH who has chosen Jerusalem rebuke you! Is this not a brand plucked from the fire?" Now Joshua was standing before the angel, **clothed with filthy garments**. And the angel said to those who were standing before him, "**Remove the filthy garments from him**." And to him he said, "**Behold, I have taken your iniquity away from you, and I will clothe you with rich apparel**." And I said, "**Let them put a clean turban on his head**." (Zech. 3:1–5a)

Through this prophecy, we see a picture of YHWH seeing his Son clothed with the sins of the world, which are represented by the filthy garments. We also see Satan following Jesus into heaven in order to accuse him of unrighteousness, due to the sins of the world that he had taken upon himself. We then see YHWH recognizing the perfect sacrifice Jesus made for his people and stating that he should instead by clothed with the garments that only the high priest was worthy of wearing. The day Jesus ascended into heaven for the Feast of Firstfruits, he was clothed with the rich apparel of the high priest, like every other high priest before him, including the turban that had a plate of pure gold attached to it, which read, "Holy to YHWH." At this time, Jesus took his rightful place at the right hand of his heavenly Father in the Holy of Holies.

The New Law

The year that Jesus became our High Priest is the year the law changed and the old covenant sacrifices became obsolete.

> Now **if perfection had been attainable through the Levitical priesthood** (for under it the people received the law), **what further need would there have been for *another priest* to arise ... For when there is a change in the priesthood, there is necessarily a change in the law as well**. (Heb. 7:11–12)

What many people do not understand is that Jesus did not die on the cross in order to eliminate the entire law. Quite the opposite is true. While Jesus walked this earth, he himself was a living testimony to what our lives would look like if we kept the law exactly as YHWH gave it. God's commandments will always be the commandments because God's truth will always be the truth. God still asks us to lead holy lives by following his laws. What has changed, now that the Holy Spirit lives within us, is that God's law can be written upon our hearts, making it easier for us to resist temptation and to flee from Satan, thereby allowing us to keep YHWH's commandments. What has changed, with Jesus's death and resurrection, is the law concerning the way we are forgiven of our sins.

Before the sacrificial law for the forgiveness of sins was changed, the main sacrifices made on the Day of Atonement involved two male goats. After Aaron offered a bull as a sin offering for himself and his household, he would bring the two goats before YHWH. Aaron would cast lots upon the two goats, one lot for YHWH and the other lot for Azazel. The goat on which the lot fell for YHWH was offered as a sin offering for the people of Israel. The blood of this goat would be sprinkled over the mercy seat of the ark of the covenant in order to atone for the sins of the entire assembly of Israel. Aaron would then present the live goat chosen for Azazel and confess over him all the iniquities of the people, thereby placing the sins of the nation onto this goat. This second goat chosen for Azazel was led outside the city into the wilderness, a solitary land, symbolically taking the sins of the nation with it, never to return (Leviticus 16). Before the second goat was led outside of the city into the wilderness, the high priest would take a piece of white wool and dip it into the blood of the sacrificed first goat. He would then tie one piece of this wool to the horn of the second goat and the other piece of the wool to the temple door. If the sins of the people were forgiven after the second goat was led out of the city, then the bloodstained wool on the temple door would miraculously turn white, thereby giving them confirmation.

This same ceremony was performed year after year, just as YHWH had commanded it, and every year the bloodstained strip of wool miraculously turned white. It turned white, that is, until the year YHWH raised Jesus as our eternal High Priest. Six months after Jesus died for our sins as the Passover Lamb, the bloodstained strip of wool failed to turn white on the Day of Atonement.[1] In the year of Jesus's death, resurrection, and ascension into heaven, the Jewish people did not receive confirmation that their sins had been forgiven. I can only imagine the questions that went through everyone's minds on that particular Day of Atonement. The high priest on that day must have questioned his procedures, thinking that maybe he had done something wrong. What they didn't realize is that the law concerning the sacrifices changed the day that Jesus, the Son of God, established the new covenant. It is recorded in Jewish history that for forty years following Christ's death and resurrection, the wool failed to turn white, which means that for forty years the Jewish people, the ones who did not come to know Christ as their Messiah, continued in the first covenant laws and did not receive forgiveness of sins as in previous years. And yet, for forty years they kept trying. Finally, YHWH allowed the Romans to destroy the second temple in AD 70, thereby eliminating this sacrificial system.

God had given these Jewish people forty years to ask themselves, "What is it? What have we done wrong? Why did the wool stop turning white?" He wanted them to start asking themselves, "What happened in that first year when we no longer received proof that our sins were forgiven?" When the Jewish people never came to the right conclusion that Jesus, the Son of God, had been sent to forgive them of their sins, YHWH finally allowed the temple to be destroyed, thereby ending the old covenant sacrifices along with it. He tried to place the name of his Son, Jesus, on the Jewish people, but most of them just could not see the truth. So God allowed the second temple to be destroyed so that they could no longer take his name in vain by continuing with the sacrifices. His Son had become the perfect and everlasting Passover Lamb who takes away the sins of the world.

> "Come now, let us reason together, says YHWH: **though your sins are like scarlet, they shall be as white as snow**; though they are **red like crimson, they shall become like wool**. If you are willing and obedient you **shall eat the good of the land**; but if you refuse and rebel, you shall be eaten by the sword; for the mouth of YHWH has spoken." (Isa. 1:18–20 ESV)

With our new High Priest came a new, perfect way to ask for forgiveness of sins, and the animal sacrificial system was no longer the way. From then on, Jesus was "the Way." Only through Jesus can sins be turned as white as snow.

Jewish Feasts

A few years ago, I did not know the first thing about the Jewish feasts. In fact, I did not even know that God had commanded his people to celebrate seven feasts every year. It was not until I discovered that a lot of our traditions during Christmas and Easter are actually taken from pagan traditions that I became determined to figure out the proper ways of celebrating Jesus's birth, death, and resurrection. So in the year 2010, my friend and I decided that our families were going to celebrate Jesus's death and resurrection through the feast of Passover. Since I knew nothing about Passover, I made a prayer request at Bible study for God to give me the knowledge on how a Christian should celebrate this biblical feast. I needed the information quickly because Passover was only one month away. On that very day, one of the ladies in my group went home and started cleaning her bedroom. As she was dusting around her husband's nightstand, she discovered a book. Even though she had been dusting around this book for about a year, she had never noticed its title until this day. The book's title is *Haggadah: From Exodus to the Cross, A Christian Passover Celebration Guidebook* by Steven B. Weiss.[2] Needless to say, she brought the book to me the following week and said, "Will this help you?" That first year and for the years ever since, we have been using this very book to celebrate Jesus's death and resurrection through the celebration of Passover. What is truly amazing is that God provided me with the book I needed to celebrate his feast before I even put any effort into researching Passover on my own. My prayer was quickly answered, I believe, because YHWH obviously thinks his feasts are important.

The Passover observance that Jewish people celebrate today is an incredible foreshadowing of Jesus's death and resurrection, and they don't even know it. Christians who celebrate Passover in conjunction with the Lord's Supper get a full picture of God's plan for salvation and how it began, since the days of Moses. It is a picture of why God commanded his people to celebrate Passover year after year. He did not want his people to forget this important piece of history, because he was going to do it again through his Son, Jesus, and he was going to do it on the same day.

I can honestly say that celebrating Passover that first year was the most fulfilling celebration that I had ever experienced. For the first time in my life, I felt that I had worshipped YHWH and Jesus the way he wanted me to. The morning hours were spent preparing my table, the food, and the Seder plate as instructed. Once our friends arrived, we started our celebration with a recounting of when YHWH led the Israelites out of Egypt, and the evening culminated with celebrating the Lord's Supper. It was done around my dining room table with my dear friends and family. The entire celebration took approximately three hours, and I really feel that it was the first time our celebration of Jesus's life, death, and resurrection was concentrated solely on him. There were no outside social pressures or traditions involved, such as Easter eggs and bunnies and buying gifts for our children. It was an extraordinary day spent celebrating Jesus, as YHWH had ordained it in the days of Moses. It was as if, for the very first time, while celebrating Passover, I saw the connection between the Old and the New Testaments. The entire celebration was an "aha" moment for me.

After I experienced Passover for the first time, I prayed that God would teach me about his other six feasts. As I should have expected, this prayer was also quickly answered. Approximately six months later, my girlfriend bought me a Jewish calendar, which explained all of the major Jewish feasts. She was buying this calendar for herself, and she just happened to think I might also find it interesting. Or was it God whispering in her ear, "Buy this for Judy also"? What God knew is that I would need the calendar for the writing of this book. He therefore prompted my girlfriend to buy the calendar for me months before I even knew I was writing a book about him and his holy name. It wasn't until I was six months into writing this book that I just happened to look at the name of this calendar, which I had never noticed before. It was called, "Names of God." Now what are the chances of that! When I saw the name of the calendar, I knew that it had been another gift from YHWH. Again, I realized that when we ask God to teach us his truth, he will go to great lengths to provide us with all of the necessary resources in order to find it.

Without the revelation of who Jesus is, the biblical feasts don't make much sense anymore to the Jewish people. Since they haven't had a temple now since AD 70, the sacrifices required for these feasts can no longer be fulfilled as YHWH instructed them. As of now, on the Day of Atonement, all they can do is pray and hope for the best since they don't receive proof anymore that their sins are forgiven. What the Jewish people do not realize is that only with Jesus Christ do the seven feasts now make sense and that through his first and second coming he will fulfill them all.

Most Christians do not realize how important an understanding of the Jewish Old Testament laws, feasts, and history is to understanding the purpose of Jesus's life. Now that I personally understand this connection, it truly boggles my mind that the church does not celebrate Jesus's death and resurrection on the same days as the Jewish people celebrate Passover, the Feast of Unleavened Bread, and the Feast of Firstfruits since they occurred on the same days and Jesus came as their fulfillment. I think of how powerful a witness the church could be to the Jewish community if we only chose as Christians to celebrate Jesus's death and resurrection during YHWH's feasts. If we did, maybe then the Jewish community would realize why their sacrificial law was taken away from them in the first place; and through this understanding they might personally come to know their Messiah.

Jewish Month of Nissan

We discussed in the previous chapters that it was during the *last* three feasts, which occur in the seventh month of the Jewish calendar, that Jesus was dedicated in the temple forty days after his birth. We discovered that the meaning of this seventh month is "beginnings." And now we have seen that Jesus's death, resurrection, and ascension all occurred on the exact dates of the *first* three feasts. These first three feasts all occur in the first month of the Jewish calendar, the month of Nissan. The word *Nissan* is a cognate to the word *nissim*, meaning "miracles, redemption." The Babylonian name for this month means "sanctuary, or first month." The Canaanite meaning of this month means "to move or start." The Sumerian meaning is "first fruits" or "offering."[3] All that occurred through Jesus in Nissan is explained through the meanings of this special month in these different languages. What *began* in the seventh month with Jesus's being dedicated *holy to YHWH* came to fruition in the first month of Nissan, which brings light to its Canaanite meaning of "to move," or "to start." Jesus was sent into this world to *establish* a new covenant as our Passover Lamb and High Priest. In the month of Nissan, with its various meanings of miracles, redemption, sanctuary, first fruits, and offering, Jesus successfully accomplished all that his Father sent him to do.

Before a grain of wheat is able to sprout new life, it first has to fall to the ground and die to itself. Only after it dies to itself is it able to miraculously produce new life. Because Jesus took it upon himself to stand between life and death, his dead body was resurrected to new life after being placed before God's divine name and his Word. From YHWH's dead, righteous branch came not only buds and blossoms but also the fruit of the Holy Spirit. On the day of Jesus's resurrection, he received a glorified body to be joined with his sinless Spirit, along with everlasting life. He was also, once again, given direct communication with his Father.

On the day of Jesus's resurrection, he was raised from mortality to immortality, and he became alive in YHWH. Being alive forevermore, Jesus became the mediator of the new living covenant. Because he is the mediator, the same fruit of the Holy Spirit that Jesus received is available to those individuals who believe that he came to forgive them of their sins and to be their LORD and Savior. The new covenant isn't for everyone; it is just for those who believe Jesus was and is the Great I AM.

The LORD's Prayer

For those who do believe this and decide to follow Jesus, he gives eternal life and forgiveness of sins, enabling us to have a direct relationship with our Father. One of the best gifts that Jesus gave us was to teach us how to pray to the Father in his name. As our High Priest, Jesus knew that

Encountering the Great I Am

we would need to know the names by which we should pray in order for there to be full communication. So when the disciples asked Jesus how to pray, he gave them what we call the LORD's Prayer.

> **Our Father who art in heaven,**
> **Hallowed be thy name**.
> Thy kingdom come,
> Thy will be done,
> On earth as it is in heaven.
> Give us this day our daily bread;
> And forgive us our debts,
> As we also have forgiven our debtors;
> And lead us not into temptation,
> But deliver us from evil.
> (Matt. 6:9–13)

Through this prayer, Jesus gave us YHWH's preferred title of *Father*. In fact, it is how Jesus addresses YHWH throughout the Gospels. Jesus wanted us to know that our heavenly Father is a personal God who invites us to call him *Abba Father*. He wanted us to know that YHWH is the one and only true Father who created us, adores us, provides, disciplines, forgives, and unconditionally loves us as his children. Jesus wanted us to know that by addressing YHWH as *Father,* we are addressing him with more than just a title. Just as it is rare that a child calls his or her earthly father by his given name, YHWH prefers us to call him Father because it truly represents who he is to us. Jesus wanted us to know that YHWH is indeed our ultimate heavenly Father, who cares deeply about our personal lives. When we dare to call him Father, YHWH knows that we have moved beyond the impersonal titles of *God* or *Lord* and have instead moved into a personal familial relationship with him—a loving relationship, where daily communication can take place.

Jesus then told his disciples that anything they prayed to the Father should be asked in his name: "Whatever you ask in my name, I will do it, that the Father may be glorified in the Son; *if you ask anything in my name, I will do it*" (John 14:13–14). Being our High Priest, Jesus knew that communication with the Father is only complete when both the Urim and Thummim are pondered with our heart, soul, and mind. By asking us to pray to the Father, in Jesus's name, we are being asked to ponder on the holiness of both the Father's and the Son's names—the names of both the first and the second covenants. Because Jesus manifested YHWH's name to us while he walked on this earth, we can be sure of to whom we are praying when we pray to the Father. And when we pray in Jesus's name, YHWH is sure that we know that it is only through what Jesus did on our behalf that we have communication in the first place. By praying in Jesus's name, we are acknowledging that it is Jesus's blood that covers our sin and makes us righteous before the Father. Jesus gives believers this key to communicating with our Father because that is what YHWH truly desires, an open and direct relationship with his children. Jesus knows firsthand that it is when we ponder on both the Illuminator's and Completer's names that we receive communication and revelation through God's voice, his Word, dreams and visions, and his Shekinah glory.

The consequence of sin is death, and it always will be. Just as Jesus died once in order to take on the sins of the world, we are all appointed to physically die once for our own individual sins. But because of Jesus Christ's perfect sacrifice, death has finally lost its sting. At the time of our deaths, no longer do believers lose communication with their heavenly Father. Because we receive YHWH's Holy Spirit in Jesus's name and it becomes one with our spirits, on the day of our physical deaths, our spirits ascend to be with the Father until the day our bodies are raised from mortality to immortality and are reunited with our spirits. In addition, while we walk this earth, we are given full communication with our Father because of what Jesus did on our behalf. And even better yet, because Jesus is currently sitting at the right hand of the Father, he daily intercedes on our behalf in regard to the desires of our hearts.

While Jesus walked this earth he was YHWH's ultimate Prophet. At his death, Jesus became the ultimate Passover Lamb. Finally, at his resurrection, Jesus attained the role of High Priest. He is now sitting at the right hand of our Father in heaven. While he walked this earth,

Jesus knew the earth was not his home, and now he is finally back in heaven where he is once again "one with the Father," a place he desires for us all.

> "And I am no longer in the world, but they are in the world, and I am coming to you. **Holy Father, keep them in your name, which you have given me, that they may be one, even as we are one.**" (John 17:11 ESV)

Chapter 18

The Holy Spirit

"**If you love me, you will keep my commandments. And I will pray the Father, and he will give you another Counselor, to be with you for ever**, even the Spirit of truth, whom the world cannot receive, because it neither sees him nor knows him; you know him, **for he dwells with you, and will be in you.**" (John 14:15–17)

"These things I have spoken to you, while I am still with you. But **the Counselor, the Holy Spirit, whom the Father will send in my name, he will teach you all things, and bring to your remembrance all that I have said to you. Peace I leave with you; my peace I give to you.**" (John 14:25–27a)

Jesus breathed the Holy Spirit onto the disciples on the evening of his resurrection. This was the day the disciples genuinely believed all that Jesus had told them. They believed that Jesus was who he said he was and that he was truly the Son of God, sent from the Father. They believed he was sent to die for their sins and to defeat death. They believed they were sinners in need of a Savior, and they believed that Jesus was that Savior, their Messiah, sent to lead them out of the enemy's hands. Because of their belief, they received the gift of YHWH's Spirit, sent in Jesus's name, to reside within them.

Jesus knew that his disciples would want to know who would go with them after he left this earth and ascended to the Father. These men had spent three years in Jesus's presence, and by his presence they had been made distinct from all the people on earth. The thought of not being with Jesus or hearing his voice daily would be too much for them to bear. YHWH knew this would be the case, and therefore he chose to send his Spirit so that they would not have to live without the voice of God in their lives ever again. By receiving the Counselor, these men would continue to be made distinct from all people because they would have direct communication with their heavenly Father through Jesus, our High Priest. The day YHWH sent his Holy Spirit to dwell within his disciples, YHWH's prophecy to Moses came true once again: "I will dwell among the people of Israel and will be their God" (Exo. 29:45). By receiving the Holy Spirit in Jesus's name, the disciples were made righteous in front of God. The day Jesus breathed on them was their "salvation day." From there on, they could be sure that they would spend eternity with their heavenly Father.

The Journey

For the disciples, their journey was far from over. In fact, their journey as redeemed children of God had really just begun. Suddenly, upon receiving the Holy Spirit, everything that Jesus had spoken to them over the years came flooding back to their minds and now made complete sense. For the questions the disciples still had, Jesus filled in the holes for the next forty days as he continued to speak to his men about the kingdom of God. Now that they finally believed, Jesus continued to teach them face to face in order to solidify their faith. He continued to let them hear him speak so that they would recognize his voice when he spoke to them through the Holy Spirit.

At some point during these forty days, I can imagine the disciples asking Jesus what they could do to contribute to the kingdom of God. Jesus had already done so much for them; they would want to know what they could do for him. So immediately before ascending into heaven, Jesus gave his disciples their mission.

> "**All authority in heaven and on earth has been given to me. Go therefore and make disciples of all nations, baptizing them in the name of the Father, and of the Son, and of the Holy Spirit, teaching them to observe all that I have commanded you**; and lo, I am with you always, to the close of the age." (Matt. 28:18b–20)

The pieces of God's puzzle, through Christ's death and resurrection, had come together beautifully for the disciples and had formed a picture of salvation for all men. However, there was one missing piece. Who would take this good news of Jesus Christ to the world? Jesus had told Peter the day he met him that he would teach him how to be fishers of men. Now was the time for Peter to use all that Jesus had taught him. Jesus could not wait any longer. He was going to ascend to be with his Father in heaven to sit at his right hand, so he told his disciples not to leave Jerusalem and to wait for the promise of the Father. "But you shall *receive power* when the Holy Spirit has come upon you; and you shall be my witnesses in Jerusalem and in all Judea and Samaria and to the end of the earth" (Acts 1:8). Once Jesus defeated death, his disciples had conclusive evidence that he was the Son of God. The day Jesus rose from the dead was the defining moment in their lives that could not be denied. There were no more questions and no more doubts on the identity of Jesus.

During the years of Jesus's ministry, he was personally molding and shaping his disciples' lives. By speaking YHWH's truth into them daily, Jesus was slowly changing their identities. Through it all he was cleansing them of their sins and their sinful ways so that their thoughts and actions would start reflecting Jesus's thoughts and ways. Because they literally followed in Jesus's footsteps, their identities started looking more Christ-like day by day. What Jesus was doing during their time together was preparing his disciples for the ministry that he had planned for them before they were even born. Because Jesus had already spent three years speaking truth into their lives, it didn't take much time for them to be prepared for their mission. At this point, they just needed to wait in Jerusalem together until they were *clothed with the power of the Holy Spirit.* This power from above would give them the ability to complete what Jesus had called them to do. Remember, even Jesus was not ready for his mission in life until YHWH bestowed upon him the power of his Holy Spirit. It wasn't until the day that Jesus was baptized and commissioned that Jesus was empowered for the position to which he had been called.

> **When the day of Pentecost [Feast of Weeks] had come,** they were all together in one place. And suddenly a sound came from heaven like the rush of a mighty wind, and it filled all the house where they were sitting. **And there appeared to them tongues as of fire, distributed and resting on each one of them. And they were all filled with the Holy Spirit and began speaking in tongues, as the Spirit gave them utterance.** (Acts 2:1–4)

John the Baptist said that Jesus would not baptize with water but with the Holy Spirit and fire. In these passages we see tongues as of fire distributed and resting on each one of the disciples. Without further details, we do not know exactly how these tongues of fire rested upon them, but these passages remind me of what happened to Isaiah when YHWH appointed him as a prophet to the nation. As recorded in Isaiah 6, after Isaiah was given a vision of YHWH on his throne, surrounded by his seraphim, he proclaimed that he was lost and a man of unclean lips and that he dwelt in in the midst of people of unclean lips, and therefore he was not worthy of being YHWH's prophet. The seraphim placed a *burning coal from the altar onto Isaiah's lips* and God said, "Behold, this has touched your lips; your guilt is taken away, and your sin forgiven." In response to God's incredible gift of forgiveness, when Isaiah was asked again by God, "Whom shall I send, and who will go for us?" Isaiah confidently replied, "Here I am! Send me."

I believe that in the same way Isaiah was appointed as YHWH's prophet, the disciples were appointed as Jesus's prophets. Imagine *red-hot burning coals* being placed on the disciples' lips. From afar, what would it look like? From the witness' point of view, the burning coals might look like *tongues as of fire* resting on their lips. I believe what God did on this day of Pentecost was take burning coals from his altar where Jesus's body had been sacrificed and place them on the disciples' unclean lips, like he did with Isaiah. When this was done, it symbolized that their sins were forgiven and their guilt was wiped clean. On this day, the disciples were given a new position in God's kingdom. From this day forward, the men who simply followed in Jesus's footsteps for three years became prophets of Jesus and would forever be known as the apostles.

More Witnesses

After the *power* of the Holy Spirit "*descended upon them and rested,*" the apostles were given the ability to speak in multiple languages, as the Holy Spirit gave them utterance. Because Pentecost was the fourth feast ordained by YHWH to celebrate every year, there were men in Jerusalem from every nation under heaven. The Feast of Weeks, also known as Pentecost, was one of the three pilgrimage feasts in which every male was instructed to appear before YHWH in Jerusalem. These three pilgrimage feasts are the Feast of Unleavened Bread, the Feast of Weeks, and the Feast of Tabernacles (Deut. 16:16–17). Because all males were instructed to travel to Jerusalem each year in order to fulfill the requirements for these feasts, it meant that there were a lot of God's chosen people in Jerusalem on these particular days. What this requirement ensured is that there would be a lot of witnesses to the extraordinary events YHWH had planned for his people.

We have already discussed the fact that Jesus's death, resurrection, and first ascension to the Father were fulfilled on the exact days of Passover, the Feast of Unleavened Bread, and the Feast of Firstfruits. Because the seven-day Feast of Unleavened Bread immediately followed Passover and incorporated the Feast of Firstfruits, there were a lot of witnesses to Jesus's death and resurrection. The multitudes of males who came to Jerusalem for the pilgrimage feast of Unleavened Bread would have seen or heard firsthand all of the miraculous events that had taken place the day Jesus was crucified and would have been in the city to hear the buzz of his resurrection.

After Jesus's resurrection, Scripture tells us that Jesus made ten distinct appearances, including first to Peter, then to the twelve, and finally to five hundred brethren at one time. It is likely that some of the five hundred who witnessed Jesus alive were some of the males who had made their pilgrimage journey to Jerusalem for the Feast of Unleavened Bread and decided to stay in the city for a little while longer to see what happened. And now, fifty days later, all of the same males would have returned to Jerusalem to fulfill the requirement for the second pilgrimage feast, the Feast of Weeks. Those males who saw firsthand the tongues of fire resting on the apostles would have known that something incredible was occurring because they would have remembered what they had seen or heard during the Feast of Unleavened Bread. Those who did not see the Holy Spirit descend on the apostles firsthand would soon hear of what happened since word of this miraculous event would have spread quickly. Once these men heard the apostles suddenly speaking to them in their own languages, they had to have known that what they were witnessing was an act of God. All of the disciples started powerfully preaching the gospel of Jesus Christ and the kingdom of God, which Jesus had adequately prepared them to speak about. Many people who heard the apostles speak knew that what they were hearing was absolute truth, and, as a result, three thousand souls were baptized on that same day during the celebration of the Feast of Weeks.

The Feast of Weeks was a feast that occurred in the third month of Sivan. It was on this day, according to Jewish tradition, that YHWH had spoken to the Israelites on Mount Sinai and given them his name and his Word, his first covenant. On this day when YHWH spoke, there were many witnesses. And now, hundreds of years later, YHWH was speaking again, this time through the power of his Holy Spirit given to Jesus's apostles. The words the apostles spoke to all present were the words of the second covenant and the new covenant name, the good news of Jesus Christ. These two monumental events in history occurred on the very same day of the year—the Feast of Weeks (Pentecost).

What I have discovered through all of God's teachings concerning his seven feasts is that they form a timeline of his extraordinary events. YHWH instructed his people to keep these feasts so that they would not miss out on his wonderful gifts that he would present to them in the future. The dates of YHWH's feasts are the dates that God did extraordinary things, first for the people of Israel and then for the world through Jesus. They are the dates when God provided deliverance from the enemy, forgiveness of sins, his Word, and his truth. All of the previous celebrations of YHWH's feasts were simply "holy rehearsals" of their ultimate glory through Christ.

Jewish Month of Sivan

It should be no surprise that the third month of Sivan has several incredible meanings, just like all the other months in which the feasts take place. To the Jewish people, the meaning associated with *Sivan* is the power "to walk, to move, and to accelerate" in our service of God. During Sivan the Jews receive the ability to walk strongly and steadily on two legs. This month is considered the month of "vision" because their forefathers saw the revelation of YHWH on Mount Sinai. In addition, the Babylonian meaning of the name of this month is "brick-making," while the Canaanite meaning is "to appoint" or "to mark."[1]

Again, I cannot think of better meanings to describe what happened on the Feast of Weeks. On the day YHWH spoke to his people on Mount Sinai, he marked and appointed them as his children by giving them his name. Likewise, on the day the apostles were given the power of the Holy Spirit, they spoke about the good news of Jesus Christ. On that very day, *three thousand* individuals were marked and appointed as the first children of the new covenant. The giving of the Holy Spirit, through their baptism in the name of the Father, the Son, and the Holy Spirit, allowed these people to be made distinct as disciples of Jesus. With the Holy Spirit residing within them, they were given the ability to walk strongly and steadily in their service to YHWH because of their new ability to communicate with him. On this day, YHWH made the very first *bricks*, or *living stones*, that would eventually build his church.

During the Feast of Weeks, it was a requirement for the high priest to present an offering of new grain to YHWH in the temple. Therefore, since Jesus was the new High Priest, he needed to present an offering of "new grain" of the new covenant to YHWH. What Jesus presented to his Father on this particular Feast of Weeks were the three thousand individuals who were baptized in YHWH's holy name. What a righteous offering it was.

On the day the tongues of fire rested on the apostles, YHWH's "sacred fire" was back for all to see. And as we learned from the prophet Elijah so long ago, "You call on the name of your god and I will call on the name of YHWH; and *the God who answers by fire, he is God*" (1 Kings 18:24a). For the ten days that the apostles waited for the power of the Holy Spirit to descend upon them, Scripture tells us that they gathered together, and with one accord they devoted themselves to prayer. During this time, the apostles called on the name of their heavenly Father YHWH and his Son, Jesus, and asked for all that Jesus had promised them. I imagine that the disciples spent their time praying the LORD's Prayer exactly as Jesus had taught them, asking YHWH *for his will to be done on earth as it is in heaven*—in Jesus's holy name. YHWH answered their prayers through his sacred fire sent from heaven. With YHWH's sacred fire, the disciples received Jesus's power, authority, and boldness to literally change the world.

Clothed with the Power of the Holy Spirit

Just as there is a difference in knowing the name of Jesus and *knowing* Jesus intimately, there is a difference in *receiving* the Holy Spirit on the day of our salvation and *being clothed in the power* of the Holy Spirit. It happened on two separate occasions for both Jesus and his apostles. I can personally testify that is how it also happened to me. Twelve years after I asked Jesus to be my LORD and Savior, YHWH brought about "an awakening of the Holy Spirit" within me that has changed me forever. After God spoke to me through my own sacred fire, I came to know without a doubt that he existed. Not too long after that, I asked his Son, Jesus, to be my LORD and Savior. I remember the day I was saved like it was yesterday. The moment I asked Jesus to reside in my heart, I immediately felt chills from my head to my toes for an entire two minutes. Since I was alone and driving, I remember this experience very clearly. At the same time that I was trying to stay focused on my driving, I was being filled with YHWH's Holy Spirit sent in Jesus's name. There was no doubt in my mind that an incredible event had just taken place. On that day, Jesus came into my life and started to teach me how to follow in his footsteps. He started immediately because he knew that we had a lot to accomplish and that it would take years.

The first order of business was to get me to hear and read his Father's Word on a weekly basis. He knew I needed truth spoken into my life before any changes would ever be possible. So the first thing the Holy Spirit prompted me to do is to dust off my Bible that I had not opened since high school and start reading God's Word. Because I had a lot of questions, I started to talk about YHWH openly with my friends at work and with my neighbors. Now that I had heard God's voice and accepted his Son as my LORD and Savior, I figured that I needed to find out more about them.

The second thing Jesus prodded me to do is to start attending church again. Occasionally, my husband and I would attend a local church that was close to our home; however, it seemed that we stayed home on Sundays more often than not. My attendance at church prior to receiving the Holy Spirit was more out of guilt than a true desire to be there. So Jesus prompted one of my husband's friends to invite us to North Point Community Church. We had heard that North Point was a nondenominational church, was extremely large, had a rock band, and that the preacher spoke for thirty minutes every Sunday. My husband and I had been raised in very conservative churches that had fifteen-minute sermons. Even though we were hesitant to attend, our friends assured us that we would not be disappointed. All I can say is that particular day changed our thoughts about church forever. The service was simple. We worshipped and praised YHWH and Jesus for the first thirty minutes. We then heard God's words spoken directly from Bible and learned how to apply these verses to our lives. I had never been to a church quite like this one. The churches my husband and I had attended our entire lives were steeped in man-made traditions. This church was different.

For the first time in my life, I actually remembered the content of the sermon beyond the day that it was spoken. It became commonplace for my husband and me to discuss our pastor's sermons throughout the entire week. This was new territory for us, and it was exciting. For the first time in our marriage, we discussed our beliefs in God, we shared our questions and wonders, and we grew in our faith as a couple. By attending North Point Community Church, I could feel my Spirit coming alive, which is exactly why Jesus sent us there. It was during this time that I came to realize that it is so much more fulfilling to talk about YHWH and what he is up to in this world than my own life.

So Jesus had me back in church hearing his Father's Word weekly, and I was reading my Bible on my own, but he knew that more would be needed. That is when YHWH introduced me to my friend Rachel. Because God was involved, our friendship was a match made in heaven. YHWH knew what he was doing when he introduced us. Because we both liked talking about God and sharing the things we were learning, we became fast friends. Together, our faith in Jesus Christ grew.

Then one day Rachel asked me to attend a Bible study with her. I knew the invitation was most likely from YHWH, so I agreed to join her. That decision was the best decision I have ever made. From day one, I felt like it was exactly where God wanted me to be. For the first time since I had begun reading my Bible, my study of YHWH's Word became more structured. I attended the same Community Bible Study for the next eleven years. During these years of truly digging into YHWH's truth, I learned so much about YHWH, Jesus, and myself. I encourage you if you haven't already joined a Bible study to try it. It was a life-changing decision for me.

In my new resolve to walk with Jesus, every day I was being shaped more and more like Christ. But as I said, when Jesus first met me, he knew it would be a long journey. During this time, several events happened in my life and my husband's life that made us start questioning exactly what we were doing. Like many forty-year-olds, we started questioning what life was all about, along with our habits and our relationships. So God began to prune things out of our lives. Everything that was harmful to my life was cut out of it: unhealthy relationships, worldly habits, and distractions. Anything that kept me from furthering my relationship with him was eliminated. At the time I did not understand what was going on, and it was very painful; but YHWH did understand because he was the one doing the pruning. It was like a gardener pruning a rosebush. In order for a rosebush to continue to blossom, year after year, all of the dead blooms have to be cut off. Sometimes entire branches need to be removed in order for the sun to reach the healthy branches. As every gardener knows, pruning is done so that, in the following year, the rosebush will be more beautiful and stronger than ever before. Well, that is exactly what was happening to me, even though I didn't know it at the time. YHWH had different plans for my life, and he needed me to be able bloom more than ever, so he cut all the unhealthy branches out of it.

Then one summer, I read and studied a book called *Waking the Dead: The Glory of a Heart Fully Alive* by John Eldredge.[2] My friends and I studied this book over a ten-week period, and because of it, my life changed forever. The premise of this book is that in order to have the Holy Spirit truly reside in your heart, you have to get your whole heart back. Because of a lifetime of Satan attacking and breaking your heart into pieces, there is no home for the Holy Spirit. Even though that is where our Father sent his Holy Spirit to reside, there is too much noise going on inside to ever be able to hear him speaking. Only after you get your whole heart back by dealing with all of the broken pieces will there truly be peace and clear communication.

For ten weeks, I made a concerted effort to deal with all of my past hurts, my insecurities, and my lack of self-esteem. Through these ten weeks I came to realize the power Satan has over us in our everyday lives. The devil doesn't want us to have whole hearts, because with whole hearts we are able to clearly hear what YHWH has to say. Therefore, Satan does his best to keep our hearts in as many pieces as he can manipulate. Throughout this entire study, I asked YHWH to help me get my whole heart back, and that is exactly what he gave me.

After spending time allowing God to mend my heart, I can honestly say that I had never before felt such peace. Almost immediately, the destructive self-talk that had plagued me my entire life was completely gone.

I came to understand that all of that self-talk was lies spoken to me by Satan himself. He wanted my thoughts to be so preoccupied with my own self-doubts that nothing else could formulate in my brain. He didn't want me to hear from my LORD and Savior or know his will for my life. Well, no more! I said goodbye to Satan's lies. I covered myself with the blood of Jesus and told Satan that he had no more hold of me. Finally, for the first time, I felt a complete peace throughout my entire being that was beyond understanding. It was a true, joyful peace that only YHWH could have brought into my life. Unbeknownst to me, I felt this peace because Jesus had finally completed his preparations for me to receive God's mission for my life. My heavenly Father had determined that I was finally ready to be "clothed with the power of the Holy Spirit."

Let me tell you what YHWH did. I find it so interesting how God accomplishes his will for his children. On November 4, 2010, YHWH gave me (or allowed to me to catch) a cold. After about five days, my cold went away, except for a residual cough. I didn't really think much about it, until about week twelve. I decided to finally see a doctor, or should I say doctors. After seeing many specialists and enduring many tests, I still had no answer for why I was coughing. It was during this time that I found myself standing in front of the Christian Inspiration aisle at a bookstore. I needed something to read, so I asked YHWH, "What do you want me to read?" Out of the corner of my eye I caught a glimpse of a book on healing, titled *Power to Heal* by Joan Hunter.[3] I thought, *Well, maybe it will help me with my cough*. So I bought the book. As I began to read, I quickly realized that the author of the book had received the gift of healing from the Holy Spirit. When she lays her hands on people, they are healed. Her parents had this gift as well. So I continued reading the book, and by the time I was finished, I was jealous. That's right—I was jealous once again. I wasn't even thinking about my cough anymore or how I could receive my own healing;

instead, I was thinking about how jealous I was of this woman's gift. Not that I wanted the gift of healing, but I wanted my own gift from the Holy Spirit. Of course, YHWH knew this would be the case. Many times during my walk with him, he has used my jealousy in order to push me further down the path he has planned for me.

Asking God for Everything

On the night I finished the book, I did something I have never done before. I had just turned the lights off and was alone in my bedroom. In complete darkness, I lifted my hands into the air toward heaven and boldly said, "*God, I want everything the Holy Spirit has to offer me! Don't hold back!*" It was a request that I had never made before. Because YHWH had brought me to a place of peace, I could finally see all that he had done for me through the years. Therefore, I was ready to do whatever he called me to do for his kingdom. On that night, I asked my LORD and Savior to send me *everything* the Holy Spirit had to offer me. I had nothing in mind when I made that request; I just knew that I wanted it all! On that night, it was as if I were saying, "Here I am, LORD! Send me."

Nothing magical happened on that night that I was aware of, other than I felt like YHWH and I were a little closer in our communication. It wasn't until about ten days later that I knew my prayer had been heard. A few weeks prior to this night, I had stumbled across the fact that God has a divine name. I found it to be a very interesting topic and thought I would write an opening for my Bible study group. My friend Rachel, who had since become the teaching director of our Bible study, told me that an opening on God's name would be great. So on one Sunday afternoon in March 2011, I spent four hours writing my opening. I was so excited when I finished that I immediately called Rachel to find out the scheduled date. To my surprise and dismay, my friend told me the open slot had already been filled. She had forgotten to tell me. She tried to make me feel better by telling me that maybe

YHWH was going to show me more about his name. So that was that—or so I thought.

Was it really Rachel that had forgotten to tell me, or was that part of YHWH's plan? He knew that if I didn't write what I already knew about his divine name on that day in March, I would not be ready for what he had in store for me. I would not be prepared for my gift. It was the next day, while completing my Bible study in the Gospel of Luke, that YHWH began to show me his divine name throughout the New Testament. Up until then, I had only looked for his divine name in the Old Testament. I can only explain that day as supernatural. God had me flipping through my Bible like a woman on a mission. He took me to Scripture passages that day that I had never read before but were critical to my understanding of his name. It was something I had never experienced; divine intervention is the only way I know how to describe it. On that day, it felt as if YHWH was personally guiding my hands, my eyes, and my understanding with regard to his Word.

That day began what I call "YHWH's three-week download period." For three weeks solid, God downloaded so much information on me that my head was spinning. Day and night, I was reading and searching the Bible for clues. The puzzle pieces were coming at me fast and furiously. Several times during this time frame, at exactly 3:00 a.m., YHWH would wake me from a deep sleep to either write or research a topic. He wanted to help me understand what I was discovering; and what better time to do it than at the quietest time of the night—God's time. One night, at the beginning of Daylight Saving Time, he woke me up once again at 3:00 a.m. Because he wanted me to research something on the computer, I went downstairs. When I looked at the clock on the oven, it read 2:00 a.m. So which clock was right—the bedroom clock or the oven clock? Then it dawned on me that it was Daylight Saving Time. I realized the bedroom clock showed the correct time. I immediately started laughing, for even with a time change, YHWH wanted me up at his hour to do his work. I knew at this point that it was not my internal clock waking me up at 3:00—YHWH was!

Throughout these three intense weeks I was getting very little sleep, and when I was awake I was reading his Word. And yet I was more energized than ever before. I had a sudden passion for YHWH that was unexplainable. I knew that what he was showing me was extremely important, and several times I was overcome with so much emotion that I found myself on the floor in my house, with my face to the ground, crying so hard that I could not speak. I didn't understand why he had chosen me to reveal this information. It was at this time that YHWH gently reminded me, "Judy, you asked me to." I replied, "Oh, yeah, that's right." I had prayed for God to send me everything that the Holy Spirit had to offer me. Prior to March 8, 2011, all I knew was that God has a divine name. In a matter of just three short weeks, I knew what YHWH was asking me to do. He was asking me to step out of my comfortable life of being a stay-at-home mom and start writing a book about him, the book you currently have in your hands.

It is simply amazing how YHWH orchestrated it all. As I previously mentioned, God prompted my husband to talk me into writing a book in January of that year, before I even knew what the topic was going to be about. At the same time, my friend Rachel bought me a Jewish calendar. God knew what I was going to need before I even knew that I needed it. He led me to read the book *Waking the Dead* in order to get my whole heart back so that I would be able to hear him clearly when the time was right. On many occasions he woke me up from being dead asleep so that he could share his thoughts with me. What an awesome God we serve! YHWH chose me to become a writer because he knew writing would become my passion. And to top it all off, because this book is a book on communication and encounters with him, YHWH had to personally show me how he encounters and communicates with his children in his amazing ways.

Since I have been working for YHWH's kingdom for several years now, my mind has been completely transformed and renewed. I am now able to interpret God's Word with clarity and have a boldness to speak about YHWH and Jesus to everyone. I have been given the ability to remember everything the Holy Spirit ever spoke to me through our long journey together because, of course, telling stories is what YHWH has called me to do. Best of all, YHWH's voice, which used to be so very small and quiet in my life, is now very loud and clear. Our relationship has become very intimate, something I wish for everyone. No longer are my days spent pondering my life. They are now spent pondering the greatest love story ever told. I feel as if the "tongues of fire" have descended on me and rested. YHWH's sacred fire has been placed within my spirit and soul, and it cannot be extinguished. Daily I feel his loving warmth within me. The fire that opened the seeds of his gospel so long ago has finally accomplished its purpose and has given me a new life.

Ask, Seek, Knock

> "And I tell you, **Ask**, and it will be given you; **seek**, and you will find; **knock**, and it will be opened to you. For every one who asks **receives**, and he who seeks **finds**, and to him who knocks **it will be opened**." ... "If you then, who are evil, know how to give good gifts to your children, how much more will the heavenly Father **give the Holy Spirit** to those who ask him!" (Luke 11:9–10, 13)

Because of my own personal experience, I have come to have a new understanding of the above verse. I had never noticed that this Scripture is specifically talking about the giving of the Holy Spirit until the week I was writing this chapter. As I was pondering these verses, God told me to look at the order: ask, seek, knock; ask, seek, knock. I kept saying these words over and over again until I got it. Asking comes first, followed by seeking, and finally by knocking. Could Jesus's words have been given so that we know the steps that are needed to receive the fullness of the Holy Spirit in our lives? Ask, seek, and knock are three distinct action verbs that have three different meanings.

From my own experience, it makes perfect sense. On the day I asked Jesus to be my LORD and Savior, I know without a doubt that I received the Holy Spirit. However, just because I had felt the Holy Spirit filling me up does not mean that I miraculously knew how to hear his voice or that my life changed overnight. I spent the next twelve years seeking out the voice of the Holy Spirit. On some days I could hear his voice, while on other days his voice seemed silent and very far away. But I kept seeking him, and he kept seeking me. With practice, over and over again, I found his voice. Finding his voice gave me great peace and joy. Finally, the day I raised my hands in the air and asked God for everything the Holy Spirit had to offer me was the day I started knocking on the door of YHWH's kingdom. As a result of my knocking, YHWH's door was opened wide. Having the door to God's kingdom wide open allowed me to receive my own special gift of the Holy Spirit, the gift that YHWH had saved for me since the day I was born.

The purpose of my gift was so that I would start boldly sharing with others what I had learned through the years about my heavenly Father and his Son. My gift was not for me alone. The parable Jesus told to accompany the "ask, seek, and knock" verses is about a man persistently knocking on a friend's door. The man who was knocking had a friend visiting and therefore was in need of three loaves of bread. Jesus tells us that because of the man's persistent knocking, the door was finally opened, and the man received the three loaves of bread that he had requested. I can only think of one thing those loaves represent, and that is the knowledge of the Father, the Son, and the Holy Spirit. The man in the parable wanted these three loaves, the Bread of Life, not just for himself but also to share with his friend.

For a small minority of people, the day they ask Jesus to be their LORD and Savior and receive the Holy Spirit is the day they are also *clothed* with the power of the Holy Spirit. However, for the majority of believers, being clothed with the Holy Spirit's power usually occurs after a period of seeking and knocking and truly coming to a place of desiring MORE of God. Some believers never move beyond asking for their salvation because they are unaware that they need to then seek and then finally knock. As a result, their lives never reflect the fullness of God's light, peace, or abundance. And finally, unfortunately, there are some people who know about Jesus but have never asked him to be their LORD and Savior. As a result, they have never received YHWH's Holy Spirit into their hearts and therefore are not YHWH's children.

So I must ask you the most important question you will ever be asked if you are a follower of Jesus: "Did you receive the Holy Spirit when you believed?" (Acts 19:2). If you are a believer in Jesus Christ and you have asked him to be your Lord and Savior, then you can be certain that YHWH's Holy Spirit, given in Jesus's name, came to dwell within your heart on the day you believed. If you are a believer, and have the knowledge that you have been living with the Holy Spirit in your heart since the day of your salvation, you need to then ask yourself if you have truly begun seeking out his majestic voice. For it is only by seeking out his voice and finding it that your life will start to change, your heart will be made whole, and you will feel his peace that passes all understanding. And finally, if you have found his sweet voice, you must ask yourself if you have started knocking on the door of YHWH's kingdom. Start today if you haven't already because *your actions* as a child of God have the power to dramatically transform your life.

When I received everything the Holy Spirit had to offer me, I encountered YHWH and Jesus in a way I had never known possible. Suddenly, I was hearing YHWH daily through many avenues: the Bible, dreams, visions, creation, words of knowledge, personal prophecy, music, and angels of the LORD. Because I made myself completely available to work for his kingdom, he opened up a whole new way of communication, which is available to everyone who submits himself wholly to furthering YHWH's kingdom. When I asked God for everything the Holy Spirit had to offer me, what he gave me was great knowledge of his divine name. What I came to realize over the years of writing this book is that with the receiving and understanding of YHWH's divine name comes *everything*!

So what are you waiting for? Go ahead—be bold. Ask YHWH for *everything* the Holy Spirit has to offer you, and then prepare yourself for the ride of a lifetime. Make sure you allow Jesus to mend your heart before you do because he will want your whole heart in order for you to feel all of his glory. Trust me, you do not want to miss out on the mission God has planned for you—the mission he planned before you were even born.

Chapter 19

The Name above All Names

> And being found in human form he humbled himself and became obedient unto death, even death on a cross. **Therefore God has highly exalted him and bestowed on him the name which is above every name, that at the name of Jesus every knee should bow**, in heaven and on earth and under the earth, and **every tongue confess that Jesus Christ is Lord, to the glory of God the Father**. (Phil. 2:8–11)

Because YHWH had a mission for Jesus's apostles, it was God's plan for his Son to depart from their presence. If Jesus had stayed with them, the apostles would never have separated from one another, and the good news of Jesus Christ would not have been spread to the ends of the world. As a result of Jesus's leaving, all of the apostles traveled to different areas of the world to start preaching the gospel and baptizing believers in the name of the Father, the Son, and the Holy Spirit, making disciples of all nations, just as they were instructed. Everything they accomplished was done in the name of Jesus Christ, the *"Name above all Names."* By being clothed with the power of the Holy Spirit, the apostles were given the authority to cast out demons, heal the sick, and raise the dead. Because everything they did was in the name of Jesus, they were able to continue doing everything they saw Jesus do while he walked this earth. Because of the power of the name they were working for, with

Encountering the Great I Am

boldness they were able to literally change the lives of the people they encountered and touched, both physically and spiritually.

Before the disciples started following Jesus, many of them had been fishermen, one was a tax collector, some of them might have been husbands and fathers, and none of them were theologians. They were ordinary folks with ordinary jobs and lives. In a sense, these men were remarkably unremarkable. We do not know anything about these men's lives prior to their first encounter with Jesus. However, from that day forward, the rest of their lives became history. Twelve ordinary men with unremarkable lives suddenly became extraordinary men with remarkable lives. And all they did to make it happen was to say yes to Jesus's invitation to follow him.

The apostles knew firsthand that before they became followers of Jesus, they were not able to do any of the miracles that they were suddenly capable of doing. They knew they were being followed by the masses only because of the *Name above all Names*, by which they proclaimed these miracles. Why, even Jesus didn't proclaim in his own name but in his Father's name alone. So why wouldn't the apostles, instead of making a name for themselves, simply work for Jesus? By working for Jesus and his Father, there were no limits to what they could accomplish because Jesus had already made a name for himself.

In many cultures, people have a great desire to be known by others. From the beginning of time, dads have been instructing their sons and daughters to go out and "make a name" for themselves, either by hard work or simply by marrying into a good family. And even more importantly, regardless of what they accomplished, they were by no means to disgrace the family name. Finally, it has always been important for a male to be born into a family so that the family name can continue on. Today you can find website after website coaching both men and women, young and old, on how to make their names known. What are the motivations for the people looking at these websites? Do these individuals want to be celebrated by the masses, or is it out of greed that they want their names known so that they can become rich in this life? Is it their desire to see their names in lights or to achieve a fleeting fifteen minutes of fame? Just thinking about purposely going about making a name for oneself seems shallow, self-absorbing, time consuming, frustrating, and lonely.

Regardless of what we personally achieve in our short lives, once we physically die, most of our names and the details of our lives are lost within one generation of our death. And after a little more time elapses, no one will know or care that we ever existed. In contrast, by working for YHWH's kingdom, the details of our lives are forever recorded in the only history book that matters and the only one that survives throughout the ages: the Book of Life. Not only will our names be listed there for eternity, but also all that we accomplished in Jesus's name will be recorded for all to see. The adjectives that will accompany our names will be *righteous, favored, blameless, trusted son or daughter, loving wife or mother, devoted husband or father*. In addition, one day we will forever be in the presence of the most famous individual who ever walked this earth. Just by being in Jesus's presence for eternity, we will have status beyond what we could have achieved on our own.

The apostles understood all of this, so for the rest of their lives they claimed the name of Jesus for everything they accomplished. Even after consistently being threatened by imprisonment and death by the rulers and religious leaders, not one of them denied his name ever again.

One day, while Peter and John were about to go into the temple, a man who had been lame from birth asked for alms. Peter directed his gaze at the man and said, "I have no silver and gold, *but I give you what I have; in the name of Jesus Christ of Nazareth, walk*" (Acts 3:6). After Peter spoke these words, the man was able to rise up and walk for the first time ever. By the world's standards, Peter was a poor man because he owned no silver or gold. However, even though he lacked material wealth, Peter was a spiritually rich man. What Peter had was the power to make a lame man walk—something that no wealthy, ordinary man could ever obtain. When the religious rulers and elders saw the miracle take place, instead of being overjoyed that a healing had occurred in their presence, they felt the need to interrogate Peter and John for their actions.

"**By what power or by what name did you do this?**" Then Peter, filled with the Holy Spirit, said to them, "Rulers of the people and elders, if we are being examined today concerning a good deed done to a cripple, by what means this man has been healed, be it known to you all, and to all the people of Israel, that **by the name of Jesus Christ of Nazareth**, whom you crucified, whom God raised from the dead, by him this man is standing before you well. … And there is salvation in no one else, for **there is no other name under heaven given among men by which we must be saved**." (Acts 4:7b–10, 12)

When asked the question, "By what power or by what name did you do this?" Peter could have replied with pride that it was by his name that this miracle occurred. But that is not what happened because Peter knew very well that it would only be upon the *Name above all Names*, upon the cornerstone of Jesus's name alone, that the church would be built. Peter knew that without Jesus's name, there was nothing that he himself had to offer the world.

Even though the rulers and elders could not deny that what they saw had actually happened, they could not put aside their pride and accept the truth that Jesus Christ was their long-awaited Messiah. They could not see that it was because of the risen Messiah that these apostles were able to miraculously heal the sick. They didn't seem to grasp that if they, too, accepted Jesus as their LORD and Savior, they would be given the same job of spreading the gospel, healing the sick, casting out demons, and raising the dead. In essence, by rejecting Jesus, these men literally placed limitations upon themselves. To this day, we do not know the names of the men who questioned Peter and John as they have all been forgotten, even though two thousand years ago these men held prestigious positions and were considered wealthy. Today, in the history book of the Bible, they are simply known by their titles because these men chose not to have their given names written into the Book of Life. Instead of accepting Jesus as the Son the God, these leaders, who were obviously being influenced by Satan, decided they would instruct the apostles to stop talking about Jesus so that the stories could no longer be spread throughout the land.

> "**What shall we do with these men**? For that a notable sign has been performed through them is manifest to all the inhabitants of Jerusalem, and we cannot deny it. But in order that it spread no further among the people, **let us warn them to speak no more to any one in this name**." So they called them and charged them not to speak or teach at all in the name of Jesus. But Peter and John answered them, "**Whether it is right in the sight of God to listen to you rather than to God, you must judge; for we cannot but speak of what we have seen and heard**." (Acts 4:16–20)

Immediately after Jesus's resurrection, Satan tried to spread the rumor that Jesus's body was either stolen from the grave or that he really wasn't dead when they took him from the cross. Satan wanted to discredit the story that the Messiah had actually been raised from the dead. However, that didn't work for very long, especially after Jesus appeared to five hundred brethren at one time before his ascension. There were just too many witnesses, and every time one of them gave their testimony of seeing Jesus alive, there was a passion in his or her words. Their stories were too credible to deny, and therefore more and more people believed and were daily being baptized into God's kingdom. When Satan's tactic of lying about Jesus's resurrection didn't work, he thought he would do the same thing he did back in 300 BC. He would just get the religious leaders to convince the apostles to stop saying Jesus's name. Since he had successfully accomplished getting the Israelites to stop saying YHWH's name, why not try the same strategy again?

What Satan soon found out is that there was a major stumbling block that he had not previously encountered. Because the Holy Spirit was residing in the apostles' hearts and was speaking truth to them daily, it was as if Jesus were still in their presence. Because they could hear Jesus's voice loud and clear, there was no way that Satan could deceive them into denying the name of Jesus. It was as if their LORD and Savior was truly still dwelling among them. The Pharisees kept telling the apostles, "Just stop saying his name and your life will be much easier." The apostles refused to comply with the Pharisees' commands because they knew intimately that Jesus's name was the *Name above all Names* given among men, and they would die before they stopped saying his name. They no longer looked for validation from man, as the Pharisees did. Their validation as human beings now came from YHWH himself and no one else. They finally understood that Jesus's name is what made them holy before their Father, and they would therefore never deny this precious gift.

To personally claim Jesus as your LORD and Savior means that you are claiming Jesus's name as your own. It means you have been blessed with the family name. When a marriage takes place and a bride takes a bridegroom's name, the subsequent name change signifies several things. For the bride, taking on her husband's name represents a change of course, a new position in life, a new way of doing things, and new duties. By marriage, a man and a woman agree to no longer live two individual lives but to become one with each other. And because of the great love a bride has for her bridegroom, she will have a desire to honor him by submitting to and respecting his family name. The more and more time they spend together, the more a man and a woman start to reflect each other's character. Just like a bride claiming her husband's name as her own is a serious matter, claiming Jesus's name as your own is the most important decision that you will ever make and should not be taken lightly. The last thing you want to do is take Jesus's name and then profane it regularly, as the Israelites profaned YHWH's name for hundreds of years.

Remember, as a result of YHWH's name being profaned, he took all communication away from his people for 430 years. YHWH was fed up with all of the hypocrites who were claiming to be his people when their thoughts and actions conveyed something completely opposite. They were pretending to be his children and had claimed his name as their own, and yet they did not love him with all their minds, hearts, souls, and strength. They just made sure they kept enough commandments in order to deceive their fellow man and receive their approval.

The third commandment says, "*You shall not take the name of YHWH your God in vain*; for YHWH will not hold him guiltless who takes his name in vain" (Exo. 20:7). Most people would explain the meaning of this commandment as using God's or Jesus's name alongside a swear word or profanity, but that is not how I see it at all. The Hebrew word for *vain* is "shav." The meaning of the word *shav* is "emptiness, deceit, lie, and falsehood."[1] Therefore, to take the name of YHWH in vain means so much more than using his name as a swear word. To take YHWH's name in vain means to openly claim his family name when your heart and actions tell a completely different story. All of the Pharisees, the religious leaders of the day, had claimed the name of YHWH as their own, and yet Jesus said that the majority of them would not see the kingdom of God because of the way they took YHWH's name in vain. There was a falsehood and emptiness to these leaders' claims of being followers of YHWH. If they truly loved God with all their minds, hearts, souls, and strength, they would have recognized Jesus for who he was, the Word of God. Instead, these men took on YHWH's name for the prestige and wealth that his name afforded them. They followed their own will and Satan's will in everything they did. In other words, they were living a lie and were hypocrites. Even Jesus defined the word *hypocrite* for these men.

> And he said to them, "Well did Isaiah prophesy of you **hypocrites**, as it is written, '**This people honors me with their lips, but their heart is far from me; in vain do they worship me, teaching as doctrines the precepts of men.' You leave the commandment of God, and hold fast the tradition of men**." (Mark 7:6–8)

Those who take YHWH's name in vain will not see the kingdom of heaven.

> "**Not every one who says to me, 'Lord, Lord,' shall enter the kingdom of heaven, but he who does the will of my Father** who is in heaven. On that day many will say to me, 'Lord, Lord, did we not prophesy your name, and cast out

demons in your name, and do many mighty works in your name?' And then will I declare to them, '**I never knew you; depart from me**, you evildoers.'" (Matt.7:21–23)

Judas was a perfect example of a person living for his own name. From all appearances, it looked as if Judas had given up on making his own name great in order to follow the only name that mattered. For three years he followed in Jesus's footsteps. But what we know from Scripture is that he claimed Jesus's name only while it fit his lifestyle. Because it was advantageous for Judas to live under Jesus's name for three years, he did. However, once he felt things weren't going according to his will, he betrayed Jesus's name. He decided it was time to make his own name rich by betraying Jesus in return for money. Once Judas realized what he had done, it was too late. His hypocrisy was made obvious for all to see. All of his pretending to honor Jesus over the previous three years came to a sudden end. Judas ended up killing himself because he could not bear the pain of knowing the role he had played in causing the death of the greatest name who ever lived.

So ask yourself, "Am I taking Jesus's name in vain?" If you don't know the answer to that question, then ask your heavenly Father. I am positive that he will let you know. I know for a fact that I took Jesus's name in vain while I was in college. Whenever someone asked me if I was a Christian, my answer was always a resounding yes. But I can tell you now that I was so far from being a Christian it is laughable. My heart was as far from God and Jesus as it could have possibly been, and I was surely not worshipping him. I had left every commandment of God for the traditions of men and Satan. I was living for my name alone and was simply pretending to be a Christian. I was a hypocrite through and through.

Taking on the name of Jesus should be the most important decision you ever make and should not be taken lightly. If you take Jesus's name in vain, the commandment tells us that you will be found guilty. However, if you finally give up on your name being great and instead lovingly and honorably identify with Jesus's name, your life will be forever changed. By forming an intimate relationship with God and working for his kingdom, in the name of Jesus, you too will have the power to cast out demons, heal the sick, and have the boldness to share the *Name above all Names* with others, just as the apostles did. You will find a peace that you have never felt before because it is only in Jesus's name that heavenly peace is found. What you will discover is that Jesus's name is the *only* name worth living and dying for.

Kamal's Story

I want to end this chapter with a story of a man who had died to himself and to making his name great. He did it for the sake of the *name* he thought was the *Name above all Names.* His parents had taught their son from a very young age the importance of dying to his own name and to be passionate for the only name that mattered, the one and only true God. From all appearances in this man's culture, he had gotten everything right. He was religious, he was passionate, and he was living the will of his god. He loved his god with all his mind, heart, soul, and strength. Yet, with this man there was one major problem; the name this man was taught to be the "Name above all Names" was the wrong name. The name this man worshipped with every fiber of his soul was "Allah."

What God saw in this man were all the right qualities and characteristics; he simply had the wrong name. YHWH knew that all it would take is one encounter with the one and only true God for this man to be transformed for his kingdom, just like Paul was transformed on the road to Damascus after just one encounter with Jesus Christ.

I came to know about this man's story one day as I was researching the meaning of a verse about God's divine name. On this particular day, something on my computer caught my eye. I noticed a video in the very bottom right-hand corner of my screen. The heading was "Kamal Saleem: A Muslim Cries Out to Jesus." Because the title piqued my interest, I listened to his story. I could not believe the words I heard. It was Kamal Saleem's testimony of how he came to know the one true God. Even though Kamal's childhood history was one I had heard many times before, what I found so special about this man's story is in the way God showed up in this man's life and the words he used to introduce himself.

Kamal Saleem was born in Lebanon to a devout Muslim family. As early as four years old, he remembers sitting at the kitchen table while his mother taught him about the Koran and his duty to Allah and jihad. She told him that one day he would be a martyr. By dying for the sake of Allah, he would exalt Islam. When Kamal was seven, his parents sent him to Muslim training camps to learn how to use weapons to engage and kill the enemy. He was also taught another, more subtle form of warfare—"culture jihad." By his twenties, Kamal was chosen to wage cultural jihad on America. So Kamal moved to the Bible Belt because he considered it to be where the strongest Christians lived. He entrenched himself in a small town and began targeting men from poorer neighborhoods to recruit them to the Muslim faith.

One afternoon, while recruiting, he had a car accident, and suddenly his life was in the hands of those he hated the most. The car wreck was so severe that he was ejected from his car, he landed on his neck, and it broke in two places. A man came running to Kamal and said, "Don't worry. We're going to take care of you, and everything's going to be all right." The ambulance picked up Kamal and took him to the hospital. The orthopedic ER surgeon looked at his chart and said, "Son, we're going to take care of you, and everything's going to be all right." The second day, Kamal woke up in the hospital, and the head of physical therapy came in, read his chart, and said the very same thing: "We are going to take care of you."

At first, Kamal was frightened by their words because these men were all Christians, and he didn't trust them. Surgeries to repair Kamal's broken neck were successful, but recovery would take weeks. Since Kamal would need someone to care for him while he recuperated, the orthopedic surgeon opened up his own home. Kamal was put in the choicest of rooms in the house and quickly became part of the family. He noticed that the Christians didn't seem any different from Muslims.

Kamal was overwhelmed with the outpouring of Christian love and even met and ate with Jewish people during his stay with this family. When Kamal was able to take care of himself and return to his apartment, the doctor had another surprise for him. He blessed Kamal with a new car. When Kamal finally returned to his home, he noticed how cold and dusty it seemed. Immediately, he knew he had to settle an issue with his god. Here are Kamal's exact words about what happened next:

> So I walk inside, I shut door. I go right to the eastern window, fall on my knees, put my hands to the heavens and I cry out, "Allah, Allah my lord and my king. Why have you done such a thing to me? I'm okay with the car wreck. I'm ok with all this, but why did you put me among Christians? I'm confused. These Christians and Jews, they are good people. There's nothing wrong with them. They don't want to kill us. They're not the same thing that I learned about. Allah. These people have relationship with their God. These people cry out to their God, and He answers them. I want to hear your voice. I want to hear you love me. If you're real, speak to me. I want to hear your voice." Guess what Allah said that day? Absolutely nothing.

Kamal felt that because he questioned his faith, the honorable thing to do was to end his own life.

> So I went to reach out my gun, put it in the right place and clock out. I heard a voice. The voice knew me by name. It said, "Kamal! Kamal! Kamal! Why don't you call on the Father of Abraham and Isaac and Jacob?" Now I fell on my knees and put my hands to the heavens immediately as I heard the voice. I cried out with every fiber within me. "God, the Father Abraham, if You are real, would You speak to me? I want to know You." Well, God of Abraham came to the room. He filled the room with His glory. His name was Yahweh, the Lord is one. He has holes in His hands. He has holes in His feet. His name is Jesus. I said to Him, "Who are you, my Lord? Who are you?" He said, "I am that I am." I said, "I am a simple man with a simple mind. What is that supposed to mean?" He said, "I am the Alpha. I am the

Omega. I am the beginning. I am the end. I am everything that is in between. I have known you before I formed the foundation of the earth. I have loved you before I formed you in your mother's womb. Rise up! Rise up Kamal. Come. You are my warrior. You are not their warrior." I said to Him, "My Lord, I will live and die for you." He said, "Do not die for me. I died for you so that you may live."

That day, instead of taking his life, Kamal gave his life to Jesus. He now has a new mission and travels the country challenging Muslims to question their allegiance to Allah. Kamal says this about God:

> He is real. If you've never experienced God before in your life, if you never tasted God, if you think you've got nothing to lose ... when you're sitting in your home, whether you're a Muslim or a non-Muslim or a non-Christian or whatever you are, call on the Father of Abraham, Isaac, and Jacob and say, "If You are real, speak to me. I want to hear Your voice." [2]

When Kamal cried out for the one and only true God, YHWH spoke to him. For me, hearing Kamal's testimony was so very special because of the way God introduced himself. These are the words God audibly used to describe himself on that day just twenty years ago.

> **I am** the Father of Abraham, Isaac, and Jacob
> **I am** Yahweh, the LORD is one
> **I am** Jesus
> **I Am that I Am**
> **I am** the Alpha
> **I am** the Omega
> **I am** the Beginning
> **I am** the End
> **I am** everything that is in between
> **I have known you**
> **I formed you**
> **I have loved you**
> **You are my warrior**

You are not their warrior
I died so you can live

On that day, after encountering the Great I AM for the first time ever, not only was Kamal saved but he was also clothed with the power of the Holy Spirit to be God's warrior for his kingdom. He was given the power to be God's witness to the ends of the earth. Because Kamal had been preparing his entire life for this one moment, Kamal knew who Jesus was the very first day he met him. It has been over twenty years since Kamal left the Islamic faith, and even threats of violence and death cannot stop him from sharing his story.

To receive salvation, all Kamal did was search for the truth, listen, and then accept Jesus as his LORD and Savior. After that, YHWH gave Kamal the ability and power to witness for him to the ends of the earth. And because Kamal was willing to obey the voice of God, because he said, "Hineni. Here I am, LORD," Kamal is now living his life abundantly. He has peace, understanding, and freedom to live for the God he loves and for the God that he now personally knows. YHWH has given Kamal a purpose to spread his Word to the 1.5 billion Muslims who are living out there but who have not tasted the freedom of God and his Son, Jesus. It should keep him busy for the rest of his life.

"In my distress I called upon YHWH; to my God I called. From his temple he heard my voice, and my cry came to his ears" (2 Sam. 22:7). Kamal had knowledge of Jesus's name. In fact, he had been instructed his whole life that people who believe in Jesus and YHWH are infidels. He had been trained to kill Christians and Jews. Just like Paul, his goal in life had become to eradicate the world of Jesus followers. Fortunately for Kamal, before he was able to do exactly what he had been trained to do, YHWH put a roadblock in his way. Because of Kamal's accident, he was introduced in a very personal way to the very people he was taught to hate. God gave Kamal a pause in his life in order to introduce him to the truth.

After pondering the truth, Kamal had the wisdom to ask questions of his god. However, Allah didn't answer Kamal; there was no voice, and no one heeded. Allah didn't answer Kamal because Allah does not exist, just like Baal did not exist in biblical times when the prophets begged Baal to answer them. But YHWH does. And because Kamal was searching for the truth with all of his mind, heart, soul, and strength, YHWH showed him love, grace, and mercy when he said, "Pray to the God of Abraham, Isaac and Jacob." When Kamal did just that, YHWH revealed himself and his Son, Jesus, to him. As a result of Kamal's encounter with the living God, he turned away from everything he knew: his brothers, his mother, his father, and his homeland. Once YHWH communicated with Kamal, there was no turning back. Kamal was now YHWH's warrior, who YHWH would use to drop the seeds of the gospel into other people's lives. However, this time it would not be through violence but through love.

Just like God gave the Urim and Thummim to Moses to place behind Aaron's breastpiece over his heart, God continues to place his name and his Son's name into his children's hearts. With God's divine names on our hearts, we are first forgiven of our sins, made completely righteous, and then given full communication with our heavenly Father. Once communication has been established, as we ponder on the names that have been placed in our hearts through the Holy Spirit, YHWH will reveal the answers to our questions, his will for our lives, and his unconditional love for us.

> **For this reason I bow my knees before the Father, from whom every family in heaven and on earth is named**, that according to the riches of his glory he may grant you to be **strengthened with might through his Spirit** in the inner man, and that **Christ may dwell in your hearts** through faith; that you, **being rooted and grounded in love**, may have power to comprehend with all the saints what is the breadth and length and height and depth, and **to know the love of Christ** which surpasses knowledge, **that you may be filled with all the fullness of God**. (Eph. 3:14–19)

Kamal was passionate for his god, Allah. He thought he was doing everything right. He thought he was honoring the one and only true God. He prayed five times a day, had given his life to follow the will of Allah, and was willing to give up his life for him. The problem was that Kamal had devoted his life to the wrong name. Only after the one and only true YHWH introduced himself to Kamal did his life sprout new life. When he claimed Jesus's name as his own, I believe Kamal was clothed with the power of the Holy Spirit on the exact same day. Because he was already passionate for whom he thought was the one and only true god (Allah) and was willing to end his life for him, on the day he finally met the one and only true God (YHWH), he was ready to take on his true mission in life, and that was to bring other Muslims to the knowledge of Jesus, the Savior of the world.

Just as Paul had an encounter with the living God, so did Kamal. If Kamal had continued on his path of worshipping Allah and had succeeded in killing Christians and Jews, his name would have been reported on the local news, and Kamal would have gotten fifteen minutes of fame. However, in a matter of days his name would have been forgotten and his title of "terrorist" is all that would be remembered. Instead, by working for Jesus, Kamal has literally changed the lives of countless individuals by introducing them to their Savior. His position in life was changed in the matter of one day and, because of it, Kamal's name has been written into the Book of Life as one of Jesus's beloved disciples. His name appears right alongside all of the other apostles', prophets', and saints' names who have lived throughout the centuries.

YHWH knows that every man, woman, and child has an inherent desire for his or her name to be known. God knows this because he is the one who placed that desire in our souls. Our heavenly Father gave us all individual names so that a relationship with him would be possible. YHWH then gave us all the desire to be known—with the hope that one day we would desire to be known by him.

So what about you—do you long to hear God's voice like Kamal did? Are you praying to the right name? Have you cried out to the God of Abraham, Isaac, and Jacob? Have you have been introduced to the Name above all Names? Do you know Jesus? Do you have a personal relationship with your LORD (YHWH) and Savior (Jesus)? Whose name are you living for? Your answers to these questions are critical to whether or not you will ever communicate and form a personal relationship with the one and only true God.

Chapter 20

Love Languages

> Jesus answered him, "Truly, truly, I say to you, unless one is born anew, he cannot see the kingdom of God." Nicodemus said to him, "**How can a man be born when he is old**? Can he enter a second time into his mother's womb and be born?" Jesus answered, "**Truly, truly, I say to you, unless one is born of water and the Spirit, he cannot enter the kingdom of God.**" (John 3:3–5)

Just as God has to breathe into your nostrils the breath of physical life, God has to breathe into our beings the breath of the Holy Spirit in order for us to have spiritual life. When we are physically born into this world, it is because of our Creator that we are able to take our first breath. However, just because we are born into this world doesn't mean we are prepared for or capable of surviving on our own. In fact, because we come into this world as babies, if we were left alone after our births we would simply perish. That is why God gave us mothers and fathers to nurture us along the way and to meet our every need for the first years of our lives. Because our parents identify our needs through our cries, they are able to keep us satisfied by keeping us fed, clothed, warm, and loved. In addition, from the day we were born, our parents started speaking, singing, and reading to us and, by doing so, began teaching us the language of the physical world in which we live.

In homes that operate the way God intended them to, our parents become our teachers, whose primary goal is to teach us their language, a gift that allows us to communicate. In a matter of only a few months, we are able to say our first words, and after a few years we usually know enough words to express our physical needs more readily. Communication becomes easier as our parents continue to teach us their language. By mastering the intricacies of our parents' language, we are eventually able to vocalize our emotional needs as well as our physical needs. Through this language we are taught everything we need to survive on our own.

With all that we are taught by our parents in our first eighteen years of life, we are able to finally leave their home to start life on our own. Even though we physically leave their home, we still communicate with our parents because, over the years, we have formed an intimate and loving relationship with them. Only when we begin living on our own do we really begin to understand all that our parents sacrificed for our survival. We start realizing that it was because of our parents' love for us that our physical and emotional needs were met.

Being born of the Spirit can be thought of in the same way. When we are born anew into the spiritual world, it is as "baby" Christians. We are born into a new world that we are ill-equipped to navigate on our own. If left alone, our newborn spirit would simply perish because Satan's physical world of sin would seek to destroy it. Therefore, when YHWH gives us our new life, he breathes into us his Holy Spirit. The Counselor is sent to nurture us in the new spiritual world into which we have been born to protect us from Satan's attacks and to start speaking to us so that we can begin to learn our heavenly Father's language. However, just because we receive a Counselor to help us learn God's spiritual language does not mean that it will necessarily come easily or quickly. The language of the spiritual world is quite different from the language of the physical world. The physical world has become Satan's world, and therefore the everyday physical language that surrounds us is Satan's. Therefore learning God's language may seem difficult, and it is guaranteed that Satan will use everything in his power to keep us from being successful. But it can be done, with a daily sacrifice of time and the Holy Spirit's help.

Learning the language of the spiritual world can be compared to learning a foreign language. It is common knowledge that the best way to become fluent in another language is by total immersion. When you leave the comforts of your own country and physically go to a foreign land, at first the new words you hear being spoken will be confusing and you may be extremely overwhelmed and frustrated. However, within weeks you will learn the essential words needed to meet your physical needs; and by staying in that country, you will soon become fluent in the language you desired to speak. If you continue to live in the foreign country, not only will you learn their language, but you will also learn their culture. In fact, you just might begin to feel welcomed, loved, and comfortable living in the foreign land.

To become immersed in YHWH's language, you have to purposely decide to do things that allow you to see, hear, read, and speak his words regularly. And in order to become fluent quickly, you have to hear or ponder the meaning of his words daily, as if your physical life depends upon it. The Counselor will explain the meaning of God's words to you, but, in order to hear the Counselor's words, you also have to seek out the sound of his voice so that you can hear him through the noise of the physical world. That is why going to church regularly, joining a Bible study, becoming part of a small group, and surrounding yourself with other Christians becomes critical. The people you meet in these unfamiliar territories will be learning or speaking YHWH's language as well, and those who are already fluent in YHWH's spiritual language can help you interpret the meaning of God's words.

Just as learning to be fluent in a physical language can take years, so does becoming fluent in YHWH's spiritual language. At times you will not be able to vocalize your needs or the desires of your heart, and you will only be able to cry out to God like a child. In those moments, the Holy Spirit will interpret your cries and intercede for you, making your needs known to YHWH in the same way parents interpret for their infants and toddlers before they have mastered their language. *"Likewise the Spirit helps us in our weakness; for we do not know how to pray as we ought, but the Spirit himself intercedes for us with sighs too deep for words"* (Rom. 8:26). Even though your journey may take years, from the very first instant of spiritual birth you will start forming a loving and intimate relationship with your heavenly Father that will continue to grow throughout the years, just as you started a personal relationship with your parents the day you were born.

Jesus spoke the words of being born anew to Nicodemus, who was a religious leader. Nicodemus was extremely familiar with YHWH's words since he had been immersed in Scripture his entire life. In addition, Nicodemus was living for the name of YHWH. However, even though he followed the commandments of YHWH to the best of his ability and was considered righteous in the eyes of his fellow man, there was still something missing: communication with his heavenly Father. Without being born into the spiritual world, even though Nicodemus knew YHWH's words, he was not yet fluent because the Holy Spirit had yet to be offered to man. Without the Holy Spirit, up to this point, Nicodemus had only received man's interpretation of Scripture. Only by being born anew would Nicodemus ever enter into the spiritual world, where YHWH himself would explain the true meaning of his words. In the spiritual world, Nicodemus would discover that the language YHWH speaks is not a language of rules and regulations but a language of love—a language that would never be learned by simply following God's law. God's love language can only be learned through a personal relationship with him. That is the whole reason Jesus died on the cross for our sins, so that personal relationships between God and his children could form.

The Greatest Commandment

When asked what the greatest commandment in the law was, Jesus replied as follows.

> And he said to him, "**You shall love YHWH your God with all your heart, and with all your soul, and with all your mind. This is the great and first commandment.** And a second is like it, **You shall love your neighbor as yourself. On these two commandments depend all the law and the prophets.**" (Matt. 22:37–40)

Similarly, on the night of Passover, Jesus said to his disciples,

> "**A new commandment I give to you, that you love one another; even as I have loved you**, that you also love one another. **By this all men will know that you are my disciples**, if you have love for one another." (John 13:34–35)

Jesus proclaimed that all of the law and everything the prophets ever spoke could be summed up by just two commandments. By loving YHWH with all our hearts, souls, and minds, we willingly keep the first four of the Ten Commandments; and by truly loving our neighbors as ourselves, the remaining six commandments are kept. Jesus expounded on the principle of what it means to love your neighbor as yourself by saying that we are to love one another "as I (Jesus) have loved you." This new commandment was truly new because, until God's Word became flesh and dwelled among his people, God's children could not feel the extent of YHWH's unconditional love for them. A new kind of love is what Jesus was asking of his disciples—the same love that they felt Jesus shower on them for three years. Jesus's new kind of love includes gifts, offerings, and sacrifices that come directly from the heart.

With the establishment of the first covenant, YHWH commanded Moses to set up a system of offerings that were to be given from the people to God. These offerings fell into one of the five categories: burnt offerings, meal offerings, peace offerings, sin offerings, or trespass offerings. These freewill gifts were to be given individually by the people to YHWH for various reasons. Since only the best of the best was to be given, the offerings required the givers to sacrifice either their finest animal or grain to YHWH.

When Jesus came as the perfect sacrifice for all mankind, this system of sacrifices became obsolete. But simply because they became obsolete did not mean that these sacrifices did not serve a purpose. Remember, everything that came with the first covenant was a shadow of either what Jesus fulfilled himself or what he commanded of us in the second covenant. Until Jesus established the second covenant, the sacrifices from the people to God were the people's way of communicating with YHWH. They were their freewill offerings or gifts made to God.

As I was thinking about these five offerings becoming obsolete with the new covenant of Jesus, I wondered what took their place. God reminded me of the book that I had read many years prior, titled *The Five Love Languages: How to Express Heartfelt Commitment to Your Mate* by Gary Chapman.[1] I read this book at a time when I was struggling in my ability to *feel* my husband's love, even though I knew in my heart and mind that my husband loved me and that he was truly my soul mate. What Chapman suggests is that not all people communicate their love in the same manner because different people have different love languages. These various love languages are completely diverse forms of communication or ways of expressing and interpreting love. As a result, many marriages suffer when two people who live together speak two completely different love languages and therefore never communicate their love to each other effectively. Through Chapman's research, and thirty years of experience as a marriage counselor, he has identified five universal and comprehensive love languages. They are as follows:

- *Words of Affirmation*: words of love or praise, letting the other person know he or she matters and is noticed
- *Quality Time*: full, undivided, one-on-one attention
- *Receiving or Giving Gifts*: receiver or giver of gifts thrives on the love, thoughtfulness, and effort behind the gift
- *Acts of Service*: any sacrificial act of service that benefits the receiver
- *Physical Touch*: physical touches that show care, excitement, concern, and love, such as hugs, pats on the back, holding hands, and thoughtful touches on the arm, shoulder, or face

Chapman maintains that most people will have one main love language, with maybe one or two other minor languages. After reading this book, I came to realize that my main love language is physical touch, followed by words of affirmation. I questioned my husband on his love language and found that quality time ranked number one, followed by acts of service. Well, no wonder I didn't *feel* love from my husband; my main love language of physical touch wasn't my husband's love language. What he needed to feel loved was quality time and acts of service, which were not on my list. It was a wonder that either of us felt any love at all from each other since the ways we were choosing to love each other was in the languages we desired to be loved ourselves.

Once I realized that my husband and I were speaking different love languages, it became easier for me to understand why he didn't give me physical touch daily—because it was a foreign language to him. He was constantly giving me quality, undivided attention and always doing acts of service, and yet I never before understood what he was "saying" to me through these languages. By doing these things, he thought he was expressing how important I was to him and how much he loved me. Because these weren't my languages, I never "felt" his love. It wasn't until we came to understand each other's languages that we started to feel each other's love, the love that had been there the whole time. We acknowledged the importance of each other's love languages and started making sacrifices to learn the languages that were foreign to us. Because of our new knowledge of how love is communicated and our willingness to practice the new languages, our marriage has been strengthened.

Just as humans need and desire to feel love from their spouses and from others, God also desires to feel love from his children. His language, spoken through the Holy Spirit in Jesus's name, is a love language. Of the five universal love languages that have been identified, we can be certain that God designed them all since he is the Creator of all things. I believe these love languages were designed by YHWH to take the place of the five sacrificial offerings of the first covenant since love has always been the driving force of everything YHWH has ever done for mankind. When you study the history of YHWH and his Son, Jesus, dwelling among his people, you can easily see the sacrificial love that he displayed over the centuries and the desire YHWH had to be loved in return.

When you consider Jesus's birth, ministry, death, and resurrection, you see all of YHWH's universal love languages being expressed to mankind. Just by his Son's physical presence on the earth, we know how important God's people were to him. He sent his Son to dwell among them for the sole purpose of giving them *quality time* so that his people could see, feel, and hear his love. Jesus was sent to fellowship with humans so that he could explain the true meaning of God's Word. And for those who didn't understand that language, YHWH instructed his Son to lay his hands on them and heal them of their ailments so that they would begin to understand the depth of his love through his *physical touch*. And yet, others needed something different. Some people needed Jesus's *words of affirmation*, that no matter what they had done in their past, they were worthy of their heavenly Father's love. But YHWH didn't stop there. He instructed his Son to express his love for all of mankind by the ultimate *act of service*. Jesus took the sins of the entire human race upon himself and offered his life for the last and final sacrifice so that we could live eternally with his Father. YHWH loved his people so much that he gave them the ultimate *gift* of salvation at the expense of his Son's death. And after Jesus's resurrection, YHWH gave them the *gift* of His Holy Spirit in his precious Son Jesus's name so that they never again would have to go through life without physically feeling his presence within them. Through Jesus's life we see that YHWH is truly the ultimate giver of gifts and blessings.

Because the apostles felt Jesus's love languages while they dwelled with him and then saw him physically lay down his life for them so that they could have life, they understood the meaning of the new commandment to love one another as Jesus loved. And since Jesus's love continued being felt with the giving of the Holy Spirit, they were able to obey this new commandment. We see through the book of Acts and the entire New Testament the great acts of love that the apostles poured upon the people in the name of Jesus. Everything they did was possible because of YHWH's unconditional love that they finally *felt* in their hearts and souls. Because they were able to feel God's love for themselves, the apostles were able to pour this same kind of love out to others, even if it resulted in laying down their own lives.

The same unconditional love that the apostles felt through Jesus's daily physical presence while he lived among them is also available to believers through the Holy Spirit. Because the Holy Spirit was sent so that we would always have YHWH's presence available to us, we also can feel his love for us daily. However, to feel the same unconditional love that the apostles felt, we need to have the willingness to practice God's love languages with him. Only when we have truly felt God's love for us will we ever be able to love others as Jesus loves us, regardless of how fluent we may have become in learning God's words through Scripture alone.

Heart Knowledge

Growing up, I was taught by my mother, preachers, and Sunday school teachers about YHWH's love for his children. However, just because I had the knowledge that God loved me did not mean that I could really feel his love for me. Just like I couldn't feel my husband's love because we were speaking different love languages, I could not feel YHWH's love because I honestly don't think I was ever truly taught how to hear the Holy Spirit's voice or speak his love language in return. It wasn't until my first encounter with YHWH through the sacred fire in my dryer that I personally felt God's love for the very first time. And it wasn't until I had my first encounter with Jesus through the healing of my abortion that I felt the sacrificial love of YHWH's Son for me. I finally understood in my heart that Jesus laid down his life for me, for my sins. In just two encounters with the living God, all of the head knowledge I had been taught my entire life became heart knowledge, and I was born again of the Spirit. All of a sudden I had a willingness to begin practicing YHWH's love languages with him. Because we started speaking the same language, I soon discovered God's unconditional love for me—an unconditional love that had been there the entire time. As a result, I was able to express my love for him and others in return.

I discovered how to truly love YHWH with all of my heart, soul, and mind by spending *quality time* with him Spirit to Spirit and heart to heart, studying his Word, listening to his voice, and wanting to do his will and not mine. I also realized how much YHWH desired to hear my *words of affirmation* of him through worship on Sunday mornings and through my prayers. He taught me that serving in church and local charities are *acts of service* for him, where I could *physically touch* his other children through my hands and feet. I learned that giving of my time and money to YHWH's kingdom were my personal *gifts to God*. He desired for me to speak these languages because they were freewill offerings given from my heart. At first, practicing these love languages felt like sacrifices and work, but the more I did them the more I looked forward to expressing my love in these ways. I actually began to long for quality time with my LORD and Savior and desired to do his will. As a result, I began to hear his voice more frequently, to feel his daily presence more often, and to feel his love for me over and over again. Every time I gave YHWH a freewill offering, he sent his sacred fire from heaven to light my sacrifice as he did for the Israelites after they built his tabernacle and temple and made their first sacrifice to him. God's lighting of my personal sacrifices warms my soul and fills me with passion for him and his kingdom. I found that loving others became much easier because YHWH himself was filling my love bucket. No longer was I continuously searching for love from others. Instead, I was capable of outwardly expressing the love I felt from God to others. I sincerely started to want to love others as Jesus commanded of his disciples. Therefore, because I started asking YHWH for his will instead of mine, God started letting me know pretty regularly how I could serve him in his kingdom. When he spoke, I listened and obeyed.

Through all of the acts of service and gifts of time and money that YHWH has requested of me over the years, he has convinced me that there is one love language that he desires of his children above and beyond the rest, and that is our *gift of words*. The gift of words that he desires most from us is telling our own personal stories of when we hear his voice, answered prayers, how he redeems us out of sin, our salvation stories, and the ways he interacts in our lives. The telling of our testimonies is a love language like no other because it is our stories that *physically touch* God's heart, our own hearts, and the hearts of the people we are speaking to. Our testimonies are detailed accounts of what happens when we spend *quality time* listening to the voice of the Holy

Spirit. They are *words of affirmation* that YHWH exists and wants to have an intimate relationship with us. They are *acts of service* for his kingdom—telling others what is possible when we listen and obey. Our testimonies encompass all five love languages at once. Our stories confirm to nonbelievers that we serve a living God.

When the apostles went out into the world to share the good news of the gospel, many times a day they shared the stories of their personal experiences with Jesus. The stories that they shared over and over again with the Jews and the Gentiles included everything from the first time they met Jesus to the very last day when he ascended into heaven. I'm sure their stories included their own personal testimonies of how they came to know that Jesus was truly the Messiah, the Son of God, and how Jesus continued to love them even when they feared, doubted, and struggled with walking in his footsteps. It was only through these very detailed and intimate stories that the apostles became credible witnesses to others. Their passion for Jesus was surely felt by everyone they spoke to. It was simply by their testimonies that thousands came to know Jesus Christ and then received the Holy Spirit. Every day when the apostles told their stories, it was as if they were experiencing their days with Jesus all over again. By reliving their stories, the memories of all that had taken place became imprinted on their brains, and their faith became so solid that no one could ever make them deny Jesus's name ever again. It was through the retelling of their testimonies and the solid faith that it produced that they were able to overcome Satan's attacks and threats of death and to fulfill God's will for their lives.

When Jesus came to this world, his mission was to tell man what he personally knew about his heavenly Father. He did this because he knew it was YHWH's will. God allowed signs and miracles to accompany Jesus's words to help people believe that the words Jesus was speaking were truth. Likewise, the apostles went out into the world to tell mankind what they personally knew about Jesus because God's will for them was to make disciples of all the nations by baptizing them in the name of the Father, the Son, and the Holy Spirit. Accompanying the apostles' words were signs and miracles to help the people believe that the words they spoke were also truth. Because the apostles did as they were commanded, the story of the gospel of Jesus Christ and his Father YHWH has reached every continent. Because they became bold in telling their personal stories, we have been given the incredible opportunity of new life through Jesus Christ.

But the stories that convinced me that Jesus was worthy of following were not the stories of the apostles. The stories that finally convinced me were the everyday stories of people I personally knew who had come to know Jesus Christ. It was the signs and miracles they had experienced and the passion in their voices that made these people credible witnesses for Jesus. It was their testimonies that eventually made me jealous enough to want what they had. If I had never heard their stories, if they had remained silent, I would never have asked God, "Do you exist?" Therefore, just as it was YHWH's will for Jesus and the apostles to tell their personal stories, so it is YHWH's will for us to tell our stories.

Storytelling

Since I have always been a storyteller, sharing my personal God stories has always been easy for me. One of my favorites is my dryer story. I have told that story so many times that I have lost count. Every time I tell it, I relive it, and as a result what YHWH said to me on that day has been imprinted on my brain. Every time I tell it, YHWH reconfirms to me that he exists. I remember once telling a new friend this same story. I will never forget the day because it was September 11, 2001, the day the Twin Towers in New York came crashing down. As we were watching the story unfold before us and people started asking the questions, "Where is God?" and "Does God exist?" I was able to relay my story. I already knew God existed because of my own personal experience of hearing his voice. As we were looking at the ashes of the fallen towers, I conveyed to my friend what YHWH had said to me the day I was looking at the ashes in my dryer: "Judy, this is life without me!" God's words, which he had spoken to me years before, were now spoken to my friend. On that fateful day of September 11, 2001, YHWH's words were once again profoundly significant.

Approximately twelve years later, I ran into this same woman. As we were catching up with what was going on in our individual lives, I told her I was writing a book about God's divine name and how he communicates with us. Her first question was, "Will it include your dryer story?" I said in amazement, "Wow, you remember my story?" She replied, "Yes, of course I remember your story, because of the impact it had on you." So whether it was the passion in my voice, the signs and wonders that accompanied my story, or the context in which the words were spoken that made her remember, I will never know. But what I do know is that on that day of 9/11, I was a credible witness for the one and only true God and, as a result, YHWH's words were remembered.

Abortion Story

Because my dryer story has always been a fun story to tell, I never hesitate to share it with the new people I meet. However, there are some stories that are not enjoyable to tell. I will never forget the first time YHWH asked me to share the story of my abortion. One day my friend Rachel encouraged me to give my testimony in front of our Bible study group. I looked at her as if she were crazy and immediately told her no. Even though I had shared my story with other women in smaller settings, I had no desire to share it in front of one hundred women. Well, as God would have it, Rachel would not accept no for an answer. She asked me to pray about it and to ask YHWH what he wanted me to do. So for an entire week, I totally ignored God and the subject as I went about my week, hoping it would all go away. But of course it didn't. It wasn't until the following Sunday before church, when I had some quiet time with YHWH, that I voiced my question directly to him. On that very day, YHWH chose to let me know his will through our preacher.

The Bible verses that morning were from the Gospel of Mark. James and John asked Jesus who among them was great. Jesus replied, "But it shall not be so among you; *but whoever would be great among you must be slave of all.* For the *Son of Man also came not to be served but to serve,* and to give his life as a ransom for many" (Mark 10:43–45). Our pastor said that in order to be truly great, we must take every opportunity to leverage the needs of others before our own. Immediately, upon hearing my pastor's words, I felt as if Jesus was speaking directly to me through Scripture, and I knew God's will. I understood with great clarity that my testimony of my abortion was not going to be for me or for my agenda but for the needs of others. By speaking my testimony I would be serving my God, for his agenda and for his kingdom.

My husband and I used to have a saying in our household when our boys were young and would complain that they didn't like how vegetables tasted. We would frequently tell them, "We don't always eat certain foods because they taste good. Sometimes we have to eat certain foods because they will make us stronger." I would say that theory applies to our spiritual lives as well. Even though I had absolutely no desire to give my testimony, I knew that somehow through it I would be made stronger in Christ. So a few weeks later I humbled myself. In front of one hundred women, I confessed that I was a sinner in need of a Savior. Through tears, I was able to convey my first encounter with Jesus Christ and my story of redemption. I shared with these women all that had taken place so many years ago, including the spiritual healing, signs, and wonders that followed the miracle of being forgiven and set free. Upon giving my testimony, I immediately knew that I had experienced even more healing. I came to understand that we are all sinners in need of a Savior, that we all have our own stories of redemption, and that my sin was not greater or less than anyone else's sin. By giving my testimony I acknowledged that it was only because of Jesus Christ's unconditional love for me that I was given new life. On that day, my faith truly became stronger because YHWH used me as a credible witness to the healing powers of Jesus Christ.

YHWH blessed me for my obedience, for my love language. On the following Tuesday, I received a letter from one of the women who had been in the audience. She wanted to thank me for my strength and for humbling myself to speak in front of everyone. My words spoke directly to her, for she had experienced two abortions in college and, like me, had told no one. My words caused this woman to become jealous of my healing and to desire the same for herself. So on the day that I spoke, she went home and told her husband all about her past. My strength had given her power to reveal all of her deep, dark secrets for the very first time. In addition, over the following twelve months, she was able to share with her parents all that had happened in college, including all of the other issues that had plagued her since she was a teenager. As a result, light was brought into the darkness, and peace and joy became commonplace in her life. Approximately one year later, this same woman took the stage of our Bible study and shared her testimony in front of one hundred women. It wasn't easy for her, as she also gave it through tears. Through it all, she shared with us the miracles, signs, and wonders that accompanied her healing because of the redeeming power of Jesus in her own life. Oh, what a powerful testimony it was, and what a credible witness she became for Jesus Christ. In the sharing of her testimony, this woman's faith in the redeeming power of God's Son also became stronger.

Because I was willing to take a step out of my comfort zone, everything worked out exactly as God had planned. It always amazes me how strategic YHWH is in his commands. God knew who would be in the audience on the day I shared my testimony. He knew my story would be needed for the process of healing to begin in this woman's life. Sometimes I wonder what would have happened if I had decided to remain silent instead of being obedient to YHWH's will. I wonder how much longer she would have suffered in silence until God used someone else to speak into her life. As a result of this experience, I have never hesitated to share any of my stories. I realize that my words could be exactly what YHWH wants the person sitting next to me to hear. Because I have become so faithful in telling my personal God stories, I know with all my heart that is why YHWH continues to shower me with more and more stories to tell, with just as many miracles, signs, and wonders to accompany them. He knows that he can trust me with sharing the words he has personally placed on my lips. In telling his stories, YHWH has convinced me that I am helping to accomplish his will on earth—as it is in heaven.

Judy Jacobson

My Baptism

So when YHWH asked me in the spring of 2012 to speak in front of thousands of people, my answer was a resounding yes. In January of that year, our preacher asked us to identify the one thing that God was asking us to complete for him that year. At that time, I thought the answer was that I was to finish writing this book. It wasn't until the next Sunday when our preacher spoke on baptism that I knew without a doubt the one thing that I was to complete. Through studying the book of Acts the previous year, I had already come to the conclusion that there was one very special event that was missing in my life. Throughout my entire life, I had assumed that being baptized as a baby was biblical because it was my denomination's tradition. It wasn't until I studied God's Word for myself that I became convinced that this was simply not true. So the Holy Spirit's voice spoke to me through our preacher that Sunday morning and convicted me that I needed to be baptized as an adult. That thought was confirmed when I heard the words of the last song we sang that morning, which was "One Thing Remains" by Brian Johnson, Christa Gifford, and Jeremy Riddle.[2] It was something I knew that I needed to do to be spiritually complete.

The Holy Spirit knew that my baptism in 2012 was of much more importance to YHWH than finishing my book. So on March 8, I was baptized in the name of the Father, the Son, and the Holy Spirit in front of a thousand people. Before my physical baptism took place, my prerecorded testimony (okay, so I didn't *actually* speak in front of thousands of people) was played on screen for everyone in the audience to see and hear. This time, the story YHWH wanted me to share in front of others was not my dryer story or my abortion story, but it was my story about being clothed in the power of the Holy Spirit. He wanted me to share with others what is possible when we ask for *everything* the Holy Spirit has to offer us.

I knew I was doing YHWH's will by being baptized because of the signs and wonders that accompanied it. Somehow he managed to schedule my baptism for a Thursday night during our Night of Worship instead of on a typical Sunday morning as it is normally done. It took place exactly *one year from the day* that God gave me his gift from the Holy Spirit. In addition, the song that was sung immediately before my baptism was "One Thing Remains"—the same song YHWH chose to convince me to be baptized in the first place. This particular song is a love song about God's love never failing or running out. YHWH knew how much meaning the date and the song would have for me. On that night, God wanted me to personally know that his love will always be available to me. Because I *felt* his love for me so strongly, I will never doubt it again.

In essence, my baptism was my gift of words to God—my love language to publicly thank YHWH for all that he has done for me over the years. He had given me so many incredible gifts that I felt the least I could do is to tell another one of his love stories. By publicly proclaiming that Jesus Christ is my LORD and Savior, I said to YHWH that night, "Here I am, LORD; I am forever yours!" My words to God were words that he had been waiting to hear from me since the day I was born.

Because I have discovered how to speak YHWH's love languages, I am able to feel his love. If you have never personally felt YHWH's love, that doesn't mean that his love is not available. It simply means that you have not learned to speak his love languages. When you decide to start making sacrifices to learn his spiritual languages, you will be rewarded with feeling his unconditional love, a love for you that has been there your entire life. When you give your love freely to him, he will light your sacrifices with his sacred fire—his Holy Spirit within you. He will light a passion and warmth in your heart that you have never felt before. As a result, your relationship with YHWH will grow into the loving relationship that he always desired to have with you.

Giving Your Best

Just as the Israelites were to offer the best of the best to YHWH through their animal offerings, we are also to offer the best of the best when it comes to our love offerings. Unlike animal and grain offerings, love offerings have the capability of changing the world one heart at a time.

If we are boldly proclaiming Jesus's name through our own personal stories, then we are doing God's will by being credible witnesses for his living Word. When we tell our stories and speak our other love languages, we are dropping YHWH's seeds exactly as he designed us to, just like those pine trees in Yellowstone National Park. We make the seeds of the gospel of Jesus and of his love readily available to others so that when their own sacred fires are lit, new life will be possible. It is not only our belief in God but our true-life stories that have come about through the Holy Spirit that make us distinct from all the other people in the world. And it is the love that we show others through the love languages of the Holy Spirit that prove that we are Jesus's disciples. It is the love languages that we speak that eventually draw others to Jesus's love for them.

When we share our stories in Jesus's name, we are talking in the *new tongues* that Jesus promised would be a sign that followed believers (Mark 16:17). We are Jesus's witnesses for this generation. We are his disciples, his humble prophets. We must speak YHWH's words, even if they fall on deaf ears like most of the prophets' messages did. We must speak boldly about our encounters, or the unthinkable could happen—the truth about Jesus could be lost to our children's generation.

So I challenge you today to think of the one thing that you need to complete this year for YHWH's kingdom so that you too can be a credible witness to others for Jesus. Because of the power of the name you are working for, you will be able to literally change the lives of the people you encounter by your obedience, both physically and spiritually. If you start every day by asking God, "What does love demand of me today?" I promise that you will start hearing YHWH's voice very loudly and very clearly. Because YHWH knows firsthand that love has the capacity to change the world, this question is one of his favorites. When we love others as Jesus loved us, we are giving our heavenly Father our biggest sacrifice of all—a piece of our heart to someone else. And when we love through God's sacred fire—his Holy Spirit—it is guaranteed that people will take notice because YHWH's sacred fire *never* goes undetected.

Chapter 21

The Antichrist

Now war arose in heaven, Michael and his angels fighting against the dragon. And the dragon and his angels fought back, but he was defeated, and there was no longer any place for them in heaven. **And the great dragon was thrown down, that ancient serpent, who is called the Devil and Satan, the deceiver of the whole world—he was thrown down to the earth, and his angels were thrown down with him**. And I heard a loud voice in heaven, saying, "Now the salvation and the power and the kingdom of our God and the authority of his Christ have come, for **the accuser of our brothers has been thrown down**, who accuses them day and night before our God. And **they have conquered him by the blood of the Lamb and by the word of their testimony, for they loved not their lives even unto death**. Therefore, rejoice, O heavens and you who dwell in them! **But woe to you, O earth and sea, for the devil has come down to you in great wrath, because he knows that his time is short!**" (Rev. 12:7–12 ESV)

Until he is thrown out of heaven for good, Satan's primary and most successful strategy since Christ's death and resurrection has been to convince people that either God truly does not exist or that Jesus is not the Son of God. Satan knows that if he can get people to deny either the Father or the Son's name, eternal hell will be their consequence. He is well aware that both of YHWH's names are needed in order for the voice of God to be heard. When the voice of God is not heard, the only voice people hear is their own or Satan's, which is exactly how he likes it. Without the voice of God in someone's life, the devil knows that spiritual love languages are rarely expressed.

Another strategy of Satan's has been to convince the world that he himself does not exist. As long as you do not know that there is a real spiritual enemy in this world named Satan, you will never know that you need to resist him or fight against what he is doing in your life. By convincing people that he does not exist, he successfully deceives them into believing that *all* of their thoughts are either their own thoughts or given to them by God. It never becomes apparent to these people that the true source of the majority of their self-destructive talk is from the Father of Lies, Satan himself.

In addition, by convincing people that he does not exist, Satan also successfully convinces people that the book of Revelation must simply be a fairy tale. You see, the book of Revelation is all about him. Therefore, Satan is very interested in keeping people from reading or studying it.

For people who do believe in the name of the Father and the Son and also believe that Satan exists, the devil uses the more subtle approach of convincing them that faith is a private matter and should not be discussed with friends, family, or colleagues. By doing this, Satan has actually created a new way of denying Jesus—by simply being silent. Satan has convinced believers throughout the ages that it is fine to believe what you want to believe but not to share your faith with others, because even Satan knows the power of God's stories. He uses this tactic because he knows Jesus's own words: "So everyone who acknowledges me before men, I also will acknowledge before my Father who is in heaven; but *whoever denies me before men, I also will deny before my Father in heaven*" (Matt. 10:32–33).

Both Judas and Peter denied knowing Jesus before men. The difference between these two men, as far as we know, is that Judas never repented of his grievous sin before he died. He therefore did not receive eternal life at his death. Peter, on the other hand, truly repented of his sin and, as a result, never again denied Jesus's name before man. Instead, he proclaimed Christ's name for the rest of his life. When believers remain silent about Jesus, they are essentially telling Jesus that he is not a priority in their lives, because it is the people we love that we talk about the most. If you never talk about Jesus with others, then you may need to question yourself about your love for him.

Even though Satan's methods of deceiving YHWH's people have changed throughout the centuries, there has been one common theme in his tactics. His main goal is to use whatever means possible to keep people from hearing YHWH's voice. When there is no voice, there is no relationship. One day, not so far in the future, Satan and his demons will finally be thrown out of heaven forever. On this day, his game plan will change one last time. At this point, he will know that his time is short, and, because of it, he will come to earth with great wrath. Satan will make war with the saints because his full power will be unleashed. For the first time in history, he will be able to physically kill believers for their belief in the names of YHWH and Jesus.

> **And I saw a beast rising out of the sea.** ... And to it **the dragon gave his power and his throne and great authority**. One of its heads seemed to have a mortal wound, but its mortal wound was healed, and the whole earth marveled as they followed the beast. **And they worshiped the dragon, for he had given his authority to the beast, and they worshiped the beast, saying, "Who is like the beast, and who can fight against it?"** And the beast was given a mouth uttering haughty and blasphemous words, and it was allowed to exercise authority for **forty-two months**. It opened its mouth to utter blasphemies against God, **blaspheming his name and his dwelling**, that is, those who dwell in heaven. Also it was allowed to make war on the saints and to conquer them. And authority was given it over every tribe and people and language and nation, and **all who dwell on earth will worship it, everyone whose name has not been written before the foundation of the world in the book of life of the Lamb who was slain**. (Rev. 13:1–8 ESV)

Just as YHWH sent his Son, Jesus, to complete his mission, Satan will send his Antichrist to complete his. In these verses, Satan is described as the dragon, and the Antichrist is described as the beast. The Antichrist will receive all of Satan's power, his throne, and his great authority in order to achieve his goal. Just as YHWH's Holy Spirit descended from heaven and remained on Jesus, Satan's spirit will enter the Antichrist. In a similar way that he was allowed to enter Judas on the night he betrayed Jesus (Luke 22:3), Satan will enter the Antichrist. Unlike Jesus, who came down from heaven in his Father YHWH's holy name, the Antichrist will ascend from the sea, the bottomless pit, in his own name and will claim to be God. He will embody all of the pride of Satan by exalting himself, not only against YHWH but also against everything that bears his holy name. Satan's deepest craving will be for all people to bow down to his name as their god. His spirit will dwell within the Antichrist with one goal in mind—to destroy mankind.

> Then **I saw another beast which rose out of the earth; it had two horns like a lamb and it spoke like a dragon**. It exercises all the authority of the first beast in its presence, and **makes the earth and its inhabitants worship the first beast, whose mortal wound was healed**. It works great signs, even making fire come down from heaven to earth in the sight of men; and by the signs which it is allowed to work in the presence of the beast, **it deceives those who dwell on earth, bidding them make an image for the beast which was wounded by the sword and yet lived**; and it was allowed to give breath to the image of the beast so that the image of the beast should even speak, and **to cause those who would not worship the image of the beast to be slain**. Also it causes **all**, both small and great, both rich and poor, both free and slave **to be marked on the right hand or the forehead, so that no one can buy or sell unless he has the mark, that is, the name of the beast or the number of its name**. This calls for wisdom: let him who has understanding

> reckon the number of the beast, **for it is a human number, its number is six hundred and sixty-six**. (Rev. 13:11–18)

The Antichrist will have an accomplice to assist him in his mission. Most people refer to this second beast as the False Prophet. The job of the False Prophet will be to "prepare the way" for the Antichrist, just as John the Baptist prepared the way for Jesus. His goal will be to deceive all of mankind into worshipping the first beast. While in the Antichrist's presence, the False Prophet will be given the ability to work "pretended" signs and wonders in front of humans in order to deceive them into worshipping the Antichrist. His wicked deception will work because it is prophesied that people will make a graven image of the Antichrist and then will bow down and worship it. In addition, the False Prophet will cause all people to receive a mark of the beast, either on their right hands or their foreheads.

Those who choose not to bow down to the image of the beast will be slain. In addition, those who choose not to receive the mark of the beast will not be able to buy or sell anything, including food. The resulting consequence of not receiving the mark of the beast will be starvation. Remember when I said that if Satan could outright kill us, he would? He doesn't currently have that ability because YHWH and Jesus have been restraining him since he deceived Adam and Eve in the garden of Eden. They have been restraining him so as to protect mankind from his pure evil. Currently, we do suffer harm from Satan, and the consequences of following his ways can result in death, but he himself cannot slay us at will. That will continue to be the case until Satan's power is unleashed on the day he is no longer allowed access to heaven. During this time, Satan will be speaking the physical language of death and starvation in order to intimidate believers into denying Jesus Christ's name.

Since the garden of Eden, we know of many instances throughout Scripture of people being possessed by Satan's demons, but never before has his entire being been able to embody another human being—or he would have done it a long time ago. Yes, there have been individuals throughout history who have been possessed by Satan's demons, such as Hitler and Stalin, but the evil these men portrayed does not even come close to the evil that the Antichrist will bring to the world. These historical figures may have deceived and murdered many people, but in the end all of these men were ultimately destroyed by the good and truth found in other men. In contrast, when Satan is finally unleashed to the earth, his evil will so completely embody the Antichrist that the only entities capable of destroying him will be YHWH himself and his Son, Jesus. The ultimate goal of Satan entering into the Antichrist is so that he can "play God" and be worshipped. It all goes back to the reason for his rebellion in the first place, which is pride. Satan wants to be on YHWH's throne so badly that he is willing to do whatever it takes to assume that position, even if it's just for the short time he is allowed to physically reign on earth in human form.

Man of Lawlessness

> Let no one deceive you in any way; for that day [Jesus's second coming] will not come, unless the rebellion comes first, and **the man of lawlessness is revealed**, the son of perdition, who opposes and **exalts himself against every so-called god or object of worship, so that he takes his seat in the temple of God, proclaiming himself to be God**. (2 Thess. 2:3–4)

To achieve his goal of complete control of the world, Satan will exalt himself through the Antichrist against not only YHWH but every other so-called god or object of worship as well. His deception will be made possible because it is prophesied that the Antichrist will appear to suffer a fatal wound to his head by the sword, from which he will be healed. It will seem to those watching that he died and was raised from the dead. And because of the belief that only God can raise the dead, the majority of the nations will worship the Antichrist as god. At this point in history, Satan will take the seat he has desired from the beginning of time, the seat in the temple of YHWH in Jerusalem.

Before Satan is cast out of heaven, we know from Scripture that a third temple will be built in Jerusalem. The Jewish people have been waiting for this moment since Herod's temple was destroyed in AD 70, at which point all sacrifices ceased. Although attempts have been made over the centuries to rebuild the temple, they have all failed. However, sometime in the future, YHWH will allow the Jewish people to finally construct a third temple and sacrifices will resume. It is in this temple that I believe Satan will take his seat. When we consider the details of Solomon's temple, which the third temple will likely be built to resemble, we know that there was no seat in the temple of God except for the mercy seat over the ark of the covenant. Remember, the ark of the covenant represents God's throne that is in heaven. So by sitting on the mercy seat of the newly rebuilt ark of the covenant in the Holy of Holies, Satan will symbolically be sitting on the throne of YHWH on earth.

By sitting on the mercy seat of the ark of the covenant, Satan will be taunting YHWH with the power that he has used throughout the centuries to get YHWH's people to disobey his commandments. He will be reminding God of how he influenced his people to stop saying his holy name and to break commandment after commandment. Satan will remind YHWH of how he has distracted people over the centuries from hearing the voice of YHWH or Jesus. I believe Satan will be reminding YHWH that it was because of him that YHWH had to send his Son, Jesus, to die on the cross in order to atone for all the sins of the world. With pride, Satan will be saying to YHWH, "Take a look at the world now, and see who your people are worshipping. Look at who has finally taken over your temple and is sitting on your throne on earth in the Holy of Holies."

As god, Satan will have the desire to mark his people with his seal, like YHWH seals his people with the Holy Spirit. So in the end times he will choose to mark his people with *either* his name *or* the number of his name, which is 666. One of these identifying seals will be placed on either the forehead or the right hand of everyone throughout the world. Anyone without these marks will be refused the right to buy or sell. When individuals accept this mark, Satan will be claiming them as his own.

Judy Jacobson

The Number 666

Many Bible scholars believe that when the letters of the Antichrist's name are converted to numbers (gematria), they will equal 666. That may be the case, but until we know who the Antichrist is, we will not know for sure if that is what Jesus meant. And really, what good will that knowledge accomplish? Some will say that it will help us to identify who the Antichrist is. I don't see why that is necessary when Scripture already gives us so many identifying signs. Scripture clearly tells us that the Antichrist will be a man who claims to be god, who receives a mortal wound to the head, and who is brought back to life. He will sit on the seat in the rebuilt Jewish temple in Jerusalem and will at some point demand that everyone bow down to his graven image and take his mark. YHWH gave us this information so that we will know the Antichrist when we see him. For those who know YHWH's truth, there will be no doubt in their minds of the identity of the Antichrist. We will not need to determine if his name adds up to 666 in order to come to this conclusion. Therefore, I believe the number 666 represents so much more than the total value of the Antichrist's name.

Jesus tells us through the apostle John that the number 666 is a human number. The number six is considered a human number in the Bible because it was on the sixth day that man was created. Each human being consists of a body, a soul, and a spirit. Our bodies are our physical beings. Our minds, will, and emotions compose our souls, while our spirits are the first breath of God that brings us to physical life. So when I see the number 666 and consider it a human number, I see the three 6's as representing our bodies, souls, and spirits.

After man was created on the sixth day, it wasn't until the seventh, or Sabbath, day that man was invited to rest in the presence of God. So our human number 6 is one number short of being in the eternal presence of YHWH. Since the number 7 represents spiritual completion and perfection, when it comes to our body, soul, and spirit, our human number of 666 represents our imperfect human condition. Only when we ask Jesus into our lives to be our Savior and then start spending time resting in the presence of our Creator and communicating with him will the number of our beings ever change and move beyond our imperfect human condition.

When you receive YHWH's Holy Spirit in Jesus's name, your spirit and YHWH's Spirit become one. Your spirit becomes a new creation because instantly you have the Creator of life residing within you. No longer is your spirit the spirit of the world, which is considered dead in God's eyes (Eph. 2:1–22). By receiving God's Holy Spirit, your spirit is made brand new and perfect, and it consists of God's will, the mind of Christ, and all the fruits of the Spirit—which are heavenly emotions. However, at the moment of receiving your new spirit, your soul still consists of your own free will, your mind, and your earthly emotions. It's only after you start spending daily time in the presence of your LORD and Savior that your soul is refreshed. Over the years of spending time with your heavenly Father, your mind will be renewed and start looking like the mind of Christ. Your will becomes God's will, and because of it your emotions start reflecting *all* the fruits of the Spirit, regardless of your circumstances. When this happens, you begin to live abundantly and to the fullest. Because when your soul becomes renewed through the Holy Spirit within you, your hands, feet, and mouth become the hands, feet, and mouth of Jesus. No longer is your body controlled by a troubled soul but by a soul that has been redeemed, restored, and renewed—a soul that is Spirit-led.

By receiving YHWH's Holy Spirit in Jesus's name, you are also guaranteed that, one day, your body will be raised gloriously from the dead. On that day your body and soul will completely reflect the perfect Spirit who lived within you while you walked the earth. Your entire being will finally have reached perfection. You will be in your Creator's physical presence for eternity. The moment you see YHWH face to face, you will finally understand with certainty that the purpose of your life was, and always has been, to spend time daily in his Shekinah glory.

So the number 666 can really be seen as *our own human number*— before we put our faith in the names of YHWH and Jesus and start speaking their spiritual language. Therefore, unbelievers who receive the mark of the beast will really just be receiving their own number. Satan knows this to be true because the number 666 has represented his condition from the day he rebelled against YHWH and was renamed. From the very beginning he rejected the names of the Father and the Son and therefore obtained his new number, and he will never achieve spiritual perfection. In addition, when it comes to Satan, the number 666 represents not only himself and his name but also the evil trinity between himself (the Dragon), the Antichrist, and the False Prophet. Satan's trinity represents the epitome of sinful man and what will be possible when all of Satan's evil power is unleashed to do whatever he pleases, with no one stopping him.

Bowing to Satan

When Satan claims that he is god and deceives people into believing him, the majority of people will bow down to his graven image. When they do this, they will be breaking the first and second of YHWH's Ten Commandments. And when they choose to receive the mark of the beast on their right hands or on their foreheads, they will be breaking the third commandment by profaning YHWH's holy name. By bowing down to the Antichrist's image, they will be worshipping Satan's name. This brings us to the fourth commandment:

> "**Remember the sabbath day, to keep it holy**. Six days you shall labor, and do all your work; **but the seventh day is a sabbath to YHWH your God**; in it you shall not do any work, you, or your son, or your daughter, your manservant, or your maidservant, or your cattle, or the sojourner who is within your gates; **for in six days YHWH made heaven and earth, the sea, and all that is in them, and rested the seventh day; therefore YHWH blessed the sabbath day and hallowed it**." (Exo. 20:8–11)

The fourth commandment was given to Israelites as a sign that YHWH was their God and they were his people. It was on this seventh day of every week that God asked his people to rest from their work and their daily lives and instead to spend it resting in his holy presence. On the Sabbath day, it is believed that YHWH's Shekinah glory physically descended upon the Jewish people and into their homes. If the people refused to rest on this day, then they missed out on resting in YHWH's holy presence. By consistently spending time together, God knew that his people would begin to hear his voice, feel his presence, and become distinct, and that is why he made this day holy.

From the time God spoke the fourth commandment until AD 321, the Jewish people and then the followers of Christ kept the seventh day as the Sabbath. However, in AD 321, the emperor of Rome, Constantine, decided to change the day of the Sabbath from the seventh day to the first day of the week. Since the time of Moses, the seventh day of the week began Friday night at sunset and ended Saturday night at sunset, with the first day of the week starting on Saturday night and ending Sunday night. The Catholic Church decided to follow Constantine's orders to change the day of the Sabbath and eventually claimed the change as their own idea. We know through documentation from the Catholic Church, and also the Protestant churches that later followed suit, this change was made to reflect the day Jesus rose from the dead. All of these churches agree that this decision to change the Sabbath day was made on their own, without approval from YHWH.[1] Therefore, since AD 321, most Christian believers have been breaking the fourth commandment every week—not because it is a sin to worship YHWH on Sunday but because we are not "resting in his presence on the seventh day," as he has commanded us.

I believe the moving of the Sabbath day from Saturday to Sunday is one of Satan's deceptions that he was able to accomplish through church leaders long ago. I believe he did this so that when his Antichrist is reigning, he will be able to profane YHWH's seventh-day Sabbath in a way that only he could. When the Antichrist comes and claims that he is god, it would be expected that he will demand his followers to worship him on the seventh day of the week as Scripture commands. He will take this seventh day as his own, so that instead of YHWH being worshipped on this day, he will be worshipped. If people believe he is the one and only true god, he might even be able to deceive them into thinking that since they have been breaking the fourth commandment for centuries now, it is time to bring the Sabbath day back to its appropriate day. The prophecy of Daniel says this about the Antichrist: "He shall speak words against the Most High, and shall wear out the saints of the Most High, and *shall think to change the times and the law*" (Dan. 7:25). I believe the *law* that Satan will think to change is the *time* of the Sabbath day. I believe he convinced the leaders of the church to change the day of the Sabbath back in AD 321 so that when his Antichrist comes, he can change the Sabbath back to YHWH's holy day in order to commit the ultimate sin. Worshipping the Antichrist on the seventh day will make YHWH's Sabbath day anything but holy.

When people around the world are bowing down to the Antichrist on the seventh day, I imagine that Satan will be taunting YHWH, saying, "Look what has happened to your holy Sabbath Day, and look at whose name the people of this world are worshipping on this day." What Satan won't understand is that this will not be offensive to YHWH. Since the new covenant of Jesus Christ and the giving of his Holy Spirit to those who believe in Jesus's name, it won't matter what Satan does to the Sabbath day because YHWH knows that his believers can now rest in his presence any day of the week. YHWH's holy presence has already descended upon his believers and has remained.

Jesus summed up the first four commandments as loving YHWH your God with all your heart, with all your soul, and with all your mind (Matt. 22:36–38). By forcing people to break the first four commandments, Satan will be trying to ensure that the people are sinning against Jesus's most important commandment. We can also be sure that during the Antichrist's reign, the fifth through the tenth commandments will be broken regularly because, undoubtedly, he and his henchmen will be murdering, stealing, lying, coveting, committing adultery, and dishonoring their fathers and mothers.

So with all the evil that will be in the world during this time, how will true believers be able to navigate when they will be threatened with death and starvation if they disobey? We must keep in mind that everything Satan will be doing through his Antichrist and his False Prophet will be for the purpose of influencing humans to give up their inheritance to be with God for eternity. By worshipping the beast and his image or by receiving the mark of the beast, people will deny Jesus's name before man in the ultimate way, and Jesus will therefore deny their names before his Father. Those who are deceived and receive Satan's mark will lose their inheritance. If this happens, they will be spending eternity with Satan in hell.

> "**If anyone worships the beast and his image, and receives a mark on his forehead or on his hand, he also shall drink the wine of God's wrath**, poured unmixed into the cup of his anger, and he shall be tormented with fire and sulphur in the presence of the holy angels and in the presence of the Lamb. And the smoke of their torment goes up for ever and ever; and **they have no rest, day or night, these worshipers of the beast and its image, and whoever receives the mark of its name.**" (Rev. 14:9–11)

Two Options

There will be two options: give in to Satan's tactics, live comfortably for forty-two more months (which is the length of the Antichrist's reign on earth), and then spend eternity in hell; or decide ahead of time never to bow down to any graven image or receive the mark of the Antichrist. The consequence of the latter decision will most likely be immediate death or starvation for those people and their families, and yet they will spend eternity in heaven resting in their Creator's presence. So you will truly have a decision to make. And you really should make that decision today, when the pressure of the terror of the Antichrist is not yet in the world. By being convicted of your decision today you will be more likely to make the right decision on the day when it really matters.

When I think of these threats from the Antichrist, I can't help but think of the story of Daniel's friends being thrown into a fiery furnace after they refused to bow down to king Nebuchadnezzar's golden image.

> Shadrach, Meshach, and Abednego answered the king, "O Nebuchadnezzar, we have no need to answer you in this matter. **If it be so, our God whom we serve is able to deliver us from the burning fiery furnace; and he will deliver us out of your hand, O king. But if not, be it known to you, O king, that we will not serve your gods or worship the golden image which you have set up.**" (Dan. 3:16–18)

Because Daniel's friends believed YHWH's promises and had complete faith that they were worshipping the one and only true God, their decision to not bow down to Nebuchadnezzar's image was easy. Some time in their past they had sought out God, and he had revealed himself to them. He had revealed himself to them in a way that no one could disprove. Their faith was strong because of past communication. They did not care that their lives hung in the balance, because ultimately they knew they would not lose their inheritance through physical death. They knew that whether they lived or died, YHWH would ultimately deliver them out of the enemy's hands.

Also, do you remember the story of Esau and Jacob when Jacob took Esau's inheritance away from him?

> Once when Jacob was boiling pottage, Esau came in from the field, and he was famished. And Esau said to Jacob, "**Let me eat some of that red pottage, for I am famished!**" ... Jacob said, "**First sell me your birthright.**" Esau said, "**I am about to die; of what use is a birthright to me?**" Jacob said, "Swear to me first." So he swore to him, and sold his birthright to Jacob. Then Jacob gave Esau bread and pottage of lentils, and **he ate and drank, and**

rose and went his way. Thus Esau despised his birthright. (Gen. 25:29–34)

For the people who choose to receive the mark of the beast, the day they receive the mark will be the day they sell their birthrights to the enemy. On that day they will value their physical lives more than their future spiritual inheritance. On that day they will be able to buy food and drink, eat, and go on their merry way, just like Esau. However, at some point they will realize what they have done, and, unfortunately, at that point it will be too late. Their decision concerning whom they worship will have been made. At that point, even if they repent in tears, it will be too late. Remember, once God shut the door of Noah's ark, it was not reopened.

So we all need to be careful to not fall into the same trap that Esau did of selling his inheritance for just one meal. I know that by not bowing down to the Antichrist and by not receiving his mark, my physical life may end; but considering the evil that will be going on in this world at that time, death may seem like the best option and I may welcome it. If I die during these times, then I will have the satisfaction of knowing that I died for the God who loved me so much that he sent his Son to die for me. But I also believe that in the same way Shadrach, Meshach, and Abednego were miraculously saved from the fiery furnace when death looked imminent, YHWH will be working miracles during this time. Do you remember who was seen walking with Shadrach, Meshach, and Abednego after being thrown into the fiery furnace?

> Then King Nebuchadnezzar was astonished and rose up in haste. He said to his counselors, "**Did we not cast three men bound into the fire?**" They answered the king, "True, O king." He answered, "**But I see four men loose**, walking in the midst of the fire, and they are not hurt; and **the appearance of the fourth is like a son of the gods**." (Dan. 3:24–25)

The fourth man seen walking among them, having the appearance like a "son of the gods," could only have been Jesus Christ since there is only one Son of God. Because these three men believed in YHWH with all their hearts, souls, and minds, Jesus loosed them from their bondage and walked among them. When they came out of the fire, Scripture tells us that the fire had not had any power over their bodies. The hair of their heads was not singed, their mantles were not harmed, and there was no smell of fire upon them (Dan. 3:27). These men had been thrown into a fire, and yet they were not consumed. Regarding this miracle, King Nebuchadnezzar said, "Blessed be the God of Shadrach, Meshach, and Abednego, who has sent his angel and delivered his servants, who trusted in him, and set aside the king's command, and *yielded up their bodies rather than serve and worship any god except their own God*" (Dan. 3:28 ESV).

I have no doubt during the time of the Antichrist that Jesus will be walking among his people, just as he did with Shadrach, Meshach, and Abednego, to save us from our hour of trial and imminent death when we refuse to deny YHWH and Jesus's name and bow down to the Antichrist's graven image. Although I believe that some of us will be miraculously saved from death during these days, I also believe that some of us will die a martyr's death like Stephen, the first martyr for Jesus (Acts 7:1–60). Because of Stephen's strong belief in Jesus Christ, no one could convince him to deny Jesus's name, and he was eventually stoned to death. However, just before Stephen died, he gazed up into heaven and said, "*Behold, I see the heavens opened, and the Son of man standing at the right hand of God.*" Because Stephen was seeing the glory of God at the moment he was being stoned to death, I believe that Stephen did not feel any of the physical pain that was being inflicted upon him; but instead, through all of his senses, he felt God's Shekinah glory like never before.

As far as not being able to buy and sell food as a result of refusing the mark of the beast, I believe that YHWH will honor our faith by supernaturally providing food and drink for some believers during these times. The story that comes to my mind is about the widow who was asked by Elijah the prophet to make him a meal during a severe famine that was caused by YHWH. At the time of Elijah's request, the widow had only a few morsels of bread and oil left in her jars and was planning to make herself and her son a meal to eat and then prepare to die. Elijah said,

> "**Fear not**; go and do as you have said; **but first make me a little cake of it and bring it to me,** and afterward make for yourself and your son. For thus says YHWH the God of Israel, '**The jar of meal shall not be spent, and the cruse of oil shall not fail, until the day that YHWH sends rain upon the earth.**'" (1 Kings 17:13–14)

And that is exactly what happened. Because the widow obeyed Elijah's command and served him first, before herself, she and her son were saved from starvation and death. In return for the widow's faith and obedience, God provided food for her and her son until the rains came and the famine ended. I believe we will see this very thing happening to those who stand firm and serve YHWH first by not denying his Son Jesus's name before man during the time of the Antichrist.

For those of us who have a personal relationship with YHWH, I know with certainty that our Father in heaven will be speaking to believers through his Holy Spirit during these difficult times. YHWH said that in the last days he would pour out an even greater portion of his Spirit upon all flesh. Sons and daughters will prophesy, young men will see visions, and old men will dream dreams (Acts 2:17–19). I believe his voice will be very loud and clear, and we will feel YHWH's presence in undeniable ways. As a result, we will be thoroughly convicted to make the right decisions so that we do not mistakenly sell our birthrights to Satan. If you have open communication with your heavenly Father, then there is no need for fear. As parents warn their children about danger, you can be assured that YHWH will also warn his children about the Antichrist when the time is right.

Just like the people whose job it is to detect counterfeit money don't spend time studying counterfeit bills, you do not need to spend a lot of time studying or worrying about the Antichrist. All you need to do is study the truth of Jesus Christ and seek out his Father's voice through the Holy Spirit so that when you hear the Antichrist's voice you will be able to readily identify him as Satan. Because you will have spent your life listening to YHWH's voice and speaking his spiritual love languages, you will easily detect the Antichrist when you see him.

One Final Note

Have you ever wondered why Satan wants his name or his number on our right hand or our forehead? Well, I did, and because I am a puzzle maker, I knew I wouldn't be satisfied until I had discovered all of the pieces. Here is what I discovered. A long time ago, YHWH commanded Moses to celebrate Passover as a commemoration of the day he led his people of Egypt, out of the bondage of slavery.

> "And you shall tell your son on that day, 'It is because of what **YHWH did for me when I came out of Egypt.' And it shall be to you as a sign on your hand and as a memorial between your eyes**, that the law of YHWH may be in your mouth; for with a strong hand YHWH has brought you out of Egypt." (Exo. 13:8–9)

YHWH was telling Moses that he would place a sign on the *hands and foreheads* of those who remembered what he had done for them in delivering them from Egypt. Their celebration of Passover was a sign of the covenant that YHWH was their God and they were his people; and they were therefore marked because of it.

When Jesus came as the Ark of the new covenant, he instructed his disciples that Passover would now be a day when they should remember what he did when he laid down his life in order for their sins to be forgiven. He said, "Do this in remembrance of me" as he was breaking the bread and drinking the wine that represented his body and his blood, given for the sins of mankind. Paul stated that by celebrating Jesus's death and resurrection through the LORD's Supper, believers are remembering the day Jesus delivered them from death and from the bondage of their enemy, Satan. So, just like YHWH placed a sign on the people who were delivered from Egypt, YHWH also places a sign on those who truly celebrate Christ's death and resurrection, the new Passover celebration, on their hands and foreheads.

I personally can only think of one sign YHWH would place on our hands and foreheads that would represent the new covenant of Jesus Christ, and that is YHWH's two divine names. When his names are placed on our foreheads, it symbolizes what happens when our minds spend time reflecting on his names. Just like the high priest pondered the Urim and Thummim, when we ponder the names *YHWH* and *Jesus,* we are given full communication with our heavenly Father. With full communication, we feel his unconditional love, are forgiven of our sins, and are given God's purpose and will for our lives. By dwelling on YHWH's divine names, God knows that our hearts will be lifted in praise and worship, our mouths will start to speak his love languages, and we will use our hands and feet to do the work of his kingdom, which his Son, Jesus, modeled for us while he walked on this earth. It is through our hands and through our voices that we express love to our heavenly Father and to our neighbors, and we shine Jesus's light into this dark world.

Satan becomes defenseless when love is spoken because love is the most intimate spiritual language there is. Therefore, in end times, Satan will try to conceal YHWH's names on our foreheads and our hands in order to cover the seal of the Holy Spirit. He will attempt to cover YHWH's names with his name in order to defeat God's love. Satan does not want us meditating on the names of YHWH and Jesus or doing God's will. He wants us brooding over our own physical lives, on when and where we will be getting our next meal. Don't let Satan win this battle in your current life or during the times of the Antichrist. From this day forward, contemplate only on the names worth exalting, and let YHWH be your protector, your provider, your deliverer, your LORD and Savior—your God.

"**Do not labor for food which perishes, but for the food which endures to eternal life**, which the Son of man will give to you; for on him has God the Father set his seal." (John 6:27)

"The Devil Lost This One!"

Chapter 22

The Great Physician

"Come now, let us reason together, says YHWH: **though your sins are like scarlet, they shall be as white as snow; though they are red like crimson, they shall become like wool**." (Isa. 1:18 ESV)

In January of 2012, I was given the opportunity to go to the Hippocrates Health Institute in West Palm Beach, Florida. Hippocrates, for whom this institute was named, was a Greek physician born in 460 BC. He became known as the founder of medicine and was regarded as the greatest physician of his time. Hippocrates held the belief that the body *must be treated as a whole* and not just a series of parts. He believed in the natural healing process of *rest, a good diet, fresh air, and cleanliness.* Today Hippocrates is known as the Father of Medicine.[1] When I was given the opportunity to visit a place that was not only named after him but also uses his natural principles in physical healing, I jumped at the chance.

I was so excited before my trip because I knew without a doubt that this trip was going to be another adventure orchestrated by God. I wasn't sure what YHWH had in store for me, but I was confident that I would see his glory shining through it all. The Scripture that kept popping into my head the entire week before I left was Jesus's reply to Satan as he was being tempted in the wilderness. "It is written, 'Man shall not live by bread alone, but by every word that proceeds from the mouth of God'" (Matt. 4:4). As I was reflecting on this verse all week long, I couldn't help recalling all of the personal spiritual healing that I had experienced through God's divine Word. I remembered all of the times I had heard God's voice and the peace, joy, and love that had filled my soul because of it. Because I had personally experienced the power of YHWH's living Word, I knew Jesus's words were truth. So I went to Hippocrates with very high expectations. After my one-week stay, all I can say is that my expectations were not only met but exceeded by leaps and bounds.

The majority of people who go to the Hippocrates Health Institute do so with the hope of healing their physical bodies of all different kinds of diseases. Men, women, and children all flock to this place with cancerous tumors of all kinds, high blood pressure, skin disorders, obesity, heart disease, intestinal issues, addictions, lung disorders, depression, and many other ailments. People come for many different reasons, but they all have one thing in common: they have all decided to take the healing of their physical bodies out of the hands of their doctors, who recommend surgery, chemo, radiation, and medications, and put it into their own hands. They have all reached a place in their sicknesses where they are tired of only having their symptoms masked by medications and instead desire true healing.

Visitors to Hippocrates are allowed to stay for only three weeks. During this time, they are fed a 100 percent organic, raw, vegan diet consisting of sprouts, vegetables, fruits, and whole grains. Nothing on the menu is ever cooked, so the food is loaded with all the vitamins, minerals, and enzymes that YHWH designed them to have. Everything served for consumption is what is considered to be "alive." The foundation food at Hippocrates is wheatgrass, one of the richest natural resources of vitamins A, C, D, K, and B-complex. It is also the richest source of chlorophyll, which is the blood of plants. Since it is one of the most direct and highly concentrated forms of the sun's energy, it is an optimal energizer when it is juiced. Just two ounces of wheatgrass juice is nutritionally equivalent to five pounds of fresh vegetables, and it contains 103 vitamins and minerals. The list of attributes of wheatgrass is extensive, and the benefits of consuming wheatgrass juice have filled many books. Wheatgrass has been termed "the complete food."

After consuming only living foods, most people who visit Hippocrates leave three weeks later as changed individuals. By the time they leave, their tumors are shrinking, their skin is healing, their depression is lifting, their blood work has improved, and their lives are being transformed. They leave Hippocrates feeling empowered to eat and live differently, and, as a result, their bodies are able to miraculously heal themselves of their physical illnesses. During the week I visited, I was amazed by the many stories of miraculous healings that took place for the people who continued this eating lifestyle once they arrived home. All of their healings took place without the use of medication.

Regardless of the illness that an individual comes to Hippocrates with, the prescription for true healing is always the same. It doesn't matter what the specifics of the diseases are because a diet of living foods is always the answer. Their physical bodies all respond to this natural prescription because this new diet is free of the toxins that had perhaps caused their illness in the first place. As a result of removing the toxins from their bodies, their physical bodies are able to heal on their own, just as they were created to do.

So I went to Hippocrates, not because I had a serious illness in need of healing, but simply to rest, detox, learn, and observe. Or so I thought! The normal process for someone who stays for three weeks consists of a really bad first week, a mediocre second week, and an incredible third week due to the detoxifying effects of the new diet on the body and the emotions. Since I was only going to be there for one week instead of three, I did not know what I would experience. What I should have realized is that YHWH wanted me to experience it all, so he shortened the process of detoxifying so that I, too, could experience healing.

My Healing Journey

I arrived at Hippocrates on a Sunday afternoon. Other than introductions, a tour of the facility, and settling in, nothing much occurred on this day except for our first meals of living foods. By Monday evening I was already starting to feel the effects of eating pure food. In a matter of minutes, I went from feeling really good to having a bad headache, feeling nauseated and dizzy, and then hyperventilating. All I could think of is how much I wanted to be in the comfort of my own home with my own foods. I really didn't enjoy being told what I could eat and what I couldn't, even though I was well aware of the benefits of healthy eating.

None of this really made any sense to me since I had only been there for twenty-four hours. The employees assured me that what I was feeling was the beginning of the detoxifying effects of the wheatgrass, so I decided to persevere. By Tuesday I was very frustrated and overwhelmed by all of the lectures and information that was being thrown at me, and I was very tired. My emotions were all over the place, and I cried a lot. I wasn't crying about anything in particular; I just found myself weeping the entire day. All I could figure out is that my heart and soul must be detoxing as well. The staff promised me that I would soon feel better, so I continued on.

On Wednesday morning, I woke up feeling incredible. My head was clear, and I was starting to be able to focus. Wednesdays at Hippocrates are juice-fasting days for all those who want to participate. So the entire day, I consumed only highly nutritious juices, which included wheatgrass. Since I was familiar with fasting, I knew what to expect. What I didn't expect is that Wednesday, January 25, 2012, was going to be one of the most incredible days of my life. After working out in the morning hours, I decided to find a quiet place on the grounds to read my Bible. The place I found was truly spectacular, with lush gardens and a small pond surrounding me. All I could hear were the sounds of the birds chirping and water bubbling from the fountains and waterfalls. I spent four hours in this beautiful location, consuming God's living Word. Because I was fasting, the passages I came upon this day were extremely clear.

While I was sitting there, a gentleman approached me. Out of curiosity, he asked me what I was studying. I told him my story about writing this book about God's divine name, and I told him that I was searching my Bible in order to gain more understanding. We then launched into a conversation that I now know God wanted to take place. This gentleman was a very well-read individual who had discovered many years ago that God's divine name is YHWH. He had also believed in his past that Jesus Christ was the Son of God. At one point in this man's life, he was truly convicted that these facts were the absolute truth. He even indicated to me that he had had many past conversations trying to convince others that Jesus was the Son of God, sent from heaven to save the world from their sins.

However, for some unknown reason, this man had since lost the truth concerning both of God's divine names. At this point in his life he considers himself to be a very spiritual man; however, he now believes in the connectivity of the universe and that everything in nature, including man, is connected by one consciousness. So I asked him, "Whom do you worship, now that you no longer believe in the names of YHWH and Jesus?" He really couldn't answer that question. All he could really indicate to me was that his beliefs had since "evolved" and that he no longer held onto the names of YHWH and Jesus. He now believes that there is a god but there are many ways to him. Although he believes in creation and the universe, he no longer believes in the Creator of the universe that he himself had discovered was specifically *named* in the Bible.

I was so incredibly astounded that this individual had given up the precious gifts of YHWH's divine names and the life that comes with them. And yet I knew that Satan was the one who had deceived this man into denying the names of the Father and the Son. This man reminded me of a Jewish man I had recently met who had given up his belief in YHWH and had become an atheist. These two men seemed so similar in the way they had both lost their beliefs to the teachings of Satan's world. The only thing I could think of to explain this gentleman's new belief is that his prior belief in YHWH and Jesus was based only on head-knowledge; because if this gentleman had experienced a close encounter with the living God, Satan would never have been able to change his faith so drastically.

After this gentleman left me to my thoughts, I reflected on our conversation. I wasn't exactly surprised by his words. I know there is an abundance of people in this world who believe there are many ways to God. But what I couldn't get over is that this man at one point in his life had the knowledge of both YHWH's and Jesus's names and all that they stood for. He had the Illuminator's and the Completer's names in his hands; the Urim and the Thummim were his to hold. For some reason, this man decided to let these precious treasures go, which were more valuable and priceless than all the riches of the world. He discarded them in his mind as if they were worthless. Maybe he simply didn't understand their true value. His new beliefs seemed very empty to me. He seemed at peace, and yet he didn't exactly know whom he worshipped. So I prayed, in the name of Jesus, that YHWH would use my conversation with this man as his seed to someday restore the knowledge of his divine names to this gentleman.

After praying, I picked up my Bible to continue my search for truth. As I was thinking about this man and his false belief that there are many ways to God, YHWH immediately placed a passage in front of me that addressed this very issue.

> The wilderness and the dry land shall be glad, the desert shall rejoice and blossom; like the crocus it shall blossom abundantly. ... **And a highway shall be there, and it shall be called the Holy Way**; the unclean shall not pass over it, and **the fools shall not err therein**. No lion shall be there, nor shall any ravenous beast come up on it; they shall not be found there, **but the redeemed shall walk there. And the ransomed of YHWH shall return**, and come to Zion **with singing; everlasting joy shall be upon their heads; they shall obtain joy and gladness, and sorrow and sighing shall flee away**. (Isa. 35:1–2, 8–10)

YHWH wanted me to see this passage at that very moment, and he wanted me to focus on his highway called "the Holy Way." And because I was fasting, he knew my focus was ultra-sharp. When I read this verse, I immediately remembered John the Baptist's words: "As it is written in the book of the words of Isaiah the prophet, 'The voice of one crying in the wilderness: Prepare *the way of the Lord*, make his paths straight'" (Luke 3:4). John was preparing the way for Jesus, the Son of God. When John said these words, he was referring to Isaiah's prophecy of YHWH preparing a way. "A voice cries: 'In the wilderness prepare *the way of YHWH*, make straight in the desert a *highway for our God*'" (Isa. 40:3).

Both passages are referring to God's divine names as being "the Holy Way." The names of YHWH and Jesus form the highway called the Holy Way. God led "the way" for the Israelites for forty years in the desert and then in the promised land through his name, the ark of the covenant, his sacred fire, prophets and priests, Shekinah glory, and the Urim and Thummim. YHWH then sent his Son, Jesus, to continue leading people down the holy highway. According to Isaiah, the fools and the unclean shall not walk along this highway—only the redeemed. Jesus told his disciples: "*I am the way*, and the truth, and the life; *no one comes to the Father, but by me*" (John 14:6). There is only "one way" to God. In the Old Testament it was called the "Holy Way." In the New Testament it is called "the way." But I think Jesus could sum it up in a few sentences. "I am the only way which produces truth; I am the only way which produces life. If you follow me along my way, I will lead you straight into the arms of my Father."

The God Equation

When it comes to science and the physical world, everyone believes in absolute truths. Two plus two always equals four. An apple tree will always produce apples and never oranges. Gravity will always pull things toward the earth, not away from it. The earth will always revolve around the sun, not the sun around the earth. Truth in the natural world is black and white. There is no gray. If there were no absolute truths in the physical world, there would be no mathematical or chemical formulas that scientists could rely on to explain the world in which we live. There would be no laws of physics or laws of chemistry. The world would be full of chaos because the outcome of any action would always be changing.

So since it is widely accepted that there are absolute truths when it comes to our natural world, or creation, why then is it so hard for people to believe there is only one absolute truth when it comes to God and the spiritual world? Since YHWH is the only one who knows the truth about the spiritual world, why would God allow there to be various conflicting truths about the spiritual world when he knows very well that it would result in chaos? He wouldn't!

History has proven that when the truth about God is left up to man, there will be no consensus. When left up to man, the truth about God will never be crystal clear. This becomes apparent when we begin to study the different religions, denominations, and faiths of this world and realize there are a myriad of ideas on who God is and how you reach him. In these various faiths, there are just as many beliefs on what happens when we die. I don't think the God of absolute truths would allow there to be so many "truths" about him. As a result of all these various beliefs concerning God there has never been peace, and many wars have been fought based on these differing religions. "There is *a way* that seems right to a man, but in the end it leads to death" (Prov. 16:25). "For the time is coming when people will not endure sound teaching, but having itching ears they will accumulate for themselves teachers to suit their own likings, and will turn away from listening to the truth and wander into myths" (2 Tim. 4:3–4).

There is only *one* absolute truth, or it would not be called truth. And because YHWH is the only one who knows the absolute truth about the spiritual world, he knew that he would personally have to reveal himself to mankind in order for people to know with certainty the truth about him. As we have learned through the pages of this book, that is exactly what YHWH did through Moses, his name, his Word, and communication with the priests and prophets. YHWH revealed the absolute truth about himself to the Israelites so that they would not be in the same state of confusion as the rest of the world.

When the truth about YHWH was not accepted by the Israelites, the first covenant was made obsolete so that YHWH could reveal his truth to the world. Knowing that only he could once again reveal the truth about himself, YHWH sent his Son, Jesus, down to earth in flesh and blood so that his Son could tell mankind in person about the Father who sent him. Jesus came to reveal YHWH's truth to us. Jesus came as God's revealed Word in YHWH's name. God sent John the Baptist to prepare the holy way for his Son, Jesus. John the Baptist prepared the Jewish people for the arrival of their long-awaited Messiah, just as Moses prepared the way for the introduction of YHWH to the Israelites. Jesus communicated YHWH's truth in person for three years, until the new covenant was solidified through his own blood. After Jesus died for our sins and rose again from the dead, the new covenant through the blood of Jesus became the absolute spiritual truth for eternity. When Jesus left this world, God sent his Holy Spirit in Jesus's name to continue to teach us spiritual truths about him. Finally, YHWH knew that there would always be a hunger for the truth about him, so he provided mankind with the written truth about himself in what is called the Bible, which includes both the Old Testament and the New Testament, the old covenant and the new covenant.

The Absolute Truth

When there is an absolute truth about something, we can trust that the outcome will be the same every single time. That is exactly what happens when we put our trust in the absolute truth about YHWH and Jesus. When someone believes in the truth about Jesus, the result is the same. When we acknowledge that we are sinners in need of a Savior and we put our trust in the Son of God, who died on a cross for our sins, rose on the third day from the grave, ascended into heaven, and sits at the right hand of the Father, Jesus forgives us of our sins and makes us children of God. Every single time the result is the same, no matter our background, our past sins, our age, gender, and so on. When it comes to God, the truth never changes. When we believe in the absolute truth with all of our hearts, we will receive what every other believer receives—a personal relationship with YHWH through Jesus Christ and eternity with YHWH. I have termed this absolute spiritual truth about YHWH as "the God Equation."

YHWH + JESUS = HEAVEN

It is so simple and yet so true. That is what is so beautiful about it. God gave us an equation, and, being an engineer, I like equations. Equations are what we use every day to figure out the world into which we have been born. Equations express truth that can be trusted to give us answers to our questions about this world. Jesus stated the God equation beautifully to his disciples.

> "Let not your hearts be troubled; **believe in God, believe also in me**. In my Father's house are many rooms; if it were not so, would I have told you that I go to prepare a place for you? And when I go and prepare a place for you, **I will come again and will take you to myself, that where I am you may be also**." (John 14:1–3)

While Jesus walked on this earth, he revealed to mankind all the pieces to the spiritual puzzle. He said, "Believe in God, and believe also in me." When we do as he commands and believe in the names of the Father and the Son, YHWH plus Jesus, we can be assured that heaven is where we are going when we die. When Jesus comes again, he told us we would be going where he is going, and that is to be with our Father in his home. The God equation works because YHWH and Jesus are well-known constants. They do not change! There are no variables in this equation. YHWH and Jesus have been the same yesterday as they are today and will be tomorrow because they are absolute truths. Jesus restated the God equation to his disciples on the night of Passover as he was praying.

> "Father, the hour has come; glorify thy Son that the Son may glory thee, since thou hast given him power over all flesh, to give eternal life to all whom thou hast given him. **And this is eternal life, that they know thee the only true God, and Jesus Christ whom thou hast sent**." (John 17:1b–3)

YHWH + JESUS = ETERNAL LIFE

While Jesus was here on earth, he spent his entire ministry being a witness to YHWH. Jesus openly acknowledged that everything he did was only possible through the power of his Father. The miracles he performed and the words he spoke were testimony of the One who sent him. And YHWH witnessed for Jesus as well. YHWH's testimony for his Son, Jesus, began the day of his baptism and culminated in Jesus's death and resurrection, allowing Jesus's name to be the Name above all Names by which salvation is received. What a beautiful picture of both YHWH and Jesus witnessing for one another, for all mankind to see and to believe that what they had individually revealed to mankind was the absolute truth.

Even though all people in this world have or will eventually have God's absolute truth available to them, unfortunately very few will embrace it. Because of pride, mankind has demonstrated that it knows better when it comes to the spiritual world, even though all humans live in the physical world. Hence, there is a belief in society that there are many ways to God. Mankind has come to this conclusion, even though it is historically documented that once upon a time there actually lived a man named Jesus, who claimed he was the Son of God and that he had been sent to tell us the truth about his heavenly Father. He proved his divinity with miracles, signs, and wonders—including raising dead people to life. It is simply inconceivable to me that humans cannot see YHWH's truth about the spiritual world through his Son, Jesus.

The Only Way

What YHWH did for me on that particular day, as I was super-focused on his Word, is to convict me that there is only one holy way. Jesus is the "Only Way" that provides everlasting peace and joy every single time. After I came to this conclusion, I packed up my Bible and went on with my day.

Later that night, I visited the heated mineral pools. After changing into my bathing suit, as I was leaving the bathroom, I happened to glance at myself in the mirror. The mirror was only big enough for me to see my face. Usually my first instinct, like most women when looking in a mirror, is to immediately focus on my flaws. But that is not what happened on this night; this night was different. Remember, on this day of fasting, my focus was crystal clear, and I had just spent four hours consuming God's living Word. So on this night, as I glanced at my face in the mirror, I was *unable* to see any of my physical flaws. Instead, for the first time in my life I saw only "beauty" smiling back at me. It was the most amazing sight that I have ever seen. For the first time, I saw myself *the way* YHWH sees me, as a beautiful child of God.

The joy I felt was so immediate and so overwhelming that I couldn't help but smile back at myself in the mirror with a huge grin. I felt truly beautiful for the first time in my life. But it wasn't a physical beauty that I saw in the mirror that night; it was a spiritual inner beauty that I had never seen in myself. That night I felt God's love for me in *a way* that I had never experienced. What a special gift!

> **Your beauty should not come from outward adornment**, such as elaborate hairstyles and the wearing of gold jewelry or fine clothes. **Rather it should be that of your inner self, the unfading beauty of a gentle and quiet spirit, which is of great worth in God's sight**. (1 Peter 3:3-4)

The next day as I was thinking over what happened, God really impressed upon me that when I remove all the poisons out of my life, from my food, from my heart, and from my mind, great healing can take place. When the toxins are removed, the truth becomes very clear; with truth, healing of the body, soul, and spirit becomes possible. YHWH planned for this experience to take place while I was visiting a place of great healing in order for me to truly understand what he wanted me to see. You see, the Hippocrates Health Institute is all about life. For an entire week, I was surrounded by YHWH's beautiful creation, seen in the lush gardens. I ate and drank foods that were full of life and the sun's chlorophyll, the blood of plants. Nothing "dead" touched my lips. Nothing "dead" was consumed. I could feel hope and joy in the air, because the people who surrounded me were empowered to defeat their illnesses and their enemy. I saw daily what could happen to people when they remove the toxins from their diets. And although I myself had not gone to Hippocrates needing physical healing, God knew that I still needed another form of healing.

YHWH reminded me that when he spoke to me through my dryer so many years ago, he had shown me a picture of the condition of my soul and spirit without him. He said, "This is life without me." All that I saw on that day was darkness, deformed metal, and ashes. He showed me how my heart was in a million pieces and was basically dead. On that day, God told me to give him my heart and said he would mend it for me. And that is what I did. So what I saw in my reflection in the mirror on this particular night was simply a visual representation of what he had accomplished. On this night he wanted me to know that he had indeed taken my heart, had completely mended it through his Son, Jesus Christ, and had turned my dark "ashes" and all of my sorrows "white as snow." On the day I discovered that YHWH truly existed, the health of my spirit was dead. Now, fifteen years later, YHWH wanted me to know that my spirit was full of life and shining so brightly that others could see it. When I looked at myself in the mirror, it was as if he were saying, "*Judy, you now have life in me. You have been changed and made brand new. You are now simply beautiful and radiantly bright white, inside and out.*" YHWH wanted to provide me with proof, once again, that he exists and that with him nothing is impossible. What a beautiful ending to a prayer made so long ago, one that asked for proof of God's existence and that he cared about me and my family.

Through the years of learning about YHWH and Jesus, I had been surrounded by God's truth and beauty. Through YHWH's Word, his voice, his sacred fire, his Holy Spirit, and his Shekinah glory, he had taken my heart from death and had brought it to life. Because I had been daily consuming YHWH's living truth for the last fifteen years, on this night I was able for the first time to see Jesus's life shining through me so brightly that I caught a glimpse of my LORD and Savior in the mirror—through my own reflection. YHWH wanted me to see that my inner beauty through Jesus Christ is a beauty like no other.

Judy Jacobson

Treating the Whole Body

Hippocrates was a physician who knew that the body must be treated as a whole in order to achieve wellness. Hippocrates knew that for healing to occur, a prescription of rest, a good diet, fresh air, and cleanliness was all that was needed. Jesus Christ was sent to be our Great Physician. He also treats the body as a whole because he knows that it is a body, soul, and spirit that make us whole. Because he created us, Jesus knows that when one part of a person is not well, the whole body is not well. He knows that the root cause of the majority of physical and psychological ailments is due to the unhealthy condition of our souls. He also knows that when the soul is healed, by regularly taping into God's Holy Spirit that dwells within us, great healing will take place in our overall well being as well as in our physical bodies. Therefore, Jesus knows that the prescription to treat whatever ails us consists of resting in his heavenly Father's presence, daily consumption of YHWH's Word, the Holy Spirit's voice (which is a breath of fresh air), and the ultimate cleanliness—the forgiveness of our sins. By following these instructions, we can be assured that Satan's toxic voice, lies, deceptions, and curses will be cast out of our bodies, our souls, and our spirits. Then and only then will we be free to live life abundantly.

Jesus is our Great Physician. No matter in what condition Jesus finds our hearts, the prescription is always the same. For every person, for every situation, Jesus Christ can heal everything that spiritually ails us with his body and blood that he has given for us. Consuming Jesus's living body and blood is what healed my soul and spirit through YHWH's Holy Spirit, given in Jesus's name. His blood entered into my being and healed me one thought at a time, thereby removing the root cause of my spiritual illness. Jesus's blood is available for you as well.

If everyone embraced the absolute truth about God and his Son, we would witness a healing of this world that is beyond comprehension. We would all be worshipping the same God and would all have the same values. There would be no more wars over religious beliefs and no more denominational feuds. Everyone would have the Holy Spirit in his or her heart and would communicate with YHWH on a daily basis. There would be spiritual joy all around us, as well as a great peace. And that is why Jesus is eventually coming back to earth to reign for one thousand years. We saw a glimpse of what he can accomplish while he walked on this earth; but this time he will come back as the glorified Jesus, who now sits on the right side of YHWH. When Jesus comes back, he will lead us down the holy highway, back to the Tree of Life located in the garden of Eden. Back in Paradise, death and sin will no longer be found—only life.

I now know that Jesus spoke truth when he said, "Man shall not live by bread alone, but by every word that proceeds from the mouth of God" (Matt. 4:4). Because of my experience at the Hippocrates Health Institute, I came to believe with all my heart, soul, and mind that I am to live *only* by the words that come directly from the mouth of YHWH and Jesus. I came to understand that *only* the daily bread sent from heaven is truly capable of producing an abundant life. Finally, I realized all that we have to do in order to sprout new life from the seeds that have been dropped into our lives is to truly believe the words YHWH sent his Son, Jesus Christ, to speak to all mankind:

"Your Sins are Forgiven."

Chapter 23

To Those Who Conquer

> **But you are a chosen race, a royal priesthood, a holy nation, God's own people**, that you may declare wonderful deeds of him who called you out of darkness into his marvelous light. **Once you were no people but now you are God's people**. (1 Peter 2:9–10a)

Since I was a small child, rainbows have always intrigued me. Even today whenever it is raining and sunny all at the same time, I get excited, thinking that today I might get to see YHWH's glory displayed in the clouds. So one week when I heard rainbows referenced three times in a matter of three days, I knew what God was asking me to do. It was his way of saying to me, "You need to find out more about my bows." And when God asks me to do something these days, I just do it, with no questions asked. I know YHWH's glory will be revealed through what he is about to show me.

Earlier in the same week I had been thinking about the number 7 in the Bible. I had been thinking about the seven biblical feasts in the Old Testament. I also knew that priests were consecrated for seven days before they could serve God. In addition, there are seven days in a week, of which the seventh day is the Sabbath. In the book of Revelation, there are seven lampstands, seven angels, seven seals, seven trumpets, seven bowls—the list goes on. In this same week, my husband said to me, "Did you know there are seven colors in a rainbow?" Because I had already been thinking about the number 7, this fact piqued my interest because I knew a rainbow in the clouds is the sign that was given to Noah to represent God's very first covenant with mankind. The next day my son's friend said to me, "Ms. Judy, I saw a triple rainbow this past weekend. It was so cool." Two days later, the same child said, "Ms. Judy, I dreamed last night about the triple rainbow. All night long I was allowed to look at its beauty."

Biblically, the number 3 means resurrection, divine completeness, and perfection.[1] We know that Jesus walked this earth for three years and was crucified in the third hour. There were three hours of darkness while he hung on the cross, after which he gave up his life at 3:00 p.m. He defeated death and rose gloriously on the third day. Jesus described himself as the way, the truth, and the life. The number 3 represents the trinity of the Father, the Son, and the Holy Spirit, as well as the trinity of man's body, soul, and spirit. That particular week, the numbers 3 and 7, in relation to rainbows, were referenced three times in a matter of three days. Coincidence? Remember, nothing is coincidence in God's kingdom. There was a reason I needed to look into this further.

I started by drawing the outline of a rainbow on a piece of paper. As I did this, I saw that a rainbow forms a semicircle over the horizon. I also drew the seven rings that represented the seven colors seen in a rainbow. As I was looking at my semicircle, I thought, *If the horizon was not in the way, and I continued drawing my rainbow, it would form a complete circle. Hmm, I wonder what circles represent in the Bible.* YHWH brought to my mind that circles represent covenants. Male circumcision, which is in the shape of a circle, represents God's everlasting covenant in the flesh between God and his people. The marriage covenant is sealed by the giving of rings, which are never-ending circles. Kings used to seal their written words or promises with the face of their rings, which were typically circular. The high priest had a crown in the shape of a circle that had "Holy to YHWH" written upon it. And finally, the stone that was rolled in front of Jesus's grave was round. This stone is what sealed the new covenant. Just by their shape, circles represent something that never ends because they have no beginning and they have no end. So biblically, circles represent God's everlasting promises.

But the rainbows that we see in the clouds do not form a complete circle. They only form semicircles over the horizon. So how could a rainbow have anything to do with representing YHWH's covenants? As I was contemplating all this, I remembered what I learned in geometry class so long ago. I recalled that a portion of a circle is called an *arc*, which once again brought to my mind the ark of the covenant. As you will remember, the ark of the covenant carried God's divine Word and his divine name and was designed to provide salvation for God's people. So what was God trying to tell me about rainbows? What divine words had YHWH given us regarding his bows?

The first place God references his "bow in the cloud" is in Genesis. Remember, after the flood had passed and Noah and his family were on dry land, God established his very first covenant with Noah.

> "Behold, **I establish my covenant with you and your offspring after you**, and with every living creature that is with you, the birds, the livestock, and every beast of the earth with you, as many as came out of the ark; it is for every beast of the earth. **I establish my covenant with you**, that never again shall all flesh be cut off by the waters of the flood, and never again shall there be a flood to destroy the earth." And God said, "**This is the sign of the covenant** that I make between me and you and every living creature that is with you, for all future generations: **I have set my bow in the cloud, and it shall be a sign of the covenant between me and the earth. When I bring clouds over the earth and the bow is seen in the clouds, I will remember my covenant that is between me and you and every living creature of all flesh**. And the waters shall never again become a flood to destroy all flesh. **When the bow is in the clouds, I will see it and remember the *everlasting covenant* between God and every living creature of all flesh that is on the earth.**" God said to Noah, "**This is the sign of the covenant** that I have established between me and all flesh that is on the earth." (Gen. 9:9–17 ESV)

As a small child, I was taught that these verses were God's promise that he would never again destroy the earth by means of water. It wasn't until I read them again that I saw for the first time that God repeats his promise to Noah *three* times and, in doing so, the word *covenant* is used *seven* times. Surely these verses had another hidden meaning as well. YHWH said to Noah, "I set my bow in the cloud as a sign." He continued by saying, "When the bow is seen in the clouds, I will remember my *covenant*, which is between me and you." He finished by saying, "When the bow is in the clouds, I will look upon it and remember the *everlasting covenant*." That is when I saw the word *everlasting* when referring to God's covenant. In referring to his everlasting covenant, YHWH was promising much more to Noah and his descendants than never flooding the earth again with water. God established this covenant with Noah after he had destroyed the entire world, with the exception of Noah and his family. They were saved from God's wrath because Noah had formed a relationship with God. It was because of this relationship that YHWH found favor with Noah and therefore blessed him with salvation and life.

Rainbows usually appear after the worst part of the storm has passed, as the sun's light is penetrating through the darkness to bring forth brilliant colors for all to see. As I was thinking about the Antichrist and the great storms that he will bring to this earth during his reign of forty-two months, I couldn't help but think of all the evil and wickedness that will be widespread throughout the land. In those times, God will find favor with those individuals with whom he has a relationship. In the same way he saved Noah from his wrath, God will save these individuals. Once again, YHWH will destroy the wicked and reward the favored with his eternal presence.

Revelation Rainbow

The book of Revelation tells us that one day we will see a rainbow like no other: "Then I saw another mighty angel coming down from heaven, *wrapped in a cloud, with a rainbow over his head,* and his face was like the sun, and his legs like pillars of fire" (Rev. 10:1). This mighty angel just happens to be the seventh angel, who blows the seventh trumpet. God said, *"When the bow is in the clouds, I will look upon it and remember the everlasting covenant."*

> And the angel whom I saw standing on sea and land **lifted up his right hand to heaven and swore by him who lives for ever and ever**, who created heaven and what is in it, the earth and what is in it, and the sea and what is in it, **that there should be no more delay**, but that **in the days of the trumpet call to be sounded by the seventh angel, the mystery of God, as announced to his servants the prophets, should be fulfilled**. (Rev. 10:5–7)
>
> Then **the seventh angel blew his trumpet**, and there were loud voices in heaven saying, "**The kingdom of the world has become the kingdom of our Lord [YHWH] and of his Christ, and he shall reign for ever and ever**." And the twenty-four elders who sit on their thrones before God fell on their faces and worshiped God, saying "We give thanks to thee, Lord God Almighty, who art and who wast, that thou hast taken thy great power and begun to reign. The nations raged, but thy wrath came, and the time for the dead to be judged, **for rewarding thy servants, the prophets and the saints, and those who fear thy name, both small and great, and for destroying the destroyers of the earth**." Then God's temple in heaven was opened, and **the Ark of *his* Covenant was seen within his temple**; and there were flashes of lightning, voices, peals of thunder, an earthquake and heavy hail. (Rev. 11:15–19)

When I saw these verses in relation to rainbows, I knew what God was revealing to me. Today, when we see rainbows in the sky after a storm, we should remember that God made an everlasting covenant with all flesh that is upon the earth. We need to remember that this everlasting covenant is more than just a promise that he will never destroy the entire earth again by flood. This everlasting covenant is the one YHWH established through his Son, Jesus. The everlasting promise to those who believe in his Son's name is that, although they will experience physical death, through Jesus Christ they will be given eternal life. On a future day, a mighty seventh angel will descend in a cloud with a rainbow over his head. He will blow the seventh trumpet, and the kingdom of God will finally be at hand. In those moments, God's temple in heaven will be opened and everyone will see Jesus—YHWH's everlasting *"Ark of his Covenant."*

Jesus's Second Coming

Jesus's second coming will occur in the same way that his heavenly Father first descended upon Mount Sinai and met his people. Just as YHWH did not come quietly, Jesus will not come quietly. Instead, Jesus will come with a loud trumpet blast, voices, peals of thunder, flashes of lightning, an earthquake, and heavy hail. Everyone on earth will be able to see, hear, and feel Jesus's visible presence. "Behold he is coming with the clouds, and every eye will see him" (Rev. 1:7).

> **"Immediately after the tribulation of those days** the sun will be darkened, and the moon will not give its light, and the stars will fall from heaven, and the powers of the heavens will be shaken; **then will appear the sign of the Son of man in heaven**, and then all the tribes of the earth will mourn, and **they will see the Son of man coming on the clouds of heaven with power and great glory**; and he will **send out his angels with a loud trumpet call, and they will gather his elect from the four winds**, from one end of heaven to the other." (Matt. 24:29–31)

The purpose of Jesus's second coming is threefold. The Son of God will first of all come to gather his children together in order to reward his servants—the prophets and saints—who have feared YHWH's name and have kept the faith throughout the centuries. Second, he will come to finally destroy the destroyers of the earth and therefore put an end to sin and its consequence of death. But even more importantly, the purpose of Jesus's coming will be to reign with his children for eternity.

So when will all of this happen? I believe it will all occur in the seventh month of Tishrei, the month of spiritual completion and perfection, whose very name means "to begin." Remember, there are three feasts of YHWH's seven that have not yet been fulfilled with Jesus's first coming. The Hebrew word for feasts is *moadim*, which literally means "appointed times."[2] We learned that the first three feasts, Passover, Feast of Unleavened Bread, and the Feast of Firstfruits, were all fulfilled with Christ's death, resurrection, and first ascension into heaven in the first month of Nissan, which means "to start, to move, and firstfruits." The fourth feast, called the Feast of Weeks (Pentecost), occurred in the third month of Sivan, which means "to mark, to appoint." It was during this feast that God marked and appointed his disciples with his Holy Spirit. All four of these appointed times occurred on the exact days of the first four feasts.

Jesus said that until heaven and earth pass away, *not an iota, not a dot, will pass from the law until all is accomplished* (Matt. 5:18). And remember that part of the law is the seven mandated feasts that YHWH commanded the Israelites to keep every year. That leaves us with three unfulfilled feasts, which occur in the fall of the Jewish calendar in the month of Tishrei, which is the holiest month of the entire year.

All three of the remaining feasts, the Feast of Trumpets, the Day of Atonement, and the Feast of Tabernacles, mark the birth and dedication of Jesus, when YHWH's Word first became flesh. These three feasts marked the beginning of the new covenant; therefore, I believe these feasts that once signaled Jesus's first coming will once again signal the second coming of our LORD and Savior. Remember, the month preceding these three feasts announces the coming of a "King in the Field" who is out to inspect the produce of his land. At Jesus's second coming, the King of kings will once again physically leave his heavenly throne, descend to inspect the world, and then begin his eternal reign with his children.

The Events

When Jesus comes again, we know from the book of Revelation that several events will take place. These events are the gathering of the elect (which is often called the rapture); the wedding feast of the Lamb; judgment of the Antichrist, his false prophet, and their followers; Jesus's one-thousand-year reign; judgment day for the rest of mankind; and the coming of the new heaven, new earth, and New Jerusalem, which is the eternal city. Scripture tells us that the first event to occur is the rapture.

> **Lo! I tell you a mystery. We shall not all sleep, but we shall all be changed, in a moment, in the twinkling of an eye, at the last trumpet. For the *trumpet will sound*, and the dead will be raised imperishable, and we shall be changed**. For this perishable nature must put on the imperishable, and this mortal nature must put on immortality. **When the perishable puts on the imperishable, and the mortal puts on immortality, then shall come to pass the saying that is written:**
>
> "Death is swallowed up in victory.
> O death, where is thy victory?
> O death, where is thy sting?"
> (1 Corin. 15:51–55)
>
> For the Lord himself will descend from heaven with a cry of command, with the archangel's call, and **with the sound of the trumpet of God. And the dead in Christ will rise first; then we who are alive, who are left, shall be caught up together with them in the clouds to meet the Lord in the air**; and so we shall always be with the Lord. (1 Thess. 4:16–17)

When the last trumpet is sounded by the seventh angel, our bodies will be changed from perishable to imperishable, and we will be raised gloriously to meet Jesus in the air. I believe this day will occur during

YHWH's Feast of Trumpets, on the first day of the seventh month of Tishrei. This future day will forever mark the beginning of the fulfillment of the everlasting covenant promised to Noah so long ago—when the bow is seen in the clouds.

Once YHWH's saints have safely entered into Jesus's presence, into the Ark of Jesus, the seven bowls will take place. "As it was in the days of Noah, so will it be in the days of the Son of Man. They ate, they drank, they married, they were given in marriage until the day when Noah entered the ark, and the flood came and destroyed them all" (Luke 17:26–27).

After those who are found favored, righteous, and blameless are caught up in the air with Jesus and enter into his Ark, God's wrath will come upon the rest of the world. The seven bowls described in Revelation Chapter 16, which represent God's wrath, seem to come pretty rapidly in succession. They remind me of the ten plagues that took place in order to release God's people from Egypt. I believe these seven bowls are released during the ten days between the Feast of Trumpets and the Day of Atonement. These bowls represent judgment for the evil ones, the people who denied the divine names of the Father and the Son. During this time, foul and evil sores will come upon men who bear the mark of the beast and worship its image, and the throne of the beast and its kingdom will be thrown into darkness, a darkness that I imagine will be felt. Finally, Satan will gather the nations, his followers, for one last battle in a place called Armageddon. Jesus will meet Satan there, along with his warriors, the raptured believers.

> **Then I saw heaven opened, and behold, a white horse! He who sat upon it is called Faithful and True**, and in righteousness he judges and makes war. His eyes are like a flame of fire, and on his head are many diadems; and he has a name inscribed which no one knows but himself. He is clad in a robe dipped in blood, and **the name by which he is called is The Word of God**. And the armies of heaven, arrayed in fine linen, white and pure, followed him on white horses. **From his mouth issues a sharp sword with which to smite the nations.** ... On his robe and on his thigh he

has a name inscribed, **King of kings and Lord of lords**. (Rev. 19:11–16)

I believe this future Day of Atonement is the day the King of kings and Lord of lords will smite Satan, his Antichrist, the False Prophet, and all those who follow them. Scripture tells us that Jesus will accomplish this by issuing from his mouth a sharp sword. Just as he knocked the men down in the garden of Gethsemane before his crucifixion, I believe Jesus will simply have to say, "I AM YHWH; I AM HE," and the nations will fall. Nothing more will need to be said. *"Therefore, behold, I will make them know, this once I will make them know my power and my might, and they shall know that my name is YHWH"* (Jer. 16:21).

During this battle at Armageddon, the Antichrist and the False Prophet will be captured and thrown alive into the lake of fire that burns with sulphur. At this same time, the Dragon, that ancient Serpent, Satan, will be seized, bound for one thousand years and thrown into the bottomless pit. He shall no longer deceive the nations. Righteous judgment will be made on this ever-so-holy Day of Atonement when Satan, the creator of sin, will finally be judged for his deception and pride. On this day, death will be no more for followers of Jesus.

Following this holy Day of Atonement will be the celebration of the Feast of Tabernacles. Remember, the Feast of Tabernacles is an eight-day feast that has always been characterized by great rejoicing. In the year of Jesus's second coming, there will be a celebration like no other. Can you imagine the rejoicing that will be going on around the world after Satan is captured, bound, and thrown into the bottomless pit? This feast that first represented YHWH dwelling among his people in the wilderness and then Jesus dwelling among his people after his dedication forty days after his birth will finally commemorate Jesus's second coming to begin reigning with his chosen people for one thousand years. Oh, what a feast it will be! Jesus will once again be living on earth among YHWH's chosen people.

The Elect

The elect who are caught up in the air with Jesus on the Feast of Trumpets will be YHWH's chosen race, his holy nation, his royal priesthood. On the day of rapture, believers in God's only Son will take over the priestly duties from the tribe of Levi, just as Jesus took over the duty of the high priest from the line of Aaron.

Do you remember the last two verses that we discussed that refer to the Urim and Thummim's being missing? If you recall, these words were spoken when God sent his people back to Jerusalem to rebuild the temple after their captivity in Babylon. At that time, the genealogies of many individuals were unknown because a high priest with the Urim and Thummim could no longer be found. As a result, Nehemiah had to exclude these people from the priesthood.

> These sought their registration among those enrolled in the genealogies, but it was not found there, so they were excluded from the priesthood as unclean; the governor told them that they were not to partake of the most holy food, **until a priest with Urim and Thummim should arise**. (Neh. 7:64–65)

Well, the time has finally come. A High Priest has "risen," whose name is Jesus. Jesus himself is the Thummim, the Completer, who sits at the right hand of the Urim, the Illuminator. As High Priest, one of Jesus's duties will be to determine who is included in the holy priesthood. Only Jesus knows the genealogies of all the people who have ever walked this earth and the names of those who have been written into his Book of Life. Only he can determine who will be given the gift of partaking of the most holy food in YHWH's temple.

The Seven Gifts

The book of Revelation is a book of prophecy given to us by Jesus through his most beloved apostle, John. It is a book of promises and a book of gifts. It is the culmination of God's perfect plan finally coming to fruition. The book of Revelation begins with Jesus speaking to seven of his churches—his seven lampstands. In these seven letters, Jesus promises seven gifts that he will personally deliver to "those who conquer." Those who have not denied the name of the Father or the Son and have kept the faith will be greatly rewarded. I want to first list these gifts as they were given to John and then explain their importance. When all of these priceless gifts are gathered together in one place, they form a beautiful picture, and you can see what a significant role followers of Christ, YHWH's priests, will play in Jesus's millennium kingdom.

> "To him who conquers I will grant to **eat of the tree of life**, which is in the **paradise of God**." (Rev. 2:7b)

> "He who conquers **shall not be hurt by the second death**." (Rev. 2:11b)

> "To him who conquers **I will give some of the hidden manna**, and I will give him **a white stone, with a new name written on the stone** which no one knows except him who receives it." (Rev. 2:17b)

> "He who conquers and who keeps my works until the end, I will give him **power over the nations, and he shall rule** them with a rod of iron, as when earthen pots are broken into pieces, even as I myself have received power from the Father; and **I will give him the morning star**." (Rev. 2:26–28)

> "He who conquers **shall be clad thus in white garments**, and **I will not blot his name out of the book of life; I will confess his name before my Father and before his angels**." (Rev. 3:5)

> "He who conquers, **I will make him a pillar in the temple of my God**; never shall he go out of it, and **I will write on him the name of my God, and the name of the city of my**

> **God, the new Jerusalem** which comes down from my God out of heaven, **and my own new name**." (Rev. 3:12)

> "He who conquers, **I will grant him to sit with me on my throne, as I myself conquered and sat down with my Father on his throne**." (Rev. 3:21)

What incredible gifts Jesus himself will shower on his priests! I never knew so much was waiting for believers until I started investigating YHWH's divine name. "Be faithful unto death, and *I will give you the crown of life*" (Rev. 2:10b). When the dead and alive are caught up in the air with Jesus, we will be given new, glorious bodies. All that currently corrupts our bodies in this life will be no more. Our bodies will never again experience death; the second death will be reserved for nonbelievers on the final judgment day, which will take place one thousand years later. Because YHWH sees the precious blood of his Son, Jesus, on the door frames of our hearts, the second death will pass over us, just as the angel of death passed over the Israelites in Egypt.

The white garments we will be clothed with will represent the purity of our souls and spirits because they will have finally reached perfection. Our clothing will be a reflection of our hearts since God will have removed the ashes and made them as white as snow. Because we will be found righteous and blameless, Jesus will confess our names to YHWH as holy. We will be given a crown of life to reflect our righteousness, like Jesus did when he ascended into heaven after his death. Our gold crowns will be inscribed with the words "Holy to YHWH."

Jesus tells us that we will become pillars in the temple of YHWH. On our pillars will be written the name of YHWH, the name of New Jerusalem, and Jesus's own "new" name. Because we will be within the temple, Jesus tells us that we will be allowed to sit with him on his throne, just as he conquered and sat down with his Father on his throne. We will also be given a new name written on a white stone. By being in Jesus's daily presence, we will be able to freely eat the fruit from the Tree of Life.

As priests, we will rule the nations with Jesus in New Jerusalem. As priests, we will serve Jesus and will help teach the people how to follow in his perfect footsteps. With Satan out of the way and Jesus reigning as King, the nations (the people left on earth who didn't take the name of Jesus or the mark of the beast during the time of the Antichrist) will experience a peace like no other because only YHWH's truth will be spoken during these times. Because of the overwhelming peace, the nations' swords will be made into plowshares and their spears into pruning hooks. They will not lift swords against other nations, and they will not learn about war anymore (Micah 4:3). The name of the eternal city in which we will rule with Jesus will be *YHWH Shammah*, which means "YHWH is there"[3] (Ezek. 48:35b). Of course that is the name of the eternal city. That is what God had planned from the very beginning: to dwell among his people once again.

All of these extravagant gifts will be showered upon believers in Jesus Christ simply because we have conquered by not denying the names of our heavenly Father or his Son, Jesus. When we receive these incredible gifts from Jesus, we will feel YHWH's unconditional love for us in a way that we have never felt before.

Jesus's New Name

On the night that YHWH instructed me to gather all of the "to those who conquer" verses into one place, I noticed something that I had never seen before. I noticed for the first time that Jesus receives a "new name" and that he writes his new name upon believers, along with his Father's name and the name of New Jerusalem (Rev. 3:12). How interesting! Jesus receives a new name! This was new information to me. Why would Jesus get a new name? And even more importantly what is Jesus's new name?

God explained to me on this particular night that when Jesus defeated death and ascended into heaven, presenting his own blood as his sacrifice, Jesus received a *new name* to reflect his *new position* in God's kingdom, just like Abraham, Sarah, Israel, Peter, and Paul all received new names to reflect their new identities in God's kingdom.

This only made sense! Throughout Scripture, God was always changing peoples' names, so why wouldn't Jesus's name change as well after he became YHWH's High Priest?

> When he had made purification for sins, he sat down at the right hand of the Majesty on high, **having become as much superior to angels as the name he has obtained is more excellent than theirs**. (Heb. 1:3b–4)

> And being found in human form he humbled himself and became obedient unto death, even death on a cross. Therefore, **God has highly exalted him and bestowed on him the name which is above every name**, that at the name of Jesus every knee should bow, in heaven and on earth and under the earth. (Phil. 2:8–10)

Remember, when Yeshua became flesh and blood, he temporarily gave up his name of YHWH and received a man's name. Because of his common name, Jesus became a little lower than angels (Heb. 2:7); however, once Jesus became the perfect sacrifice, defeated death, ascended into heaven, and took a seat at the right hand of his Father, he was renamed once again. Scripture tells us that after Yeshua sat down at the right hand of the Majesty on high, he received a name more excellent than the angels, a name above *all* names.

Well, there is only one name that is above *every* name. I believe that when Jesus ascended into heaven, he received the name that he had had since the beginning of time, and that is his Father's name, YHWH. And if you think about it, why wouldn't he? Remember what the apostle John said: "In the beginning was the Word, and the Word was with God, and the Word *was* God" (John 1:1). Well, God's Word is now sitting back at YHWH's right hand, so why wouldn't God highly exalt Jesus and bestow on him the name that is rightly his?

We have proof that Jesus received his Father's name on the day of his ascension in the book of Jeremiah. If you investigate all of God's various names listed in the Bible, you will notice that the majority of God's names were given to him by various individuals in the Bible to describe one of YHWH's characteristics. But, there is one name for God that is actually a name prophesied for the future. This name is found twice in the book of Jeremiah. When you study these two almost identical Scripture verses, you realize that this name is not yet another name given to describe one of God's characteristics but instead is his Son Jesus's *new name* in disguise.

> "Behold, the days are coming, says YHWH, when **I will raise up for David a righteous Branch, and he shall reign as king and deal wisely, and shall execute justice and righteousness in the land**. In his days Judah will be saved and Israel will dwell securely. And this **is the name by which *he* will be called: 'YHWH is our righteousness [YHWH Tsidkenu]**.'" (Jer. 23:5–6, Jer. 33:14–16)

Jesus is the righteous Branch that was raised up for David to reign as king to execute justice and righteousness in the land. And one day, Scripture says that Jesus *will be called* YHWH Tsidkenu. Now, your Bible and my Bible won't say *YHWH Tsidkenu* because the translators replaced *YHWH* with *LORD* and *Tsidkenu*, a formal name, with its meaning, "righteousness."[4] What your Bible and my Bible say is that he will be called, "the LORD is our righteousness." Can you see how when the Scripture was translated, the true meaning of these verses was lost? What these verses tell me is that, one day, we will not be calling Jesus, Jesus. We will be calling him YHWH Tsidkenu, so that all of the nations will be calling Jesus by the same name during his millennial reign. No longer will there be confusion on whether Jesus's name is Jesus, Iesous, Iesus, Yehoshua, Yeshua, or any other name that he is called due to the different languages throughout the world. During Jesus's millennial reign, we will all call him by his "new name." We will all call him YHWH Tsidkenu. What an appropriate new name for Jesus, God's only Son, who provided us with righteousness through his perfect sacrifice.

So throughout history Jesus's name has changed. From the beginning of time Jesus was YHWH. Then when Jesus became flesh and blood, his name became Yeshua, which means "YHWH is salvation." Then after ascending into heaven, Jesus obtained his rightful name of YHWH, and he will one day be called YHWH Tsidkenu by his people, which means, "YHWH is our righteousness."

In Revelation 3:12, Jesus says he will write three names upon us: his Father's name, which is YHWH; New Jerusalem's name, which is YHWH Shammah; and his *own new name*, which is YHWH Tsidkenu. These names that Jesus promises to write upon us all have our heavenly Father's divine name within them. Jesus writes these three names upon us because we have conquered, and because we have conquered, Jesus is writing on us the divine names of our *heavenly family and our heavenly home*. YHWH's names are being written upon us because we too have ascended, like Jesus, into heaven and are being given our family names because of our new positions in YHWH's kingdom.

YHWH Tsidkenu

In light of this information about Jesus receiving a new name, when someone accepts Jesus as their LORD and Savior and they receive the Holy Spirit from their heavenly Father into their hearts, in what *name* do you think the Holy Spirit is sent? Since Jesus received his new name immediately after he ascended into heaven and sat down at the right hand of his Father, the name by which the Holy Spirit, the Counselor, came to live inside of you must be YHWH Tsidkenu, Jesus's new name. Again, it only makes sense. YHWH's Holy Spirit would never be sent in a common man's name. It would only be sent in the holiest of *all* names. What this means for believers is that not only is Jesus's name living inside of you, but so is YHWH's name.

Being created in YHWH's image makes humans extremely beautiful. But what makes believers holy is YHWH's divine name. Just as the ark of the covenant, the tabernacle, and the temple were holy, we are holy when YHWH's name is placed inside of us through his Son Jesus's new name. More new information, I know! This is how God explained it to me:

Encountering the Great I Am

Judy, the day that you accepted my Son, Jesus, as your LORD and Savior is the day that I sent my Holy Spirit to reside in your heart. Remember, I promised you that if you would believe in me and in my Son, I would send you the Counselor to guide you in all of my ways. And remember, I said I would **send you the Counselor in Jesus's name**. What you did not know at the time is that the Counselor who came to reside in your heart **was sent in Jesus's "new name."** Remember, Jesus received his new name the day he ascended into heaven on the day of his resurrection. Therefore the name that has been residing in your heart and in your spirit the whole time you have been my child is the name **YHWH Tsidkenu**. On the day of your salvation you received my holy name and my Son Jesus's holy name, so that we could communicate with one another and therefore form a relationship. I knew that in order for you to be in my presence, you would need to be made holy through my Son's perfect sacrifice for your sins. So I sent you my Holy Spirit in my Son's name, which is also my name, in order to make you **righteous and holy**. Remember what my Son, Jesus, said to his disciples, "**Whoever receives me, receives *not me*, *but him who sent me***" (Mark 9:37). Remember also what Jesus prayed for his disciples on the night before his death: "**Holy Father, *keep them in your name*, which *you have given me*, that they may be one, even as we are one**" (John 17:11).

Jesus is and always has been the Word of God. So when we received God's Holy Spirit in Jesus's name, not only did God place his Word into our hearts, but he also inscribed into our hearts his name. We received YHWH's most precious gift—his divine name. Just like YHWH inscribed his name and words on tablets of stone for Moses and the Israelites, he inscribed his Word and divine name onto the hearts of believers in Jesus Christ. And even better yet, his divine name has been inscribed on our hearts from the day we asked his Son, Jesus, to be our LORD and Savior.

What that means is that when we pray to our heavenly Father in

Jesus's name, we are actually praying in YHWH's name as well. Remember, in order for the high priests to receive full communication from YHWH, they had to ponder on both of the names written upon the Urim and the Thummim—YHWH and Jesus! YHWH and YHWH Tsidkenu! Likewise, YHWH knew that only when believers ponder on both his name and his Son's name will they ever have full communication with him. When YHWH's two divine names were placed over the high priest's heart, he was made holy and righteous to stand in YHWH's presence. And so are we! We were given his names so that we could stand in his presence through prayer while we are flesh and blood and one day be able to stand in his very presence in our glorified bodies. Now that is an inheritance like no other! YHWH planned all of this from the very beginning of time, and he did it all for his name's sake.

Rainbows

So today, when you see a rainbow in the sky, you need to remember what God promises us will happen in the future and the everlasting promises and gifts that will be given to us. When the seventh angel is seen in the clouds with a rainbow over his head, he will blow his trumpet and the kingdom of God will be at hand. Today, rainbows are only seen as semicircles because the covenant of Jesus Christ has not yet been completely fulfilled. There are still more events that have to take place. However, once the covenant is fulfilled by the completion of the seven feasts, we will see the rainbow as a complete circle around YHWH's throne. We will see it for the first time because we will not be viewing the rainbow as mortal men and women but as God's children from YHWH's perspective. "At once I was in the Spirit, and lo, a throne stood in heaven, with one seated on the throne! And he who sat there appeared like jasper and carnelian, and **round the throne was a rainbow** that looked like an emerald" (Rev. 4:2–3).

Remember, I said there are seven colors of a rainbow. The colors are violet, indigo, blue, green, yellow, orange, and red. Would you believe that the seventh color, the largest color making up the outside ring of the rainbow, the one that covers all the other colors, is red. Coincidence? No, just a heavenly design. The outside ring is red because it represents Jesus's blood that was shed for our sins to seal God's covenant. Whoever believes in Jesus will have everlasting life in heaven. Just as the red color of the rainbow seals the rainbow, Jesus's blood seals God's everlasting covenant of salvation. Those inside the covenant, inside the circle, with God at the center are protected from their enemy, Satan, by Jesus's blood. Those who believe in the power of the Ark of Jesus will receive salvation. However, to those who are outside of God's covenant, outside the blood of Jesus, the red color of the rainbow does not represent salvation. The red color to those people who do not believe in the Ark of Jesus represents their sins and the fire that will ultimately consume them by God's wrath.

My prayer for you is that you will never look at rainbows in the same way again. From what we have discovered through Scripture, a rainbow is a promise of YHWH's everlasting covenant of eternity with him. Remember, YHWH is your God and you are his child. One day you will see him face to face as you stand before his throne, and surrounding his throne will be his rainbow. The rainbow will consist of God's glory shining through the water of your baptism, along with the millions of his other children standing beside you. The rainbow around YHWH's throne will for eternity be a complete, never-ending, *everlasting circle*. Promise fulfilled!

Chapter 24

The White Stone

"To him who conquers I will give some **hidden manna**, and I will give him **a white stone, with a new name written on the stone** which no one knows **except** him who receives it." (Rev. 2:17b)

Of all the extravagant gifts that will be showered upon believers in Jesus Christ, there are two gifts that I view as having value above and beyond the rest—two gifts from Jesus that would be enough for me just by themselves. They are the hidden manna and the white stone.

Now when I first started contemplating the white stone, I had many questions for God. What is the white stone? What new name will be written upon it? Why is Jesus handing it to all believers? How in the world will I know this new name, like the scripture says, when I will be just receiving it? *And* what does the hidden manna have to do with any of it?

I knew this new name was important but was not sure why. So in order to make sense of it all, I started to think about the specifics of what could be taking place surrounding the receiving of this white stone. Remember, the church has just been raptured, and we are now being rewarded individually for our faith with all of these gifts. So what is taking place?

Then I heard what seemed to be the voice of a great multitude, like the sound of many waters and like the sound of mighty thunderpeals, crying, "**Hallelujah! For the Lord our God the Almighty reigns. Let us rejoice and exult and give him the glory, for the marriage of the Lamb has come, and his Bride has made herself ready**; it was granted her to be clothed with fine linen, bright and pure"—for the fine linen is the righteous deeds of the saints." And the angel said to me, "Write this: **Blessed are those who are invited to the marriage supper of the Lamb**." (Rev. 19:6–9)

At this point in time we will be at the wedding feast of the Lamb meeting our bridegroom, Jesus. So ask yourself, what happens to a bride's name after the bride and groom are married? Why, the bride takes on the name of the bridegroom, doesn't she? In this moment, what Jesus will be formally handing us will be our new family name in order to reflect our new position in YHWH's kingdom. On this day, we will all be receiving our memorial family name that the prophet Isaiah spoke of.

"**O YHWH, we wait for thee; thy memorial name is the desire of our soul.**" (Isa. 26:8)

So what is the new name we will be receiving? Per the prophet Isaiah we will be receiving the name of our heavenly Father, which only makes sense because a name not only makes you unique, but it also defines for others the family you belong to. It identifies your heritage. Just like the followers of Jesus knew who he belonged to because his name was Jesus the "Son of God," from this day forward we too will be officially known as either a son or daughter of YHWH." On this day, our heavenly Father will be formally claiming us as his righteous children by giving us his name. What a gift!

All the receivers of YHWH's name will *know* it because it is the name we received when we received the Holy Spirit. We will recognize the name because this name has been living inside of us since the day we asked Jesus to be our LORD and Savior; since the day YHWH sent his Holy Spirit is his Son Jesus's new name of YHWH Tsidkenu into our hearts.

> For this reason I bow my knees before the Father, **from whom every family in heaven and on earth is named**. (Eph. 3:14–15)

But that's not all. What makes humans so special is our uniqueness to God. Therefore, along with your new family name of YHWH, which can be thought of as your last name, you will also receive on this white stone your new first name.

So what is your new first name? YHWH explained to me that your new first name will be the name by which he physically spoke you into existence into your mother's womb. It will be the name by which he created you into the unique, individual person that you are. Just as God created light by speaking the words, "Let there be light," God brought you into existence into your mother's womb by uttering one word. He brought you into existence by speaking your own unique name, his own personal word for you that created your unique qualities and characteristics.

That is why Scripture says that when you receive your new name, you will know it—you will have heard this name spoken to you once before by your heavenly Father. On the day you were spoken into existence, your heavenly Father's name for you was written into your soul and spirit; it was imprinted into your DNA.

Now scientists will tell you that you were brought into existence when your father's sperm and your mother's egg came together, which is true. But what science cannot explain is why every human being on earth is different from every other human being on earth. Even though we share 99.9 percent of the same genes with one another, there is a 0.1 percent difference between us all, which equates to 3 million differences between your genome and anyone else's. That's a lot of differences when you look at it that way. Not even identical twins, who are created from the same egg and sperm, are truly identical. There is always one difference between identical twins—their fingerprints. I look at the 0.1 percent difference between every human being as being the very fingerprint of God. YHWH's fingerprint chosen just for you is what makes you so special in his eyes.

For thou didst form my inward parts, thou didst knit me together in my mother's womb. I praise thee, for thou art fearful and wonderful. **Wonderful are thy works**! Thou knowest me right well; my frame was not hidden from thee, **when I was being made in secret**, intricately wrought in the depths of the earth. Thy eyes beheld my unformed substance; in thy book were written every one of them, the days that were formed for me, when as yet there was none of them. (Ps. 139:13–16)

"***Before* I formed you in the womb** I knew you." (Jer. 1:5)

"... **every one who is called by my name, whom I created for my glory, whom I formed and made**." (Isa. 43:7)

What is so cool about your new name is that no one in the universe will have your same name. Everyone will have their own unique heavenly name given to them by their heavenly Father, and you will be called by this name for eternity. And of course this new name will accurately describe your identity because this name is who you truly are.

So ... *What Is the White Stone?*

The Greek word that has been translated as "white" in Revelation 2:17 is "leukos." The definition of *leukos* is "light, brilliant, bright."[1] It is the same word that was used to describe Jesus Christ's clothing during his transfiguration that became "dazzling white." In addition, *leukos* is used to describe the clothing of the angels found in Jesus's tomb, the garments of the twenty-four elders around YHWH's throne, and the garments that believers will finally be clothed in for eternity. This word describes the color of the garments of those who are exalted to the splendor of the heavenly state. There is something about the whiteness of these garments that is brilliant and bright and that shines light.

So what white stone is Jesus handing us that has these heavenly qualities of illumination? When I asked God this question, he told me very clearly to investigate diamonds. Here is what I discovered. Diamonds start out as carbon, the most common element in all of creation. It is out of this element that YHWH forms the rarest of gems. Diamonds are initially formed ninety miles under the earth, under intense pressure, at two-thousand-degree Fahrenheit temperatures, at which time they are brought to the surface of the earth by a volcanic eruption. When diamonds are mined, they are not capable of reflecting light; they are found dirty and dull. Only after a gemologist holds the diamond in his hands, cleans it, and then cuts it will it ever bear light. Because the gemologist carefully cuts facets and polishes the diamond in just the right manner, it becomes capable of reflecting brilliant light through its surface. When the gemologist is finally finished with his work, the rarest of diamonds will be found blemish-free and flawless.

As I was researching diamonds, I couldn't help but think that what a gemologist does with a diamond is exactly what Jesus does after YHWH physically places us into his hands. Jesus first cleans us of our sins and the filth that have accumulated from living in Satan's world, after which he then creates facets and polishes our lives in a way that only he can. When we first allow God to find us, we are messy, dull, and dirty. It is only after following in Jesus's footsteps that our lives start to shine his light back into the dark world from which we came. As we continue to allow Jesus to hold us in his hands, fine-tuning everything about our lives, we start reflecting his brilliant light to those around us.

Diamonds have been chosen by man throughout the centuries to represent ultimate love between a man and a woman because a diamond stone is the hardest substance known and will last forever. Therefore, it has become tradition for a bride to receive a diamond ring from the bridegroom to represent their everlasting covenant. I personally cannot think of a better *white stone*, a diamond that illuminates YHWH's pure white light, that could be used by YHWH to represent the everlasting marriage of agape love between Jesus and his Bride, his church, his children!

The Hidden Manna

So what is the hidden manna, and what does it have to do with the white stone? We have discovered that the stone is a dazzling white diamond, and the name written upon this diamond will be our new name for eternity, our new identity as one of YHWH's righteous children. Jesus himself will hand us this diamond at the wedding feast of the Lamb. But as marvelous as the white stone and the name written upon the stone will be to believers, the hidden manna is beyond marvelous. The hidden manna is magnificent and has everything to do with what is written on the white stone.

The hidden manna that Jesus wants us to think about is the manna that was sent down from heaven to feed the Israelites. It was the daily bread that fed them for forty years in the wilderness and is the holiest food ever to be consumed by man. It is the food that physically nourished their bodies on a daily basis. Remember, an omer of this manna was placed into the ark of the covenant as a memorial of God's provision to his people. After the manna no longer came down from heaven, only the high priest had access to this "hidden" manna.

Well Jesus is now our High Priest. So what would Jesus want to give us from the ark of the covenant that we would need? We already have YHWH's written word in the Bible, and, at this point in time, we will be standing in the very presence of Jesus. So what else would we need? What would feed us spiritually that Jesus knows we would not be able to live for eternity without?

> "Thus say YHWH who made the earth, YHWH who formed it to establish it—**YHWH is his name: Call to me and I will answer you, and will tell you great and hidden things which you have not known.**" (Jer. 33:2–3)

This is when God woke me from sleep at exactly 3:00 a.m. to consider the verse about the hidden manna, the new name we receive on a white stone, and all that I knew about "texting." It seemed like a strange request, but I obeyed. Here is what I wrote on that particular night at 3:00 a.m. while pondering on our new name as either a son or daughter of YHWH.

> God's divine name is YHWH.
> YHWH is written in the language of Moses's day.
> It was a language that did not use vowels.
> Even without the vowels, Moses and the people knew how to say God's divine name because it was pronounced daily.
> It is like texting today, when texting first came into use.
> Texters will tell you that "I lv u mm" means, "I love you mom."
> Texting is the language of our day.
> When texting first came about, the vowels were typically not typed, and yet we knew how to read the words.
> It's as if the vowels were "**hidden**" in the text messages.
> Unfortunately, unless we are given the missing vowels in YHWH's name, we will never know how to pronounce it.
> Therefore, at some point, **God will need to give us the hidden vowels**.

Hidden vowels ... hidden manna ... *Oh my, the "hidden vowels" are the "hidden manna."* Jesus says that he will give us the hidden manna, and then he says we will receive a white stone with a new name written upon it. The puzzle pieces were all coming together at once. *The new name written on the white stone is our heavenly Father's divine name—with all the hidden vowels included in YHWH's name.* We are being given something we have been waiting to receive from the beginning of time: *our everlasting memorial name* that was promised to us by the prophet Isaiah. Because Jesus is our High Priest, he has access to the hidden manna, and since he knows who is in the Book of Life, he also has the names of those who are YHWH's children.

> "I will give in my house and within my walls a monument and a name better than sons and daughters; **I will give them an everlasting name which shall not be cut off.**" (Isa. 56:5)

We are given the hidden vowels in our Father's name because Jesus knows we will want to know everything there is to know about the name above all names, because from this day forward communication with our Creator will be face to face.

Remember, after YHWH's name was no longer said, starting in 300 BC, YHWH's name was still available to the high priests because it could still be found written in the Hebrew Scriptures. However, to the rest of the congregation, God's written divine name and its pronunciation were all but lost. In its place, the word *LORD* was spoken when referring to YHWH. But that is not what YHWH ever desired. He gave his name to his people because he wanted them to worship, to speak, to praise, and to pray to him by his given name. After YHWH gave Moses his name, he said, "*This is my name forever; this is what I want to be known as for all generations.*" What broke YHWH's heart is when, instead, his chosen people started profaning his name. That is why YHWH purposely took his name away and gave the world his Son's name of Jesus for the new covenant name. He wanted more than anything for his name to once again be called upon and for personal relationships to develop between his people and their God. He therefore allowed his divine name to temporarily be lowered to titles so that his Son's name could be the name upon which his followers called. However, one day, because it has always been his desire, we can be sure that his divine name of YHWH will be said again.

On the same day that you are raptured and are receiving your white stone, surrounding you will be believers from *all* generations receiving their white stones as well. YHWH did it! I wasn't sure how he was going to make his name remembered throughout all generations since his name has already been missing for over 2,300 years. But in the end it will happen exactly the way YHWH ordained it. And YHWH's name will be remembered and spoken by his children forever.

Just like YHWH engraved his words and his name on two stone tablets at the time of Moses, YHWH will engrave our new heavenly names into stone. He will then place these stones into our hands as personal gifts. The finality and permanency of who we are to him will finally be complete. Our family position will be official and will continue for eternity.

> **Your words were found, and I ate them**, and your words became to me a joy and the delight of my heart, **for I am called by your name, O YHWH**, God of hosts. (Jer. 15:16 ESV)

Chapter 25

YHWH Shammah

Blessed be his glorious name forever; may his glory fill the whole earth! (Ps. 72:19)

On the same day that YHWH prompted me to think about circles, rainbows, and everlasting covenants, he put it into my mind to discover what a square represents in the Bible. On this particular day, my head was swirling with geometric shapes.

Because I am an engineer, I remembered from geometry classes that a square is defined as a four-sided polygon, characterized by right angles and sides of equal length. I also knew that a square has four corners. As soon as I said "corners" in my mind, it hit me: all of this had something to do with corners. I knew of a Scripture verse that used the word *corner*: "Behold *I am laying in Zion for a foundation a stone, a tested stone, a precious cornerstone*, of a sure foundation" (Isa. 28:16a). Of course! A square would have a cornerstone if the square represented the shape of the foundation of a structure. From this verse alone, I knew that God wanted me to see that a *perfect square*, with *Jesus as a cornerstone*, represents a *sure foundation*. So I asked myself, *What else in Scripture is described as a perfect square?* It was at this moment that a vision of what God was trying to get me to see appeared in my mind.

I began by drawing a perfect square on a piece of paper. Now keep in mind, I was knee-deep in writing my chapter on the Urim and Thummim when God gave me this picture in my head. So at the same time I was drawing the square on my paper, I also had an image of what the breastplate of judgment looked like, and I remembered this verse: "And you shall make a *breastpiece of judgment*. ... It shall be *square* and double, a span its length and a span its breadth" (Exo. 28:15, 16). Amazing! The breastpiece of the high priest was perfectly square, and it held YHWH's divine names—but did it represent a sure foundation? I wasn't sure. So I asked myself, *What else in the Bible is described as a square?*

> So Solomon built the house, and finished it. ... The **inner sanctuary he prepared** in the innermost part of the house, **to set there the ark of the covenant of YHWH**. The inner sanctuary was **twenty cubits long, twenty cubits wide, and twenty cubits high**; and he overlaid it with pure gold. (1 Kings 6:14, 19–20a)

Another piece of the puzzle! In Solomon's temple and in the tabernacle that preceded it, the Holy of Holies formed a perfect cube, with its foundation a perfect square. It was in the Holy of Holies that the ark of the covenant was placed, which contained YHWH's divine name. I was getting excited. Not only was the high priest's breastpiece that he wore in the presence of YHWH a square, but the place where God communicated with the high priest through the Urim and Thummim also formed a square. I asked God, "What are you trying to show me? Is there more? What else in your Book of Truth is a square?" And that is when God took me to the final chapters of the book of Revelation.

> "Come, I will show you the Bride, the wife of the Lamb."
> And in the Spirit he carried me away to a great, high mountain, and showed me the **holy city of Jerusalem** coming down out of heaven from God, having the glory of God, its radiance like a most rare jewel, like a jasper, clear as crystal. ... And he who talked to me had a measuring rod of gold to measure the city and its gates and walls. **The city lies foursquare, its length the same as its breadth**; and he

measured the city with his rod, twelve thousand stadia; **its length and breadth and height are equal**. (Rev. 21:9b–11, 15–16)

Wow! The eternal, holy city of Jerusalem, promised to all believers, will have a square foundation. It will form a perfect cube, just like the Holy of Holies found in the tabernacle and the temple. Could it be that the high priest's breastpiece had anything to do with the prophesied eternal city of Jerusalem? They were both in the shape of perfect squares and of great importance. Could it be that the high priest's breastpiece so long ago was made to represent God's eternal city that has yet to come?

So I went back to the square that I had drawn on my piece of paper, and I imagined it as the outline of the breastpiece of the high priest. Within the square, I drew the twelve circles to represent the stones that represented the twelve tribes, God's chosen people. I drew these circles in four rows of three stones, exactly as they were placed on the breastpiece. As I looked at this square, I imagined what it would look like in three dimensions. I thought of the lines that form the square of the breastpiece as foundation walls made of stone, and I imagined them rising off of the paper so that the height of the walls were the same as its length and width. I imagined these foundation walls having the names of the twelve apostles of the Lamb written upon them (Rev. 21:14). At the same time, I looked at the twelve round circles and imagined them as pillars of stone rising off the page. On these pillars, I saw the names of believers, which were inscribed by Jesus himself (Rev. 3:12)

Now, as I imagined this cube forming off of my page, in my mind I turned it on its side. What I first saw as just a cube became a box and then a structure that was made strong by the foundation walls and the pillars inside. Because of the pillars and the foundation walls, this structure would be able to support a roof. And then, I realized what I was looking at. I was looking at a house, and not just any house, but *"the house"* where Jesus said in the God equation he was preparing a room for us.

> "Let not your hearts be troubled; believe in God, believe also in me. **In my Father's house are many rooms**; if it were not so, would I have told you that I go to prepare a place for you? **And when I go and prepare a place for you, I will come again and will take you to myself, that where I am you may be also.**" (John 14:1–4)

But that's not all. Remember, the Urim and Thummim were placed behind the breastpiece in the high priest's garments. If the breastpiece were laid flat on a table, the Urim and the Thummim would physically be below it. Therefore, as I thought of the cube as my Father's house that Jesus has been building, I imagined these sacred stones, inscribed with the names of YHWH and Jesus, being physically below it. By being below the house, the Urim and the Thummim represent the "rocks" that YHWH's house is built upon.

> "Why do you call me 'Lord, Lord,' and not do what I tell you? **Every one who comes to me and hears my words and does them**, I will show you what he is like: **he is like a man building a house, who dug deep, and laid the foundation upon rock**; and when a flood arose, the stream broke against that house, and could not shake it, because **it had been well built**. But he who hears and does not do them is like a man who built a house on the ground without a foundation; against which the stream broke, and immediately it fell, and the ruin of that house was great." (Luke 6:46–49)

It made perfect sense. YHWH is the "everlasting rock" that his house is built on, and Jesus is the "cornerstone" of his sure foundation. But as I once again looked at my square and imagined God's house rising off the page, I remembered that the placement of the Urim and Thummim were over Aaron's heart, which would place YHWH's divine names not only below the house, supporting it, but also in the very center of it.

> **And I saw no temple in the city, for its temple is YHWH God the Almighty and the Lamb**. And the city has no need

of sun or moon to shine upon it, for the glory of **God is its light, and its lamp is the Lamb.** (Rev. 21:22)

There shall no more be anything accursed, but **the throne of God and of the Lamb shall be in it,** and his servants shall worship him; **they shall see** *his face*, **and** *his name* **shall be on their foreheads**. (Rev. 22:3–4)

One day in the future YHWH and Jesus, YHWH and YHWH Tsidkenu, the Urim and the Thummim, the Illuminator and the Completer, Light and Perfection, will be located directly in the center of YHWH's holy city, the New Jerusalem—YHWH Shammah, YHWH is there. They will be shining their light for all to see. Oh, what a glorious city it will be when YHWH's light shines through the millions of believers surrounding him, forming his beautiful rainbow of colors around his throne.

> And **I saw a new heaven and a new earth**; for the first heaven and the first earth had passed away, and the sea was no more. And **I saw the holy city, new Jerusalem, coming out of heaven as a bride adorned for her husband**; and I heard a loud voice from the throne saying, "**Behold the dwelling of God is with men. He will dwell with them and they shall be his people, and God himself will be with them**; he will wipe away every tear from their eyes, and death shall be no more, neither shall there be mourning nor crying nor pain any more, for the former things have passed away." (Rev. 21:1–4)

YHWH's Resting Place

It has been a long journey through the history of God communicating with his people, but YHWH has finally found a resting place for his name. He first gave his divine name to Moses out of a burning bush and told Moses to give his name to the Israelites, his chosen people. YHWH then audibly spoke his name in front of two million men, women, and children so they would know the name of the God who wanted to dwell among them. After this, he personally inscribed his name for his people on two stones, along with his Ten Commandments. He told Moses to place his name inside the ark of the covenant and to build a tabernacle around it. At the same time, YHWH inscribed his name and his Son's name on two stones and told Moses to place them behind the high priest's breastpiece. With the Urim and Thummim over the high priest's heart, he would have communication with YHWH. He also assigned the entire tribe of Levi to protect his name and to serve him in the tabernacle. Finally, YHWH's Shekinah glory continuously dwelled over his name through a cloud by day and a fire by night.

However, YHWH never planned for his name to remain in a sacred box in the wilderness. He had much grander plans indeed. "So they set out from the mount of YHWH three days' journey; and *the ark of the covenant of YHWH went before them three days' journey, to seek out a resting place for them*" (Num. 10:33). Everywhere the Israelites went, the ark of the covenant led the way. When the ark moved, they moved. When the ark rested, they rested. However, even after forty years in the wilderness, the ark did not find its ultimate rest. God's Shekinah glory was living among his people in the desert, but not in the way he had intended. Once the ark entered into the promised land after a few hundred years, YHWH's name did eventually find a resting place in Solomon's Temple, for a period of time. Here it rested until 587 BC, when YHWH allowed Solomon's Temple to be destroyed. It was at this time that YHWH removed his name and the ark of the covenant from among his people and told them to stop profaning his name.

It wasn't until YHWH sent his Son, Jesus, into the world that his name once again found a resting place in his Son's heart. Jesus became YHWH's Ark of the New Covenant, and Jesus's body was the new temple in which YHWH's name resided. It was through the Ark of Jesus that YHWH's name, through his Holy Spirit, found its way into the hearts of millions of believers throughout the two thousand years since Jesus's death and resurrection. Our bodies became the physical tabernacles in which YHWH's Spirit could communicate with our spirits.

But this still was never the final resting place for YHWH's divine name. God knows that our physical bodies are mortal and temporary, and he has always wanted more than that for us. Since the garden of Eden, God has always desired spiritual perfection when it comes to communing with his children; therefore, YHWH will not rest until spiritual completion has been fulfilled. So long ago, YHWH sent out his ark into the wilderness to find a resting place for his name. The ark went on a journey for three days to seek out the promised land. When it arrived at the city of Jerusalem, it had reached its final destination. "For YHWH has chosen Zion; he has desired it for his habitation: 'This is my resting place for ever; here I will dwell, for I have desired it'" (Ps. 132:13).

That is why the country of Israel is and always has been the focus of all the nations. That is why so many people have tried to lay claim to it over the years. There is something different about that land, something spiritual that cannot be grasped. This sacred land is different because it is where YHWH's divine name physically walked, sat, and enjoyed fellowship with his children. Israel is where YHWH's divine name loved, cried, mourned, and laughed with friends and family and enjoyed being in their presence. It is in Jerusalem where YHWH's divine name gave up his own life so that others could live. And that is why Jerusalem is where YHWH will dwell for eternity. It is a land that has been chosen as an inheritance to those who dwell with him—because that is where he first experienced life with his children through Jesus. New Jerusalem is the eternal city where YHWH desires to walk with all of his children once again.

Those saints who will eventually live on this land for eternity will be made distinct from all other people, from all other nations, because they will bear YHWH's name. His name will be written on their foreheads, and placed in their hands will be their new family name, written upon a white stone. They will see YHWH's face and will be in his presence. They will be worshipping him by praising his name—with all the vowels included.

> And he who sat upon the throne said, "**Behold, I make all things new**." And he said, "Write this, for these words are trustworthy and true." And he said to me, "**It is done! I am the Alpha and the Omega, the beginning and the end. To the thirsty I will give from the fountain of the water of life** without payment. He who conquers shall have this heritage, and **I will be his God and he shall be my son**." (Rev. 21:5–7)

On that day, there will be spiritual perfection like no other. After Jesus's one-thousand-year millennial reign, a new heaven, a new earth, and a new Jerusalem will be created. Found within the new Jerusalem will be our Creator YHWH and his Son, YHWH Tsidkenu, and surrounding him will be his chosen people, who have all received his name. It will be a day of great rejoicing in his presence. Our Lover will finally be living among us. When we finally see YHWH face to face, it will be an encounter like no other—an encounter that words will have a hard time explaining. How each of us will respond to being in YHWH's presence will vary according to our previous encounters with him. Some will be dancing with joy; some will be crying with relief. Some will be overcome with laughter, while others will be taking everything in through silence. What all of us will experience is complete awe that our LORD (YHWH) and Savior (Jesus) has chosen us to be in his presence, and we will sing and praise his name for eternity.

Love Story

I want to leave our time spent together studying Genesis to Revelation, from Exodus to the cross, and from creation to eternity with one final story. It is a personal love story between a lost child and the one and only true God.

Every year, after our women's Bible study comes to an end, we all come together for what we call "Share Day." During these two hours, we fellowship with one another and share what God has taught us through another year of studying his Word, his truth. Many incredible stories of communication with God are conveyed year after year. Most years, God places something on my heart that I know he wants others to hear, so every year I put away my fear of public speaking and speak what God has placed on my lips. However, this particular year, Share Day was only one week away, and God had not yet given me a clear indication of what he wanted me to share. I really felt like this year YHWH wanted me to remain silent and just enjoy listening to others. I even told a friend that I didn't think I would be speaking this year since God had not yet placed anything on my heart. Well, wouldn't you know it, on that very night, as I was writing about Satan and his Antichrist, God indicated to me that I needed to share with others what I had learned about the Antichrist's number of 666.

Throughout this particular year's Bible study we discussed end times, the Antichrist, and the Day of the LORD, so sharing the meaning of the Antichrist's number was relevant to our study. So on that day I made sure I went first because I always like to speak before my nerves get the best of me. I shared with everyone, as I shared with you, what God had placed on my heart about the number 666 being a human number that represents our bodies, souls, and spirits and our own human condition before we place our trust in YHWH and his Son, Jesus. I explained that our numbers will increase in this life only by spending one-on-one time with our LORD and Savior. As a result of loving God through quality time with him, we will begin to experience peace, joy, and love in this life, regardless of our circumstances. I concluded by saying that today I was very thankful that YHWH's Spirit in Jesus's name is dwelling inside of me. Ever since the Spirit of YHWH in Jesus's name entered into my heart, he has been slowly increasing my number, and on the "Day of the LORD," my body, soul, and spirit will finally reach perfection. I had come to realize that on that day, *my number will no longer be 666, but it will be God's number of 777.*

After I finished speaking, a girl I had never met literally ran up to the stage for her turn. She practically stiff-armed another woman who was getting up as well so that she could be next. This seemed strange to me because it is rare that someone wants to take the stage so quickly. Holly began to share her story of how God had spoken to her throughout the year while she read and pondered God's truth. Holly explained that she has a passion for running. She had been running since she was fourteen and had completed many races, including numerous marathons. She told us that the running numbers she wore during these races lined the walls of her garage. Her numbers were reminders of her accomplishments, of what she was good at.

Holly shared with us that she had recently qualified for the Boston Marathon and had started training in December of 2012. By February, she was halfway through her training, had paid her entrance fee, and had booked her hotel. During this same time period, God had also been working in her life by speaking to her heart through his Word. This was Holly's first year in Bible study. During this year, she had spent time actually reading and reflecting on the words of the God she claimed to believe in. It was during this time that she went to a fellowship with the other women in her group. She left the fellowship with a deep conviction that *if* what she desired in life most was to become a godlier woman, wife, and mother, *then* she needed to start pursuing a path for achieving it. She realized on that day that running had become her idol and that her running successes alone would never make her happy. So a few weeks before the Boston Marathon took place, Holly heard God's voice clearly telling her that he didn't want her to run Boston. What followed was a week-long struggle with her LORD and Savior. Here are entries from Holly's personal journal that she wrote during this time:

> I had been spiritually treading water for many years, probably since college. I had become the most despised Christian … a lukewarm one. I realized I had been treating God as if he were a waterfall. I would view the waterfall from a distance. I would see how incredible the waterfall was, see its power, be awestruck by its beauty, see the changes it made to the earth that it touched.
>
> But I would leave the waterfall and no one would know I had been there. No one could see evidence that I had been at the waterfall; I wouldn't mention the waterfall with others.

I did not love the waterfall as openly as so many of my mature Christian friends.

I was saddened and deeply convicted. God had been pulling on me since the birth of my firstborn to start growing spiritually. As he kept tugging on me, I would make excuses. Too hard to find childcare while I did small group or Bible study. I would do it as my kids got older. I would wait for my spouse to be the spiritual leader. ... I continued to just view the waterfall on Sundays.

But I did find time for running, for doing things I liked to do ...

And that is when Jesus broke me. I became mad at myself for creating excuses for not growing spiritually. How could I desire something so right and not put any effort into achieving it? What was getting in my way?

The lack of time and the desire to run!

Jesus wanted me to take a break from running and racing. He wanted me to stop putting running in front of him and my family. I broke down in agony. "But why Lord, why take the one thing that I am adequate at? I'm not a good friend. I'm not a good wife or mother. But I am a good runner. Why would you take the one thing I am adequate at?" And the Lord replied, "Because I am adequate." I said, "But no... wait... I run to calm my nerves ... as an outlet." He replied, "My Word will calm you."

After a week of trying to find a compromise with God, I finally came to realize he just wanted my heart. He wanted my commitment. He wanted me to put him first again. I wanted to know what would come of my commitment. He replied, "But that is not faith." He wanted me to commit by faith alone.

So for the first time in her life, Holly stepped out in faith and went on a running fast for two weeks. She quickly dove into establishing a routine for quiet time with her LORD and Savior. Holly spent time waking up early, before her children woke up, to read God's Word in order to absorb everything God placed in front of her. Because she was fasting from running, things were very clear and, as a result, God became very real to her for the first time in her life. She gained a new appreciation for him for always pursuing her and loving her. In addition, Holly began to freely speak the name Jesus in her household.

Normally Holly would run a half marathon about a month before each scheduled marathon. This time, since God was asking her to take a fast from running, she decided to forgo the Publix Half Marathon. Since she would not be running Boston, she saw no reason to run the Publix race. However, she still wanted her Publix number so that she could place it on her garage wall. This time her unused number would have a different meaning for her. This time her number would be a milestone marker of what God had done for her. So one week before the Boston Marathon, Holly asked a friend to pick up her Publix race number.

Four days later the bombing at the Boston Marathon took place while Holly sat safely in her home in Georgia. When she heard about the bombings, her heart sank. That day is the day Jesus broke her of her pride. She was filled with humility because God had never given up pursuing her, even after she had ignored him for so long. She was filled with embarrassment and shame that she had actually asked God to tell her why he was asking her to fast from running, when all he wanted to do is save her from all the curses that could have followed if she had disobeyed. She was filled with gratitude that God's lesson, his "sacred fire," was accomplished in Georgia and not in Boston. She was overwhelmed by the fact that she didn't have to be involved in the chaos that followed the bombing; and she didn't have to wonder if her husband, who would have been standing at the finish line, was alive, dead, or maimed. She understood that this was the first time she had ever stepped out in faith for Jesus and, as a result, God had rewarded her immensely.

Encountering the Great I Am

It was during this time that Holly opened her unused Publix race number. The number that God chose for Holly, for the races that she never ran, was 11777. For several weeks, Holly had been running the race of faith with her LORD and Savior and, since she had been spending time with him, he wanted to give her a new number, one that represented what a personal relationship with him would accomplish. When she saw her number she knew it was special because she knew the number 7 had significant meaning in the Bible. She saw her number as a sign that God was truly pursuing her, and she asked him for guidance on how she could glorify his name. She prayed for God to flow over her and through her.

Holly heard God's voice asking her to give her testimony on Share Day. Speaking about God was something she was not good at, even though she had already been forced out of her comfort zone to share with her runner friends the reason why she wasn't running Boston. So she prayed for courage to be obedient to YHWH's wishes. The day before Share Day, her child got sick. Satan was obviously trying his hardest to keep Holly from telling her amazing story. But God had other plans and no one, not even Satan, would thwart them. So YHWH removed all of Holly's obstacles, and he successfully got her there.

On the day of Share Day, Holly's nerves were getting the best of her. She told her leader that she would rather run a marathon in the clothes she was wearing than to speak what God had placed on her lips. She had decided that she would not share her number because someone might think it was hokey. She thought that maybe her number only meant something to her. That all changed when Holly heard me speak.

When I mentioned the number 6, she said her jaw dropped. And when I continued speaking about the numbers 666 and 777, she was so moved because, *again*, God was making his presence known to her. Finally, she understood why her number was so important. YHWH wanted Holly to know that *"when you spend 1 on 1 time with me, I will make you a '777.'"* Her new number represented the many blessings she would be rewarded with for running the race of faith with God by her side. This new race would eventually result in physical and spiritual perfection, which would be her ultimate reward.

That's why Holly was so excited to share and had literally run up to the stage with her number in her hand. The words YHWH had given me to speak gave her all the confidence she needed to share her testimony. As she told her story, we were all in awe; and when she finally unrolled her number for everyone to see, the three 7's were shining so brightly that there were audible gasps in the room. On that day, YHWH's presence in the room could be physically felt through all of our senses. He had successfully used two individuals who had never met each other to communicate to his children what is possible when we listen to his voice. YHWH's Shekinah glory and power was revealed for everyone to see. First came obedience—from both of us—and then understanding!

Through the whole experience, Holly finally came to know what the Holy Spirit's voice sounds like and has vowed that she will never doubt his calm, patient voice again. The day Holly shared her "God story," she successfully glorified her LORD and Savior's divine name. Her entire experience was her first "close encounter" with the living God. Through Jesus, she now has a solid foundation, a cornerstone upon which her faith can be built. For the first time, she personally discovered that YHWH truly exists and that he cares about her and her family. Not even Satan will be able to convince her otherwise. Finally, she had gotten so close to the waterfall that she had been viewing from afar for so long that she felt its living waters flowing over her and through her. And now, because she has felt his power, she can't help but share her story with others.

> Then he showed me **the river of the water of life**, bright as crystal, **flowing from the throne of God and of the Lamb through the middle of the street of the city**; also, on either side of the river, **the tree of life with its twelve kinds of fruit**, yielding its fruit each month; and the leaves of the tree were **for the healing of the nations**. (Rev. 22:1–2)

Ask YHWH to Wow You!

What makes Holly's story even more special for me is that just weeks before Share Day, I asked my heavenly Father to speak to me again in one of his amazing ways of communication. I told him how much I loved to hear his voice. I said, "Father, in these last few chapters of my book, please 'wow me,' and I promise I will write about it." All I can say is that the God I serve does not disappoint. What a perfect ending to a beautiful story of how YHWH loves each and every one of us so much that he will go to great lengths to prove his love. Was I ever wowed on that day, along with everyone else who was present.

God wants to wow you too. YHWH wants to give you his name—a name that means light and perfection. He will give it to you engraved on the most beautiful diamond you will ever be able to imagine. But he has to know you in order to claim you as his child. In order to know you, there has to be communication. There has to be a relationship, a loving relationship. It begins with deciding who Jesus is. So who do you claim Jesus is? If you accept and believe with your whole heart, mind, and soul that Jesus is "Christ, the Son of the living God," then the next step is to ask him into your heart. You have to invite Jesus to be your LORD and Savior. He will not force himself upon you; he will not come into your heart until he is asked. So you have to take the first step. After you have invited him in, YHWH will send his Holy Spirit, in Jesus's new name, into your heart. YHWH's Spirit will reside in your heart forever. It is here, from your heart, that you will communicate through the Holy Spirit to YHWH and Jesus—your LORD, your Savior, your Father, your Creator, and your God. And it is through this communication that the most intimate, personal, and loving relationship that you have ever experienced will form through YHWH's spiritual language.

The wedding feast is not for strangers; it will only be attended by well-known family members. Just like you would never get married to a stranger or even an acquaintance, neither will YHWH. The wedding feast is for those who have conquered, reserved only for intimate lovers. Now is not a time to be lukewarm with your faith. Now is a time for your God-given radiant life to shine into the depths of darkness that invade this world. Now is the time to be bold, to fight the good fight. It is time to claim Jesus as your LORD and Savior so that you can put on your breastplate of righteousness (Eph. 6:14), defeat the enemy, and reign with YHWH for eternity. It is time to be wowed!

Once you were no people but now you are God's people. (1 Peter 2:9)

Blessed be the name of YHWH from this time forth and forevermore! From the rising of the sun to its setting the name of YHWH is to be praised! (Ps. 113:2–3)

Chapter 26
Conclusion

YHWH was known by Noah as *Elohim*, which means "God." YHWH introduced himself to Abraham, Isaac, and Jacob as *El Shaddai*, which is translated "God Almighty." To Moses and the nation of Israel, God introduced himself as *YHWH*, "I AM WHO I AM." After YHWH's name was all but lost, God reintroduced his second covenant name to the world as *Yeshua*, which means "YHWH is salvation." Yeshua taught the world how to worship and praise and to address YHWH as *Father*. Once Jesus died and was resurrected, his name was exalted to *YHWH Tsidkenu*, which means "YHWH is our righteousness." Because YHWH is "The Great I AM," he used different names for different seasons of his eternal plan in order to dwell with his people.

YHWH knew that his people would forget his name and replace it with a title. He prophesied that it would happen.

> "How long shall there be lies in the heart of the prophets who prophesy lies, and who prophesy the deceit of their own heart, who think to make my people **forget my name** by their dreams which they tell one another, **even as their fathers forgot my name for Ba'al**." (Jer. 23:26–27)

The meaning of the word "Baal" is "Lord, master, owner, possessor, husband."[1] When you replace the word *Baal* with its meaning of "Lord," this verse takes on a whole new meaning.

> "even as their fathers **forgot my name for LORD**."

However, one day, YHWH's name will be remembered and used once again. On that day everyone will confess that the one true God's name is YHWH.

> Therefore, **God has highly exalted him and bestowed on him the name which is above every name**, that at the name of Jesus every knee should bow, in heaven and on earth and under the earth, and **every tongue confess that JESUS CHRIST is LORD** to the glory of God the Father. (Phil. 2:9–11)

Or in other words,

> every tongue will confess that **JESUS CHRIST is YHWH**.

Jesus is YHWH. YHWH is Jesus. YHWH gave his Son his name because the Father and the Son are one. Remember the words YHWH placed on Jesus's lips to speak: "I and the Father are one." Therefore, because they are one, there will be a day that YHWH and Jesus's names become one.

> And YHWH will become king over all the earth; on that day **YHWH *will be one and his name one*.** (Zech. 14:9)

Scripture tells us that on the day when YHWH is finally living among us, the entire world will have one language. At that time the world will no longer be filled with thousands of different physical languages, but instead we will all be speaking one spiritually pure love language, the language of YHWH himself. I personally cannot wait for that day.

> "Yea, at that time I will **change the speech of the peoples to a pure speech**, that all of them may **call on the name of YHWH and serve him with one accord**." (Zeph. 3:9)

The day that YHWH and Jesus become one will be the day that YHWH's Word will have accomplished and prospered in all that it was sent out to do. Remember, YHWH said that his Word (Jesus) would not return to him empty handed. Jesus is currently sitting at YHWH's right hand because there is still more work that needs to be done. However, one day YHWH's Word will completely return to him, and Jesus and YHWH will become one once again. We can be assured that day will not occur until *after* Jesus personally hand delivers *all* of his Father's children to YHWH himself. Mission complete!

So what's in a name? It really is a good question to ponder. When YHWH said, "I AM WHO I AM," what he meant is, **I AM the Father, I AM the Son, I AM the Holy Spirit**. That is why we baptize in the name of the Father, the Son, and the Holy Spirit. We don't say *names*; we say *name*! One God, one name—YHWH!

What YHWH wants you to leave our time together knowing is that the one and only living God has a name. He wants you to know that, if you are a believer, it is his holy name that he has physically placed into your heart through his Son, Jesus. YHWH placed his Holy Spirit and name within you so that you can enter into your heavenly Father's presence whenever you want to. For YHWH knows that it is in his presence that you can fellowship with one another and hear his precious voice. It is your Creator's precious voice that has the power to heal you, cast out your demons, and feed you daily revelation. Christians who enter into YHWH's presence regularly live extraordinarily abundant lives because of the heavenly voice that is daily guiding, instructing, and protecting them.

What I hope you leave here understanding is the true power and authority of the name that lives inside of you. Remember, it was YHWH's name and Spirit that gave Jesus the power and authority to raise the dead, so YHWH's name that resides in you also has the power and authority to release you from your own bondage and prison walls. So worship YHWH and Jesus' holy name ... ponder it ... meditate on it ... thank your heavenly Father for it every time you enter into his presence. Be careful to never underestimate the *power* of the truly majestic name that lives inside you. Then allow YHWH's name to set you free!

When I asked God five years ago for everything the Holy Spirit had to offer me, it was the mystery of his name that he sent. What I have discovered is that with YHWH's name comes absolutely *everything*!

> May YHWH bless you and keep you.
> May YHWH make his face to shine upon you.
> May YHWH lift his countenance upon you and give you peace.

God Bless <><

Notes

Chapter 1: What's in a Name?

1. Dorothy Astoria, *The Name Book*, (Minneapolis, MN.: Bethany House Publishers, 1982), 7–9.

Chapter 2: God's Divine Name

1. Timothy J. McHyde, *Know the Future: A Bible Prophecy Breakthrough from Overlooked Keys in the Words of Jesus*, (Litografia e Imprenta LIL, S.A., 2009), 74.
2. *Merriam-Webster.com*, 2011, http://www.merriam-webster.com (8 May 2011), s.vv. "god," "father," "almighty," "savior," "creator."
3. Merrill C. Tenney, *Zondervan's Pictorial Bible Dictionary*, (Grand Rapids, MI.: Zondervan, 1967), 408.
4. Tenney, 833.
5. "Hebrew Streams," www.hebrewstreams.org/works/Hebrew/hashem/html, (26 September 2016).
6. McHyde, 72–74.
7. Brent Curtis, and John Eldredge, *The Sacred Romance: Drawing Closer to the Heart of God*, (Nashville, TN: Thomas Nelson, 1997), 96.

Chapter 3: Proper Names

1. Revised Standard Version of the Bible, copyright © 1946, 1952, and 1971 National Council of the Churches of Christ in the United States of America, (page v of the Preface).

Chapter 4: The Ark of the Covenant

1. Tenney, 249.
2. Tenney, 248.
3. "The Rod and Staff of the Lord," *Dawn Bible Students Association*, http://www.dawnbible.com/2009/0908cl-2.htm, (26 September 2016).
4. Tenney, 507.

Chapter 5: Sacred Fire

1. Tenney, 831.

Chapter 6: Shekinah Glory

1. Tenney, 782.

Chapter 7: The Spirit of Prophecy

1. Tenney, 685.

Chapter 8: Urim and Thummim

1. Tenney, 878.
2. "Urim and Tumim," *Ohr Somayach*, http://www.ohr.edu/2032 (26 September 2016).

3. Ed F. Vallowe, *Biblical Mathematics: Keys to Scripture Numerics: The Significance of Scripture Numbers as Revealed in the Word of God*, (Columbia, SC: The Olive Press, 1998), 80.

Chapter 9: Satan

1. W. S. Lasor, "Sennacherib," *The International Standard Bible Encyclopedia,* (Grand Rapids, MI: William B. Eerdmans Publishing Company, 1988), http://biblehub.com/topical/d/day-star.htm.
2. Tenney, 215.
3. Tenney, 2.
4. *The Encounter*, directed by David A. R. White, (Scottsdale, AZ: Pure Flix Entertainment, 2011), Film.

Chapter 10: The Silent Years

1. Tenney, 831.
2. Tenney, 833.
3. Ibid.
4. Linda Cochrane, *Forgiven and Set Free: A Post-Abortion Bible Study for Women*, (Grand Rapids, MI: Baker Books, 1996).

Chapter 11: Noah's Ark

1. Merriam-Webster.com, s.v. "ark."
2. *Merriam-Webster.com*, s.v. "covenant."

Chapter 12: The Ark of Jesus

1. "Yeshua," *Wikipedia: The Free Encyclopedia,* https://en.wikipedia.org/wiki/Yeshua.
2. Tenney, 156.

3. Tenney, 172.
4. Vallowe, 85.
5. Tenney, 162.
6. *Merriam-Webster.com*, s.v. "consecrated."
7. *Merriam-Webster.com*, s.vv. "consolation," "comfort."
8. Tenney, 278.
9. *Merriam-Webster.com*, s.v. "redeem."
10. The Galilee Experience, *The Names of God: 16 Month Biblical/Jewish Calendar, September 2010 through December 2011*, (Haifa, Israel: AAA Printers).

Chapter 13: The Word Became Flesh

1. "אלול - Elul and Selichot,"" אלול - Elul and Selichot, http://www.hebrew4christians.com/Holidays/Fall_Holidays/Elul/elul.html, (16 July 2014).
2. "List and Names of Months of the Jewish (Hebrew) Calendar," *Jewish (Hebrew) Calendar,* http://www.angelfire.com/pa2/passover/months-of-the-jewish-calendar.html, (15 July 2014).
3. Vallowe, 66.
4. "List and Names of Months of the Jewish (Hebrew) Calendar."
5. "Elul," *The Jewish Magazine*, http://www.jewishmag.com/13mag/elul/elul.htm, (26 September 2016).
6. Vallowe, 74.
7. "List and Names of Months of the Jewish (Hebrew) Calendar."

Chapter 14: My Beloved Son

1. Tenney, 528.
2. John Ortberg, *If You Want to Walk on Water, You've Got to Get Out of the Boat*, (Grand Rapids, MI: Zondervan Pub. House, 2001).
3. Tommy Newberry, *The 4:8 Principle: The Secret to a Joy-Filled Life*, (Carol Stream, IL: Tyndale House Publishers, 2007).

Chapter 16: The Passover Lamb

1. *Merriam-Webster.com,* s.v. "manifest."
2. Charles R. Swindoll, *Jesus: The Greatest Life of All*, (Nashville, TN: Thomas Nelson, 2008).

Chapter 17: Our High Priest

1. Mitch and Zhava Glaser, *The Fall Feasts of Israel*, (Chicago, IL: Moody Publishers, 1987).
2. Steven B. Weiss, *Haggadah: From Exodus to the Cross, A Christian Passover Celebration Guidebook*, (Steven B. Weiss, 2005).
3. "List and Names of Months of the Jewish (Hebrew) Calendar."

Chapter 18: The Holy Spirit

1. "List and Names of Months of the Jewish (Hebrew) Calendar."
2. John Eldredge, *Waking the Dead: The Glory of a Heart Fully Alive*, (Nashville, TN: Thomas Nelson Publishers, 2003).
3. Joan Hunter, *Power to Heal*, (New Kensington, PA: Whitaker House, 2009).

Chapter 19: The Name above All Names

1. *Strong's Exhaustive Concordance: New American Standard Bible*, 1995, Updated ed. La Habra: Lockman Foundation, http://www.biblestudytools.com/lexicons/hebrew/nas/shav.html, s.v. "shav."
2. "Kamal Saleem: A Muslim Cries Out to Jesus," *The Christian Broadcasting Network*, Inc. http://www.cbn.com/700club/guests/interviews/Kamal_Saleem_052010.aspx. (11 November 2011), Copyright 2014 The Christian Broadcasting Network, Inc. All rights reserved.

Chapter 20: Love Languages

1. Gary D. Chapman, *The Five Love Languages: How to Express Heartfelt Commitment to Your Mate,* (Chicago, IL: Northfield Pub., 1995).
2. Christa Black-Gifford, Brian Johnson, Jeremy Riddle, *The Loft Session [Bethel Music]*, ChristaJoy Music Publishing, Bethel Music, Mercy/Vineyard Publishing, CCLI#5508444, 2010.

Chapter 21: The Antichrist

1. "Did Constantine Change the Sabbath from Saturday to Sunday?" *The Ten Commandments,* http://www.the-ten-commandments.org/did_constantine_change_sabbath.html, (26 September 2016). "How the Sabbath was Changed," *Sabbath Truth,* http://www.sabbathtruth.com/sabbath-history/how-the-sabbath-was-changed, (26 September 2016).

Chapter 22: The Great Physician

1. "Hippocrates," *KOS Greece Island,* http://www.kosisland.gr/en/kosisland-history/hippocrates-from-kos.html, (26 September 2016).

Chapter 23: To Those Who Conquer

1. Vallowe, 53.
2. "God's Plan for the Church and the Jewish People, Part Four, Moadim: The Appointed Times," *Nikirk Ministries,* http://www.nikirkvoice.org/moadim.htm, (26 September 2016).
3. Tenney, 408.
4. Ibid.

Chapter 24: The White Stone

1. *Strong's Exhaustive Concordance: New American Standard Bible,* 1995, Updated ed. La Habra: Lockman Foundation, http://www.biblestudytools.com/lexicons/greek/nas/leukos.html, s.v. "leukos."

Chapter 26: Conclusion

1. Tenney, 87.